The Quest of the Folk

D0145288

CARLETON LIBRARY SERIES

The Carleton Library Series, funded by Carleton University under the general editorship of the dean of the School of Graduate Studies and Research, publishes books about Canadian economics, geography, history, politics, society, and related subjects. It includes important new works as well as reprints of classics in the fields. The editorial committee welcomes manuscripts and suggestions, which should be sent to the dean of the School of Graduate Studies and Research, Carleton University.

The Quest of the Folk

Antimodernism and Cultural Selection in Twentieth-Century Nova Scotia

IAN MCKAY

Carleton Library Series 212

McGill-Queen's University Press
Montreal & Kingston · London · Ithaca

© McGill-Queen's University Press 2009
ISBN: 978-0-7735-3536-7

Legal deposit first quarter 2009
Bibliothèque nationale du Québec

Printed in Canada on acid-free paper that is 100% ancient
forest free (100% post-consumer recycled), processed chlorine free

First published 1994 by McGill-Queen's University Press

McGill-Queen's University Press acknowledges
the support of the Canada Council for the Arts
for our publishing program. We also acknowledge
the financial support of the Government of Canada
through the Book Publishing Industry Development
Program (BPIDP) for our publishing activities.

Library and Archives Canada Cataloguing in Publication

McKay, Ian, 1953–
    The quest of the folk: antimodernism and cultural selection in
    twentieth-century Nova Scotia / Ian McKay.

    (Carleton Library series; 212)
    Includes bibliographical references and index.
    ISBN 978-0-7735-3536-7

    1. Folklore – Nova Scotia. 2. Culture and tourism – Nova Scotia.
    3. Tourism – Social aspects – Nova Scotia. 4. Nova Scotia – Social life
    And customs. 5. Folklorists – Nova Scotia. I. Title.
    II. Series: Carleton library 212

FC2319.M35 2009   306.409716   C2008-906618-9

Typeset in Palatino 10/12
by Infoscan Collette, Québec City

For David, and to the memory of Naomi

Contents

Acknowledgments

My sincere thanks go to colleagues and friends whose encouragement, criticisms, and advice have influenced my investigation of twentieth-century antimodernism in Nova Scotia: Gary Burrill, Mike Earle, Judith Fingard, Erik Kristiansen, Norman MacDonald, Alan MacEachern, Ken MacKinnon, Scott Milsom, Suzanne Morton, Del Muise, Rosemary Ommer, George Rawlyk, Neil Rosenberg, Eric Sager, and Mariana Valverde. Jeff Brison was kind enough to share his research notes on the Rockefeller Foundation Archives with me. I also thank Andrew Nurse, Linda Little, and Michael Boudreau for research assistance, and archivists and librarians at the Dalhousie University Archives, the Public Archives of Nova Scotia, the National Archives of Canada, the Canadian Museum of Civilization, the interlibrary loans department at the Douglas Library, and the Queen's University Archives. I also owe significant debts to St. Mary's University and the Gorsebrook Research Institute, to Dalhousie University, and to Queen's University for providing me with money and intellectual stimulation over the past seven years. The Social Sciences and Humanities Research Council of Canada gave me a Canada Research Fellowship, and I have also been assisted by a research grant from the Principal's Development Fund at Queen's. I also thank the Public Archives of Nova Scotia for giving me permission to quote extensively from the papers of Mary Black and Helen Creighton, with the sole restriction that I not quote from the closed files within the Creighton papers, and the Folklore penter for permission to consult her taped interview with Helen Creighton. Finally, I should like to thank Kathy Johnson for copy-editing the text, Kathy Sutherland for preparing the index, and George Rawlyk for his unstinting practical support in a testing time.

Having thanked all these people and institutions, I take full credit for the mistakes in fact and interpretation that remain in my work.

Foreword to the Carleton Library Series Edition

The Quest of the Folk was published in 1994, reprinted in 2006, and now makes its appearance in the Carleton Library Series. For me, the *Quest* is rather like the good ships doted upon by Simeon Perkins in his renowned eighteenth-century and early nineteenth-century Nova Scotia diaries.[1] Like Perkins, keenly awaiting news from the *Polly* and the *Betsey* as they went about their run-of-the-mill coasting exercises, interspersed with the odd bit of privateering and hurricane-dodging, I often scan my e-mail for word of the *Quest*'s latest adventures. Quite frequently I get letters – sometimes from the book's admirers pursuing topics closely related to the book (such as the rise of tourism, the impact of folklore, and twentieth-century Nova Scotia) or those rather more distant from it (like postmodernity in contemporary Japan), and sometimes from its detractors, who tell me they've thrown it across the room in rage (and, reading between the lines, might well find it therapeutic to do something similar to its author). It's good to think that as a Carleton Library title the good ship *Quest* might yet have a few more voyages.

What is it about this modest vessel that sparks a warm welcome in some ports and something more like a "lock-up-your-children" moral panic in others? I think the *Quest* arouses such controversy because it documents, and then often critiques, everyday things that have a "taken-for-granted" feel to them. The book is very much based on original documents and a close reading of particular files; as a historian I am acutely aware that there are risks in going beyond such particular sightings to a much grander, more universal narrative about "the region" or "late capitalist modernity." Yet the book also takes a stance that is critical of the neo-liberal orthodoxies that now form so much of the fabric of our own time. Through an investigation of the empirical, it ventures toward an exploration of the politics and ethics of possessive individualism. In some respects, from a twenty-first-century radical perspective, it rather soft-pedals the enormity of historical reinvention in the age of total commodification. Armed with many more documents, and a hardened anti-capitalist perspective, I would today envisage *Quest*-like books that raise less decorously and more directly the questions about power and representation I was only starting to explore in the early 1990s.

The background of the *Quest* really lies in *New Maritimes*, that radical regional magazine edited by Lorraine Begley, Gary Burrill, Ken Clare, Michael Earle, and Scott Milsom, and sustained by a host of other writers and activists, on which I worked in the 1980s and early 1990s. (Pointing this out in no way dilutes my personal responsibility for the text nor implies the full or even partial agreement of my comrades-in-arms with its analysis). It was while working on *New Maritimes* that I first engaged systematically with the problems of tourism and history, epitomized in the 1980s by the Parade of Sail, the Gathering of the Clans, and the annual tourist invasion of Peggy's Cove. The workshop within which *Quest* started to take shape was an ill-heated country newspaper office in an Enfield basement. *New Maritimes* comes from the 1980s, that Dark Age before Facebook, U-tube, and e-mail, not to mention (at least until about 1986 or so) accessible lay-out software. So the Enfield, N.S., basement office in which the magazine took shape was strewn with scissors, paste-pots, and strips upon strips of typeset columns – the proofreading of which required many after-midnight pursuits of particular letters in just the right font and size ("Does anyone have an 'E' in Garamond, size ten"?) It was a good place to reflect on the down-to-earth elements of any struggle to change the commonsense assumptions of the surrounding world.

Maritime radicals of the 1970s and 1980s confronted a paradox or, more accurately, a contradiction. The region was alive with struggles – against the war machine, environmental devastation, racism, and exploitation, among many others – that gave the magazine a ready market. Yet Maritime history was perceived, by insiders as well as outsiders, as a cozy conservatism – as static and comfy as a vast overstuffed Victorian sofa. And this imagery was relentlessly pushed, especially in the corporate yet state-sponsored extravaganzas that achieved new prominence in the 1980s. (As we began to discover, the roots of these festivals of the not-so-oppressed really stretched back to the 1920s). Why would so many people, in what was plainly a modern, class-divided society engaged with all the burning questions of the day, buy into a patronizing and reactionary vision of their own past – in essence, take up positions as characters within a vast state-sponsored historical fiction, one that awkwardly erased oppositional people and unpleasantly conflictual moments? It was especially hard for someone immersed in the sources of an earlier day, and trained to think about social structures and conflicts, not to notice the extraordinary extent to which a tourism-oriented politics of commemoration entailed the wilful eradication of a challenging past. All that was historically radical, one might say, had melted into postmodern air. So I was led to the empirical exploration of similar phenomena in the region's past and (with greater reservations and many detours) to the political and cultural theorists who might illuminate them. In essence, in this little workshop many of the questions and themes of the *Quest* were taking shape. And behind this project was the assumption, which I confess I still maintain, that it is possible for historical research and theoretical reflection to explore the actual conditions of our shared lives – and, on the basis of this critical and realist spade-work, to speak a certain historically grounded truth to power.

Herein, perhaps, is the nub of some of the debates aroused by the book.[2] It arose at a moment, not yet past, when the very concepts of "truth" and "power" were under intense interrogation, above all in the liberal academy. Because it treats questions of class, race, gender, and sexuality, *Quest* was seen by some poststructuralists and Foucauldians as the work of a fellow-traveler, when a more careful reading, especially of its closing pages, would have raised warning-flags about any such appropriation. In truth *Quest*'s Gramscian design, one that since 1994 I have come to understand better and embrace more fully, is built on critical realist and historicist assumptions quite different from those of most of the critical theory once popular in the late twentieth century. In contrast to late-twentieth-century assumptions that contemporary capitalist social and cultural *forms* are, so to speak, *light* – contingent, fragmentary, performative, ungrounded, and playful – the Gramscian working in this more critical realist vein is apt to see such contemporary *relations* as *heavy* – necessary, unified, materially based, organic, and oppressive. Geoff Eley and Keith Nield have put this distinction well with respect to discussions of power: "Gramsci reminds us, or allows us not to forget, that as well as being insidiously dispersed, power is also organized, accumulated, engrossed, stockpiled, put aside for a rainy day, configured into institutions, concentrated into forms of agency, normalized and systematized into a public sphere, naturalized, made opaque."[3] I take some pride in noting that *Quest* was already articulating something of this insight in 1994, yet I would also advise anyone who wants to pursue this journey further to engage much more extensively than I could then in the struggle for a realist and critical framework within which to position the many discoveries still awaiting us in the archives. The questions implicitly raised by *Quest* can now be posed more sharply. What ethical and methodological principles should govern the representation of the other? What is the status of truth under conditions of postmodernity? On what grounds can the ethical and epistemological relativism characteristic of late-twentieth-century marketing culture be critiqued? And how can this critique be made a force in a planet facing a global meltdown of its physical and social structures? Are there, or should there be, any limits to possessive individualism? To modernity itself? What are the costs – personal, environmental, political, spiritual – of living lives of possessive individualism?

I think that these central themes of the *Quest* explain the fierceness with which it has been resisted when it enters certain hitherto calm, liberal harbours. But it is in this very fierceness that I see grounds for hope that *Quest*'s coming decades may be as interesting as its first. What once seemed like an isolated raid on the continent of capitalist culture by one small sloop from Nova Scotia may well come to be seen as a forerunner of more powerful transnational armadas of anti-capitalist rebels and critics. May the research continue, the questioning persist, and the activism intensify. And may the *Quest* have a few more adventures yet in the stormy waters of the twenty-first century.

Ian McKay

Prologue: A Postcard from the "Shore of Songs"

In the Public Archives of Nova Scotia there is a postcard depicting a scene from Mill Cove, Lunenburg County, one of many fishing settlements ringing St. Margaret's Bay on Nova Scotia's Atlantic coast. The photograph is of a small cabin with weather-beaten boards, encircled by a rough-hewn rock wall and sod for insulation: a rickety ladder leads to a loosely shingled roof, deeply stained by the soot from the stove chimney. In front of the house stand seven people, presumably its occupants: on the left, two men, one an old man with a full white beard, the other a man of younger years; in the centre, a woman in front of a tub, with a bent back and gaunt face; on the right, four children – two girls in pinafores, and two boys, one of them still in a young child's dress. In the foreground, rocks are everywhere, and in the distance, one can just discern the far horizon of the hills on the opposite shore of the Cove.[1]

Surrounded by the hills and the sea, and above all by rocks: these people are firmly (and surely intentionally) "fixed" within a natural frame, represented as small figures in a stark landscape that engulfs them: the faces of the two young boys almost vanish into the rocks around them. And they are "framed" by the photographer in at least two further senses: explicitly by the caption, which "explains" the significance of the representation ("A simple Life, House 8 x 10 Mill Cove N.S."), and implicitly by the edges of the postcard, which defines the scene as a commodity of a particular sort, suitable for the sightseer to this rockbound coast as a way of remembering,

"A Simple Life, House 8 × 10 Mill Cove, N.S." Postcard, c.1890s. PANS N-2382.
Mill Cove is located on the west side of St Margaret's Bay in Lunenburg County.
St. Margaret's Bay, within easy driving distance of Halifax, came to be viewed as the
archetypal Nova Scotia landscape in the twentieth century; Peggy's Cove, the
province's most famous coastal village, is located at the entrance to the Bay.

advertising, or authenticating his or her vacation among the fisherfolk.

This much is obvious: but what does the photograph mean? What
"sense" can we make of, or with, it? On the mundane level of
identifying obvious traits, most people, particularly "insiders" initiated into western ways of seeing, would be able to attain a consensus:
this photograph represents seven people (with some doubt as to
whether the smallest figure is a boy or a girl), many rocks, a cabin.
Stepping on to somewhat riskier ground, one might infer that these
people constitute a family grouping and that, given the identifying
location of the photograph and the evidence of their clothes and the
state of their (permanent or temporary) habitation, that they are poor
people who depend on the fishery for their livelihood.

This photograph has in fact been used as a "realistic" representation of the "way things used to look" circa 1890–1900 in the local
history devoted to this area.[2] Here it functions as an illustration
incidental to a narrative largely focused on the church and the Canadian Forces base nearby. In this purely local context, the photograph
documents a beloved landscape, and perhaps, for some readers,

beloved ancestors; descendants of this family may find that the photograph as a faithful image of those now dead has a meaning, a "power of authentication," that exceeds its "power of representation."[3] They would bring to the photograph a perspective quite different from that of the intended audience of the original card. Such ways of seeing the photograph, suitable to their context, nonetheless leave us with the problem of the two framing devices – the postcard form and the caption – that provide us with clues to its intended audience. They leave us accepting the "truth" of the photograph, but, as Allan Sekula has observed, "Although the very notion of photographic reproduction would seem to suggest that very little is lost in translation, it is clear that photographic meaning depends largely on context. Despite the powerful impression of reality (imparted by the mechanical registration of a moment of reflected light according to the rules of normal perspective), photographs, in themselves, are fragmentary and incomplete utterances."[4] John Tagg takes this sense of the complexity of the nature of the photograph further: "The indexical nature of the photograph – the causative link between the pre-photographic referent and the sign – is therefore highly complex, irreversible, and can guarantee nothing at the level of meaning. What makes the link is a discriminatory technical, cultural and historical process in which particular optical and chemical devices are set to work to organise experience and desire and produce a new reality – the paper image which, through yet further processes, may become meaningful in all sorts of ways."[5]

John Berger, working from a quite different perspective, remarks: "The way we see things is affected by what we know or what we believe ... We never look at just one thing; we are always looking at the relation between things and ourselves. Our vision is continually active, continually moving, continually holding things in a circle around itself, constituting what is present to us as we are."[6] In attempting to understand the meaning of a photograph from the past, we cannot escape from this circle of interpretation to gain access to the "neutral data" or "brute facts," because such data acquire meaning only within a prior enabling framework. The sense that we can make of a given photograph, for example, depends very much on the relationship between the photograph and the "frame work" performed by those who, working in a particular context, develop implicit or explicit stories within which a given representation makes sense.

The past no longer exists, and is accessible to us only through partial and fragmentary sources: and these sources are generally silent on the motivations of a photographer and the impact of his representation on a wider audience. Still, this particular photograph sends out important clues. Given the postcard format, the photographer's motivations were most likely commercial, and the caption suggests that there is little likelihood that the postcard was ever intended for the consumption of those who lived in Mill Cove. And that caption surely takes us some way to a plausible interpretation of the contemporary meaning of the photograph in its time and place. It is because, in this case, the "frame work" has been so plainly set out for us, through the text and the form of the image, that we can infer, with some security, the interpretive framework within which it once made sense.

A small experiment will illustrate the point. Transform, in your mind, the words "A simple Life, House 8 x 10 Mill Cove N.S." into "The Heathen Poor upon Our Coasts." Then replace those words with "Starvation and Suffering through Capitalist Underdevelopment." The "meaning" of the photograph changes, even to the extent of the details that are readily noticed. And these are not alternative captions chosen at random: they constitute the historically existent alternative ways of seeing people such as these.

"The Heathen Poor upon Our Coasts": in the mid-nineteenth century, when descriptions relied upon written words more than visual images, Victorian missionary reports developed a compelling case, strengthened by many apparent details, for this rockbound coast as a veritable hell on earth. The fisherfolk, it was said, were "wild" people who lived in small, half-finished wooden houses, and subsisted on fish, potatoes, tobacco, and rum. The average wife could be found "working as hard as a slave both about the fish and the land," with her many ill-clad children running about her. From the perspective of the mid-Victorian missionary, here was a damned landscape of disease and destitution, polygamy and drunkenness (and even – and this can be corroborated in other sources, such as contemporary newspapers – "starvation" when the fishery failed in 1867–68).[7]

"Starvation and Suffering through Capitalist Underdevelopment": since the 1970s, regional social history, often of neo-Marxist provenance, has developed a starkly different interpretive framework, within which the photograph would mean something. This same representation of the fishing family would call up a history, never adequately synthesized, of the suffering and also the resistance of producers along the coast. For feminists, it would illustrate the indispensable role of women, whose separate and unequal burdens are suggested by the positioning of the figures in the image. In either case, the acute distress and "starvation" reported in the nineteenth century would be seen not as the inhabitants' just reward for their feckless and ungodly ways, but as the dire consequence of an oppressive form of mercantile exploitation.

Neither of these ways of seeing can be easily accommodated to the caption before us, this apparent celebration of "A simple Life." This photograph, which "frames" an understanding of people in history, can therefore be "framed" in turn as an early moment in a transition from one way of seeing to another. Produced for the probable purpose of making a profit within a tourism economy, the postcard presents the fisherfolk as the Other, as a spectacle to be appropriated and enjoyed within the objectifying gaze of tourism. If the narrowly economic context of this photograph is the rise of the tourism industry in Nova Scotia, within which the rural "Folk" came to play the role of attraction, its cultural context, the ideological thrust of this representation, seems to be one of a liberal antimodernism: an intensely individualistic thirst for an existence released from the iron cage of modernity into a world re-enchanted by history, nature, and the mysterious.*

What makes this photograph fascinating, in this interpretive context, is that it captures not some unassailable "truth" of the fishing family, but a hesitant shift towards a new way of seeing (to borrow from John Berger) or towards a new "structure of feeling" (to borrow from the late Raymond Williams).[8] The "simple Life" is proclaimed, yet the romanticism implied by the caption is somewhat undercut by the prosaic listing of the modest dimensions of their cottage. The unflinching attention to the details of poverty, the measurements of the cabin – these dramatic elements will be subsequently purged from ever more essentialist representations of the coast, which as the twentieth century unfolds will become more and more the symbolic landscape of the simple life and the sturdy fisherfolk. The photograph marks a transition from scorning and criticizing their lives and customs to celebrating them: and apparently celebrating them on the basis of a redescription of the very grounds – "primitivism," "isolation," "distance from modernity" – that had once been the cause of so much Victorian hostility. As tourism, folklore, and handicrafts all developed in the twentieth century, the people of the fishing villages came to be seen as bearers of Nova Scotia's cultural essence: they became archetypal Nova Scotians living not on a barren patch of

---

* Throughout this book I have capitalized "Folk" as a way of bracketing the word and the concept without resorting to intrusive quotation marks. Editorial corrections to mistakes in spelling and punctuation in original manuscripts appear in square brackets at the appropriate place in the citation.

Atlantic shoreline, but on a mythified "Coast of Songs," which rang with their ballads and merriment. They came to be represented as stout-hearted, resourceful fisherfolk who led a "simple life" by the sea, untroubled by urban stresses, nourished by the natural beauty all around them: and a wholly different "structure of feeling" was laid upon this rockbound landscape, as the stern rocks became beautiful and the rough-hewn cabin was transformed into the very epitome of the rustic picturesque. These people and those like them became the Folk. They came to be celebrated, without even implicit irony or hesitation, for their Good and Simple Lives. By the 1990s, the memories of starvation, mercantile exploitation, and impoverishment had virtually vanished.

The Simple Life of the Folk: this is the enabling framework I seek to identify, to explain, and to critique in this study. I view the reduction of people once alive to the status of inert essences as a way of voiding the emancipatory potential of historical knowledge. "Class conflict," Allan Sekula has remarked, "is not simply economic and political in character. It is also a conflict of representations."[9] To rewrite the history of subaltern classes and groups in ways that ostensibly pay them homage, all the while draining their history of specificity, is one subtle and effective method of preserving their inferior position. Documenting how this operation has been carried out, analysing the "real representational practices that go on in a society, and the concrete institutions and apparatuses within which they take place," plotting "the network of material, political and ideological constraints which bear on these institutions and constitute their conditions of existence and operation," marks one small but necessary step towards a more open and more radical understanding of the past.[10]

When I look at the photograph, I imagine not the "simple Life" of the Folk but the infinitely complex lives of people who once suffered and loved and worked, and who consequently deserve to be remembered as accurately as possible. Who governed in this household? How did it feel to live in so small a house, if even for a short time? How long did people like this stay on a coast that so often meted out hunger and hardship? What songs did they sing and what newspapers did they read, if they did read? Piecing together answers, bit by bit, where we can find them, would never give us a conclusive truth. What we can attain is a more respectful and accurate interweaving of our inevitably partial truths. We can extend to the dead the respect they deserve, as people living not a supposed "simple Life," but the complicated, difficult, interesting lives of most human beings. This will cost us the reassuring images of the Folk, but it will gain us a more complicated and truthful sense of the past. "Only that historian will have the gift of fanning the spark of hope in the past who is firmly convinced that *even the dead* will not be safe from the enemy if he wins. And this enemy has not ceased to be victorious."[11] The enemy in this case is that fatal complacency, content to think in essences, which has thus far successfully thwarted that which the liberal order has most reason to fear: the oppressed in command of their history.

The Quest of the Folk

1 The Idea of the Folk

Now let me give you a little atmosphere so you'll know what it's all about.

Helen Creighton on her discovery of the Folk

"A LITTLE ATMOSPHERE": DEVIL'S ISLAND, 1929

Dark figures gathered round the sputtering embers of a camp fire. It was late spring, 1928. A picnic was in progress on the shores of the Atlantic, near the town of Dartmouth, Nova Scotia. One of the figures was Helen Creighton, a young local journalist.

"As the evening shadows lengthened we strolled along the beautiful sandy beach, leaving a small bonfire to burn itself out," Creighton later recalled in her memoirs. "On our return we found a villager, Mike Matthews, standing beside it, and in that easy way one does in the country, we began to talk. The stillness of the night, the long twilight, and the gentle murmur of waves lapping the shore turned our thoughts to earlier days and I said, 'Has treasure ever been found along this shore?'" Yes, replied Matthews, the first of Creighton's many "informants," gold pieces from buried pirate treasure had been known to appear on the shore. And there were, in coastal hamlets nearby, people who would speak of such things. They were to be found at "the end of the land," at Hartlan's Point. "I asked him to advise the Hartlans of my coming," Helen Creighton later recalled, "little realizing that a great new door had been opened and that the Eastern Passage road had become my path of destiny."[1]

The "path of destiny": Helen Creighton had a finely developed and, as it turns out, accurate sense of her own historical and cultural importance. She constructed the story of her earliest days as a folklore collector as a time of sudden discovery, rich coincidence, and trans-figuring illumination : in brief, as her second baptism. Her remem-bered Quest of the Folk began on the margins: at the edge of the ocean, at the edge of the day, when boundaries become indistinct and the familiar becomes strange, and at the edge of her home town, Dartmouth, a virtual suburb of Halifax, the capital of Nova Scotia.[2] An atmosphere of expectancy and inchoate possibility enveloped this remembered "path of destiny," which began on the borderlands of land and water, the city and the countryside, the modern and the pre-modern. And as numerous and various the adventures along this path turned out to be, Creighton's path remained on the margin, where the lights of the city met the dark, entrancing, romantic Oth-erness of the countryside beyond. It was on this margin of possibility, this liminal space in between the city and country, lightness and darkness, that Creighton found her life's purpose.

This book is about the "path of destiny" that led Creighton and countless other cultural figures to develop "the Folk" as the key to understanding Nova Scotian culture and history. It is about the ways in which urban cultural producers, pursuing their own interests and expressing their own view of things, constructed the Folk of the countryside as the romantic antithesis to everything they disliked about modern urban and industrial life. In this introductory chapter, I will examine the international context of the concept of the "Folk" and then focus on the local circumstances that made this concept an attractive one for many people in the 1920s and 1930s. I will also lay out where I think the concept of the "Folk" fits within a general phenomenon of antimodernism in the province, and provide a brief indication of where I stand in the contested terrain of cultural theory and politics. A crowded agenda, indeed: but I still want to spend a little more time on this first remembered scene, as Helen Creighton is drawn, step by step, onto her "path of destiny." It is an important moment in the cultural history of Nova Scotia and of Canada.

At the time of her "baptism" in 1929 Creighton was a journalist on the scent of fresh copy. She was also looking for something: a vocation in life. Weeks earlier, a friend at the Department of Educa-tion, Dr. Henry Munro, had shown her a newly published collection of ballads from the province. If she could find just one of the authentic old ballads, he told her, her fortune would be made. As a someone who had grown up in a bustling twentieth-century city, Creighton had no childhood memories of folksongs or ballads, but she did have a sense that the public was ready to explore the newly fashionable world of folklore. She was particularly taken by the commercial pos-sibilities of tales of treasure and romantic stories of the sea. The pirate tales that she had heard about at the picnic at Eastern Passage beckoned intriguingly.

Creighton had been born into a prosperous Dartmouth family on 5 September 1899. She was a small, wiry woman, who complained throughout her career of exhaustion and constitutional weakness, but who also enjoyed vast reserves of stamina and self-discipline. It soon became clear that her path of destiny was going to make heavy demands upon both. Her first foray onto her path took her on to a rut-filled, bone-jarring drive to visit the Hartlan family, over a road so rough that the last half mile had to be travelled on foot. Having survived the journey, she surveyed the first station of her quest: a little group of houses clustered around a larger abandoned house.

Here were the humble Hartlans. They were people of the margins, people of possibility – familiar people who would seem unfamiliar when placed in a certain light and within a certain conceptual framework. Mrs. Enos Hartlan was familiar to Creighton, because, like many people in Greater Halifax's rural hinterland, she brought her garden produce to the city and sold it to middle-class families like the Creightons in Dartmouth. But in the context of Creighton's emergent pursuit of the primitive and the archaic, the familiar vegetable grower was transformed into a guide to another world. She was an eager talker. Soon the young urban journalist discovered on her very doorstep a hidden world of ancient customs and supernatural happenings. The house at the centre of the hamlet had been abandoned because it was haunted; ghosts could be heard knocking on its doors and coming down the steps. German inscriptions on boards in the Hartlans' kitchen warned off witches. There were wondrous tales and extraordinary songs. Creighton sat fascinated by Enos Hartlan, an old man who entertained her in stockingless feet, and sang toothlessly, intriguingly, of times long past and places far away.

Creighton worked the Atlantic Coast near Dartmouth for perhaps a year, collecting songs and lore. Everywhere she went she seemed to hear of a mysterious island with a gloriously ominous name: Devil's Island. It was only a tiny spit of land, set down at the mouth of Halifax Harbour, in sight of the city, yet romantically remote from it. Asking among her friends, Creighton could not find one who had ever been there. Yet over and over she was told by her coastal informants: that is where you will find your songs.

Her voyage to the island in June 1929 was the turning point in her quest, her decisive step over the boundaries of her earlier life. Until now, Creighton had discovered some lore and some songs, but not the treasure that would validate her life decision. Devil's Island was her breakthrough. As she worked and reworked the story of her journey to the island later in life, it became her symbolic folkloristic baptism – which explains, perhaps, why in her memory she seems to have pushed the first voyage to Devil's Island back to 1928, the year she first started visiting the Folk of her area.[3] Her own sense of the dramatic significance of the island shines through in the highly romantic description she sent years later to a colleague in the Canadian Authors' Association. The island, she wrote, was set within the frothing, sublime sea, where

the cruel waves beat relentlessly upon the pebbled beach below, and the rain lashes against the exposed and coldly receptive window panes ... The undertow continues its suck, suck, sucking, always hoping for the moment when it will cease to be cheated of its prey, but even then greedily unsatisfied. Weary pebbles are tossed ashore and never allowed to remain for any rest upon the beach, and the mischievous, rollicking song of the breakers becomes a thunderous melody, menacing, terrible.[4]

Within this stormy setting, not unlike those evoked by Daphne du Maurier, was an island whose very name conjured up an image of the supernatural. But, wrote Creighton, with a wry self-deprecating humour, her crossing was disappointingly unromantic. She was taken to the mysterious island not by some gnarled pirate reeking of rum and singing the wild songs of a buccaneer, but by an anxious and inexpert tourist from Chicago. The initial appearance of Devil's Island was no less deflating. However romantic its name, the tiny treeless dot of land – just one mile in circumference and only about ten feet above sea level – was "not beautiful, and certainly not romantic." Its flatness made it "pathetically uninteresting. Its shore line is very ordinary. It is simply a negligible quantity with nothing scenic to attract. I felt horribly let down."[5]

Creighton constructed this scene of crushed romantic hopes not, one imagines, out of actual remembrance – the flatness and "ordinariness" of Devil's Island is perfectly evident from the shoreline, and it is therefore hard to imagine why she would have been disappointed when she drew closer to it – but, in the manner of a thousand ethnographies,[6] to heighten our expectations of what is to follow, what cultural treasures will emerge after the ethnographer has admirably overcome culture shock, the discomforts of travel, and disillusioned romanticism. Creighton uses the dreariness of the island's landscape as a foil for the cultural treasures hidden within it, and magnifies the reader's appreciation of her ability to see beyond initial appearances.

The friendly natives welcomed the visitor from another world with open arms, and Creighton gradually came to realize that, providentially, she had made a momentous discovery. As she would later write,

It was here ... that I found my gold mine. There are only fourteen occupied houses, but nearly all the men sing, and even the children sang me such delightful bits, as, "He kissed her cold corpus a thousand times o'er[.]" But one old man, with distorted face and voice very "tick" proved the greatest find which I suppose the whole country possesses. Alone he sang me over seventy songs, and when I saw him a few days ago he said he had remembered another twenty-five. And such a variety! He sang two of Robin Hood, one of which I though[t] of having sung. A priceless song, almost word for word like the song in Child's collection. And Robin Hood, you know, lived in the thirteen hundreds. He has also given me numerous local sea songs and ballads, nearly every time with a story attached. Comic songs, love songs, ballads long forgotten, many of them very rare – indeed whenever any other man sings for me I marvel yet again at the memory of my dear Mr Ben. And such a [picturesque] figure he is, being so horribly ugly, poor thing. But with it all so very kind and obliging. I have travelled far and wide, but I don't know of any place more interesting than this little Devil's Island. The Singing Island I call it.

What the Singing Island lacked in majestic scenery, it made up for in the extraordinary cultural wealth of its Folk. Creighton was struck by the look on the faces of the humble fisherfolk as they listened to the first of the songs, a locally composed ballad ("Meagher's Children") about the tragedy of two young girls who got lost and died in the woods near Halifax. "There was that on the faces of the islanders which told us that their hearts were warm with sympathy for the two little girls whose sad fate was being sung," Creighton remembered. "People whose lives are fraught with danger know well how to sympathise ... These kindly folk were well worth studying, although on the other hand they were no study at all. They were an open book of glorious tales of folk-lore and impossible stories."[7] Devil's Island had once seemed like a pathetically uninteresting landscape; it could now be redescribed as a fascinating, enriching, romantic haven of the Folk.

Picture the little island at your back with its miniature hills and dales, its houses perched so insecurely that you feel a breath of wind might come at any moment and blow them all away. Facing the harbour is a row of fishing shacks in which the gear of the men is kept. In front of them is a path.

Behind the log on which the men are sitting the Devil's Island harbour lies, the fishing boats rocking cosily in the soft cradle of the sea. Far away are Lawlor's and McNab's Islands, heavily wooded in vivid contrast to this island upon which we stand. Far, far away is Citadel Hill at Halifax, very familiar, but now seeming as part of a different world, so unlike is the atmosphere here at the harbour's mouth. Behind Citadel Hill is the setting sun; a glorious sun in the full pride of colourful beauty.[8]

Within sight of the city, but splendidly remote; seemingly flat and uninteresting, but harbouring deep mines of cultural gold, the "Singing Island" opened up a world of wonderful possibilities for Creighton. It was a miracle: on the doorstep of her city she had uncovered an island of cultural remoteness, a truly "different world."[9]

It may not actually have happened as quickly or as dramatically as Creighton would later remember it. As we remember our stories and our lives, we shape and reshape them, and a slow awakening to the prospects opened up to her on Devil's Island may have been telescoped in memory into this moment of discovery and rebirth. Yet whatever the balance between literal and poetic truth, Creighton was powerfully conveying a sense of being lifted out of her old life and transported, through the voice of the Folk, into a new dimension. Creighton had providentially found her calling. The hero of the narrative had been given her baptism. Her lifelong Quest of the Folk was well and truly launched.

THE EMERGENCE OF THE "FOLK" IN MODERN CULTURE

Creighton's moment of awakening can be interpreted as an example of a much more general phenomenon: the invention and diffusion of the concept of the Folk as a way of thinking about the impact of modernity. The voyage that Creighton interpreted as evidence of destiny can be located in a much broader pattern by a historian. For this providential moment on Devil's Island was surely a profoundly structured "accident."

This book is about the underlying logics – social, cultural, political – that made this "accident" possible and its consequences predictable. Specifically, it investigates when and why middle-class cultural producers – writers, visual artists, promoters, advertisers – began to think of rural Nova Scotians as "Folk," and what the consequences of that social and cultural category have been for the region in general and for Nova Scotians in particular. It focuses both on particular people and a broad range of cultural innovation within the confines of one Canadian province.

Creighton's voyage to Devil's Island in the late 1920s was part of a general cultural pattern. In the second and third quarters of the twentieth century, throughout Nova Scotia (and especially, as in Creighton's case, in the immediate vicinity of Greater Halifax), middle-class people started to voyage into the countryside in pursuit of cultural treasure. In finding something special on the rural door-step of Greater Halifax, along what she herself called the "Coast of Songs," Creighton was part of a much bigger movement of aesthetic colonization of the country by the city. "A critique of a whole dimension of modern life, and with it many necessary general questions, was expressed but also reduced to a convention, which took the form of a detailed version of a part-imagined, part-observed rural England": so Raymond Williams observes the ways in which admiration for an idealized British countryside served as the too easy antidote for urban alienation.[10] In Nova Scotia, one could draw a circle, centred on Halifax and encompassing the Atlantic coastline, extending from about Petite Rivière in Lunenburg County to the border of Guysborough County, and capture most of the "sacred ground" of the new representations of the province: Peggy's Cove, the symbolic landscapes that directly inspired the design of handicrafts, the birthplace of the schooner *Bluenose*, the popularization of "folk art," the settings for scores of novels and short stories, and so on.

Throughout the province, the period from 1927 to 1960 witnessed a widespread urban fascination with rural ways, and "the Folk" became a short, enigmatic phrase that summed up what many observers of Nova Scotia considered a self-evident truth. An explanation of this pattern requires two preliminary steps: a brief consideration of the concept of the Folk in western cultural history, and an analysis of the political, economic and social forces operating in the local context. When Creighton arrived on Devil's Island in 1929, she carried with her at least some assumptions derived from a long history of European and North American thought about the Folk. These enabled her to "place" the people she encountered in a structure of thought and feeling. On her return to the city, she was further able to orient herself by turning to various mentors and authorities as her guides to the theory of the Folk. Creighton, who began strictly as an amateur, encountered these intellectual influences gradually, in a pragmatic attempt to respond to her discoveries in what seemed to be the culturally appropriate manner.

The most salient structuring assumption was that there was within the population a subset of persons set apart, the Folk, characterized by their own distinctive culture and isolated from the modern society around them. This assumption is by no means self-evident. According to Giuseppe Cocchiara, writing on the history of folklore, it seems to have coalesced in Europe as a way of theorizing social relations in western societies after the great discoveries in America and in some measure as a result of them. Cocchiara establishes a connection between the figure of the "noble savage" of Renaissance humanism and the "noble peasant folk" of nineteenth-century Romanticism, and argues that when Marc Lescarbot, in *Histoire de la Nouvelle France*, reported on the "customs of New France compared with those of ancient peoples," he was laying the groundwork for a categorization and celebration of the "primitive folk" in France itself. "By this point the savage was a touchstone with which the classical and modern worlds could be measured," Cocchiara says of the mid-seventeenth century. "This constitutes the beginning of the history of folklore, especially when coupled with ethnology. The concept of the noble savage contained the affirmation of a new set of values from which the history of folklore was to gain a vigorous impulse: the affirmation of all that is simple and elemental, as opposed to all that is artificial and farfetched."[11] Long before the Romantic Rebellion and long before the mid-nineteenth-century invention of the word "folklore," argues Cocchiara, the concept itself was taking shape. Even during the Enlightenment, when popular traditions could be simply dismissed by *philosophes* as errors of the human spirit, Cocchiara detects the presence of early and significant counter-tendencies. In Switzerland, for example, some historians regarded Folk traditions as the foundations of the original fundamental characteristics of each of that country's founding peoples. In Britain, Bishop Thomas Percy's *Reliques of Ancient English Poetry* (1765) marked a significant turning-point in an élite fascination with "popular antiquities." Nonetheless, the rise of Romanticism in the late eighteenth and early nineteenth centuries brought about a dramatic consolidation and popularization of the concept of the Folk. The key pioneers and works were German, notably Johan Gottfried Herder's two-volume *Volkslieder* (1778, 1779), and the work of Jacob and Wilhelm Grimm, particularly their collection of nursery and household tales (1812).

Herder's significance to the emergence and stabilization of the category "Folk" is indisputable. His work was propelled by the critique of modernity and of the Enlightenment. "His battle developed on two fronts," remarks Cocchiara, "since it was inspired by two goals: (1) to combat the Enlightenment, which regarded tradition as a symbol of ignorance and fanaticism, and (2) to combat the art of his time, which followed foreign (especially French) models that were then quite at home in Germany."[12] Herder's approach was a blend of the new and the old. Following Rousseau, but shifting his analysis into a more purely aesthetic key, Herder was fashioning a conservative response to the French Revolution and the powerful eruption of

European mass politics it had dramatized. An intellectual, even of aristocratic background, could not safely deride popular traditions by invoking an Enlightenment universalism. He would be far wiser to examine popular traditions for signs of wisdom and spirituality, and for indications of stability within the fast-changing nineteenth-century world. Since Herder argued that there was more than one "*Volk*" – which in German conveyed the idea of "the people" or "the nation" – he could be said to have extended a humanitarian welcome to other peoples, hitherto carefully confined to the margins of the story of civilization. However, his thought was actually less conducive to tolerance than this gesture might imply. He was self-consciously turning to the "barbaric" and the "primitive" as ways of countering the stresses of modernity, positioning tradition and custom as almost sacred elements of collective identity, and exalting the German *Volk* above all other peoples in the world. In the arts of the Folk, not in rationality and science, was the vital stuff of life. Germans in search of their identity were better advised to consult their own "barbaric" traditions than those of the Greeks. Poesy "lived in the ear of the people," Herder proclaimed, "issuing forth from the lips and harps of the living singers: it sang of history, events, mysteries, wonders, and omens: it was the blossom of the unique character of a people, its language, and its land, its occupation and biases, its suffering and arrogance, its music and soul."[13] By *Volk*, Herder "often meant the whole of an ethnic community," but in certain discussions pivoted on the question of the state, Herder identified the *Volk* with a section of the population – the farmer, the artisan, the shopkeeper – and used the word *Bürger* to distinguish this element of the population from the aristocracy, the "rabble," and the learned class.[14] For Herder and for many subsequent writers on such subjects – and we hear a distant echo of this in Helen Creighton's description of the primitive simplicity and sincerity of the Devil's Islanders – the culture of the Folk, their tales and music and crafts, encapsulated the natural "cultural core" before it was complicated (and perhaps corrupted) by "society."[15] To put it mildly, there were many ambiguities and difficulties left in the concept of the Folk as developed by Herder. It was difficult to distinguish how much of the Folk tradition was passed along genetically (or, in a more "nineteenth-century" phrase, in the bloodstream) and how much was acquired culturally (defined most generally as those behaviours and ideas that do not seem to be biologically inherited but that are apparently acquired historically through interaction with society).[16]

The brothers Grimm developed and radicalized Herder's conceptions of Folk poetry, and in some respects Creighton, arriving on

Devil's Island as a "collector" of cultural items, was once more following in the footsteps of a distant German forerunner: the Grimms had added to the idea of the Folk an early version of the strategy of fieldwork. The Grimms would, within narrow limits, allow the Folk to tell their own stories. Their major theoretical contribution was to attribute metaphysical origins to Folk culture. Agreeing with Herder that Folk poetry must be considered a wellspring of national culture, they exalted the tradition even more than he had by arguing that the origins of this magical, anonymous, and impersonal lore were divine, the products of a providentially constituted collective spirit, the *Volksgeist*. As one of the great abstractions of Romanticism, "the Folk" came to be regarded as the epitome of simple truth, work, and virtue, the antithesis of all that was overcivilized, tired, conventional, and insincere. The Folk were closer to nature ("wild" and "lacking social organization," according to Herder) and could respond more spontaneously to "natural music." For romantic nationalists, the "Folk" were those whose very existence and culture testified to the possibility and necessity of the nation.

As a category first developed and then elaborated in European thought, and later "naturalized" by theorists in Britain and America, the Folk concept implied a certain conception of the world and the social order. Within the German tradition, for Herder and the Grimms, the Folk were essentially those who preserved an older way of life within an urban and literate society. Workers and socialists, those deracinated products of the coalfields and cities, could not be true Folk, not only because they were creating a literate and political culture, but also because in their emphasis on a politics based on class, they violated the vital nucleus of the Folk idea: the *essential and unchanging solidarity* of traditional society. And because the same word – *Volk* – was applied both to peasants and to "the people" as a whole, it was easy to make the claim that peasant customs said more about what was intrinsic to the "people" or the "nation" than did the customs of, say, workers or the aristocracy. From Herder and the Grimms, the Folk bore witness, in the eloquent simplicity of their lives and in the anonymous warmth of their common culture, to the *Gemeinschaft* – that ideal type of a society bound together by tradition, custom, and faith, and permanently rooted over generations in small, uncommercialized communities. The Folk were the living antithesis of the class divisions, secularism, and "progress" of the urban, industrial world – that *Gesellschaft* of modernity, of contracts and class divisions, and of that scourge of the oral culture of the Folk, the printed word. To visit the Folk and enjoy their songs and tales was to transcend class divisions and to live the truth of a pastoral vision of society – one in which rich and poor were bound together by ties of love and understanding. The very fact that a bourgeois could share lovingly in their culture suggested, perhaps especially when the collector was relying on the memories of an old retainer or a cherished nurse, that the Folk and their middle-class collecting friends were essentially one. Once collected and disseminated, the Folk repertoire was no less solidaristic in its wider ramifications, for it could unite people of a common national culture and of a common "race." The ways in which folk tales were both collected and used thus testified to the deep organic solidarities which modernity had not succeeded in eliminating. The deep communal ties of the *Gemeinschaft*, the little community, the warm spontaneity of "natural humanity" in its original form, could be reinvigorated, even in a fast-changing world. Such organic, natural ties as existed between the Folk and the Nation were far more essential than the superficial and transitory divisions of ethnicity, gender, or class.[17] The "lore" of the folk – their ballads, songs, games, proverbs, sayings, curses, magical beliefs, myths, and superstitions – could be seen as something that transcended such divisions and that could knit diversified and heterogeneous nations together. Small wonder, then, that (as the folklorist Neil Rosenberg has reminded us) not only in Germany, where for Herder and his followers the collection of *Volksleider* was a patriotic duty, but also in many other countries, intellectuals have drawn upon "national folklore" for "purposes of symbolic identity."[18] At the same time, the national identities created through the use of such categories could not and did not include everyone. Treating some people (normally peasants) as "Folk" (and hence the privileged bearers of "national essence") only worked if there were some who were not "Folk." These found themselves caught at the wrong end of a polarity. As the "Folk" became ever more essential to the Nation and their "culture" became identified as its cultural core, those who were unmistakably not of the Folk came, within nationalism, to be defined more and more as "unnatural," cosmopolitan, uprooted, and unwholesome. (The classic instance is that of Jews.) They either adapted to this uncomfortable situation by intensifying their own separate identity, or they sought, by assimilating, somehow to cancel the polarity.

The reactionary implications of this dichotomous social categorization are apparent. That which is unchanging, the true, solid, and possibly even providential core of a culture and society, resides within the Folk. Change was equated with degeneration and deviance – an entropic vision that is the unifying thread of the Folk concept to the present day. Identifying the true with the constant meant that discussion of the Folk and their lore stressed, with an uncanny consistency, such essentialist questions as those of *origin* and *authenticity* (authenticity being construed in the most rigid possible way: a version of a song was "authentic" only if it consistently reproduced the characteristics of the piece in its "original" form). Even where there could be no solid evidence, those who believed in Folk culture demanded assurances that they were dealing with originals, untouched by the influence of print, orally transmitted from a distant time. Attention was focused obsessively on an idealized past of the Folk. Indeed, it was because they preserved the traces of this "natural" past that the wild Folk were worthy of attention.

Herein was the logic of what might otherwise seem the bafflingly obscurantist debates over whether, for example, one individual among the Folk originated the ballad, or whether it emerged as the collective and anonymous creation of massed crowds of Folk.[19] Such arcane debates were urgent for the middle-class people engaged in them, because they spoke to the very reasons why the concept of the Folk had been taken up in the first place. The Folk were less people in their own right and more incarnations of a certain philosophy of history. One might draw a parallel with the anthropological thought of the young Marx. For the Marx of the 1844 manuscripts, history is invested with a universal meaning, as a process of humanization inherent in the human species itself, and human history is "emplotted as a single story in which *the* nature of the species, originally given as a potential, unfolds towards a full normative realization."[20] Only to the extent that workers take up their "historic mission" and create a "universal class" do they constitute a "proletariat." Marx of course subsequently transcended the essentialism and idealism of these early formulations in his study of social formations in history. Conservative thought about the Folk did not. The Folk remained an essentialist abstraction, in which an ideal was materialized within a certain social group abstractly conceived as having a historic mission. If the young Marx's proletariat was "essentially" revolutionary and his sense of history teleological and universal, Herder's Folk was "essentially" traditional and embodied the opposite, anti-Enlightenment principles of particularism and tradition. An optimistic young Marx could anticipate the coming, through the proletarian incarnation of an abstract ideal, of a better day of equality, in a perspective on history that was future-oriented and progressive. The Folk exemplified the opposite vision, an entropic sense of historical decline and cultural loss. The lost organic solidarities of their culture served as solace and a warning for those irremediably separated from them by the catastrophe of modernity. What might be called the Myth of the Enlightenment in the young Marx was countered by the antimodernist Myth of a Golden Age. This told the story of a lost age of social cohesiveness (followed by civilization's remorseless decay and degeneration). Both approaches were tendentially élitist, insofar as living workers or peasants were ascribed an abstract "historic mission" of which they might themselves have little knowledge. The place of praxis in Marx's thought, however, mitigated an élitism which in Folk theorists, with their often violently mournful and backward-looking sense of cultural decay, could run unchecked. The most élitist of the Folk theorists deprived the living human beings among the peasants of all creativity and transformed them into mere vessels of national essence, bearers of cultural treasures whose true value they themselves could never understand. A conservative vision of cultural entropy allied easily with an equally conservative sense of the cultural inferiority of the unlettered Folk. It was in the name of this vivid sense of history as entropy that so much energy could be spent in the search for pristine origins and in spinning out fantasies about what the true "Folk culture" must have been like before its sad decline. If the young Marx's "essences" were inherently dynamic, containing with themselves their own opposites, those of the conservative Folk theorists were inherently static and timeless.

For all its backward-looking quality, Folk theory could inspire a politics in the present. The ties between the Folk and romantic nationalism were strong and pervasive. As many scholars have remarked, it is somewhat misleading to think of "nationalism" arising out of pre-existing "nations"; it can be shown, instead, that nationalists, by canonizing certain texts and practices, actively helped to imagine into being the very nations about which they spoke. Creating the modern nation, Benedict Anderson has suggested, required, inter alia, intellectuals to create, discursively, an "imagined community," contexts in which people who would never meet one another or even visit one another's communities could nonetheless come to feel some sense of commonality. To do this, the consequences of time and place had to be collapsed. A good example can be found in the daily newspaper, that classic shaper of "national" sentiment, wherein a sense of common experience is created by the bringing together of unrelated events. Newspapers use the most advanced means of modern technology and culture to create a fictional community which they may even refer to as a living entity, endowed with a personality and collective interests. The "nation," Anderson argues, may be defined as an *imagined political community*. It is imagined "because the members of even the smallest nation will never know most of their fellow-members, meet them, or even hear of them, yet in the minds of each lives the image of their communion."[21] A.D. Smith qualifies this "modernist" definition of the nation with his emphasis on the importance of ethnic community as a core for many nations. The "core" of ethnicity, for Smith, resides in a quartet of distinctive "myths, memories, values and symbols"; a "myth-symbol complex provides the *ethnie* with myths of ancestry, historical memories, borders of cultural difference, a common name:" and at the core of this complex lies what Smith calls the *mythomoteur*, the constitutive myth of the *ethnie*.[22] These two interpretations, while by no means uncontroversial, both improve on many overly functionalist discussions of national identity and nationalism[23] by distinguishing clearly between imagining a community and perpetrating a hoax, thereby delivering us from the interpretive standoff between those who portray ideological leadership as a wilful process of class or ethnic manipulation, and their opponents, who naively take "nation-builders" at their own evaluation. They both suggest, rather, a process of myth-formation and cultural intervention closer to that visualized by Antonio Gramsci, for whom "hegemony" was that process through which a fundamental class (either the bourgeoisie or the working class) articulates the interests of other groups to its own, thereby exercising a moral and intellectual leadership and creating a genuine "national-popular will" as a fundamental aspect of its ability to rule.[24] As we trace the "politics of cultural selection" through which a "mythomoteur" and a "neo-nationalist" common sense were created in Nova Scotia, we shall discover that the patterns were rarely those of outright invention or hoax. They are more acceptably depicted as processes of cultural hegemony, working through the creation of an imagined community.

The usefulness of the idea of the Folk for bourgeois nationalists has long been clear. The Folk, transcending and preceding all divisions into classes, testify to the imagined organic unity of the nation, and the cultural phenomena associated with them are indispensable for the purposes of symbolic identity. As Philip V. Bohlman remarks in his penetrating study of folksong scholarship, there is a direct connection between what Folk theorists did with song and what nationalists were doing on a more general level with the idea of community. In *The Study of Folk Music in the Modern World*, Bohlman notes the revealing persistence over generations of a tautological, conservative orientation in studies of folk music. The earliest European theorists, he writes, "portrayed folk music as if it were the cultural core of noncomplex society. Speculations on the nature of folk music and the social organization of nature were tautologically circumscribed ... Folk music was the crystallization of the cultural core. As folk music was structured, so too was the rest of society."[25] Bohlman suggests that German Romantics had to imagine a basis for *das Volk*:

If they were to anthologize folk music in such a way that it could be called *deutsche Volkslieder* ... Similarly, the [Anglo-American] intellectual scions of Francis James Child proceeded to imagine communities of ballad singers and social contexts for communal musical activities that had little historical validity. The musical symbols of an imagined community are many: an identifiable corpus of folk song, usually printed for wide distribution; national songs and national anthems; folk songs that spell out the history of the nation in overt and subtle forms; and, in general, the equation of folk music with national music.[26]

Just as nationalists imagined "the nation" of which they spoke, enthusiasts of folklore imagined "the Folk" necessary for the crafts and lore that had survived to the present day. Although such an imagined folk canon was necessarily a product of modernism, and often (like the daily newspaper) a *bricolage* of unrelated cultural artifacts, it was invariably presented as whole and traditional – as a hallowed set of crafts, music, stories, and sayings reflecting the noble simplicity of the Folk in its natural state. Folk music scholarship conveyed this conservative, nostalgic image from the earliest stages of its history, and, writes Bohlman, "exceptional has been the perspective that did not turn toward the past, idealizing and revering a community of folk music before it disappeared. Many of the fundamental endeavors of folk music scholarship are steeped in this conservatism and the ideological stances it engenders: collection, classification, revival, canonization." Even radicals who attempted to conscript the concept of the "Folk" for their own use have found that its conservative logic cannot be so easily disregarded.[27] Just as nationalism did not "discover" the nations of which it spoke but rather "imagined" them into being, nineteenth-century Romantic enthusiasts of folklore did not so much "discover" the Folk past as much as they constructed it as the necessary conceptual basis for their "Folk" canons. Helen Creighton, imagining on her first visit to Devil's Island the natural origins of the community's response to the songs and believing herself to have come in touch with an organic and harmonious society, was following in a long tradition.

Although the concept of the Folk can be traced back to continental Europe and the anti-Enlightenment, twentieth-century Nova Scotia was more directly influenced by elaborations of the concept in Britain and the United States. As part of the British empire, and then as one of the provinces of Canada, Nova Scotia was very much affected in all aspects of its culture by British models. A British garrison in Halifax, a system of education strongly influenced by British ideals, the legacies of imperialism and the Great War so evident in memorials and monuments: all of these gave credence to the visitors' frequent perception of the city and province as very British in tone. At the same time, Nova Scotia was strongly attached to the United States, and more particularly to New England, where many Nova Scotians could trace family roots and to which many moved as emigration from the province became a powerful demographic force from the late nineteenth century on. If the entire Dominion of Canada could be said to have been influenced by the United States and Great Britain – as part of a cultural "North Atlantic Triangle" – Nova Scotia was perhaps unusual in how powerfully and immediately both major sets of influences were felt.

The world of folklore scholarship to which Creighton had access as a new researcher into the Folk was, by the 1920s, emphatically Anglo-American in its orientation. In Britain, the work of the American Francis James Child – especially *The English and Scottish Popular Ballads*, completed in 1898 – had focused attention on a select set of 305 ballads, which became known as the "Child ballads." Born in 1825, Francis James Child became the first professor of English at Harvard in 1876. Child's concept of the essential canon long remained an influential one, perhaps more because of the seeming completeness and authoritativeness of his collection (which weighs about six pounds) than because the logic behind his canon was apparent to his successors.[28] Child's mantle was inherited by George Lyman Kittredge, who assumed the Harvard chair of modern languages in 1894, and whose extraordinary influence was to be felt throughout North America and directly in Nova Scotia.[29] Because of his implicit stress on ballads originating in non-literate societies, Child's legacy was an exaggerated tendency among ballad collectors and others to equate change with corruption, in pursuit of the *authentic* and the *original*. By the 1920s many collectors distinguished between the Child ballads, the true aristocrats of the music of the Folk, and "other" songs – such as songs first published on broadsides in the British Isles as well as in North America, and by extension all those later forms of popular music that were patently not the anonymous, ancient products of the Folk. Some theorists intensified the élitism implicit in this notion of the canon by adhering to the view that popular lore and songs invariably came from above: only aristocratic origins could explain why the Folk so often sang of the exploits of the well-born.[30] One could easily combine a career collecting the traditional ballads sung by ordinary working people with the utmost contempt for those who had come into possession of such aristocratic heirlooms almost by accident.

Child had established, among the growing numbers of people seriously interested in the "traditional ballad," a sort of "regime of truth," a way of distinguishing what was truly of the Folk from the spurious, merely "popular," and corrupted culture of ordinary people. This boundary of truth was policed by the tune collectors of the English Folk Dance and Song Society, who collected "only the older tunes in oral circulation, [and] printed selected tunes unembellished in the Society's journal, though they took less pains with the texts."[31] In the view of the society, although contemporary England might still listen to folksongs of recent invention, few of them merited preservation.[32] To a remarkable extent, and many decades after his death, the definite article in the title of Child's book continued to exert an influence: folklorists, authorized to decide which songs were "inauthentic and modern," and which ones "genuine and traditional," did so largely on the basis of Child's belief that he had isolated and presented "*The* English and Scottish Popular Ballads," that he had unearthed the essential canon. Even after the "Child canon" had started to erode as a universally accepted yardstick of authenticity, belief in the need for canon, authenticated by those with expert credentials, persisted.

Although an American had been pivotal in the development of "their" canon, English nationalists were not slow to realize the implications of Child's work for the idea of a national music. As Alun Howkins observes, if one believed (following Herder) that the sounds of music could literally express the soul, and that this soul had a national character, it was a matter of concern that the English preferred the music of German composers to their own melodies. So, just as mock-Tudor became the preferred architectural style of stockbrokers thirsting after tradition and the "English essence," Tudor and Stuart music and folksong came to constitute the "true" English music that nationalists sought to recover and develop.[33] The key twentieth-century British collector and folklore theorist was Cecil Sharp (whose work was to have a direct impact on Creighton). Sharp broadened the parameters of the canon, while attaching folksong to a seemingly scientific neo-Darwinian schema of musical evolution. For Sharp, the folksong was the "unaided composition of the unskilled" and differed generically from composed music. At the same time, the most precious melodies might ascend the evolutionary ladder to become suitable materials for high culture. The inherent musical qualities of a given folksong determined its chances of

survival. Thus a conservative approach that had traditionally minimized human agency found support in a scientific elaboration of
ideas of "communal composition" and "natural selection."[34]

The second major international influence on Nova Scotian folklore
came from the United States. In some respects, this was a modified
version of the British tradition. The "Child/Other" dichotomy was
firmly rooted in North America. Often a folklorist's collection would
feature the "Child ballads" first, implicitly defined as essential, gar-
landed with scholarly notes and other signs of significance. The
residuum – more recent music, whether British or North American,
including music first published on broadsides, banjo music, local
songs about feuds, narratives of current events, black music – was
marginalized and treated far more casually. As the Maine folklorist
Sandy Ives observes, "The tendency was to put those Child ballads
first as the very real, best, the aristocrats of the ballad world and
then other ballads sort of tapered off toward the back and local songs
might be included in the back of the book."[35]

Folklore collectors who had internalized the Child canon were
understandably excited to discover, in the valleys and coves of North
America, ancient ballads from Britain. It was thrilling to learn that
in the modern Appalachians the Folk were still singing Elizabethan
ballads, which were sometimes better remembered (the collectors
wonderingly exclaimed) than in their English homeland! Middle-class
cultural enthusiasts went so far as to supplement the Elizabethan
ballads with such reinvented English traditions as Morris dancing,
which were wholly foreign to the traditions of the "mountain Folk,"
as well as Danish arts and crafts. The result of this earnest middle-
class mountain pedagogy was a "Folk culture" that was remarkably
English in its song and dance, remarkably Danish in its crafts, and,
for all that it advertised itself as "all that is native and fine," an
example of modernist *bricolage*.[36]

"Genuine" folk culture, according to Child, had descended from a
holistic epoch when there was such a complete community of ideas
and feelings that "the whole people form[ed] one individual."[37] Those
who, unlike Child, took this myth of the past holistic community to
its limit, in the tradition of the Grimms, believed that Folk culture
emerged as the spontaneous, autonomous, gregarious poetry of the
primeval horde's "collective soul." Others championed an individualist myth of origins, a sense of Folk culture as a legacy of the high
cultures of the Renaissance or earlier. Both groups of scholars emphasized cultural retrieval and restoration. They agreed that their mission
was to recover and understand the traditional ballads, not to place
them in their socio-historical context, and to value the true and

authentic traditional ballads, not the modern forms of music sung from memory by ordinary people, which could be contaminated by the newspaper or the radio. For the folklorist Howard Brockway, writes David Whisnant, "Child ballads and dulcimers were good; banjos and the newer music to be heard at the railheads and county seats were not ... The 'outer world' and its 'trivial and commonplace music' were a 'killing blight'; the impending social and economic changes within the mountains would bring only 'contamination.'"[38]

There was, then, a complex and powerful *Anglo-American* folklore matrix, a common trans-Atlantic entropic sensibility that structured assumptions and methods in the study of the Folk and their supposed lore, notwithstanding the major differences in outlook between the two traditions. Some of the most important American collections were created by English visitors, seeking in the New World evidence of the folk culture of the Old. Cecil Sharp, who was to become a key influence on Helen Creighton, was a leading example. His collecting in the American south was pathbreaking, but it was governed by the same preference for ballads cannonized by Child and disregard for "other materials occurring in profusion in the same 'field' – religious music, popular music, instrumental music, and recently composed ballads and songs"[39] – not to mention the music of blacks, whom Sharp disparaged.

As was the case worldwide, there was no clear a priori reason in this trans-Atlantic paradigm for including some within the Folk and excluding others. If, as David Buchan urges, we can derive a more socially specific notion of "the Folk" in the Scottish case by defining the category in terms of the non-literate inhabitants of places where tradition was transmitted largely via word of mouth, and the ballads as oral literature, originally composed and transmitted by such non-literate people, it must be remembered that such a tight definition was not available to people of the early twentieth century.[40] The categorization proceeded implicitly. The Folk did not exist either as a self-defined group or as an externally defined population; they existed in the mind of the interpreter. These interpreters, however, travelled in schools and shared a sense of history as entropy. And they all agreed that the real Folk did not live everywhere. The Folk did not generally frequent coal mines, steel mills, factories, or cities. Not only was cultural contamination rife, but the organic solidarities of the true Folk community were being undermined. The Folk did not belong to political parties or read newspapers or mount labour protests. They were the passive recipients of tradition, not its active shapers. Emphasis was placed on the retrieval and restoration of the Folk essence, on recovering the traces of individual songs and charting the evolution of the Child ballads in North America, not on placing the singing of folksongs and other traditions in socio-historical context. For many of the first Anglo-American folklorists, the point of the exercise was to preserve an aesthetic treasure-trove of Folk culture. Academic folklore emerged in the turn-of-the-century period as a powerful legitimating force, but it did not reorder the assumptions of the field. Elitism – the supposed ability of middle-class and often academic men and women to rule on the inherent worth or worthlessness of folk traditions on the basis of their "authenticity" within a closely defined canon and on an "objective" evaluation of their aesthetic worth – was durably installed as a feature of international discussions of the Folk. In this construction of the Folk, culture was a collection of decontextualized artifacts – old ballads, sayings, superstitions, customs, handicrafts – whose value lay not in the functions they performed for those who employed them, but in their status as isolated relics of an older and better time. The middle-class collector was a kind of recording angel, rescuing the cultural treasures of the international Anglo-American Folk from the uncomprehending local people who accidentally harboured them. One did not worry about how the songs or legends were used in the present day, or about the complex hopes and fears of those who made use of them; one worried instead about mining and refining and marketing this cultural resource. And merely expanding the canon, as some critics of the Child approach were inclined to do, did not undermine the very notion of a Folk canon, defined by experts on the Folk and brought to bear on cultural activities. Although both Henry Ford and Lord Beaverbrook contradicted in one sense the narrowness of the cultural politics of the nineteenth-century ballad-hunters by encouraging a much broader conception of what was valuable in "Folk" traditions, they remained faithful to the principle of "guardianship" over cultural essences menaced by economic and social change. Although neither followed the letter of Child, one might say they followed his spirit.

The key Anglo-American image was that of the "closed account," which neatly combined the notions of capital accumulation and historical entropy. The Folk tradition that mattered was no longer being created, but merely lingered on as a precious hidden fossil of an earlier time. David Whisnant notes that the publicity generated by one of the settlements in the Appalachians "uniformly emphasized cultural *survivals* – marvelous but essentially anachronistic artifacts: ballads and baskets, archaic speech and manners, dulcimers and play-party songs. Over and over again, the word went forth from the settlement schools that mountain culture was 'Elizabethan.'"[41] The ordinary people who harboured this ancient folk culture might not, indeed probably could not, be aware of what it was they had. They were the living and fast eroding walls of a cultural vault full of treasures. The collector held the key, and his or her mission was to rescue the treasure while the walls still held and the customs or songs or crafts still "survived." These assumptions seem to have been common throughout the Anglo-American cultural world, especially in the interwar period. "The ... folk tradition must not be regarded as a repository of cultural artefacts, but as an evolving expression of popular culture. In analysing culture as a form of social practice rather than a collection of products, we must pay attention to the changing technologies of expression and social relationships through which the tradition was produced and distributed."[42] The historian David Frank's sensitive observation, made in a study of the industrial folksong in Nova Scotia, is at complete odds with folklore as it was conventionally practised and diffused within a "survivalist paradigm" common to early twentieth-century folklore collectors and scholars on either side of the Atlantic.

Within this shared paradigm there were some distinctively North American aspects of folklore. These were a popular-nationalist tendency to challenge the Child canon, the early salience of anthropological approaches to folklore and consequent fissures between them and more literary approaches, and finally a more marked tendency to professionalism within the universities.

Although Child ruled in the United States, his rule was not uncontested. The United States was too heterogeneous and too nationalistic to permit so heavy an emphasis on a construction of the American Folk as the passive bearers of the British ballad. Gradually a broader category of "folksong" – characterized by oral transmission, constant formal changes, "vitality" over a "fair period of time," and the loss of all sense of individual authorship and provenance – came to supplement the narrower category of the Child Ballad.[43] Right-wing industrialists and racists, worried about the popular spread of black music in the 1920s, were significant for this emergent concept of the folksong. In the 1930s and 1940s the Left, no less essentialist in its cultural politics, championed the folksong within an aesthetic united front, and the Folk were vaguely defined as the "working class" or "ordinary people," whose songs invariably expressed inchoate longings for a society of justice and freedom. The folk revival of the twentieth century was influenced by the cultural policies of the Communist party of the United States, which were (according to R. Serge Denisoff's distinctly unsympathetic account) in turn shaped in part by Stalinist aesthetics, by the rather more complex critiques of the emergent cultural industries, and finally by the encounter of Communists and singing rank-and-file protesters in such massive strikes as those in Gastonia and Harlan County.[44] Communist enthusiasm for the Folk in the 1940s and 1950s might also have reflected many of the same antimodernist impulses that can be documented in other aspects of cultural life.

A further difference that distinguished the American from the British development of a shared survivalist paradigm was the greater salience in the United States of anthropological influences. In the United States there were substantial differences between the approaches taken by anthropological and literary folklorists. The Folk of the anthropologists tended not to be illiterate peasants within literate societies, as they were in Europe, but rather the non-literate members of "primitive" societies. Moreover, anthropologists, who were generally researching cultures without writing, could not blithely accept a definition of folklore as "that which was transmitted orally," since this would incorporate all aspects of the culture under their purview.[45] The paradoxical consequence was that "folklore" was more narrowly defined within anthropology – as "verbal art" or "oral literature" – than it was within literary folklore, where it could include all aspects of the "traditional lifeways of the people." (A similar division could be traced between curators of art galleries who valued objects for their intrinsic aesthetic interest, and curators of museums, who insisted upon contextualizing the object as a clue to the past.) "Thus," Rosemary Zumwalt wryly observes in her study of American folklore scholarship, "one might surmise that the literary folklorists adopted an anthropological approach, and the anthropological folklorists a literary one."[46]

The literary approach intensified the elitism inherent in the category of the "Folk" because it tended to assume that the collection, preservation, and understanding of literary forms was an appropriate end in itself, justifiable in terms of absolute standards of taste. "It was the text that interested them," Zumwalt says of the literary folklorists. "And it was the *origin* of the text that concerned them. They asked: What is the *Ur* form and from whence did it come?" Anthropological folklorists were more likely to ask, "What does the narrative tell about the people, and from whence did they come?"[47] Although the literary approach was long predominant in Nova Scotia, it did eventually have to defend itself from criticisms derived from its anthropological alternative.

Professionalism suggested a third way in which American traditions diverged from those of Britain. Creighton's "path of destiny" was relatively unmarked by socially accepted milestones of professional acceptance. There were few working models of professionalism to guide her. Not until the mid-twentieth century did folklore studies attain a limited academic respectability in the United States (the first Ph.D. was awarded in 1953). Those preoccupied with the folk were, until then, divided into two camps. In the first were members of departments of English or anthropology in the university, who wrestled with each other for control over the definition of folklore. In the second were the dedicated amateurs, who tended to be less specialized and more interested in tapping the growing popular market for things pertaining to the Folk. Even in today's Britain, "folklore" has yet to attain the academic status it enjoys in North America. Creighton, entering this field in the 1920s, thus had to define herself vis-à-vis the literary–musical British model, the literary–anthropological American model, and the expectations of an emergent mass market for things of the Folk.

The Canadian reception of these patterns was, as befits a country that is very much a social and cultural archipelago of distinct nations, regions, and societies, immensely complex. Although the emergence of folklore as a major interest of the National Museum and the eventual inauguration of professional folklore instruction at Laval and Memorial universities signalled a movement towards professionalism in Canada, it occurred significantly later than the parallel developments in the United States. Although professionalism did eventually emerge as a powerful force in the field, it worked slowly and unevenly. Prominent "folklorists," particularly in the Maritimes, were left in the somewhat anomalous position of "semi-professionalism." As for the division between literary and anthropological approaches, this seems to have reflected which part of Canada had been colonized by an American academic influence. Anthropologically inclined folklore played a very significant role in the west coast (Franz Boas) and at the National Museum in Ottawa (Marius Barbeau), but the dominant approach in the east was literary, perhaps because of the regional prestige of nearby Harvard, the centre of that approach. Yet as the National Museum in Ottawa gained in power and stature as a force in regional folklore, those whose main interests were literary and musical were brought into contact with, if never wholly under the control of, those who represented this potentially more holistic anthropological approach to the Folk.

The Nova Scotian interpreters of the Folk tended to be more conservative, more Anglocentric, and more fiercely essentialist than those of the United States. Canadian patriotism and a lingering British imperialism inclined Nova Scotians to maintain their ties with the predominantly aesthetic criteria of the British school. Nova

Scotian approaches to the Folk rarely paused to spell out their theoretical assumptions. The implicit theory might be best captured in a tautology: the Folk were those who guarded the lore of the Folk. They lived, generally, in fishing and farming communities, supposedly far removed from capitalist social relations and the stresses of modernity. The Folk did not work in factories, coal mines, lobster canneries, or domestic service: they were rooted to the soil and to the rockbound coast, and lived lives of self-sufficiency close to nature. The Folk and their lore were special and rare. Only in certain areas could one find the dying embers of an old organic Folk culture: Folk superstitions, Folk songs, Folk games, Folk handicrafts – they all survived, but only in rare pockets. The Nova Scotia Folk were difficult to define. As in Europe, the Folk were apparently peasants, telling old tales, singing old songs, making old crafts in traditional ways, living lives of quiet stolidity in centuries-old villages. They were most often "fisherfolk." We note in these assumptions both the impact of the Anglo-American nexus and the tendency in Nova Scotia to make it even more conservative than it already was.

No one, to my knowledge, ever attempted to make the claim that Nova Scotia was literally a "Folk society" (as some Quebec nationalist intellectuals attempted to do).[48] This is perhaps because it is extremely difficult to make anything like a cogent case for the existence of a "Nova Scotia peasantry." In fact, presenting most communities in Nova Scotia as exemplars of the ideal of the *gemeinschaft* (an organic community rooted to tradition and the soil) is problematical. Settled thousands of years ago by natives (the Micmacs), and then by the French (the Acadians), Nova Scotia passed to British control in the mid-eighteenth century. It received waves of immigrants from New England, from Protestant German-speaking principalities in Europe, from the mid-Atlantic states (with the Loyalist emigrations after the American Revolution, including numerous blacks), and from Scotland, Ireland, and England. Each ethnic group retained customs peculiar to itself, and, far from resembling the organic solidarity of a folk community, the early nineteenth-century province seethed with tensions and rivalries, ethnic, religious, and ideological. By the mid-nineteenth century, Nova Scotia (including both the peninsula itself and the island of Cape Breton, once a separate colony but annexed in 1820) was a significant factor in world shipping and in the fishing industry. Mines – the largest in British North America – had been started on the province's coalfields. The rapid growth of secondary manufacturing, the explosive growth of the coal industry, and a greatly expanded iron and steel sector gave Nova Scotians of the 1880s and 1890s a sense of living in a rapidly advancing province. The crisis that befell the province's economy after this period of expansion will long be a matter of debate. Manufacturing had passed into the control of externally based companies, and many plants established in the 1880s to take advantage of high tariff protection were closed in the early twentieth century after being merged with central Canadian enterprises. Yet before the 1920s there was remarkably little sense of economic crisis, perhaps because the coal and steel sector, itself dominated by outside interests, continued to post remarkable increases in production. For Nova Scotians of the 1910s, the most discussed issues were those raised by rapid and unplanned industrial growth. How could social order be maintained if massive industrialization created zones of high infant mortality, low education, and disease? Should children work in the mines? How should workers and others respond to the labour wars that raged in the province's coalfields – including one episode of industrial strife that lasted twenty-two months and was ended only by the use of armed force? How should Halifax, devastated by a massive explosion in 1917, be rebuilt in order to live up to the progressive demands for rationally planned working-class housing?[49] Then came the 1920s, and an immense change in economic and political life. The Nova Scotia coalfields were thrown into chaos by layoffs and labour wars; across the province, secondary manufacturing and resource industries declined; and tens of thousands of young Maritimers and Nova Scotians left home for the United States and central Canada. A strong provincial labour movement, which had once confidently predicted the death knell of the old order in the province, and which had allied with the farmers to create the official opposition party in the province, was thrown into disarray. A "Maritime Rights" movement led by small businessmen and professionals emerged to fight for the interests of all three Maritime provinces, although it never completely succeeded in developing a sense of a "Maritime" interest that rivalled strong identification with individual provinces.[50]

This is not the history of a settled, ordered Folk society, but of a region that experienced many of the contradictions of capitalist modernity. Even precapitalist eighteenth-century Nova Scotia scarcely fit a model of Folk tranquillity and rootedness. The eighteenth-century "South Shore" (which extends along the Atlantic from Halifax to Yarmouth) was more like a refugee camp than a haven from the storms of modernity. Acadians thrown to the four winds after their expulsion by the British, the Loyalists, the foreign Protestants dumped onto these shores by political and religious upheaval, the blacks facing their first Nova Scotian race riot in Shelburne: none of these groups resemble the idealized "Folk." As the province developed socially and economically, it diverged more and more from the Folk ideal. Widespread mass literacy and an extensive print culture centred on Halifax but affecting the entire province have coexisted since the early nineteenth century. Religious denominations and an extensive religious press brought to the majority of Nova Scotians the complex traditions of American and European theological discussion. With the partial and not widespread exception of places where estate agriculture was practised in the eighteenth and early nineteenth centuries, there never was a "peasantry" tied to the land in the European sense in Nova Scotia. Those primary producers who were worked up as European-style "Folk" did not live in tranquil villages, nor did they lead lives of quiet stolidity. Geographical mobility (moving from place to place in search of waged work or better access to fish stocks), occupational pluralism, and (from the mid-nineteenth century on) widespread outmigration to cope with diminishing opportunities in the region made many villages in rural Nova Scotia resemble transit stations more than quiet havens of tranquillity. If one disqualified from the "Folk" those who had worked as employees in coal mines, or on fishing schooners, or in the lumber camps; if one insisted upon life within a world of oral culture; if one required isolation from the world of modern ideas, from newspapers, radios, books; if one needed relatively self-contained "small communities" with their own standards, cultures, and traditions; if one required distance from the "cash nexus" of merchants, banks, department stores, "acquisitive individualism" – if all of these were required for the Folk, very few, if any, Nova Scotians would have qualified by the 1920s. A century of capitalist development, beginning with the start of large-scale coal-mining in the 1820s, did not augur well for the survival of a supposedly organic and pre-modern society. The fishing industry, which would provide so many images of Folk picturesqueness, has served up episodes of near starvation, bitter battles between merchants and producers, various forms of unequal exchange, and some of the most graphic illustrations of the perils of monopoly capitalism the twentieth century can provide.[51] The idea of an isolated, sheltered fisherfolk, far removed from the storms of modernity, depends not upon empirical evidence but upon age-old European conceptual paradigms; yet this idea has proved highly influential as a way of narrating what is essential in Nova Scotia's history. It has become a privileged way of understanding history and culture, and through them the "Spirit of Nova Scotia."

The paradoxes and ambiguities of developing the idea of the Folk in this particular context have been significant. The Nova Scotia Folk were implicitly defined as the carriers of folklore (that is, stories and songs characterized by oral transmission, traditionalism, anonymity, tendency to formula, and presence in a number of versions). At the same time, this lore was not truly theirs, and it could be saved only if it was transferred to other hands and other, more modern, means of cultural transmission and storage. Vanishing, isolated in small cultural enclaves, as reclusive as nocturnal animals, the Folk had to be hunted down and then coaxed into parting with their essence. Thus the trope of the "romantic quest" was firmly installed in the narratives in which the middle class described its ventures onto this primitive terrain. These emissaries of modernity braved dirt, isolation, and social danger to retrieve the true nuggets of authenticity concealed in the primitive countryside. When Creighton pushed beyond the margins of the known world in visiting the Hartlans, and when so many others painted the fishing coves and wrote of the simple lives of their people, they underlined the Otherness of the Folk: they were simple, isolated, different: they were Other, and not "us." And yet, paradoxically, the Folk were more "us" than we ourselves, more *essentially* Nova Scotian (or Canadian), the last true products of our soil and the last authentic producers of our culture. There were echoes of Spencer and Darwin in the folklorists' argument that the Folk were the prototypical Nova Scotians, and neither their poverty nor their isolation, both seen as part of an eternal and unavoidable fate, affected the treasure they unknowingly carried.

Inspired by international precedent, those who first conceptualized Nova Scotians as Folk were driven by the notion of saving decontextualized items, whether "traditional" ballads or bits of superstition and lore. The Folk were called forth by the very body of international theory and practice that purported to speak about them. "The Folk" is a category that can work only in relation to other classifying categories. In twentieth-century Nova Scotia, it was not generally a way in which a group of people designated themselves ("We, the Folk ...") As everywhere, "the Folk" had to be created through framing and distilling procedures carried out in thought, and then set into practice through processes of selection and invention. Collectors were editors, animators, and producers who selected certain informants, rewarded certain cultural acquisitions, marginalized that which was not "of the Folk" – indeed, literally erased those songs and sayings which true members of the Folk would regard as an embarrassment, as an untruthful representation of who they really were. Whatever flexibility might creep into the determination of "the canon" of "folksong" or "folk art," that such boundaries needed to be set and adjudicated by experts has never been in doubt.

When Creighton set out for Devil's Island as a journalist in 1929, she was also voyaging into an international matrix of words and things that defined the true Folk and determined what would count as true statements about them. Her significance was that she mediated the lived experience of songs and traditions as directly experienced on the coast and the complex international tradition that had grown up to interpret such phenomena worldwide. Becoming a folklorist meant gradually adopting this grid of significance, this ability to separate the genuine from the spurious, to distinguish the true gold originating in the lost Atlantis of the Folk community from the clinging dross of artificiality and modernity. Creighton's "discovery" of Ben Henneberry on Devil's Island was a significant and eventful accident. What was even more significant, and less accidental, was that she was looking for him in the first place, and knew what to do with his "gold mine" of songs once she had uncovered it.

REGIONAL CRISIS, ANTIMODERNISM, AND THE FOLK IN NOVA SCOTIA

This leads us to the third way of telling the story, on an intermediate level of medium-range synthesis, where this book will do most of its work. This involves asking why the local cultural producers – the writers, artists, photographers, musicians, publicists, and other enthusiasts of the arts – took up the international concept of the Folk just when and how they did. Why, in the short period from 1900 to 1950, and in the context of an emphatically non-Folk society, did so many people strain to see, and select out for cultural esteem, those elements which could be accommodated to the Anglo-American Folk ideal?

They did so as part of a broader antimodernist movement within the region and the province. This local variant of antimodernism can be called *Innocence*. Innocence emerged in the period from 1920 to 1950 as a kind of mythomoteur, a set of fused and elaborated myths that provided Nova Scotians with an overall framework of meaning, a new way of imagining their community, a new core of a hegemonic liberal common sense. Innocence discerned the essence of the society. The province was essentially innocent of the complications and anxieties of twentieth-century modernity. Nova Scotia's heart, its true essence, resided in the primitive, the rustic, the unspoiled, the picturesque, the quaint, the unchanging: in all those pre-modern things and traditions that seemed outside the rapid flow of change in the twentieth century. True Nova Scotians were those who could trace local roots from the pre-modern era. Innocence denotes the local development of antimodernist conceptions of history and society through a network of words and things diffused by the urban middle class and corresponding, in a complex, indirect, and general sense, to its social and cultural interests.[52] Innocence was a mythomoteur fuelled by *essentialism* – that is, a concept of reality as composed of the two levels of essence and existence, with essences as the final, perfect states towards which existents are striving or from which they have originated – and a kind of *antimodernism*, whose dominant form can be defined (following Jackson Lears) as "the recoil from an 'overcivilized' modern existence to more intense forms of physical or spiritual experience."[53] From the late nineteenth century on, and across the western world, scepticism about "progress" and fear that unprecedented social and economic changes were destroying the possibility of "authentic" experience (and even undermining the bases of selfhood itself) shaped social thought and cultural expression across a wide ideological spectrum. For a number of reasons, antimodernism had an especially powerful resonance in Nova Scotia, where, in the second quarter of the twentieth century, it transformed representations of the provincial identity. Innocence was a network of words and things that established powerful and pervasive ways of seeing and feeling. Innocence was both the imposition of externally derived categories on Nova Scotian social realities – through tourism, for example, Nova Scotia came to be defined more and more unequivocally as a "therapeutic space" removed from the stresses and difficulties of modern life – and an internally generated set of ideas about Nova Scotia which local cultural producers considered to be self-evidently true. In fact, Innocence blurred the distinction between "internal" local knowledge and "external" objectifying stereotypes. Local cultural producers, themselves thoroughly integrated into North American urban culture and often acutely sensitive to international cultural patterns, tended to highlight in their novels, paintings, broadcasts, and photographs those aspects of Nova Scotian society and history which they knew would succeed in the international cultural marketplace. Innocence was a way of seeing and thinking through which the pre-modern "Otherness" of Nova Scotia was "naturalized" (that is, made to appear an obvious and commonsense interpretation).

There were five particularly dramatic changes in perception and practice entailed in Innocence. The new doctrine that the province was essentially Scottish was fortified with invented traditions and emblems; the province's history was seen anew as a collection of static artifacts testifying to the lost splendours of a vanished golden age; the symbolic landscapes of the province became those which emphasized insularity, rockbound coasts, and an omnipresent sea; and representations of the archetypal Nova Scotian came to emphasize muscle-bound masculinity and prowess. Finally – and this is the theme this book sets out to explore in depth – Nova Scotia came to be seen, at least on the level of its myths and symbols, as *essentially a "Folk society."* Victorian Nova Scotians had exalted their society's newspapers, scientific achievements, novels, universities, and religious institutions: in short, all those things, and they were numerous indeed, which suggested that Nova Scotians were in step with the march of improvement throughout the industrializing world. Innocence undermined this canon. It established, at the core of the reimagined Nova Scotian identity, folklore, folksong, witchcraft, superstition, the "simple life," and the so-called oral tradition. In the photographs of Wallace MacAskill, the paintings of Marsden Hartley and Stanley Royle, the novels of Frank Parker Day and Thomas Raddall, the histories of F.W. Wallace we find the same new vocabulary of region, the vocabulary of Innocence, whose keywords were the Highlander, "heritage," the sea, the hardy fisherman, and (perhaps most powerful of them all) the Folk. In this "golden age" of regionalist redescription, regionalism discovered a golden age: not in an idealized Britain, not in the radiant industrial future, but in the past – and in that past lay the essence of what it meant, and still should mean, to be "one of us." The little fishing communities, once regarded as backward and primitive, became tranquil havens of simple Folk; history was reconceptualized not as the *telos* of material progress but as a stable collection of embalmed artifacts; living men and women were revisualized as embodiments of older, nobler, more traditional (and yet more "natural") family relations. Merely to name these key redescriptions is to suggest the scope and depth of the discontinuities and shifts. The "new truth" emerging from the mythomoteur of Innocence was that the province was still enchanted, unspoiled, a Folk society, natural, and traditional: that the fall into capitalism and the "disenchantment of the world" had not affected this society's essential innocence of everything negative suggested by the phrase "modern life." The call of the blood and the racial memories of the Folk, the timeless traditions of the fishing coves, the unceasing battles of male adventurers against an eternal sea, the pull of strong families bound together by tight knots of tradition and religion: these were some of the new particular myths produced by the general mythomoteur of Innocence. For all its apparent "organicism," however, Innocence as a mythomoteur functioned within, and strengthened, a "liberal order" defined by possessive individualism, the strict division between public and private, and a self-limiting state.

By calling the antimodernist impulse in twentieth-century Nova Scotia "Innocence" I am suggesting that, although always influenced by and contributing to cultural trends on the international level, a loose network of cultural producers in Nova Scotia created their own distinctive variant of antimodernism. Internationally, antimodernism has often been an ideologically mobile force whose impact has been felt on the Left and on the Right. From the 1920s on, Innocence was far less equivocal in its right-wing politics. Elsewhere we need to speak of antimodernism's Janus face, pointing to accommodation with and resistance to capitalist hegemony. Raymond Williams brilliantly reminded us of this doubleness of pastoral antimodernism in *The Country and the City*, a critical study of the tradition in Britain.[54] However, the Nova Scotian pattern, shaped by the province's precarious socio-economic position in the second quarter of the twentieth century, was much more one-sidedly reactionary.

This social and economic crisis provided an impetus to antimodernism in general and to the category of the Folk, hitherto not much in evidence, in particular. There were three changes of the 1920s and 1930s, traceable to the crisis, which impinged directly on the emergence of the Folk *motif*. First, and perhaps most important, was the rise of the tourism economy. Since the 1920s tourism has figured centrally in strategies to cope with regional de-industrialization. Although tourism antedated the 1920s, in its earlier modes it was confined to very limited areas. Until the 1920s it had not been a permanent part of state policy either to attract tourists or to coordinate various aspects of local culture and society as part of the "tourism plant." After that decade, however, the state aggressively intervened in civil society to construct such a plant by paving highways, developing hotels, inventing new ethnic and sporting traditions, and monitoring the steady advance of the "industry." The transition to the tourism state meant an expansion in the official production of images, which was transformed from an intermittent activity to a routine state function. This in turn created opportunities for middle-class cultural producers, who could make a good dollar by creating marketable images of the Folk. At a time when, as Maria Tippett has shown, those who sought careers in the arts were severely restricted by limited state funding and the absence of large private foundations in Canada, the emergence of the tourism industry promised cultural producers a regular source of income.[55] Poets, painters, novelists, and photographers rallied to the cause of tourism, which they came to see not only as a source of revenues for themselves, but as a cause meriting the support of every patriotic Nova Scotian.

Following John Urry, this cultural turning-point could be termed the organization of the "Tourist Gaze," in which tourist impressions were no longer left to chance, but were constructed through public and private institutions.[56] By anticipating that which will attract tourism's totalizing and essentialist gaze, the state can construct the "experiences" for particular tourists, who for these purposes are also commodities to be profitably circulated through the "tourism plant." The tourism market is predisposed to essentialism, particularly that tied to the reproduction of ethnic imagery. To return home with an authentic handicraft or having had an authentic folk experience is one way of proving to oneself and others that one has indeed made the journey and found it worthwhile. What the tourist thought he or she wanted to see could be anticipated and, to some extent, simulated. In Nova Scotia, what the tourist wanted to see was something far removed from the stresses and strains of life in the large American cities of the northeast (which was for a long time the province's main source of tourists).

We may summarize the cultural impact of the transition to tourism in Nova Scotia in three ways:

1 The local production of most cultural goods would henceforth be directly influenced by tastes prevalent in the American and international marketplace. Nova Scotia's position within this political economy of cultural goods was that of a therapeutic space, an "ocean playground," and an aspect of this position was that there was a good market for romantic coastal views and books about simple families than there was for paintings of urban scenes or books exploring rural social problems.

2 The production of cultural goods would increasingly come under the influence of the state, which helped stage the first highly publicized and funded historical "extravaganza" in 1923, and which by 1953 was orchestrating the recovery or reinvention of rural crafts, publicizing regional folklore, and so on. The tourism-sensitive state became a delicate instrument for the measurement of international tastes and a massive machine for the generation of new images, new histories, and new traditions.

3 This intervention did not mean undercutting the role of capital; rather, it meant that the state, acting not on behalf of a particular class but in the interests of the stability of the socio-economic system as a whole, served as capital's pioneer, exploring hitherto uncommodified areas of cultural life that could be turned into profitable

activities. The commercial imperative was strengthened, not weakened, by the state. To the extent that provincial culture became coloured through such state activities by antimodernism, it was almost always a *commercial* antimodernism, structured by the very modern capitalism from which it seemed to provide a momentary and partial escape, and reliant upon its fast-developing technologies of persuasion.

Tourism's material impact on cultural life was pervasive and massive. It made possible a fully commercialized antimodernism, which (paradoxically) entailed simultaneously celebrating the pre-modern, unspoiled "essence" of the province and seeking ways in which that essence could be turned into marketable commodities within a liberal political and economic order.

However, tourism cannot be made to be the sole key to the emergence of the Folk, and its impact was not evenly distributed. Although images of Acadian "Folk" and "fisherfolk" were important in tourism from the late nineteenth century on, tourism's direct impact on the construction of the Folk proper was, until the 1940s, not pronounced. From the 1920s on, the state systematically created a complex network of words and things to make the "outsiders'" expectation of Innocence the "insiders'" lived experience. The "inside" and the "outside" were brought together. This procedure is not usefully described as a cheap trick, the construction of a false Folk "front" behind which "real life" could go on, or the invention of a "spurious" and superficial realm, a strictly demarcated "tourist bubble" outside which a real and authentic Nova Scotia persisted. It was rather the emergence of a new vocabulary of identity and the self, the mobilization of a new army of metaphors that seemed to give access to a deeper, pervasively influential and individualized official truth of society, history, and politics. These social and economic changes contributed to the reconceptualization of provincial identity in the 1920s and 1930s. What had once been thought essential – the cities, factories, coal mines, railways, and port facilities – were now peripheral. Now the essential Nova Scotia could be found in the unspoiled hamlets, where 'fisherfolk' lived in close harmony with nature.

A second major consequence of the economic crisis of the 1920s and 1930s was the silencing of many of the people who might have mounted a powerful challenge to the new antimodernist common sense. The crisis of the 1920s weakened a once mighty radical labour movement, sending many of its militants packing and undercutting the bargaining power of rank-and-file workers. Before the 1920s local analysts of "the social" had simply assumed a society divided into classes and the obvious centrality of the industrial "labour question." Nova Scotia was, after all, the site of some of Canada's largest and most spectacular labour revolts. But although some workers would continue to challenge the foundations of the liberal order down to the late 1940s, there can be little doubt that the dynamics of class struggle changed remarkably after the late 1920s in ways that were consistently to the disadvantage of the working class.[57]

Finally, the erosion of left-wing ideologies cleared an ideological space for other political positions, which stressed the identities of the "Maritimer" and "the Nova Scotian." These positions defy easy one-word distillations. They were "regionalist," but often worked on the assumption of provincial not regional identities, and contested the "whole" of which the region was held to be a part. They were "nationalist," but often worked against the emergent vocabulary of Canadian nationalism. Calling them "provincialist" or "parochial" underestimates their complexity and implicitly consigns them to the margins of a supposedly more central and more spacious Canadian identity; it also overpoliticizes them, and draws attention away from the extent to which cultural redefinition was an aspect of their appeal. They are perhaps best described as "neo-nationalist," which implies comparisons between what these people were doing in this local context and similar movements in other peripheral regions, although with the significant proviso (that applies fully to dominated nationalisms in Britain at most points of their history) that the goal of most of those who held such positions was not the dismantling of the Canadian state but something a good deal less politically definable.[58] Middle-class cultural producers, who had rarely sympathized with the rebellious workers, were particularly interested in this new vocabulary. Their response to the interwar crisis was multifaceted and complex. Like so many others in Canada, they felt called upon to develop a new, more distinctive vocabulary of identity. Such nation-building institutions as the Canadian Authors' Association and such nationalist artistic movements as the Group of Seven had a strong provincial resonance. At the same time Canadian nationalism, fixated on central Canadian symbolic landscapes and historical myths, created very little room for Maritimers. Like so many other middle-class intellectuals in the western world, Maritimers could identify neither with unfettered capitalism, which in the Nova Scotian case was clearly not an unqualified success story, nor with working-class radicalism. And so they turned to cultural forms which, though seemingly "of the people," carried no danger of radicalism, and which, though "Canadian," were also regional if not regionalist. The emergence of the Folk was perfectly suited to the perspective of those who were seeking new ways of imagining their communities, yet who also had every reason to hope that these new ways would entail the restoration of a comforting conservative ideal. Although there were a few exceptions (such as the poet Kenneth Leslie), those working with the key categories of Innocence were simultaneously conservative in their social imagination (idealizing the permanence and stability of the rural social order) and liberal in their political economy, defending above all the free marketplace of cultural goods and services from which they themselves made their living.

When Helen Creighton visited Devil's Island in 1929, she was both an insider and an outsider, both a Nova Scotian exploring what she could imagine to be the roots of her Nova Scotian identity and a thoroughly modern city-dweller exploring the primitive Other on her doorstep. In this she was wholly typical of her time and place. Much as they proclaimed their rootedness in their particular region and the distinctive call of their own particular blood, the cultural producers who redescribed Nova Scotia as a land innocent of modernity were far from distinctive when viewed from an international perspective. People were doing this kind of thing worldwide: attending, in many countries, to the "call of the race," and digging up folksongs and folktales as icons of eternal cultural truths. Practically everywhere in the interwar world, it seems, we find great refusals of capitalism's "disenchantment of the world," and an intellectual search for something more real, natural, authentic, and essential. Understanding the local moment of antimodernism we have called Innocence requires our seeing it, always and everywhere, as Janus-faced, as international and abstract in its cultural logic as antimodernism worldwide, and yet as fiercely parochial and determinate as the most narrowly focused local history in its pursuit of local distinctiveness. In embracing the sturdy peasant folk and attending to the call of the blood, Nova Scotian cultural producers were both imitating an international fashion *and* responding creatively to their own local conditions and their own socio-political interests.

THE CRITIQUE OF INNOCENCE AND THE STRATEGY OF THIS STUDY

It is one thing boldly to proclaim these theses, and another to provide the evidence to sustain them (or, more modestly, to show that some interesting new insights can emerge when such ideas are brought to the evidence). In a related volume, *Roads to Innocence: Tourism and the Politics of Culture in Twentieth-Century Nova Scotia*, I will look at the broad range of antimodernist forms that emerged in interwar Nova

Scotia and became part of the vocabulary of identity. This book began its life as one chapter of that longer study. In writing it, however, I gradually discovered that the subject of the Folk was so crucial and so complicated that it merited sustained attention in a book of its own.

The remainder of this book is divided into three chapters, followed by a short conclusion. In the following two chapters, I trace two contrasting strategies for "naturalizing" the notion of the Folk in Nova Scotia. Folklore is the subject of the next chapter. In folklore, the Folk were constructed as the unwitting bearers of a culture whose significance they only partially grasped. Amidst the dross of their squalid isolation and their primitive disorder, the Folk harboured a vast cultural treasury of pre-modern sayings and ways: Elizabethan words, ancient ballads, the unselfconscious authenticity and warmth of the small peasant society. The metaphors that occurred again and again in the letters and books of the folklore collectors were of "gold," "treasure," "mining," and "fortune": all metaphors that suggested that Folk culture was a kind of static ore, and the middle-class collector a combined prospector/miner/refiner/marketer without whom this ore would be lost to posterity. Our inquiry into the genesis of provincial folklore focuses closely on its central architect, Helen Creighton.

Handicrafts, the subject of the third chapter, represented a second and very different strategy. If, for ballad-hunters, the Folk could not really appreciate the ancient treasures they unwittingly carried, handicrafts planners often thought of craft workers as obstacles to the development of truly worthy rustic crafts. In handicrafts, local authenticity could not be grounded on a living, deeply rooted handicrafts tradition, but ultimately had to rest upon the idea of the handicraft as the mirror of nature, an essence squeezed from the rocks, the soil, and the local vegetation. The metaphors that recur among the promoters of handicrafts are consequently quite different from those we find in the language of the collectors: not those of mining but of pedagogy, not of recovering ore but of awakening an unconscious people to the natural forms they had somehow, over many generations, failed to see. Here the central cultural figures are not described as collectors or preservers but as inventors, organizers, and teachers. This chapter looks closely at the role of the state in the development of Nova Scotian handicrafts, and particularly at the career of the handicrafts organizer Mary Black.

However contrasting these strategies were for inventing a Folk Culture, both of them used similar categories. The dichotomous division of Nova Scotians into essentially peasant Folk on the one hand and modern, sophisticated city-dwellers on the other was mainly a twentieth-century phenomenon. Although nineteenth-century travel literature did develop the theme of "primitivism" in the countryside, it was not elaborating an ideal but satirizing or condemning a deficiency, exposing to the cold light of improvement the backwardness of the rural province. Certainly the beginnings of folklore may be traced in the writings of T.C. Haliburton and others. The beginnings of folk crafts as "collectibles" might likewise be traced back to nineteenth-century enthusiasm for the basketry and other crafts of native people. Yet these early applications of the concept of the "Folk" were marginal in two senses. First, they did not overpower the more common and powerful reading of Nova Scotia as improving, civilized, and industrializing; second, as constructs produced by and for a detached external gaze, they did not become "naturalized" within Nova Scotia itself.

"Folk" as a social category in Nova Scotia, and its promotion and naturalization as a commonsense concept, were the products of twentieth-century modernity (urbanization, professionalization, and the rise of the positive state) and the antimodernism that arose as a response to it. That Nova Scotia had never really been a peasant society in any recognizable sense was of little significance. From this nucleus of words and things testifying to a living and breathing Folk Innocence emerged cultural forms and energies that established traditions far and wide, extending from the design of souvenir ashtrays to the description of rural characters in novels. The fourth chapter analyses this pervasive impact of the idea of the Folk through literature, travel writing, and tourism promotion. In the fifth chapter, I broach the subject of the Folk under conditions of post-modernity, and speculate about the future of this element of innocence. I also discuss more fully some of the theoretical ideas that have shaped my discussion throughout the book, and readers who believe they need an explicit statement on theoretical frameworks before they can enter into a detailed discussion of evidence may prefer to start with the second section of chapter 5.

The cultural producers who reimagined Nova Scotia in the 1920s and 1930s were undertaking a politics of cultural selection. Sometimes cultural producers invented outright new forms and "traditions" to suit the tourist market and their own ideological projects. More frequently, however, selection rather than invention holds the key to Nova Scotia's cultural transformation. Tradition, Raymond Williams reminded us more than two decades ago, involves an active and continuous process of selection and reselection, and to come to terms with tradition means coming to terms not with an "object" but with the valuations, selections, and omissions of other people.[59]

Since Williams first made that observation, literary criticism has intensified our awareness of the extent to which "commonsense" and "natural" categories are socially constructed. As Benedict Anderson reminds us, imagining a community is a far different proposition than perpetrating a hoax. One of the many merits of his contribution is to release us from the interpretive dead-end of debates between conspiratorial social-control theorists who portray ideological leadership as a wilful process of manipulation and those who naively discount all consideration of the interests involved in cultural politics. The hegemonic politics of cultural selection was shaped by class, gender, and ethnicity, and by the pressure of unstated assumptions and the workings of the market.

Writing a critical study of Innocence is, then, not the same as pressing charges of insincerity against those who developed it, nor should it be seen as a straightforward exercise in debunking. In his brilliant and influential study of middle-class cultural intervention in the Appalachians, David Whisnant faced a similar dilemma of criticizing figures who were revered by many of his prospective readers. He astutely remarked: "One may reasonably display great charity for the cross-purposes, confusions, and miscalculations of fallible individuals in difficult circumstances. But insofar as those people actively intervene in the cultural (or other) lives of large numbers of people, their failures and miscalculations, however 'understandable,' become a legitimate object of public concern. For the effects of what they do touch so many, and linger so long."[60] The same could be said of the Nova Scotians who, for a very wide range of motives, constructed Innocence. Shaped by ideologies and social processes of which they were not fully aware, such cultural producers did not conspire to falsify the past. Their sincerity and good intentions are not at issue. What is at issue is the conservative essentialism they installed as a way of seeing their society.

Many Nova Scotians have warm memories of Helen Creighton, Mary Black, Will R. Bird, and the many others associated with the idea of the Folk in Nova Scotia. Sustained appraisal of their applied social thought may well seem disrespectful, negative, and unfair. This book is not intended as an exercise in revisionism for its own sake, but rather an attempt to contribute to the opening up of a debate and to the questioning of the ways in which a politics of cultural selection has made certain debatable assumptions seem like "natural" commonsense. I find in Innocence a systematic exclusion of those aspects of the past that would help people think historically about alternative outcomes, or about patterns of power and privilege in society, or about themselves as agents and victims of history.

Innocence in particular, and tourism in general, is ethically troubling because it exemplifies the transformation of living people (and their customs and beliefs) into articles of exchange. In a general ethical sense, this transformation is disturbing because it treats persons as objects rather than as ends in themselves. In a more down-to-earth sense, it also raises questions of exploitation, since the economic benefits of cultural commercialization are shared unequally and rarely accrue to those whose culture is appropriated by others. The construction of the rural "Other" in the interests of the tourist gaze is antithetical to seeing both rural and urban citizens as equals in a common project of citizenship. Both critiques can be combined, in fact, in an argument that full and free citizenship in a society of equals requires an open dialogue with the past, and such an open dialogue becomes increasingly unlikely if canons of significance, criteria of identity, and the very concept of community all come to be structured according to commercial criteria.

So there need be no disrespect in critically evaluating this body of applied social thought and assessing its current implications. The architects of Innocence were not the calculating perpetrators of a hoax, but the sincere builders of a framework of interpretation. They worked largely through mediation, passing on cultural resources they had taken from elsewhere in ways that confirmed their own socially determined "assumptions, attitudes, likes and dislikes," which "significantly determined what they looked for, accepted and rejected."[61] They were people who wielded "power through" more than they used "power over": theirs was that subtle cultural power that could define for a large number of people what is self-evident within a network of words and things. Juridical forms of power may be described as having a sort of hypothetical "last-instance" determining role in the constitution of this network, but for the most part Innocence was woven not through laws but through myths and symbols.[62] At the same time, the history of Innocence suggests the abiding importance of a neo-Marxist emphasis on the state, since it was clearly important in the lives of those who developed Innocence as a commonsense.

And it was this transformation of commonsense, of a sense of identity, of that complex of myths and symbols that told a people who they were, that was at stake in the path of destiny Creighton and so many others began to follow in the 1920s. Her voyage was ultimately important not because it signified the baptism of the region's most influential folklorist, the person whose grasp of the region's essence proved more popular and powerful than any other individual's, but because both her voyage and the career it launched fit within a much larger pattern of cultural redescription. Antimodernism had a marked impact on Nova Scotian and Maritime culture, because it emerged as a way of conceptualizing collective and individual identity at a time of profound crisis in the 1920s and 1930s. That Creighton happened upon a man with an astonishing memory for folksong and an equally prodigious repertoire was a matter of marvellous luck. That she was looking for him in the first place resulted from a general shift in concepts of identity and history. It is to her role in responding to and effecting this shift that we now turn.

2 Helen Creighton and the Rise of Folklore

When I have an opportunity of doing so, I will read more
carefully many of these ballads, which in some cases are very
amusing.

Prime Minister R.B. Bennett
on receiving the ballads of Helen Creighton

No single figure is more identified with the emergence of the idea of
the Nova Scotia Folk than Helen Creighton. From the late 1920s to
the early 1970s she stood for the idea of the Folk in the province. No
other provincial writer commands greater public esteem.[1] Her books
are widely read in the school system, and performing artists have
used songs from her collection. No balanced history of Nova Scotian
cultural life in the twentieth century would question the significance
of her contribution.

As we have seen, when Creighton went to Devil's Island as a
journalist in 1929, she was also voyaging into an international matrix
of words and things that defined the true Folk and the authentic
ballad. The folklorist was the person who could separate the gold
from the dross, the genuine from the spurious, the ballad from the
broadside. The politics of cultural selection entailed in this refining
became very significant when, as in Creighton's case, the operation
became enormously popular as a way of thinking about history and
culture. Creighton's work may well reach more Nova Scotians in a
wider range of contexts than that of any other local intellectual figure.

This chapter will examine this pivotal cultural producer in five
sections. The first looks at the most significant forerunners of
Creighton in provincial folklore – with special attention to Roy Mackenzie, whose career provides us with an instructive contrast – and
then focuses on two influences on Creighton: the popular folklore of
J. Murray Gibbon and the semi-academic folklore of Marius Barbeau
and others. The second section analyses the process through which

Creighton's identity as a folklorist was formed, with special attention to the transformative role of the National Museum in the 1940s and her relationship with Carmen Roy. The third section analyses Creighton's folklore as a kind of ideological intervention, involving powerful (but implicit) readings of class, gender, ethnicity, and Nova Scotian identity. The fourth section looks more closely at the ways in which this ideology was realized in practices of cultural appropriation and commodification as aspects of "Folk culture" that had once been considered common property became commodities to exchange. Finally, the fifth and concluding section analyses a crystallizing moment in which Creighton, by denouncing influences she perceived to be politically dangerous, showed that the conservative belief in cultural entropy that had been so prominent a part of Folk thought in Europe was no less powerfully a part of her own cultural politics.

FORERUNNERS AND INFLUENCES

As a neophyte collector of folklore, Creighton relied heavily upon the expertise and advice of others interested in the Folk. Three kinds of cultural producers helped to orient Creighton. First, there were those other folklorists who were developing a field of regional folklore in the period and, in particular, Roy Mackenzie, Creighton's most important forerunner. Second, there were the Canadian academics and the musical experts from Britain – those whose approach to folklore was deeply influenced by high culture and the literary life. Finally, there were the popularizers of Folk events, such as J. Murray Gibbon. They directly inspired Creighton and helped sustain the climate of rising interest in the Folk, which, after some discouraging years, meant that Creighton's decision to embark on a career in folklore would finally pay off.

Creighton became interested in the field at a time when the Maritimes and Newfoundland were becoming more and more famous throughout North America and Britain as places to collect folklore. From 1928 to 1935 at least six major titles were produced by academics or visiting professionals in the field of folklore in Atlantic Canada.[2] There was also a new local fascination with songs and lore. In both Newfoundland and Cape Breton popular amateur collections commemorated "old-time" songs and traditions.[3] Within the trans-Atlantic "survivalist" paradigm, it made sense to first seek the Folk in a region remote from the major areas of settlement in North America; and those folklorists influenced by Darwin and Spencer could ground this intuitive sense of where the songs could be found in their theory of social evolution.[4] Perhaps the Atlantic region was another Appalachia – another North American haven of the British ballad. Pondering why the region had suddenly become so popular, W.M. Doerflinger, an American folksong collector who concentrated on the Digby area, noted not only the snowball effect of the professional folklorists' interest in the region, but also the publicity the area had received since the 1920s in popular media. A column called "Old Songs Which Men Have Sung" in *Adventure Magazine* and the romantic sea novels of the novelist Frederick William Wallace were two significant disseminators of the Folk image. "There is a rich field for students to cover in the few years while the last deep-sea chanteymen remain on deck and old-time loggers, bards of the bunkhouse, still recall the falling of the pine and the songs that rang so bravely through the clearing."[5]

The most significant of the visiting enthusiasts drawn by this alluring prospect of the primitive was Maud Karpeles, who had helped Cecil Sharp collect folksongs and dances in England. She hoped to find in Newfoundland the same treasure-trove of traditional ballads he had earlier found in Appalachia. She was disappointed. "There are still a number of songs to be found in Newfoundland," she wrote afterwards, but added, with that sense of aesthetic standards characteristic of the English tradition, "the quality is poor. At least that again is perhaps not altogether true. If my Newfoundland songs had been the first folk songs to be noted it would be a wonderful collection, but so many of the songs are just variants of what had already been found. I had hoped that I might find a field such as the Appalachians, but that certainly was not the case."[6] The "Vassar folksong expedition" brought Elisabeth Greenleaf and Grace Mansfield to the region at roughly the same time. Arthur Huff Fauset collected folklore from blacks in Nova Scotia, and published his *Folklore from Nova Scotia* in 1931. Mary L. Fraser (Mother St. Thomas of the Angels), drew on Micmac, Acadian, Gaelic, and English lore for her 1931 doctorate at Fordham University. She was the first to prepare an extensive study of popular beliefs and legends in the province.[7]

An intensified local antiquarian fascination with "old ways" was also emerging in the early twentieth century, but it had very little to do with the category "Folk." J.B. Calkin's *Old Time Customs: Memories and Traditions*, published in Halifax in 1918, was based in part upon work he had done at least a decade earlier. It was a book aimed at a local audience still relatively uninfluenced by tourism. *Old Time Customs* contains none of the familiar landmarks of the Folk. Farmers, not the fisherfolk, are the key figures. Calkin was well removed from the entropic sensibility of international folklore. In fact, his was a quite "progressive" stance, which presented history as flowing quickly ahead, to the general benefit of Nova Scotians. Superstition is overshadowed by his discussion of the coming of free education; and even in the chapter on "signs and charms" there is no suggestion that Nova Scotians were unduly preoccupied with superstition. Their superstitions were also rather ordinary: they shared such beliefs as associating horseshoes with good luck with farmers throughout North America. To someone whose notion of "old time Nova Scotia" has been shaped by the post-1920s concept of the Folk, Calkin's book is baffling. Where is the lament for an older and better time? Where are the witches and the ghosts? Where, in fact, are the Folk? They are not to be found. Instead of magic and nostalgia, Calkin gave his readers a hymn of praise to the twentieth century's enlightened modes of punishment, industrial progress, and free education. Calkin's amateur "folklore without the Folk" exemplified the whiggish progressivism that Innocence was about to displace.[8]

For a historian detailing the emergence of titles in eastern Canadian folklore, the interwar period was clearly the period in which the field began to assume some shape. Insofar as the cultural impact of this work is concerned, however, the flood of titles may be somewhat misleading. The strictly local collections of old-time songs and tales of the pioneers often did not locate themselves within the emergent framework; those that were pitched at external scholarly audiences had a slight impact on the local audience. If the category "Folk" was to attain its full naturalization, what was needed were intellectuals who were both insiders and outsiders – insiders who lived in, or at least came from, the region, who nonetheless could place their work within the international framework. W. Roy Mackenzie (1883–1957) was the first to assume this position, and his cultural impact was substantial. He is fascinating both in his own right and as an important contrast to Helen Creighton, whom he directly inspired. Although his work is well known among folklorists both in and outside the region, Mackenzie is relatively unknown beyond the borders of their discipline. Mackenzie's relative obscurity today, as compared with the fame of his successor Creighton, suggests some interesting ideas about the dramatic change effected by the antimodernist revolution of Innocence in Nova Scotia.

W. Roy Mackenzie was an international folklorist whose work had a powerful local resonance. His *Quest of the Ballad* (1919) and *Ballads and Sea Songs from Nova Scotia* (1928) stand as major landmarks in the development of the idea of the Folk in the region and in Maritime cultural life. Mackenzie was born into a comfortably middle-class family in the small rural town of River John, Pictou County, in 1883.

Pictou County, since the 1820s the centre of coal and metal industries, was hardly a rustic backwater, and the impact of coal-mining and metal-manufacturing would have been felt among the farmers of Mackenzie's home district.[9] Nonetheless, River John was sufficiently removed from the county's industrial core that it retained the look and feel of a rural area.

Mackenzie graduated from Dalhousie University in 1902. He pursued graduate studies in English at Harvard, where he fell under the spell of G.L. Kittredge, the inheritor of the mantle of Francis James Child. The credit for alerting Mackenzie to the possibilities of ballad-hunting in Nova Scotia goes to Mary Ethel Stuart Mackenzie, his spouse, who first noticed the similarity between the ballads discussed by Kittredge and the songs Mackenzie had learned as a boy in River John, some of which were "English and Scottish Popular Ballads." "My imagination had been fired by a reading of Professor Child's great collection," Mackenzie later recalled, "and I had noted with a growing excitement that many of the best numbers in this collection were reminiscent of the songs with which, in my salad days, I had been entertained ... I began my intermittent search, then, only with the desire to preserve some local versions of the genuine old stock."[10] Mackenzie opened a direct channel of influence for the Harvard literary school (and through it the Child canon and the German essentialist tradition) to Nova Scotia.

With Kittredge's encouragement, Mackenzie returned to River John from Harvard to start collecting, and he kept coming back to the area (where he had a summer residence) after taking an appointment at Washington University in Saint Louis. As early as 1909 Mackenzie was describing Pictou County and its Folk to the readers of the *Journal of American Folk-Lore*.[11]

The Quest of the Ballad (1919) was an elegant memoir of his ballad-collecting adventures. It is a wonderful introduction to the world of an Edwardian folklorist and to the ethical and epistemological intricacies of Folk research. Mackenzie described, with an eloquence and frankness not subsequently equalled, the full context of his collecting efforts, and for this reason is regarded within folklore as an important pioneer of contemporary performance-oriented approaches. The people who sang the songs he collected come alive as characters in a novel, as colourful and quaint people of the countryside. Perhaps because he was somewhat conscious of moving into an artistic sphere normally coded "feminine," Mackenzie filled his account of collecting songs with a charged rhetoric of masculinity and adventure. The stereotypically feminine pursuit of house-to-house visiting was described in a hypermasculine language of hunting and seducing, as a romantic "quest" and as a "hunt" over the wild Nova Scotia country-side. He was no effeminate collector of songs, he seemed to be proclaiming; rather, he was "stalking the ballad," as a big-game hunter stalked the lion. "I may explain that I was still the veriest amateur at the great sport of stalking the ballad," he writes of his early days in the field, "and had not yet learned the various marks by which the more experienced hunter distinguishes his prey."[12] Once the prey is in his sights, as it were, his metaphors shift from hunting to seduction. On cajoling a cynical old woman to part with her songs, Mackenzie observed, "Many lovers, since the world began, have to their mistresses given vows of eternal fidelity, swearing by the bright moon, the stars of heaven, and the sands of the desert; but no lover did ever protest as I protested to Ann that day. She was forced to relent – or, rather, to seem to relent, for she now began to dissemble in crafty fashion."[13] (This theme of the folklorist pitted against a duplicitous woman may well have been influenced by such fictive models as that of Walter Scott's *The Antiquary*.)[14] Once the ballad-hunter conquers the virginity of the singer, however, he is home free: "If a ballad-singer can be persuaded to give you one song he will then proceed to hand over to you every song that he possesses, regretting only that he has not more to give; also, it must be remembered that old Ann and I had exchanged ballads in the process of singing to each other, and this is a ceremony as formal, binding, and sacred as the halving of a 'gold diamond ring.'"[15] Mackenzie also establishes his masculine credentials by reminding us of his early predilection for the "low company" of the Nova Scotia seaport town, which most contemporaries would perhaps have decoded as a reference not only to wharves and groggeries, but to brothels.[16] Here, in brief, was no mild-mannered professor of English but a hunter, a seductive lover, a man familiar with the rough waterfront world. An eminently Edwardian scholar, Mackenzie nonetheless suggested the romantic fascination with the "primitive" that made the Folk so popular a category in the interwar period. He also suggested, in his rhetoric of persuasion and seduction, a peculiarly masculine version of the standard pastoral trope of a beautiful relationship between the rich and the poor, the city and the country.

Mackenzie's contribution to subsequent work on the Nova Scotia Folk was immense. It was, perhaps, partly thanks to his influence that the Child canon and an Anglo-American perspective dominated early Nova Scotian works on the Folk so completely before the 1940s. Folklorists in Nova Scotia could attach themselves to a tradition that went back to the first decade of the twentieth century, and this early start was significant in terms of establishing a seemingly traditional canon. Some folklore scholars esteem Mackenzie's carefully annotated and comparative *Ballads and Sea Songs from Nova Scotia* (1928) above the more famous but less analytical work of Helen Creighton.[17]

His portrait of the Folk and their culture was, as befitted a student of Kittredge and Child, initially very selective. Mackenzie was in quest of "real" ballads, not the broadsides, children's songs, fiddle tunes, and local compositions that many people liked to sing. (One indication of how "external" this view of song was the very word "ballad," which was not a common one in the province.) As he later reflected, "The 'English and Scottish popular ballads' of Child's collection I had become familiar with; and, with Little Ned's 'Lord Thomas and Fair Ellinor' and 'Bolender Martin' haunting my memory, I had set out solely to procure variant versions of the true old stock. Everything else was dross in my sight." He might copy out other songs, but "merely to gratify my own private curiosity."[18] When he described his emotions on hearing an "authentic" Child ballad (after so many other songs), he turned (just as Creighton would in describing Devil's Island) to mining for his essentialist metaphors: "When I left the abode of song late that afternoon, with my right arm hanging limp from the shoulder, my comfort was that I had, at least, discovered one gleaming nugget in the mine of base metals."[19] Although he gradually came to see other kinds of music as something other than base metal, he would never have equated them with pure gold of the ancient English and Scottish ballads.

Mackenzie presented his findings in the "Child and other" format. He also deferred to Child by grouping his ballads according to subject-matter and by carefully noting those that were analogues of the *English and Scottish Popular Ballads*. Although he broke new ground in collating his collection with other North American collections, no reader would have missed the key point that the British ballads were the true treasures guarded, unwittingly, by the Pictou County Folk. As he put it, rather bluntly, "The art of ballad-making, indeed, has never risen to any great heights in any part of this western continent, and if we have cause for gratulation in our dealings with folk-song, as I believe we have, this is due mainly to the affectionate persistence of our singers in cherishing the ballads which they and their forefathers brought to these shores from the British Isles."[20] As a reviewer acidly remarked in the *Journal of American Folklore*, the local tunes betrayed "the clumsy hand of an ungifted muse."[21] The pathbreaking collection contained no fewer than sixteen titles (often with more than one version) belonging to the Child canon, with four others rated as close relatives. Half the volume was made up of shanties, sea songs, miscellaneous narratives, and a few lyrics.

Mackenzie's major books represented a breakthrough in Canadian folklore scholarship: they were beautifully written, assiduously annotated, elegantly presented. He was particularly original in his stress upon the "total effect" of the ballad in performance.

It is only when a ballad is rendered by a singer of the old school in the presence of one or more listeners who have by chance survived with him that the full significance of ballad-singing can be realized. The total effect is infinitely greater than that suggested by the unanimated ballad which is transmitted to the printed page, or even by the words with the music. It is both of these plus the motion of singer and listeners, an emotion manifested by the latter, sometimes in ejaculatory comments, and sometimes in an unconscious or excited joining of forces with the singer in the rendition of a line or a refrain.[22]

The American poet Carl Sandburg and the influential Nova Scotian essayist and academic Archibald MacMechan were among those who were deeply impressed by Mackenzie's work. Sandburg wrote, "I call it one of my valuable books. I esteem it highly and prove this esteem to myself at intervals by picking up the book and picking out a few songs to sing."[23] Yet Mackenzie was to be all but forgotten in his native Nova Scotia, and his books have become rare collector's items. When the local travel writer Clara Dennis wrote to Princeton University Press in 1939 to see if she could obtain Mackenzie's books, she was advised that *The Quest of the Ballad* was out of print and *Ballads and Sea Songs from Nova Scotia* (published by Harvard University Press, not by Princeton) was unknown.[24] Today, perhaps as few Nova Scotians have heard of Roy Mackenzie as have not heard of Helen Creighton.

The obscurity that engulfed Mackenzie's work had nothing to do with its quality and everything to do with its timing and ideology. Mackenzie began publishing in the field very early, well before the full flowering of Innocence. Mackenzie paid the penalty of the pioneer, writing just before the antimodernist wave and the intensification of the tourist gaze, and the penalty of American exile, which deprived him of the chance to develop a large local following. By the 1940s, similar work on folklore was publicized and promoted through the tourism state. Had he been bringing his ore to market then, he would likely have been "nationalized" by Ryerson Press, the Canadian Broadcasting Corporation, the National Film Board, and other image-disseminating agencies. None of these core institutions through which Canada took shape as an imagined community were functioning at the time his work first appeared. By the time the infrastructure of the imagined community was in place, he was a distant and almost forgotten figure.

There were two more abstract, but possibly more interesting and important, explanations for the eclipse of Mackenzie's work, which help us to understand why it was not later picked up when such a nationalist network had more fully developed. These were two respects in which Mackenzie clashed directly with the new truths of Innocence. The first was the Mackenzie tried to explain, not merely celebrate, the patterns of local ballad-singing he had uncovered. He came up with the unsettling idea that local cultures had reinvented themselves. What Folk enthusiasts took to be cultural bedrock was, in Mackenzie, more a kind of cultural reinvention. In the case of Pictou County, for example, the ballad had survived because of a process of cultural transfer.

According to Mackenzie, the ballads, brought over the ocean by the Scots, were systematically discouraged by the Presbyterian clergy; but the traditions of the Scots were passed on to other, especially French-speaking, settlers, who preserved them as part of their own culture.[25] The ballads forbidden to Calvinist Scots thus survived among the less repressed foreign Protestants. Although Mackenzie was as oriented as any of his peers to viewing folklore as a stable set of traditional artifacts, his emphasis on cultural reinvention and appropriation rather subverted this essentialist view. How could one cling to the notion of the folksong as the authentic expression of some primal horde of Nova Scotians when detailed research showed that the various ethnic groups had reinvented their identities by borrowing from each other? What did Mackenzie's notion of cultural transfer do to the concept of "racial stock" that would later be so important for Creighton? If one followed Mackenzie, one would regard as problematical and contingent the very ethnic essences that ballads (and later folk art) "represented." Ballads that later seemed to testify to those very cultural continuities of the Folk that antimodernist Innocence found reassuring were on this reading less securely founded on cultural bedrock.

The second ideological problem with Mackenzie was his concept of class. To fit in with the new cultural logic of the interwar period, he should not have made cultural differences between the classes a major theme of his work: but he did. For many middle-class enthusiasts of the Folk idea, the whole point of the exercise was that ancient ballads and traditions were accessible to all, including middle-class tourists and local city-dwellers. It was because the Folk were, in essence, an early and pure draft of the Nation that their cultural expressions were worth far more than those of intellectuals or factory workers. The Folk spoke eloquently of a time of organic unity, a golden age before class division and modernity. But Mackenzie, who had been formed intellectually long before 1919, was as candid as Victorian Nova Scotians generally were about class divisions. He thus made brutally short shrift of a pastoral emphasis on "organic solidarity" in the countryside. For Mackenzie, a fast-fading folk culture, based upon illiteracy, primitivism, and backwardness, resisted the advances of those condescending middle-class enthusiasts who would claim to know it at some deeper intuitive level of "organic" understanding. Mackenzie shared with these ballad collectors the belief that in stalking the ballad and mining the ore of the Folk, the folklorist and his middle-class readers were somehow uncovering the beliefs of their own forefathers. But he differed in imagining vividly what this encounter felt like from the other side. According to Mackenzie, the fisherfolk and farmers, the guardians of lore, were painfully aware of being looked down upon and marginalized by the modern society around them. "The persons faintly shadowed forth in this record are of a type which has long been absent from the places where the business of the world is transacted, and which is now disappearing from the face of the earth itself. Each year brings its increase of scholars and students to whom popular lore is a vital record of the beliefs of their forefathers, but the years produce few people in our time who accept as credible reports the tales and songs which scholars designate, somewhat condescendingly, as 'folk-lore.'"[26]

It is interesting to remark that as late as 1919, even the term "folklore" (initially coined as "Folk-Lore" in 1846) had not yet been fully naturalized, and it still carried connotations of patronage and condescension. Yet even before "folklore" was launched in Nova Scotia, the site of its key resources – the last refuge of the ballad – was rapidly shrinking, and soon would be entirely inaccessible to the middle-class public. Only a dramatic rescue – an exercise in "salvage ethnography" – would prevent the complete disappearance of the Folk legacy.[27]

Just as Mackenzie seems to have been far ahead of his time in emphasizing the context in which the Folk made their music, he was also unusually perceptive about the politics of cultural difference. Perhaps, as a Pictou County lad at Harvard, Mackenzie had a sharpened awareness of cultural relativism, a provincial's heightened sense of the stigma the metropolis attaches to the local and traditional. He was keenly sensitive to the pathos of economic development, and (here perhaps was his ultimate heresy) he knew full well that twentieth-century Nova Scotia was, in the main, a fast-changing capitalist society in which ballad-singing was a custom indulged in by a small and marginal minority. This is precisely the opposite of the image of the pre-modern, song-singing province later broadcast far and wide by the tourism state.

The cultural politics of Mackenzie's work is fascinating because he simultaneously idealized and stereotyped the rural ballad-singers. He was not a cultural outsider. He had learned his ballads as a child at the feet of Ned Langille, a cobbler in River John, who had "lived as completely in the past as if the clock had ceased to move, many years before, when he had reached the prime of life," and whose "garrulity and marvellous memory" were natural accompaniments of his "complete and hereditary illiteracy."[28] Mackenzie confessed that he had always been addicted to "what is frequently described as 'low company,'" and when he developed 'the nobler ambition to form a collection of the Nova Scotia ballads I had the best stock-in-trade obtainable for the purpose, a familiarity with the sort of people who now possess a monopoly of this very humble species of entertainment."[29] Mackenzie defined himself as a sympathetic outsider, able to appreciate why the ballad still spoke powerfully to common people, yet candid in his own sense of not being one of them. He saw culture as a contingent and partial expression of social realities. In culture, he suggested, we mark out our social differences from one another. His most persuasive example was the case of a popular song ("The Butcher Boy") about a lad betraying his beloved.[30] His Folk, with their belief in the literal truth of the stories contained in the ballads, reacted with genuine anger to the plight of the betrayed woman and the heartlessness of her faithless lover, the treacherous butcher boy. Yet for the sophisticated urban listener, the same song was hilariously maudlin. "Small wonder, then," Mackenzie observed, "if the few people who know this ballad and others equally old-fashioned, and who regard them with real affection and esteem, should be extremely chary about subjecting them to the merriment of unsympathetic strangers in the outer world." Mackenzie believed that his Folk regarded the ballads as true, and that in their truth lay their popular value: this is why they were preserved and admired. But this truth, in a complex and sophisticated society, was obviously a limited and local one.

It is a very obvious truth that simple amusements can be honestly appraised only by the simple. Those of us who are sophisticated may be heartily entertained by such amusements, but we cannot accept them in the spirit of the persons for whom they were originally planned.

When the child himself turns his hand to verse, we look upon the result with merriment, derision, or tenderness, as the case may be, but always with a distinct sense of our own superiority. And precisely similar is our attitude towards the popular ballad. We laugh at the "quaint language" in which the forlorn maiden expresses her sorrow for the loss of her beloved butcher boy, instead of feeling that this would be a very beautiful way for us to express our emotions if we were placed in the same tragic situation. For this, obviously enough, we sophisticated persons are not to be blamed, any more than is the ballad-singer when he senses the superiority in our bearing and refuses to expose to our possible merriment the songs which he loves and honors.[31]

This passage, and Mackenzie's entire discussion, is a discerning description of the pathos of cultural distinction in a class-divided society. It tells us exactly why only some aspects of Mackenzie's legacy were salvageable for the new mythomoteur of Innocence. He knew that within twentieth-century Nova Scotia – a class-divided, complex, industrial society – there was no evading the condescension that governed the urban appropriation of supposed rural simplicity. He was compassionate yet unsparingly unsentimental in his science of local culture. Yet it was precisely this "very obvious truth" of class difference that Innocence denied. There was in Mackenzie a far subtler and more far-reaching sense of the relativity of all cultural experience than in subsequent portraits of the Folk. For all that he spoke of "low company" and juxtaposed his Nova Scotia Folk with the civilized world, Mackenzie was keenly aware of the intractability of cultural difference and the coexistence of rival local truths.

Mackenzie's frank acknowledgement of class divisions characterized his descriptions of how he collected ballads. The collector, Mackenzie wrote, had to negotiate carefully with the Folk, opening the conversation "by discoursing gravely on topics judiciously selected from the five following classes: weather, crops, sickness, politics, and religion. Thus he will convey the impression that he is a civil, trustworthy person, and not a mere thoughtless tormentor of the old and venerable."[32] Mackenzie argued that traditional singers, once taken very seriously and "profoundly respected as dignified entertainers of the community," had to be persuaded that they were performing for someone who also respected and admired the ballads. Unless the collector convinced them of that, they were unlikely to hand over the traditional ballads "which the collector is most eager to obtain."[33] For Mackenzie, the collector of ballads was a seducer of the Innocent, and "no bashful maid was ever more coy or more elusive than is the hoary-headed vendor of outworn ballads."[34]

One can well appreciate that these passages, so candid in their class analysis and so calculating in their stance towards the Folk, offended certain Nova Scotian sensibilities, particularly those that had been shaped by Innocence. Helen Creighton later argued that a "certain damage had been done" by Mackenzie's comments about class.[35] Mackenzie viewed his Nova Scotia through the conceptual framework he had acquired at Harvard, which in turn reflected Child's, and the whole Romantic movement's, conception of the Folk. Within this paradigm, illiteracy and backwardness were seen as vital prerequisites for the survival of the ballad. But within this confining framework, and perhaps because he knew something of wrestling with the stigma of primitivism and provincialism, Mackenzie had a sensitive understanding of the depth of cultural difference in a modern society. Mackenzie wrote of the very social complexities and class-based cultural divergences which subsequent antimodernists ruled out of their vividly reimagined organic community.

Creighton's autobiography credits Mackenzie's *Sea Songs and Ballads from Nova Scotia*, pressed into her hands in 1928 by Dr. Henry Munro, with having greatly influenced her decision to enter into her early collecting career. "Dr Munro held it [Mackenzie's volume] proudly in his hands and suggested I might do for the rest of the province what Dr Mackenzie had done for the River John and Tatamagouche areas. 'If you could find only one ballad,' he said, 'your fortune would be made.'"[36] Creighton would have learned from Mackenzie the primary significance of the Child ballads and the importance of annotation, but she looked to other academics and authorities as well in her first steps in folklore.

Among these other academic influences on Creighton, those who provided her with musical expertise were of special importance. Mackenzie's volume included no music, which made sense given his attachment to an English department. The absence of music could only limit the appeal of his collection to a small, poetry-reading public. Creighton's musical training was rudimentary, and she lacked confidence in her own ability to record songs. For musical training, she relied on that which she had received years before at the Halifax Ladies' College. Her first published collection was, on her own account, seriously weakened by her lack of training in this respect,[37] and some three decades later she observed that there were flaws in the music, "because I wrote it down myself, a job for which I was not properly prepared."[38] Ernest MacMillan and J. Murray Gibbon were not alone in finding her tunes difficult to follow.[39] Yet she was resourceful enough to seek help where she needed it and to recruit as colleagues those who would fill the gaps in her training. Eventually, Creighton concluded an alliance with Doreen Senior of the English Folk Song and Dance Society. Senior brought with her the credibility of the metropolitan influence and a reputation for fine taste, although serious doubts were subsequently to be raised about the accuracy of her notations, and Creighton would rue the day that she allowed her loyalty to Senior to dissuade her from following up criticisms of her work.[40] Much of Creighton's work found academic support. Professor Archibald MacMechan of Dalhousie University, a romantic spinner of "Old Province Tales" and sea stories, was one of her strongest supporters. Even before she went to Devil's Island, he had certified some of the songs she had collected as "good."[41] Her most important academic contact was Professor John Robins, who taught English at Victoria College at the University of Toronto, and who would also influence the folklorist Edith Fowke. (Creighton had attended the university in 1921 and 1922.) Robins was an ardent admirer of the ballad, and, according to Creighton's later memory, had been about to publish a book of ballads, but lost his manuscript in a fire. [42] In 1931, after a frustrating attempt to enlist the help of a Queen's University professor, Creighton came to Robins, and he showed her "how to go through every book and read every word of every published folk song and ballad available and, when I found a variant of any song in my collection, or an outstanding line or phrase that would be comparable, to make a note of it." He also arranged library privileges, reviewed her work, and corrected her mistakes.[43] Creighton would later reflect that her first frustrating experience with the professor at Queen's had been a blessing in disguise: "Because of his ineptness, I found somebody who was very good and it was all mine. Otherwise it would have been largely his."[44] Robins later reviewed the content of every Creighton radio broadcast before it went on the air in 1938, and gave his students assignments based on problems of interpretation raised by her scripts.[45] Creighton obtained additional help from scholars at the Toronto Conservatory of Music in correcting her notation.

Marius Barbeau, the Quebec-born and Oxford-educated anthropologist, who for years was a towering figure at the National Museum, was also an important Creighton ally. Better educated in folklore criticism than most university academics, he came to exert an important influence on the entire field. Creighton herself noted the decisive influence of Barbeau in persuading her to prepare her own scholarly folklore analysis and notes.[46] Throughout Creighton's career, Barbeau would play an important and constructive, if occasionally autocratic and controversial, role. He supported her bids for financial support from various agencies and individuals, including the chief of the folklore section of the Library of Congress. ("My opinion, as you may surmise, is that Miss Creighton's research is most valuable and deserves support," he remarked in his letter, and then referred to the discrepancy between American and Canadian interest in the Folk: "I only regret that the Canadian governments should be so ill-prepared to give her full encouragement in the way that suits her best.")[47] This pattern of academic support persisted throughout her career. D.C. Harvey, a Dalhousie professor and the provincial archivist, proved supportive in getting Rockefeller Foundation money for her, and put in a good word for her to Premier Angus L. Macdonald.[48] Freelancer though she was in many respects, Creighton relied heavily on the help of high cultural figures in this first phase of her career, precisely because she was in many respects still an amateur, without the linguistic and musical skills that would have allowed her to develop confidence as a professional folklorist.

Although Creighton retrospectively gave these academic influences a great deal of weight in her autobiography, perhaps the most significant single influence was J. Murray Gibbon, a figure rather marginalized in her account but highly significant in her contemporary correspondence. He was perhaps the most important Canadian exponent of the commercial uses of the Folk. Born in Ceylon in 1875, the son of a prominent tea planter, J. Murray Gibbon was one of the new breed of cultural entrepreneurs in interwar Canada, and must rank as one of the principal figures in imagining the Canadian community in the 1920s and 1930s. His key contribution lay in his attempt to reconcile the proliferation of various groups of immigrants within the country with the drive to develop a nationalist mythology. (Without Gibbon, the now all-pervasive metaphor of Canada as a mosaic might have died an obscure death as an American writer's conceit. It was Gibbon who rescued it as the governing metaphor of the new postcolonial liberal nationalism that gradually overshadowed many Canadians' earlier identification with Britain.[49]) Gibbon held that national unity, so elusive on a political or social level, might be better pursued on the more essential level of handcrafts, Folk dances, and an emergent canon of Canadian folksong. Moreover, retention of age-old Folk customs would indirectly aid patriotism by removing the risk of the immigrants' children rebelling against their parents and destabilizing the institution of the family. Gibbon's genius for popularization meant that these ideas reached thousands of Canadians. As one of the first intellectuals to grasp the importance of folklore in a renovated Canadian myth-symbol complex, Gibbon was a seminal innovator in the organization of mass culture in Canada. As the director of propaganda for the Canadian Pacific Railway, he had a clear interest in creating tourist extravaganzas, and for him, tourism, commerce, and "the Folk" were inextricably bound together. Between 1928 and 1931, according to Janet E. McNaughton's estimate, the Canadian Pacific Railway sponsored at least sixteen major folk festivals in western and central Canada. They were pioneering efforts in a North American context, among the first (if not the first) on the continent.[50] The festivals were dramatizations of Gibbon's imagined Canada, a mosaic that was slowly emerging as a potential masterpiece under the guiding hand of history. "All we can do today is to collect and separate and perhaps ourselves fabricate the tesserae or little slabs of colour required for what that artist seems to have in mind as a mosaic," Gibbon counselled. "The foundation is provided by the geography and climate of this northern half of the North American Continent. One contribution which we can deliberately make is to discover, analyze and perfect the cements which may best hold the coloured slabs in position."[51] The CPR folk festivals were visualized as just such a unifying element. In making immigrants and their children feel at home, they would also make "ethnic questions" less worrisome for the British Canadians. The image of the tesserae set into the mosaic by an unseen hand was paralleled by the implied reduction of ethnic identification to common denominators – colourful costumes, folk music, dances – in folk festivals, which serve to minimize differences between cultures while seeming to provide an instance of democratic pluralism.[52] Gibbon put his Oxford-acquired familiarity with the national–romantic approach to folklore to good use indeed.

Although Creighton's memoirs place greater emphasis on the spiritual force of Mackenzie as transmitted via the academic Munro, her surviving correspondence of the period suggests the equal and perhaps greater role played by Gibbon's more fully commercialized model of the Folk. Gibbon naturally emphasized songs of local composition, and it may have been thanks to his influence that Creighton was prepared to collect, if not necessarily to emphasize, songs outside the Child canon. One reason Creighton could be found on the Atlantic Coast in the late 1920s hunting songs was that Gibbon had put out an all-points bulletin for local "Pirate Songs" for one of his ersatz Folk festivals (the Festival of the Sea, set in British Columbia). In 1929 Gibbon returned some songs Creighton had sent him for his festival, and urged her to send along music if she wanted her songs considered. He then added a postscript: "There are two books on

Nova Scotia folksong singing by a man Mackenzie which should be of value to you."[53]

For her part, Creighton was eager to impress Gibbon with the "gold mine" she had uncovered in her early digging. Even before she had established the extent of Ben Henneberry's repertoire, she was enthusiastically boosting him to Gibbon, as in this letter of August 1929:

My search for sea songs has resulted in the enclosed with a few ballads and love songs thrown in ... You say you will only want six songs, but I am sending them all as I know you are interested, and I hope you will advise me about continuing and where to find a market for a full collection. Every song in the collection has come from Halifax County, and if Mr Ben Henneberry has as large a [repertoire] as people say he has I think I could double it right here. I have tried to get all the native songs I could ...

I shall await your criticism with the greatest interest, and hope among them you will find some that will be helpful to you in preparing your Song Festival.[54]

This letter is important because it suggests that either before or very shortly after she arrived on Devil's Island Creighton was well aware of the commercial possibilities of folksongs and of the networks through which they might be marketed. Henneberry was, as of 30 August 1929, a seemingly still unexplored mine, but his treasures were already entering into the calculations of the new cultural marketplace.

Gibbon's influence on Creighton's early career went beyond giving it an initial push. He continued to write to her in the early 1930s, giving her down-to-earth commercial and artistic advice about folksong collecting. He warned her about the vagaries of the marketplace: "The market for this picking up of folksongs is, I fear, not remunerative in itself," he cautioned in 1929, "but if you can weave a good story round it, you can sell anything." He added: "If I could get half a dozen real pirate songs with fairly good tunes, I could pay something for these out of our festival appropriation – about ten dollars apiece. We would have to pay a composer something more to have the song harmonised."[55] Gibbon's advice may well have been highly significant for the ambitious young journalist.

Gibbon wanted "real pirate songs," and was rather dismissive in his assessment of the status of those Creighton first offered him. In accepting six of her songs for his sea festival, he passed along some direct criticisms, including Ernest MacMillan's suggestion that "you study musical notation before you do any more collecting, as the rhythm, time and accentuation of folksongs are essential if they are to be of any value to musicians." MacMillan, Gibbon reported, "said he had quite a job analysing the melodies that you had sent so as to be sure of avoiding mistakes."[56] (Ultimately the songs were never used, but Gibbon still paid Creighton sixty dollars for her efforts). In 1931 Gibbon advised Creighton to familiarize herself with the Child canon, and evidently took some pleasure in pointing out that one of her Nova Scotia songs ("The Mary L. McKay," which Creighton had presented as the "Mary L. MacKay") was not, in his terms, a true folksong at all.

In reply to yours of March 16th [1931].
There are very few people in this country who have any knowledge of balladry, though there are quite a number in the States. Why not learn something about this yourself? The chief authority is, of course, Child, whose book on this subject is the standard work of reference. If you had this knowledge of Child, it would help you very much in your work.

By the way, I discovered that the "Mary L. McKay" ballad which you sent me some time ago was written by Frederick W. Wallace, author of "Wooden Ships and Iron Men" and printed by him in a newspaper in the year 1914. One of your simple-minded sea captains must have memorized it.[57]

"One of your simple-minded captains": such was the tone adopted by one of the principal architects of "Folk" festivals and "Folk" culture in discussing the working people who sang Folk music.

HELEN CREIGHTON:
ANATOMY OF A CAREER

Creighton was hardly a passive recipient of these various influences. She was not gifted musically, and her writing style tends to a conventionalized romanticism, but she was nonetheless skilled: her skill was organization. Creighton knew where to go to get help and how to make friends with those in a position to lend her assistance. She too was one of the new breed of cultural entrepreneurs, and resembled Gibbon in that respect far more than she did Mackenzie.

Creighton's career passed through three stages. In the first (1927–32) she was the insecure young writer and ballad-collector, extremely dependent on the British school for her concepts of the Folk, and preoccupied specifically with "the ballad" rather than "folklore" in general. In the second stage of her career (1933–47) she turned more and more to popularizing the Folk as she came to terms with the difficult extra-institutional life of a freelance collector. Finally, after a transitional period in which she was the recipient of American grant money and exposed to graduate folklore education at Indiana University, she attained a position of prominence within the field, and worked "professionally" and "popularly" on both Folk music and a whole range of other issues. This third phase of her career (c. 1947–75) was the most productive and influential.

When Helen Creighton received Dr Munro's advice in 1928 to read Mackenzie's book, she was a well-connected society journalist on the hunt for new stories. Helen Creighton was caught between the roles of Victorian ladyhood and the twentieth-century professionalism of a "new woman." She was born in Dartmouth, Nova Scotia, on 5 September 1899 into a well-rooted and secure local family that had been active in the business and social life of greater Greater Halifax since the city's eighteenth-century beginnings. Creighton's father was a commission merchant and food broker, and Creighton was proud of her family's local business background. (In 1949 she proposed to her publisher that the jacket of her book incorporate the crossed flags of the prominent shipping firms of Creighton & Crassie and of Albro, "all names in my own family.")[58] Creighton summed up her class position by noting that her family "has never been wealthy, but has always been able to live comfortably."[59] This was perhaps a genteel understatement of her own sense of belonging to an important and socially prominent family.

Although the Creightons were not of Young Avenue or the North West Arm, those Halifax addresses of the very wealthy, they were not the social inferiors of those who were. Visits from lieutenant-governors and senior churchmen (the Creightons were Anglican) were not uncommon. The Creightons were well connected to the élite in Greater Halifax, and were ambitious on behalf of their offspring. Sending Helen as a day scholar to the prestigious Halifax Ladies College in 1914, and as a live-in scholar the following year, was evidence of the family's resources and social ambitions. Such class credentials were almost a requirement of joining the trans-Atlantic Quest of the Folk, at least before folklore attained more secure funding within the state and the academy. Most of those who embarked on the trans-Atlantic Quest of the Folk shared Creighton's comfortable and urban circumstances.[60]

Gender as well as class contributed to the membership of those in the Quest of the Folk. Although the senior trans-Atlantic theoreticians of the Folk – Child, Kittredge, Sharp, and later Lloyd and Lomax – were all men, a disproportionate amount of the fieldwork and research was undertaken by women. Folklore research fit easily into the traditional nineteenth-century conception of gentlewomen's artistic pursuits. As Maria Tippett remarks with regard to English-speaking Canada, "In the years around the turn of the century most teachers of art, music, dramatic expression, and elocution were women ... If they had the right connections or the money, they taught in studios that were located above stores, in church or community hall basements, or in the backs of their husbands' or fathers' offices."[61]

Creighton was emphatically an "amateur" and a "lady," a word that deftly synthesizes class and gender ideals. She did come to terms with the twentieth-century demands of "New Womanhood" and "professionalism," but only to a certain extent. In many of her customs and beliefs, she would have fit more comfortably into Victorian Halifax than she did into a Dartmouth transformed, through the remorseless processes of North American urban sprawl, into the capital city's bedroom suburb. Although she attended the University of Toronto, she never, to her regret and despite her obvious high intelligence and drive, attained an undergraduate university degree.[62] Her high esteem for academic honours is suggested by the consistency with which she used the title "Dr Creighton" after she began to receive honorary degrees.

Perhaps she was caught between two models of womanhood. According to her traditional upbringing, her proper place was in the home, as a wife and mother. She believed very strongly in the family, and explained her own divergence from the model of marriage by citing her frail physical condition and bad luck. Yet her weak constitution which she later presented as a reason for her not raising a family, seems to have been more a part of the subject-position of the Lady than an actual physical handicap. Although small in stature and afflicted later in life with cancer, Creighton in her prime did not allow her supposed weakness to get in the way of her gruelling fieldwork schedules and hours of hard labour over her typewriter. It is as if Creighton felt obliged to cite special reasons for having departed from a model of Victorian familialism she herself supported. At times, she wrote as though she did not regard herself as the independent professional woman who had decided to pursue her own career, but rather as the "spinster" who had unluckily failed to make her match. After the mid-1920s, she never really left her parental home, except for a short stint as dean of women at King's College, and to take part in events in other cities. She often found that her collecting activities were overshadowed by her responsibilities to her physically challenged sister and to her aging parents. She seems to have identified with women's traditional role, and there is scarcely a hint of feminism in her thinking. "Never have women housecleaned so willingly," Creighton remarked in 1945 in connection with fears about a second Halifax explosion, "because for so long we faced the possibility of having nothing left to clean."[63] Perhaps she came closest to making a feminist statement in observing that "women will face a supernatural ordeal that men find completely devastating."[64] Creighton joined the string of women folk collectors in the Atlantic region, some of whom, such as Mary Ethel Stuart Mackenzie, were to be overshadowed by the men for whom they worked, and others of whom were to persist as amateurs or under-paid and insecurely positioned freelancers. This gendered pattern of career insecurity may have had something to do with the importance of the cultural marketplace in determining the shape of folklore in the region.[65]

Creighton's spirited defences of her territory against all interlopers were similar to those of other ambitious cultural producers, but they were also related to her gender. She lacked the equivalence of secure tenure throughout her life, and she was particularly exercised when a challenge came from a woman. Creighton complained that one female competitor who had obtained access to "her" songs had a "way of getting what she wants. If a woman like me is susceptible to her charm, it must be doubly difficult for a man to refuse her."[66] Creighton's career illustrated both the new careers open to women and the ways in which career women could feel themselves to be on the defensive within a male-dominated society. She seems to have been uneasy with her decision not to marry and raise a family. In her memoirs she records the fear that, after a "disappointment in love," she might turn into a "nasty waspish spinster."[67] One reason the materials in her first book originated within ten miles of her Dartmouth home was that her family obligations caused her to focus her energies on a small area within easy driving distance.[68]

One can find an eloquent expression of Helen Creighton's social outlook in her writing as the regional correspondent of *Mayfair Magazine*, a publication designed, as its name suggested, for Canadian men and women who aspired to social and cultural eminence. The magazine portrayed a Greater Halifax that glittered with receptions and engagements, weddings and bridge parties: a provincial world, to be sure, but one enlivened by visitors from elsewhere. Creighton's imagined capital city revolved around the Little Theatre, the lieu-tenant-governor's residence, the military balls, the aristocrats who breezed into the splendid hotels. A few excerpts will convey the tone:

Now we have a Little Theatre in Halifax, we *have* a Little Theatre. Its arrival is rather typical of the way things are done down here. Perhaps this is the heritage of our canny Scottish ancestry. At any rate we are apt to be a bit over-cautious about embracing new ideas until we are sure we are going to take them into our midst "for keeps" ... Of course the opening night is always the best fun but alas the Guild made one mistake. It opened in a blizzard. A raging storm. Taxis agreed to take patrons but many refused to return for them. Among those who braved the storm, however, were the Lieutenant-Governor and Mrs Covert with party of ten. Chief Justice Chisholm and the French Consul, Dr and Mrs Henry Munro, and Mr D.R. Turnbull.[69]

Social life in Halifax is inevitably bound up with the sea. It may be only in the joy of a bathe in the waters of the ocean, but that is nothing to the flutter that comes to the heart of a debutante (and others not quite so young) when the ships of His Majesty's fleet come sailing up the harbor.[70]

Now a new Lieutenant-Governor has been sworn into office. Hon. Walter Harold Covert is a lawyer of exceptional ability ... Covert parties have always been distinguished due to the charming hospitality always associated with this house. Theirs is essentially a "home" family and Mrs Covert is never happier than when in the company of her children.[71]

In Halifax there have been numerous hotel dances, but of them all I think military balls in this old city are the most charming. There are so many military and naval men to attend. All wear their dress uniforms and the result is a brilliant galaxy of scarlet and gold which gives a delightful color contrast. What debutante but is thrilled to descend the winding marble staircase at the Nova Scotian [Hotel] upon the arm of [an] officer, long skirts which are still a novelty to her, sweeping the floor as did those of her great-grandmother in the romantic days![72]

The Halifax that Creighton described is not a twentieth-century Canadian city but a small imagined Agatha Christie world of Edwardian elegance, of yacht clubs and brilliant weddings, theatricals and soirées, in which the same names – the Bells, the Coverts, the Silvers – repeat themselves in a mantra of exclusivity and distinction. In this imagined community the social whirl proceeds, Depression or no Depression: wealthy travellers who arrive on glorious ocean liners have "met the business depression half way and laughed at it."[73]

The tone of elegance and refinement was, of course, what people writing for *Mayfair* were expected to dish up, but Creighton's identification with gentility went well beyond her striking this tone in her society journalism. Creighton could claim no great wealth for her family, but her tradition was undoubtedly one of gentility, comfort, and social prominence. Creighton's background at the Halifax Ladies' College and her lifelong support of private education suggested a continuity of class perspective.[74] In her autobiography Creighton describes an easy mixing with lieutenant-governors and even the governor general. When she stayed in Ottawa in 1926, friends arranged her attendance at "all important events and got me a seat in the Reserve Gallery at the House. They also arranged for my presentation to the Governor General and Viscountess Willingdon at their Drawing Room, the great social event of the year."[75] One "red letter day," 11 February 1932, is recalled with particular warmth in her memoirs: it began with a luncheon invitation from Lieutenant-Governor and Mrs Covert in honour of the governor general, Lord Bessborough. "This," writes Creighton, "was a tribute to the position I was achieving as a writer."[76] Like the figures in her *Mayfair* world who could laugh at the Depression, Creighton was insulated from some of its sterner realities. "These were days of gracious living," she said of the 1930s, "when all eight of us [friends] took our turn as hostess and each house had its maid in uniform to wait on us."[77]

Creighton's subject-position of "gentlewoman" was also in evidence in her fierce attachment to Britain as the centre of the cultural world. To an extent difficult to imagine today, genteel eyes in provincial Canada, as late as the 1930s, still turned to London for cultural standards. The *Mayfair* articles radiate a very English sense of refinement and breeding. Creighton would look to England for her first publisher and meekly defer to the expertise of English folklorists. She proudly notes in her memoirs her brother's success as a physician in London's West End, and his attendance on Princess Elizabeth and Princess Margaret.[78] Her own visit to England in the 1930s was the deferential colonial's classic pilgrimage to sacred literary and cultural shrines and figures. She paid homage to the memories of Jane Austen and Keats, and encountered her favourite author, Rudyard Kipling (to whose house, much later, Creighton made a pilgrimage, to "sit at the great author's desk ... to catch something of the aura of this writer I so admired.")[79] This passion for things English extended to her preferences in folklore: Creighton was emphatically the disciple of the English school. When she and Doreen Senior of the English Folk Song and Dance Society journeyed to Cape Breton to collect ballads, they even named the car in which they travelled "Cecil" after the eminent British folklorist Cecil Sharp.[80]

The fierce anglophilia of the Anglo-Canadian cultural élite suggests many parallels with the "medievalism" that T.J. Jackson Lears finds so central an aspect of American antimodernism. The same yearning for the old, the incense-laden, and the ritualized that sent so many interwar intellectuals off to become Anglo-Catholics could, in Canada, be blended harmoniously into liberal political orthodoxy and "loyalism." One merely needed to imagine a community united around British gentility, fine conversation in Rideau Hall, and the splendours of ancient uniforms and customs. Antimodernism and Anglophilia could be intimately tied together.[81]

Had this been all, Creighton would have merely taken her place among many thousands of other élite urban Canadians who lived, or attempted to live, in the world as imagined by *Mayfair*. But the very appearance of Creighton's writing in the magazine suggested an important tension in her life between Victorian domesticity and New Womanhood. As a freelancer writing for a mass circulation magazine, Creighton was hardly the exemplar of the carefree elegant society life she portrayed in her columns. Like so many Canadian women in the interwar period, Creighton found Victorian ladyhood confining. She searched for an appropriate role – social work, teaching, journalism – without having found, by 1928, one that was secure and fulfilling. She worked as a journalist in Ottawa and as a freelance journalist and radio broadcaster in Halifax. She often combined the ethos of traditional womanhood with her career. She did so in her society journalism for *Mayfair*, and she was the first "Station Aunt" on the Halifax radio station CHNS in 1926: "I read from my book, made woolen golliwogs for those who wrote in, wrote all the dialogue for the half-hour show, found the music, and was paid, by the *Herald and Mail*, two dollars a broadcast," she recalled in her autobiography.[82] Throughout her life she was both the Victorian lady and the twentieth-century cultural entrepreneur. If, as J.D. Tallman urges, Creighton was a "gentlewoman" – a role she seems to have embraced in her own self-conception – she was also a struggling cultural entrepreneur, driven to folklore not just by an aristocratic sense of noblesse oblige but also by a powerful drive to succeed as a writer in her own right.[83]

When Helen Creighton embarked on her Quest of the Folk in 1928, she was an energetic freelance journalist in pursuit of good copy. Throughout the 1920s she had ranged broadly in her journalistic interests. Her writings included travel writing ("Canadian Girl Witnesses Bull Fight in Mexico," "Love Making in Mexico"), children's stories ("Lois and a Potato," "The Sparrow's Wicked Deed"), and stories about music ("The Carillon of Ottawa," "Music in Ottawa"). She was particularly interested in stories about women, and wrote profiles of prominent businesswomen, female art teachers, and members of the Victorian Order of Nurses ("Miss Elizabeth Smellie, v.o.n.," "They Nurse 3,000 Patients Every Day").[84] A manuscript list of articles from 1927–28 in the Creighton Papers suggests both the range and the frustrations of her work as a freelance journalist. An entry for the poem "The Blood of the Pioneer," published on 6 September 1927 in the Montreal *Star*, is followed by the disappointed notation, "do not pay for poetry." Although "Broadcasting for Children," published in the Toronto *Star Weekly* on 24 September, fetched $28.50 and "Love Making in Mexico" brought $25 from *Saturday Night*, "Lois and the Potato" earned a mere $10 on acceptance. A monthly income ranging from $33.50 in October to $76.50 in December could hardly have given Creighton a sense of a flourishing literary market or much hope of achieving fame and fortune in the world of popular journalism.[85] Creighton needed new material. That was probably why, in the closing years of the 1920s, she so readily responded to J. Murray Gibbon's challenge and went searching for "pirate songs" within easy driving distance of Greater Halifax. Quite possibly she also was anxious to receive an income of her own. Although Creighton came from an eminent family, throughout her life she had a strong sense of economic insecurity. In later years she rented out part of her fine Dartmouth home, and in her own mind required the numerous speaking engagements and public appearances in order to make ends meet. This was the significant other side of her life. It meant that characterizing Creighton as a naive Victorian gentlewoman out of her depth in business discussions was an error of judgment – as those who attempted to sing "her" songs without credit found out to their considerable cost.

The Helen Creighton we meet in her memoirs is the archetypal young heroine, an innocent abroad, and her first collecting days are a train of serendipitous discoveries and wonderful coincidences. The thirty-year-old whom we encounter in her letters, however, was less a disingenuous innocent than an experienced and canny cultural producer. Her mastery of the Canadian cultural politics of the period was impressive. In 1932 she could advise her publisher in detail on which people would be best to review her book. ("Mr John Garvin would probably review it for 'Saturday Night.' I have met him numerous times at Canadian Authors' meetings. The Toronto Women's Press Club is interested. I gave a talk to them once on my work and they are interested on the appearance of the book. Miss McCarthy of the Mail and Empire gave me a splendid write-up a couple of years ago and will, I am sure, see that it is well reviewed for her paper.")[86] Throughout her life she portrayed her self as the innocent abroad, reliant upon the help of professionals in the field, and virtually drifting through folklore without much theoretical preparation. This was partly the proper "amateurism" of the Victorian

Helen Creighton collecting from an old man in a rustic setting. Photograph taken by E.A. Bollinger for an article in *Maclean's Magazine*, 1952. PANS 52160-177.

Helen Creighton recording three fishermen seated on lobster traps, at East Petpeswick. Photograph taken by E.A. Bollinger for an article in *Maclean's Magazine*, 1952. PANS 52160-7.

Helen Creighton collecting in a general store from two men. Photograph taken by
E.A. Bollinger for an article in *Maclean's Magazine*, 1952. PANS 52160-120.

gentlewoman, for whom it would have been unseemly to make too
open a display of ambition and entrepreneurship.[87] She consistently
downplayed her extensive apprenticeship, as a journalist, in the arts
of appealing to a wide public.

She was shrewd enough to know a prodigy when she met one.
When she met Ben Henneberry in 1929, she was startled by his
memory and his repertoire. Henneberry was an amazing phenomenon, a man who could remember seventy-eight verses of "The
Courtship of Willie Riley," and identify the "hole in the ballad" – the
spot where verses were missing. Creighton returned again and again
to Devil's Island to collect his songs. Using a heavy melodeon, which
she transported in a wheelbarrow, Creighton gathered material in
fish houses, in cottages, and at community gatherings. Often she
would sit in the door of Ben Henneberry's fish house with the melodeon at her side.

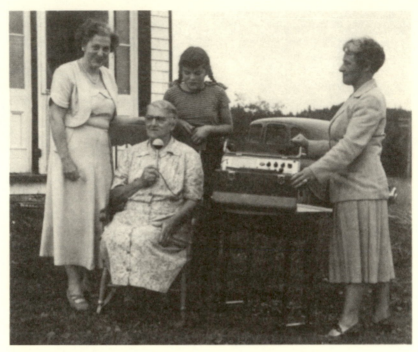

Helen Creighton collecting "A Southerly Wind" from three generations at Musquodoboit Harbour in 1951. PANS, Helen Creighton Collection, 2075.

The left hand pumps while the right hand plays the notes, and when the singer has no teeth, or has a very "tick" voice, or tumbles off the key twenty times in one song, the trials of collecting are many. Yet on the island I had to do it all this way, and in one week spent there with the lighthouse keeper and his family I got over ninety songs. In the morning in the shacks while the men mended their nets, in the afternoon the children singing their father's songs, later Mr Ben in the [solitude] of his little cottage with his wife to help me along, and in the evening the whole community at the lighthouse keeper house, staying as a rule until 3 A.M.[88]

Ben Henneberry was the key. In the evening, when he was present, no one else on Devil's Island would sing, because he had taught them their songs, and they were consequently regarded as "his." It was an old notion of ownership regulated by a collective tradition of common rights, and its days were numbered.

Creighton's voyage to Devil's Island in 1929 produced its first results in 1932, with *Songs and Ballads from Nova Scotia*, published by J.M. Dent and Sons. It was a striking book, far more elegant in

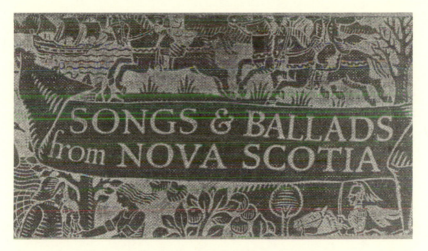

From the cover of *Songs and Ballads from Nova Scotia* by Helen Creighton, published by J.M. Dent and Sons, Toronto and Vancouver, 1932. The illustration was by Reginald L. Knowles, who repeated the motif of the medieval tapestry throughout.

appearance than Mackenzie's volumes. Included among its 162 songs were 11 Child ballads and 90 broadsides. The title of each song was printed in Old English letters. The woodcut frontispiece by Reginald L. Knowles continued the theme of Old World romance with its depiction of fair maids and dashing knights; "At the Wharves, Devil's Island," tied this theme of romance into the uneven wooden paths and the wondrous tangle of nets and barrels of the Devil's Island fishermen. These picturesque framing devices set the scene for a selection of songs disproportionately biased towards the British ballad. Professor John D. Robins's introduction expressed the hope that in demonstrating "the folk-lore wealth of the Maritimes" Creighton's collection might "stimulate activity in other sections of English-speaking Canada on the part of those who may have been daunted hitherto by the unapproachable richness of our song heritage among French-speaking Canadians."[89] The songs were listed in the "Child/Other" format, with the eleven Child ballads coming first. Robins praised Creighton for showing "true Bluenose caution" in excluding several songs "whose claim to admission among the lower nobility might have been allowed" and in selecting "songs native to this continent."[90] Although Creighton hailed the "alert mind of the Nova Scotia fisher-folk," which would "continue to create folk-songs in honour of its people," *Songs and Ballads from Nova Scotia* most warmly celebrates this alert Folk Mind when it is remembering Ancient Ballads from Other Places. "Sable Island Song," for example, is included as evidence that "the song-making instinct is not dormant," but Creighton notes that the song "has no intrinsic value."[91] Creighton's emphasis was strictly on the songs, which emerge as miraculous survivals from a remote coast. The context of the songs, the wider framework of "folklore," was not treated. Creighton was still a traditional "collector" more than she was a modern folklorist.

Songs and Ballads from Nova Scotia was an elegantly produced volume that spoke of continuities at a time of cultural crisis. Yet, as famous as the volume and the collector later became, it was not an immediate commercial success. Creighton soon had good reason to remember Gibbon's warning that there was not much money to be made from folklore. Despite Gibbon's and Barbeau's efforts, the market for folklore in Canada outside Quebec was still very limited. Creighton wound up paying her publishers $150 to cover her account with them in 1939 (and there still remained, at that point, a balance due of $99.45). "Unofficially," wrote the publisher's representative, "and in all sincerity, I can tell you that this whole matter breaks my heart, especially the paying out end ... The United States market is quite a problem in such cases. Our friends to the south of us attach little or no importance to any books that do not bear a United States publisher's imprint, or that is not the work of one of their own citizens."[92] Americans were not interested in Canadian folklore, and an English and American passion for folklore had not yet been conveyed to and copied in Canada. The Canadian market for folklore had spoken, and the message was not encouraging. Only after the Second World War would Canadian market conditions change, and even then, as late as 1946, Lorne Pierce of Ryerson Press discouraged the publication of a Creighton manuscript by noting that there was "no comparison in the interest in folk songs between Canada and the United States ... There is so little general interest [in Canada] on which to work."[93] Perhaps one reason Creighton's work did not interest a broader public hungry for antimodernism was its rather aristocratic, British aloofness: it was, curiously, an academic presentation, and not nearly as accessible as her later works.

Creighton's career slumped. She entered into an alliance with Doreen Senior, whose notations, despite her credentials with the English Folk Song and Dance Society, were not subsequently held to be beyond reproach; she continued to work the "Coast of Songs," that part of Halifax County stretching eastward of Dartmouth, which had proved so rich; the single most famous song in the Creighton collection, "the Nova Scotia Song," more commonly known as "Farewell to Nova Scotia," was found in this period. Nonetheless,

Creighton was disappointed in her career. To an extent not fully conveyed by her memoirs, she was reconsidering being a folklorist altogether, and began once again to produce reams of journalistic copy for the popular magazines.

For the historian, this hiatus in her folklore career is fortunate, for it prompted many interesting articles from Creighton's pen on subjects ranging from "fishing for albacore" to the Nova Scotian character. Once again, one is struck by the absence of any realistic assessment of the Depression or its social impact. Creighton's journalism of the 1930s focused not on unemployment and the crisis of relief, but on the strength, happiness, and colourful resourcefulness of the Folk. If one were to cite one article out of the many she produced in this period to show how well she integrated the key themes of Innocence, it would perhaps be her superb evocation of Sable Island in *Maclean's*. Victorian Nova Scotians had generally insisted on Nova Scotia's integration within the civilized world and on the province's fertility and gardenlike scenery. The interwar anti-modernists reversed these emphases with a new insistence on Nova Scotia's essential insularity, and on Nova Scotians as a "race apart," shaped by the rocks and the wind and the sea. Creighton followed the new romantic formula to perfection. She was brilliant in describing stormy seas. She pulled out all the stops in her heartfelt description of storm-tossed Sable Island.

Sable Island. For those of us who live in Nova Scotia the name is ominous. For many who live inland, perhaps, it is just a name. Yet I venture to state that in the whole of this great Dominion there is no spot more beloved by those who live upon it, no spot more desolate, no spot more awful. Here life and death walk hand in hand. Like an ill-tempered child, this mite of an island sits boldly in the Atlantic ... hiding its treacherous sand-bars beneath the sea and chortling with glee when they catch an unwary vessel in their grasp.

Upon the island the desolation must be awful, with cold sleet blowing and surf beating like thunder upon the beach. Winds whistle eerily about the houses, and sand blows around them until in time they become uninhabitable ... Beyond the shore the waves beat upon three more submerged bars which run around the island – a noise deafening to the casual visitor on Sable, but one which becomes music in the ears of those who love the sea. A steady, rhythmic beating of the surf sounds like never-ending thunder; a surf which may drown a man if he is forced to go out to a wreck. But the inhabitants do not think too much about this. Their lives have been lived beside the sea and they love it and all things pertaining to it.[94]

Here was a moving, powerful description of a distant island, populated by ghosts and legends, whose elemental nature worked a wondrous magic on all those who had breathed its salty spray and gloried in the bleakness of its wind-whipped sand dunes. Such Folk might leave the island, but what Creighton called their "simple life," their "freedom from all personal care and worry," would draw them back again and again.

The article was a striking indication of how well attuned Creighton was to emergent patterns of taste: Sable Island seemed to Creighton, as it later would to the novelist Thomas Raddall, a purer, more isolated, and consequentially more essential Nova Scotia. Yet Creighton had never been to Sable Island at the time she wrote this glowing description. The facts of the article were drawn from official government sources, and the emotional response to the landscape and the Folk was drawn purely from Creighton's imagination.[95] Only one critical reader took Creighton up on a detail that might have triggered suspicion: Creighton twice in her article mislocated Sable Island 180 miles west rather than east of Halifax. Yet readers were generally persuaded that she had actually gone to Sable Island – persuasive evidence, surely, of the extent to which a market for antimodern images of insularity and magic had emerged in the twentieth century, and how shrewdly Creighton could appeal to it.

As it was for the Folk of Sable Island, so it was with Nova Scotians in general. Creighton's journalism of the period emphasizes Nova Scotia as an island in the storm of capitalism. In an article on her own collecting work, the residents of Devil's Island, although often travelling in and out of Halifax, were still said to be "quite secluded the whole year round," and were therefore, of course and in consequence, "extraordinarily happy."[96] Creighton produced stereotypical "Stories of the Bluenose Children" and "a story of camp life in Nova Scotia" in the mid-1930s.[97] She would happily treat the Quest of the Ballad as a "romantic treasure hunt" or take whatever angle a publication might want her to select. "Would you be interest[ed]," she asked *American Girl*, "in an article upon this subject from either the scholars' or the romantic angle, with or without pictures or drawings and with or without music?"[98] Creighton's journalism fed a voracious urban hunger for the "simple life" with songs and tales and delightful superstitions, found objects from a magical coast of dreams and songs. This "gentlewoman" clearly knew the contemporary cultural marketplace.

Yet this journalistic work was not quite the path of destiny that had beckoned Creighton in 1928. How close she came to abandoning that path in the depths of the Depression is not clear, but the discouraging returns from her book and the encouraging results of writing promotional articles must have told. It was, ironically, the American folklore revival (and not any local or Canadian surge in interest) that reinvigorated Creighton's career as a folklorist. There was a roaring demand for folklore in the United States, both as a result of antimodernist yearnings for a simpler time and the innovative populist cultural politics of the New Deal. In September 1936 two American tourists in Nova Scotia telephoned Creighton. Although they had toured the "Land of Evangeline," they were in search of something more authentic and less ersatz (or, in their expression, "parky") than the manicured landscape set aside to commemorate Longfellow and the Acadian expulsion at Grand Pré. Could Creighton provide them with something better? The two women, one of whom was on the committee of the New York Folk-Festival board, engaged a conference room in a Halifax hotel, and were so impressed with Creighton's material that they invited her to bring her folksongs to New York. "They tell me," Creighton wrote excitedly to the head of the province's tourism-oriented Bureau of Information, "that at the present time there is a tremendous interest in this sort of thing."[99]

Creighton's trip to a country in which folklore was honoured and folklorists well rewarded was a revelation. It gave her a much firmer sense of merging folklore and tourism promotion. Folklore was booming in Depression America. Officially encouraged through various cultural programs of the New Deal, celebrated in novels and films, it figured centrally in the recalculation of the role of culture within liberal hegemony. (The Canadian state had locked up and isolated its unemployed single men in wretched work camps in a demonstration of its continuing reliance on coercion, whereas the American state, by creating imaginative new programs for the unemployed, demonstrated the possibilities of new ways of exercising hegemony, in which "Folk" themes were highly significant.)[100] American interest in the Folk proved a tonic for Creighton. "My New York trip has filled me with interest again, for I found there a tremendous appreciation in what had already been done, and I am sure there will be a ready market for anything I may do in the future," she wrote in 1937, adding a significant proviso: "But I want to make sure of profit somewhere."[101] The American trip proved that there were profits to be made from folklore, if only one knew how to market it. "The market is certainly there and the time is ripe because folk-interest is so high just now," Creighton remarked to her publishers in a letter that raised the prospect of her acquiring an American agent and exploiting the library market. "And last but not not least,

I think I have a moving picture house interested. If all goes well we should see Mr Henneberry on the screen. I have a travelogue in mind, featuring our folk-singers. If I can only bring it off there should certainly be profit in that."[102] To Marius Barbeau at the National Museum, whose economic security as an official state intellectual she rather envied, she remarked, "I had no idea American audiences were so responsive … I am very happy that my work is at last being recognized, and also that there will be a little profit."[103]

Creighton never regarded the commercialization and popularization of folklore as problematical. In the late 1930s she was seized with the possibilities of film. Why not make a major motion picture? she asked the Associated Screen News in 1937:

I would be very pleased to have one of your newsreel units come to see me while in Halifax, and a test would perhaps be a good thing, but that is a very small part of what I have in mind. The actual folk are not as a rule good singers because of their age and the fact that most of them have lost their teeth. The interest lies in their background, the survival of songs through them, and the use to which songs can be put at the present day. In a picture such as I had in mind I [would] have had only a minimum of actual singing by the folk, but I would have had the songs presented at the close of the picture by a glee club group at the apple blossom festival at Kentville, or in a school group.[104]

Before the Folk could be profitable, they needed to be made presentable.

Her triumph in New York led, with a certain inevitability, to some hesitant signs of acceptance in Canada. Gladstone Murray of the Canadian Broadcasting Corporation agreed to a series of some twenty broadcasts on the folksongs of Nova Scotia, some from Creighton's published book and some that had been collected with Doreen Senior since 1932. "We will have two songs in each broadcast, and I will talk on the songs, the lore surrounding them, the singers and the district from which they came," Creighton announced to her publishers. Ultimately, there were two series of ten CBC programs in 1938 and 1939, with trained and untrained singers and with folk music arrangements provided by a string quartet.[105] Creighton was becoming a nationally known figure.

The war opened many doors for Creighton. In 1942 John Marshall of the Rockefeller Foundation came to Nova Scotia as a result of that organization's intense interest in developing a continental cultural policy and bringing cultural producers in Canada and the United States into close cooperation. He met Creighton through the president of Dalhousie University, and mentioned to her that the Institute of Folklore was to be held that summer at the University of Indiana. Creighton was intrigued, especially if the Rockefeller Foundation was making an offer of financial support. With the wartime occupation of King's College by naval officers, her position there as dean of women took up less time, as she explained to the foundation, and she felt that she could devote more attention to her field interests. A fellowship was approved on 6 June 1942 for two months, to begin on 29 June 1942, to cover travel and tuition at the rate of $120 per month.[106] Creighton would later report to the foundation that her time at Indiana had been a key moment of inspiration for her.[107] In addition to greatly broadening her approach to folklore, the stay at Indiana brought her invaluable new contacts in the field. Perhaps the most decisive was Alan Lomax, who was not only a major collector in the field of folk music, but was also in charge of the Archive of American Folk Song in Washington, D.C. Lomax advised Creighton to pursue her work at the Library of Congress, and used his influence both at the library and at the Rockefeller Foundation to further Creighton's career.[108] Creighton requested the loan of a recording machine from the Library of Congress and further financial support from the Rockefeller Foundation. In normal circumstances her chances of obtaining the support of either institution were not high: the Library of Congress had made it a policy not to lend its machines other than for war purposes, and the Rockefeller Foundation did not place folklore uppermost on its crowded agenda.[109] But Creighton, probably acting on Lomax's advice, presented herself to both bodies as an exceptionally attractive wartime proposition. She took care to emphasize that her proposed project had a direct connection to the war effort: she planned to collect folksongs from servicemen passing through Halifax, and emphasized especially the "internationalist" opportunity opened up by the city's huge floating wartime population.[110] The Library of Congress was anxious to extend its collection to include more Canadian items, which were seen as a valuable opportunity to compare British and American influences; and the Rockefeller Foundation saw in Creighton a chance to further its long-term vision of cultural continentalism. Four major Rockefeller grants, administered through the Public Archives of Nova Scotia from 1942 to 1946, made a decisive difference to Creighton: she was able to use a recording machine for the first time, to go on extended folksong expeditions in Yarmouth and in other areas distant from Halifax, to conduct field research on the folklore of Lunenburg County, and to return to Indiana to write up the results under the careful eye of Dr Stith Thompson, the author of the renowned *Motif Index of Folk Literature*.[111] As a Canadian, she was seen as a special case meriting favourable consideration: in December 1943 she was the only person in North America engaged in collecting traditional songs for the Archive of American Folk Song.[112]

The Rockefeller Foundation played a pivotal role in reorienting Creighton from British ballad-collecting to the more inclusive North American approach to folklore. If the foundation had as one of its implicit purposes the knitting together of Canadian and American scholars on a continental basis, Helen Creighton's file can only be regarded as an outstanding success story.[113] As was typical of cultural workers in Canada, she was given earlier and more powerful signs of recognition from outside the country than within it. Without Rockefeller support, she might not have gone to Indiana to acquire a new vision of folklore; she might not have been able to obtain access to the Library of Congress recording equipment to record Nova Scotia songs, and she might not have had the opportunity to research her manuscript on Lunenburg folklore and have it reviewed by one of the world's leading folklorists. The Rockefeller Foundation seems to have played a key role in her transition from ballad collector to general folklorist.

Notwithstanding these promising signs, had Creighton's career ended in 1945, she would be as little remembered today as Roy Mackenzie. The late 1940s were the making of her immense regional reputation. If, in the 1920s and early 1930s, it makes some sense to emphasize the cultural context of her career over her own ability to shape it, by the 1940s and 1950s she was much surer of her direction and purpose. Her exposure to newer currents of folklore at Indiana helped her break out of the élitist embrace of the English school at the moment when Canadians in general were rethinking their ties with Britain. From the 1940s on, she was no longer a British-style "ballad-stalker" but an American-style "folklorist," now as interested in magic and superstition as in Child ballads, and consequently able to connect much more forcefully with a widespread middle-class yearning for re-enchantment. After years of marginality as a freelance journalist *cum* amateur folklorist, Creighton achieved official status and security. She came to define folklore in Nova Scotia. For many people, her vision of the true Folk culture of the province attained the same reality in their minds as her vividly described Sable Island.

It takes nothing away from Creighton's victory in the 1940s to note the auspicious circumstances in which it occurred. Slowly, English-speaking Canadians began to construct their own Folk image, as the myth-symbol complex evolved by intellectuals of the 1920s, hitherto focused on Central Canada and the Canadian Shield, was forced to become less restrictive under the pressure of war. Until the 1940s, cultural producers in English-speaking Central Canada, although taken up with various forms of nationalism, were highly uncertain about the significance of folklore from the periphery (and indeed about the Maritimes in general). For all his impact on Creighton's work, Gibbon was typical in neglecting the Maritimes by beginning his folk festivals in Quebec City and moving west. Other Canadian nationalist figures proved no less regionally biased. Gradually, however, this parochial outlook was transformed. In the 1940s a wave of Maritime books issued from the strategically significant Ryerson Press, Maritime broadcasts found a national audience, and articles on the Maritimes in the national magazines appeared more frequently. Canadians also started to visit the region in large numbers.

Wartime patriotism provides a significant key to this new enthusiasm for the Canadian, and particularly the Maritime, Folk. The doctrine of the mosaic propounded and commercialized by Gibbon before the war became something like an official "multiculturalism" during it. English-speaking Canadians became more and more interested in exploring their own folkways. Wartime propaganda, through the National Film Board and other state agencies, directed particular attention to the promotion of national unity through cross-cultural understanding, and "folklore" emerged as an important weapon in this campaign. Watson Kirkconnell, in *Canadians All: A Primer of Canadian National Unity*, issued by the Director of Public Information in 1941, extolled the benefits of the mixed human ingredients that had been poured into the "huge mixing-bowl of Canada's national life. Surely no mincemeat in the world could have more spice and flavour than the Canadian people."[114] Illustrations for Kirkconnell's pamphlet, drawn from the motion picture *Peoples of Canada*, proceeded on the assumption of fixed racial essences. Accepting, as did Gibbon, the Nazis' racial categorization of Europeans into three main subspecies (Nordic, Mediterranean, and Alpine), Kirkconnell went on to insist that all Europeans' ethnic identities were composed of mixtures, and that there therefore could be no reasonable basis for racial division in Canada. Nova Scotians provided some of the best evidence of "racial types" who remained true to themselves but at the same time were loyal, steadfast Canadians: below an illustration of shipbuilding was the caption, "From the Upper Rhine came the Germans ... their descendants are the builders of the famous Bluenose schooners." Elsewhere he referred to the "oxen of the Dutch" (meaning Lunenburgers of German descent) still treading Maritime highways.[115]

Images of "Canadian Folk" were disseminated through movies and songs of the "Canadian Folk" selected by Barbeau for the encouragement of the Canadian Forces. "Who would have thought that our folk songs collected in such peaceful surroundings, would have been put to such a use?" wrote Creighton wonderingly to Barbeau, who requested and received permission to use five songs from her collection in his propaganda effort. As she informed him, enlisting the Folk for the purposes of war was an international pattern: in Britain, songs published by Creighton and Doreen Senior were being used by the Ministry of Propaganda.[116]

Folklore's wartime popularity and the American folk revival were bargaining-points for Creighton in her attempts to interest reluctant Canadian publishers. Creighton wrote in January 1945 to Lorne Pierce of Ryerson Press to broach the subject of publishing a folksong collection. She noted the warmth of her reception in the United States:

Two years ago the Rockefeller Foundation sent me to Indiana University to take a course in folklore, and I was given an amazingly warm reception due entirely to the fact that my book was well known and they wanted to know more about the folklore of Nova Scotia ... The largest market for a book of songs such as I have prepared will be in the United States where it will be eagerly received because they know how rich our tradition is here. I would like, if possible, to publish under my own flag which may be more patriotic than practical, but Miss Senior [feels] the same way too.[117]

Ryerson Press and Lorne Pierce were cautiously supportive. On 22 January 1945 Creighton mailed "a very large and bulky parcel," the first part of her manuscript. She wanted to get the package to him right away, for if the city was devastated by a repetition of the 1917 explosion, "I would hate to see twelve years' work destroyed for it would be impossible to duplicate the collection. Neither could enough of the old timers be found to make another one with songs of the quality found here."[118]

Ryerson Press's hesitant response suggested that the Canadian folk revival had not attained the proportions of its American counterpart. Although Creighton had itemized all the evidence she could find of an awakening Canadian interest – radio interviews, stories in the Montreal *Standard*, further exposure in *Maclean's*[119] – Lorne Pierce at Ryerson was not swept off his feet. He believed, along with Marius Barbeau, that only a subvention from the Canadian Humanities Research Council or further financial aid from the Rockefeller Foundation would make publication of the book commercially realistic.[120] As he remarked to Creighton, he and Barbeau were "feeling very hopeless over the size of the work, the cost involved and our inability, not only to get anywhere near the Manufacturing Department at the present time, but to afford the heavy costs."[121]

Creighton, informed of these difficulties, continued to cite the American precedent. "I was afraid there would be [difficulties], for wartime publishing leaves much to be desired. Yet in the States they seem to go ahead without trouble."[122] Eventually Pierce did agree to give Creighton and Senior's *Traditional Songs from Nova Scotia* a second look, but only after reading a work of international criticism by Constance Rourke which suggested the new centrality of folklore in contemporary thought. Even then, he made his support of the project contingent on his obtaining financial aid from Premier Angus L. Macdonald of Nova Scotia, and exclaimed, "Somehow our Canadian governments must wake up. We are aeons behind the USA and others."[123] J. Frank Willis, writing to Creighton on behalf of the CBC in 1949, struck the same theme of Canadians' following the American cultural pattern. The folklore revival now in full swing in the United States was only just starting to have a major impact on Canada, he argued. "We have noticed," he wrote, "and indeed it is apparent all over America, that there is a great upswing of public interest in the folk song and ballad. It has already transmuted Berle Ives into a very rich man, and a great many others are cashing in handsomely on this awakening interest."[124] That the Canadian folk revival was underway was implied by the eventual publication of *Traditional Songs from Nova Scotia*; that it was embryonic was suggested by the length and difficulty of the collection's path to publication.

The publication of *Traditional Songs from Nova Scotia* marked a new stage in Creighton's career and in the idea of the Folk in English Canada. The book represented two major shifts. One was Creighton's growing independence from the English model: Creighton's agenda was to become a folklorist with a large public following whose work would cover not only music but the whole range of folklore. The second was her arrival as a national figure, who ranked with Marius Barbeau as the country's best-known authority in the area, and who had no rivals as an interpreter of the culture of the Maritimes. The key to this second development was Creighton's position as an adviser to the National Museum. Through the 1950s and the early 1960s, this institutional link was to be pivotal to her position; after the mid-1960s, it involved her in serious methodological and epistemological debates over the purposes Canadian folklore should fulfil. The years from 1947 to 1965 were those of Creighton's most complete success, and the museum was perhaps her most valuable resource.

Her first major Canadian collection signalled her emergence as one of the country's most important cultural figures. Although Doreen

Senior's name was on the cover and she was technically equally responsible for its content, *Traditional Songs from Nova Scotia* was mainly Creighton's. She was delighted by it. "I can hardly take my eyes away from it long enough to write a letter," she exclaimed to one correspondent at Ryerson. "I really think it is beautiful. I like the compactness of it, especially in these days when people don't want large bulky books."[125] The book was significant in suggesting Creighton's growing independence of the British model. Doreen Senior, ostensibly a co-editor, did not receive proofs of the book before its publication, and vigorously protested against this failure to keep her fully informed. Although the oversight was undoubtedly influenced by the sheer difficulty of collaborative cultural effort across the Atlantic, more could reasonably be read into the disagreement over editing between Senior and Creighton. Creighton was outgrowing her mentor and establishing her own claim to her own territory. In editing their joint production of *Twelve Folksongs from Nova Scotia*, published in Britain by Novello in 1940, Senior had edited out Creighton's notes, "which," Creighton later remarked, "I think quite spoiled the book." Creighton now published their major collection of Nova Scotia songs, but without first showing the music to Senior for her approval, much to her British partner's chagrin. "I only wish Miss Senior were as happy as I am. At this late date she is greatly distressed because she was not sent proofs to read, which on the face of it sounds dreadful ... I was walking on air until this happened, but it has shaken me considerably. I want to be proud of our book. I want us all to be proud of it. And now I don't know."[126] Her conception of folklore was moving in a different direction from Senior's. It was becoming much less narrowly focused on music and much less dependent on the English tradition.

The dispute with Senior was the result of a shift towards a new style of folklore that had, in some respects, already occurred in her perspective. In 1944 Creighton went to Lunenburg County to collect folklore of all types, a radical departure from her earlier emphasis on music. She was shifting from the amateur Victorian tradition of ballad-collecting to an inclusive definition of the Folk more in accordance with the developing professional tradition in the United States, to which she had been exposed at Indiana. When Ryerson Press asked her how she would like to define her position in the book, Creighton replied,

Actually I like being referred to as a folklorist, because that is the way most of my time is spent. Local papers are apt to call me a lecturer and author. I do lecture occasionally, but the term folklorist is more fitting. You might like to add two international connections with which I have been honored. I've been made a Correspondent of the International Folk Music Council who have headquarters in London, England, and a Fellow of the American Anthropological Association. Nearer home, I've been made an Honorary member of the Dartmouth University Women's Club, a gesture which particularly touched me.[127]

The most important acknowledgment of her new status came from the National Museum, which in 1947 appointed Creighton to its staff as a museum adviser. (This meant that she would annually be given money to do her research, without the need to submit new proposals for museum contract work every year.) The dominant intellectual figure at the museum for folklorists was undoubtedly Marius Barbeau, who had joined the institution in 1911 and, although about to retire, retained much influence in Folk circles. Born in the Beauce, Oxford-educated, a collaborator in Gibbon's folk festivals, a pioneering anthropologist and popularizer of native traditions, and a theorist of the impact of modernization on the "Folk society" of French Canada, Barbeau seemed to represent virtually all the major trends of cultural thought in twentieth-century Canada. "In an age of increasing specialization," writes Edith Fowke, "he ranged over the whole field of folklore and anthropology, collecting and studying and describing Indian myths, ceremonials, language, music, arts, and culture; French-Canadian folktales, songs, games, handicrafts, art, and architecture; and English-Canadian songs and art."[128] Creighton would later clash vigorously with Barbeau, especially over the politics of the Canadian Folk Music Society (a branch, founded in 1960 by Barbeau, of the International Folk Music Council.) She would later believe him to be prone to marginalize English-language folklore and to place too much emphasis on using folksong as a resource for high culture. However, she also found him a pillar of support throughout the 1940s and 1950s. If the major influences acting on Creighton were those of Child and Sharp in the 1930s, in the 1950s and 1960s she was more strongly influenced by the style of Stith Thompson at Indiana, the famous collector and categorizer of motifs in folk tales, who gave her the benefit of a close reading of her Lunenburg monography, and by Barbeau, whose influence shines through the "Sketch for the instructions to Miss Helen Creighton" drawn up by the museum in 1947.

Miss Creighton's research, during four months in the Summer of 1947, will be along the lines familiar to her in collecting the folk-songs of her province; also to expand it if she finds opportunities, into the (French) Acadian field. Phonograph records should be made and numbered on index cards of the melodies and dances (a few stanzas each song, enough to provide for transcription); texts taken in writing, and the sources noted down as remembered by the informants.

Folk-tales ... stories, legends, folk dances, sayings, riddles, proverbs, recipes, weather lore, animal lore, and other folklore should be collected, wherever they can obtained.

The rural arts may be observed, wherever they exist – hooked-rug making, spinning and weaving, wood-carving, pottery making; also old village or town handicrafts and trades.[129]

Creighton's first summer of work with the museum was spent in southwestern Nova Scotia, and she reported a rich harvest of folksongs, ballads, folkdances and games; legends, both Indian and European, anecdotes, tall tales, proverbs, sayings, riddles, jokes, nicknames, local expressions and technical terms, and epitaphs, not to mention information concerning the "practice of witchcraft, supernatural experiences, ghost stories, superstitions, dreams, premonitions, treasure hoards, weather lore, mining lore, handicrafts, folk medicine, cooking recipes, [and] quilt pattern names."[130] It would be on the basis of this lore more than on her collections of songs that Creighton's influence came to be so pervasive in the province.

Although Creighton's long relationship with the museum would be marked with bitterness, particularly at its close, the institution was on balance very helpful to her career. The museum connection gave her respectability, semi-academic standing, and a relatively steady, if far from munificent, income. Above all, it gave her credentials as an authoritative folklorist. Still, Creighton retained even in this third "professional" stage of her career many of the attributes of the amateur ballad-hunter and storyteller. She had successfully used the museum's resources to create a public for her work; and that work in turn was increasingly focused on the popular themes (particularly the supernatural) that television audiences and casual readers would find entertaining. A balanced interpretation of her experience with the museum must include the consideration that although Nova Scotia governments had provided slight support for her in the 1930s and 1940s, and the Rockefeller Foundation and Library of Congress made a more substantial contribution in the 1940s, it was the museum that supported Creighton for over twenty years in her research and publications. Until the institutional emphasis shifted to hierarchy and piecework in the 1960s, the museum attached relatively few strings to Creighton's work, and gave her a Canada-wide credibility she might otherwise have lacked.

The nation-building enterprise of constructing the Folk undoubt-edly involved exploitative relationships, particularly with collectors in peripheral regions. The museum got its folklore rather inexpen-sively in the Maritimes, and researchers there never felt they had as much security as those in central Canada. Many were women, and were not readily accorded the same professional status as men.[131] The most glaring instance of an undersupported folklore project in which the absence of state funding had an impact on the type and nature of the folklore collected was Louise Manny's work on the Miramichi in New Brunswick. Her research was firmly controlled by her benefactor, Lord Beaverbrook. He refused to allow Manny to collect any British ballads, "no matter how much they had been shaped by New Brunswickers."[132] Creighton regarded Lord Beaver-brook as "not an entirely satisfactory sponsor," who didn't even pro-vide Manny with a tape recorder; Creighton wanted the museum to help her colleague out.[133] The Manny case suggested the practical ways in which the half-hearted commitment of supposedly national institutions to Canadian culture left folklorists to scrounge money where best they could.

Creighton's relationship with the museum was far less unequal that Manny's relationship with her distant capitalist patron. Creighton had far greater freedom to define her own style of folklore and set her own agenda. Her connection with the museum allowed her to bridge the worlds of high and popular culture, the world of the academy (which the museum, at its most ambitious, aspired to be part of) and the world of the bestseller and the television broad-cast. She knew how to use the credibility acquired in the universities and the museum to maximum effect in the wider cultural world. *Folklore of Lunenburg County* (1950), *Gaelic Songs in Nova Scotia* (1962, with Calum MacLeod), and *Folksongs of Southern New Brunswick* (1971) were all published as a result of her long association with the insti-tution. In the late 1970s, at the end of her collecting days, she esti-mated that her collection contained over 4,000 songs, of which only 667 had been published.[134] In the 1950s her work entered more and more into the cultural mainstream. Films (*The Rising Tide*, 1950; the National Film Board's *Songs of Nova Scotia*, 1957; a folk opera (*The Broken Ring*, 1953); records (*Folkmusic from Nova Scotia*, 1956); a ballet (*Sea Gallows*, 1958) – all testified to Creighton's new status. In the 1960s television added to her fame. In addition to guest appearances on leading CBC shows such as "Take Thirty" (1960) and "Front Page Challenge" (1962), she appeared on programs devoted entirely to Creighton and folklore, such as "Land of the Old Songs" (1960) and

"Lady of the Legends" (1966). Her 1957 collection of ghost stories, *Bluenose Ghosts*, was a bestseller, but anything with Creighton's name on it seemed to do well. Even her first academic monograph, *Folklore of Lunenburg County*, was reissued by Ryerson in a popular format in 1975. Considered as a "hegemonic project" intended to present to Canadians as a whole an image of a state institution equitably concerned with all regions and with the disinterested preservation of people's traditions, the museum's folklore work in the region was a remarkably inexpensive success. It was no less successful from Creighton's professional perspective. The museum connection helped Creighton define a high profile regionally and nationally, popularly and professionally.

The benefits and costs of the museum connection were personified by Creighton's relationship with Carmen Roy, the head of the folklore department. The correspondence between Creighton and Roy constitutes a remarkable personal and professional archive. Creighton's letters to Roy show her warm, spontaneous response to life; her letters give us an insight into the living human being sometimes overshadowed by the media image of the celebrity. At the same time, and with growing bitterness, they dramatize the immensely complex issues raised by the Folk in Canada, as Roy and Creighton articulate sharply differing perspectives on their craft and on the practical organization of research.

Creighton and Roy had a lot in common. Roy too had done work in fishing communities and in a part of Quebec, the Gaspé, which more closely resembled the Maritimes than it did the St. Lawrence Valley. Roy was also a collaborator with Creighton in the Canadian Folk Music Society (of which Barbeau was president). After she was named head of the folklore department, she became Creighton's supervisor.

Creighton's letters to Roy bring out many many aspects of her relationship with her own province. She loved Halifax and Nova Scotia, and described with a lover's eye winter storms and the dazzling vista of the harbour as seen from Dartmouth. "Our BIG STORM was quite thrilling, and I have never seen such winter beauty," Creighton wrote in the winter of 1960. "Everybody with a camera was out taking pictures, and once we were able to walk down town everybody spoke to everybody whether you knew them or not. There was a happy spirit abroad. A lot of people were reticent about admitting they enjoyed it as though they were afraid of being considered odd. Personally I have always loved snow, and my happiest childhood memories are of playing in it."[135] For Creighton, the sights of her city prompted some of her most lyrical descriptive passages. The sight of Halifax Harbour from her Dartmouth window inspired this passage:

The waves of the harbour were rough and the sun shone so brightly that it was dazzling. We are on an elevation looking straight out Halifax Harbour and we also overlook quite a bit of the city. In the late afternoon the water sometimes becomes a deep blue. With the lights from the ships in the stream and from office buildings across the harbour the beauty is indescribable. There is often a very lovely blue in the early morning too which I see occasionally. These are the things I miss when I go away from home.

"It is a great satisfaction to be able to picture you as I write," she concluded. "Please remember me to all my friends at the Museum … I hope it will not be long before we meet again."[136] Creighton identified very closely with Roy. "I think of you very often as I drive over the country roads. I wonder how your work is going, and what you are finding, and under what conditions you are sleeping."[137] Both of them succumbed to illnesses in the 1960s, and each worried about the other. "Isn't it distressing that Carmen is ill? I don't know much about it, but will be glad when she is back at her desk again," Creighton wrote to Barbeau.[138] To Roy she wrote, "You know, dear one, that if I can do anything to help you to get well again, I will be only too happy to do it."[139] When Creighton went into hospital for surgery (a radical mastectomy) in 1964, she sought to shield Roy from news of her illness. "Unless it is necessary, let us not worry Carmen with this while she is away," Creighton wrote to Jeanne Monette, Roy's assistant. "I had to tell you on account of my summer plans, but could we spare her until we find what the surgeon discovers? But please give her my love if you are writing her. I will work until the time when I go in which might not be for another two or three weeks. Or it may be next week."[140] When Roy learned of her friend's misfortune, she reported that she had been so sad that she nearly became ill herself.[141]

The friendship seems to have been important for them both. Part of its charm was its cross-cultural nature, the atmosphere of *bonne entente*. Creighton (later an active proponent of French immersion in the private Dartmouth Academy)[142] experimented with French in her letters to Roy, sometimes closing not altogether confidently with "Très affectuessant á vous."[143] They could complain to each other about the difficulties of working alongside the imperious Barbeau, whom they saw as rather highhandedly imposing his own design on the Canadian Folk Music Society. "The more I study Dr B's program for 1961, the more it distresses me," Creighton complained to Roy, "with everything *based* on folklore, and such a minimum of the real thing. Moreover he seems to have forgotten that English Canada exists, which must be embarrassing to nice people like you and Luc [Lacourcière]."[144] Roy, a fellow member of the society, offered sympathy but felt resigned to Barbeau's eccentricities and intransigence.[145] They shared many of the same friends and the same sense of succumbing to some of the infirmities of old age.

The friendship was also a professional relationship between women who, similar in some respects, had different agendas for the Folk in Canada. Creighton retained much of the breezy independence of the amateur and the freelancer, which frustrated Roy, who was expected to supervise her and who had a more professional, bureaucratic attitude towards the work. Creighton's research proceeded intuitively and inductively. She explained to Roy that flexibility was functional in the Maritime setting, where one might encounter some villages with no songs and others with vast reserves of both songs and folklore. Why then make two trips to the richer community? Should one confine one's attention to a pre-set problem, when the Folk resources "out there" were undetermined and probably fast eroding? For Roy, the pre-selected theme should come first, and the piling up of more and more material was not particularly useful. It was almost a classic clash between an intuitive empiricism on the one hand and rationalism on the other.

Signs of difficulty in the relationship surfaced as early as 1960, when Roy complained that she was having a hard time obtaining a proposal for definite summer field project from Creighton.[146] When Roy had asked her just what it was she meant to do in the coming summer, Creighton had replied,

August seems to be shaping up quite busily. Sandy Ives wants me to go to Maine to their Northeast Folklore Society meeting and I suggested he write Dr Russell about it. I would like to do some work on Grand Manan, and might be able to slip down from there. Louise Manny also wants me for her Festival, and I think I should support her there. Then we have our own Festival of the Arts in Tatamagouche which is a fine place to display our books on folklore along with other books. They also like to fit in some of our folklore either as music or a play. Before that I have some good contacts in Cape Breton to follow up and some in Shediac. I have always more or less drifted along, following clues as they came along and I think that is much the best way. I am glad you have been in my province, for you can understand now why there is still so much to be found. And then there is Prince Edward Island where I should also go.[147]

Roy kept pushing for specific projects, and Creighton kept coming up with possibilities to be pursued separately or in tandem: a study of ghost stories involving parents and children in need; a selection of tales from Pubnico; a Gaelic collection; an annotated version of her book on ghost stories; or a study of the folklore of Grand Manan Island.[148] Roy required a definite plan for Creighton's four months of field work so she could justify to her superiors Creighton's small salary, room and board (eight dollars per day), and mileage money.[149] At the end of the season Roy wanted a good "scientific" study from Creighton on the subject of Grand Manan Island, New Brunswick, which she evidently thought was located in Nova Scotia. If, as Creighton had suspected, there were no songs there, Roy wanted Creighton to explore some of the reasons for the absence of songs. She counselled Creighton to adopt a more rigorous, planned approach to collecting, rather than collecting "inconsiderately."[150] This difference of opinion as to the proper way to design folklore research and the role of folklore in intellectual life persisted throughout the 1960s.

It was a debate over tactics, connected to deeper issues of strategy and purpose. The disagreement was really over the place of the idea of the Folk in the twentieth century. For Roy, folklore was more about modernization than about survival. It was about exploring the dynamics and tensions of Canadian society. Folklore was an emergent social science concerned with the oral transmission of cultural values. In February 1960 Roy wrote a remarkable letter to Creighton outlining her methodological differences. Beginning with a personal salutation, "Dear Helen," Roy then launched abruptly into a long manifesto calling for a new scientific folklore. The letter was a stern critique of Creighton's work. Collection should be tailored to public needs and the requirements of specialized folklorists. It should attempt, more directly, to speak to Canadian culture. It should explore the causes of cultural change. Questions should be directed towards the theoretical answers one anticipated. If Creighton had followed Roy's plan, she would have spent the summer of 1960 asking her respondents to respond to questions on the question of whether or not "the Canadian" was suffering from an inferiority complex.[151] All this was a far cry from Creighton's normal working method: collecting whatever the Folk had to offer in a given community. It would have transformed Creighton into a foot-soldier of modernization theory, particularly as it had developed at Chicago. For Robert Redfield, the key theorist, and particularly for Barbeau, whose thought is evident in Roy's manifesto for a new folklore, although "folklore" might survive in the present day it did so as an endangered form, imperilled by a monolithic process of modernization.[152]

From Creighton's perspective, however, Roy's manifesto was urging her to make a transition she had already made. Her recent work was already bringing the singer closer to the reader, and showing "the how, why, and where of folk songs, the people who sing them, and their function in that particular community. I also state something that I think important. That is that I have always considered it my part to produce the source material (words and tunes) and let the creative artist pick it up from there (for arrangements for solos, choirs, symphonies, ballets, and so forth). That is why I published as I do."[153] But Roy was not about to yield the high ground of social science, and Creighton was not about to rethink the methods and epistemology that had guided her over three decades. Roy believed that after thousands of songs had been collected and a myriad of folk tales and beliefs noted, the key problem was to find a pattern in the evidence and an argument for its contemporary relevance. Creighton resisted any systematic attempt to theorize about the social purposes served by the cultural repertoire she had preserved.

The two friends, for all their personal closeness, were thus miles apart in their positions on folklore. Creighton's *Bluenose Magic*, largely researched by her while under contract with the museum, was subjected to a withering blast of criticism from Roy. In reviewing the manuscript, Roy attacked Creighton's English (which demonstrated a certain *chutzpah*, given her own uncertain grasp of the language and Creighton's status as past president of the Canadian Authors' Association), the apparent casualness of the text's discussion of the research plan, and Creighton's reference to folklore as a "first love," which Roy considered a phrase that revealed a lack of objectivity and direction in the work. Moreover, Creighton gave no indications in her script of the statistical distribution of beliefs in various ethnic groups.[154] Creighton, initially thrown "into despair" by this criticism, mounted a spirited defence of her record. Her work had not proceeded without plan, but in the most practical and flexible way.

No, my work hasn't lacked planning or direction but I have approached it in what to me always seemed the most practical way. You can do this much more easily as a Museum Adviser than on contract. Any trip has always been first in search of songs. You know yourself that songs turn up in most unexpected ways, and to turn around and go elsewhere when the first enquiries yield no songs could mean missing very important material. I have therefore adopted a system of adapting to my surroundings to make the most of every opportunity. Take my visit to Seabright, for instance. This is only sixteen miles from Halifax and a lot of city people have summer cottages there. I expected to spend a week in Seabright at the most, but one evening I was collecting when a girl from another house came in and said her father was waiting for me to visit their house because he had some stories to give me. Fortunately I went and he told a few stories which were not terribly interesting. I soon discovered however that he had something else on his mind, and it turned out that he wanted to sing a song or two but was too shy to suggest it. The upshot of this was that he and a friend knew a great many songs, but the people in the village were not aware that he knew any. As a result, I spent the whole summer there and it proved a most profitable season for my main objective, songs, and many other items as well. I discovered the first year I worked for the Museum that wherever I found material I should stay with it and not be in a hurry to move on. I've always found this the most practical way to collect and, as I said, for general collecting it makes working as Museum Adviser more profitable in the broad sense than going out on contract.

As for statistical evaluation of material, Creighton remarked, with rather more sophistication than her "scientific" correspondent, that this could not be usefully attempted in a place that had not been uniformly covered.[155] Creighton's reply amounted to a defence of the craft of the literary folklorist against the critique of someone pressing for an approach grounded in postivist social science.

And, for Creighton, there was surely more at stake than resistance to social science in this fundamental methodological debate. Her own role as a popular intellectual, uniquely able to bridge the world of the academy and the cultural marketplace, was also at issue. Ironically, as Creighton had become increasingly professional in her institutional attachments, she had turned more and more to the most popular forms of folklore: tales of magic, superstition, and cures. The third phase of her career could be defined, in fact, as one in which she used her professional position with the museum to undertake a popular project: the diffusion of folklore to as many Nova Scotians as possible. Creighton kept a watchful eye on the bookshops of Nova Scotia, and complained to the National Musem in 1966 that by making *Folklore of Lunenburg County* so hard to get, they were stopping summer visitors and others from buying the folklore they wanted to buy.[156] Roy, more securely positioned in Ottawa, was frankly puzzled about why she was so obsessed with the popular market, but, as Creighton explained to her in 1958, popularizing folklore made sound economic and intellectual sense.

You ask why I tire myself with speaking and so forth. There are several very good reasons. One is that last year I asked Dr Rousseau what his policy was in this regard and he wants me to do it. It is a very good way of letting the public know what the Museum is doing. Also I am much more valuable to the Museum when I can travel about and speak of our work than I would be if I kept my little nose in my typewriter all the time.

Then there is the question of money. As you know I work for a distressingly small fee. I've always felt that if the Museum could, they would increase it and do the right thing by me. I hope I'm right. In the meantime I'd lead a pretty confined life on what I make. As a speaker I get around and see the world. Speaking has taken me as far afield as New York, Washington and Indiana University. Last summer it took me to St. Andrews, Lennoxville, Montreal, and Newcastle, and it put me on television in Montreal, Sydney, and Halifax. I always get soft hearted, or soft headed, when it comes to taking fees from organizations, and usually give my services, but small organizations serve the purpose of giving the speaker experience and assurance, and from their reactions one learns what an audience finds most interesting. Then when a big assignment comes up like t.v. or radio, or something that can afford to pay, I am ready for it. Some day I might do a Canadian Club tour; the speaking end wouldn't worry me, but I might find it too fatiguing. It's a nice thing to keep in mind though. Or the Museum might want to send me somewhere.

Then, of course, there is the fact of sharing. I was brought up in the belief that if I had a talent which would give people pleasure it was my duty to share it ... This season the groups I've addressed are so completely different that the one talk has served for all. That has minimized preparation and I've been able to enjoy the contacts myself.[157]

Without her strong belief in popularization, defended with both economic and more general arguments, Creighton would never have attained her present status as a definer of identity. She emerged in the magazines and newspapers, and more crucially, on radio and television programs, at precisely the right moment, when what was broadcast had an immense and lasting impact. At the same time, Creighton's work took place within and was structured by the commercial setting, particularly as influenced by the tourism industry. Creighton had no hesitation about using the Folk as tourist attractions. *Marine Highway*, the filmmaker Margaret Perry's promotional masterpiece for the Nova Scotia government, included some of Creighton's folksingers: "Ned McKay," she recalled in her memoirs, "looked picturesque with shaggy beard and kind eyes beneath bushy eyebrows, and Isaac Doyle was at ease sitting on the edge of a wharf playing with a rope."[158] *Songs of Nova Scotia*, made by the National

Film Board and drawing on Creighton's Folk, was a favourite on the tourist boat that sailed between Yarmouth and Bar Harbour, Maine.[159] A provincial tourism film, *Bluenose Ghosts*, featured superstitious stories re-enacted by a theatre group.[160]

It was on television, that most potent force of twentieth-century modernity, that many Nova Scotians first encountered the truth of their pre-modern essence. In correspondence with Barbeau in 1957, Creighton congratulated him as a successful television performer ("You televise very well, and in this way so many people have come to know about you and your great work") and told him of her own first experiences with the powerful new medium: "I had no idea how extensive the television is until I appeared to tell a ghost story from our Halifax studio. It was amazing how many people stopped me on the street to speak of it and, as a result, I was given a number of excellent stories."[161] The Creighton phenomenon was very much connected to her command of the new medium, despite the fact that she found television productions gruelling and stressful. "I thought my eyes were permanently burnt through, they were so sore from the bright lights"; but then she added, significantly, "It was a stimulating experience and kept me going as if it had been a tonic."[162]

Creighton handled television superbly. Her success in the new medium illustrated the value of the museum connection. It gave her national prominence: she and Barbeau were considered Canada's leading folklorists by the 1960s. They were both so famous that the CBC's satirical "Rawhide" program could count on listeners to understand the humour of an "April Fool's" program in 1959, in which the host was to chat "with two of his imaginary characters ... in the province who are 'the only surviving exponents of a type of folk music which seems to have been overlooked in the collections of both Dr Helen Creighton and Dr Marius Barbeau.'"[163]

Creighton enjoyed the limelight. She enjoyed being president of the Canadian Authors' Association (an office she held from 1962 to 1964) and felt that the museum should feel excited about it as well. Creighton believed that by leading the CAA (which she wanted to be a working association, not a social club) she was doing work in which the museum had a stake, and which she believed its senior officers approved. "You can tell the Treasury Board," she wrote defensively to Jeanne Monette at the museum, after her term as the president of the association ended in 1964,

that I have worked diligently day and night for the months of May and June and have proved in the last two years that I can take on an extremely difficult administrative task and do it well. With letters of congratulation and gratitude pouring in, the Musem can hold up its head with pride ... These duties have been much heavier than I anticipated, but it was agreed that I must do the job well, even if it meant doing less for the Museum during my term in office. At times I could get along well with my folklore; at other times it has had to be set aside, but that was understood with the Museum. Treasury need have no worry that I have [wasted] government time.[164]

In Ottawa, Roy may well have felt that Creighton, whom she already had thought difficult to supervise, was not giving her museum work enough attention.

Roy's reservations about publicity-oriented folklore could only have been intensified by Creighton's increasing emphasis on the supernatural, an issue that dramatized the differences between their two research styles. The spirit world came to occupy a bigger and bigger role in Creighton's imaginative life. Roy regarded the supernatural as an interesting field in which to test social psychology and the impact of modernity on folk belief; Creighton's stance was more that of a believer who contacted and counselled fellow believers. With Roy she openly shared her sense of the impact of the spirit world on her attitudes. She mentioned her speaking to schoolchildren, and her counselling those worried about supernatural experiences. One child was comforted with the "knowledge" that if one saw the devil in life, one would not see him in death. Had Roy heard of that tale?[165] Yes, Roy replied, and it might be suitable for a good study in the psychology of folk beliefs.[166] For Roy, reports of supernatural occurrences could be grist for a bigger social-psychological mill. For Creighton, some – indeed, many – accounts of supernatural occurrences were true and should be investigated by parapsychologists.

Creighton's interest in the supernatural won her a far larger audience than anything she had done before in folklore. After her ghost stories were broadcast in 1956, her local member of Parliament was among those who sent her a fan letter.[167] "I am constantly surprised at the interest it has created," exclaimed Creighton to Roy on the subject of her collection of ghost stories. "Some people keep it for bedside reading! Teen agers love it. People come to me all the time in person, on the telephone, and by letter with their experiences, knowing I will take them seriously. This should make me very useful even if it means just being nearby for consultation. What a subject folklore is; always something new developing."[168] A second cultural gold mine, and this one seemingly inexhaustible, had opened up for Creighton.

Creighton shared with Roy her personal belief in foreshadowings and spirits.[169] It became clear from the tone of Creighton's letters that she was seeing herself more and more as a lay parapsychologist, dispensing comfort to the ghost-stricken and providing empirical "data" on the hereafter.

Did I ever tell you about a haunted house I have been interested in Dartmouth? A new house with knockings which intensified, and a crucifix which was shaken many times from the wall and always fell with the smooth side downwards. The house was new and there was no possibility of any human explanation. It ended on a terrible night when the family were all in different parts of the house and the nine year old boy saw what he insists was the devil all fiery red and with horns which turned in as on a moose. The rest of the family were in different parts of the house and all suffered at the same time from shock although they saw nothing. The boy ran ... after the devil laughed and at the boy's scream disappeared leaving a penetrating smell behind him like a morgue. The family being a happy little group with no inner conflicts, and deeply devoted to their church, though not in any way fanatical, couldn't believe that anything so horrible could happen to them. Their faith hadn't been shattered, but they were terribly upset for some months and are only now recovering. They moved, and one daughter felt something heavy on her chest one night holding her down; then she was lifted up above the bed and at her scream she was dropped and fell back heavily on her bed. They therefore moved again, this time to Halifax since they had heard a ghost can't cross water.

I've written all this in detail to the Parapsychology Foundation, and Mrs Garrett even 'phoned me from New York. Her theories however don't fit the case and she won't admit there is evil in the world except that we make ourselves.[170]

Creighton was thrilled at the prospect of being offered a position on the advisory board of a proposed Institute of Parapsychology at Duke University, which, she said, would have meant much more to her than being president of the Canadian Authors' Association. "What a new door of interest it opens up," she wrote to Roy, "particularly as I am continually having experiences myself."[171]

Roy was circumspect in her response to Creighton's enthusiasm for the supernatural. She responded with a distinct coolness to Creighton's proposal that she prepare a scholarly edition of *Bluenose Ghosts*.[172] As for the haunted house in Dartmouth, Roy remarked that the National Museum was not about to commit itself to a belief in such phenomena. [173] For someone who, like Roy, saw folklore as a positive science that might speak powerfully to the modern Canadian predicament, Creighton's strategy of popularizing ghost stories without analysing their social function must have seemed like a throwback to the amateur traditions of an earlier day. It must have seemed more like a regrettable lapse than a promising new direction.

How and in exactly what combination these deep-seated differences combined to end Creighton's attachment to the museum is difficult to say, but such strong disagreements over professionalism and purpose must have played a significant role. Creighton's account of losing her semi-permanent adviser's position and being reduced to the status of an outside contractor places the emphasis on the shift to the new director, Roy, and on her own failing health: "I suppose it is because I accomplish so much that nobody realizes the long hours I have always had to spend resting, and how limited my strength is. A new director had come to the Museum who left all folklore decisions in the capable hands of Dr Roy. She has built up the Archives splendidly, and to her the Museum comes first; I knew she wasn't happy that I was giving it limited attention. I was not too surprised then when the surgical axe fell."[174]

For Creighton, everything came at once: the end of her presidency of the Canadian Authors' Association, which was marked by controversies and difficulties, the end of her adviser's position with the museum, and (she feared, because of a personal "forerunner") the end of her good health. The coincidence of these misfortunes made the transition from insider to outsider at the museum doubly painful. That the blow was seemingly administered by someone she had regarded as a close friend, and without a detailed explanation, made it even more devastating. All of these events meant that her transition to working strictly on contract (as of 1 April 1964) was an experience that was far more bitter than the impression conveyed in her memoirs. Instead of being bound in any permanent way to Creighton, the museum now hired her for set periods at a set wage (in 1964, for 192 working days at the paltry rate of fifteen dollars per day, with a consideration for mileage).[175] Roy implied to Creighton that she would fight for her when her contract came up for discussion, but repeatedly reminded her that nothing could be guaranteed. The museum would not commit itself to her work in advance of the approval of its estimates by the House of Commons and the Treasury Board. Contracts directly related to the museum's own exhibits might well be given preferential treatment over hers; and it was up to the researcher to put in a strong proposal for a contract, to help Roy fight for it in the system.[176] Whatever the complicated bureaucratic rationale for these changes – which might plausibly be interpreted as the intellectual equivalent of the bureaucratic "deskilling" of once-autonomous craft workers by a centralizing authority – Creighton could hardly help taking them personally. She already felt underpaid and exploited by the museum. "As you know I work for a distressingly small fee," she wrote to Roy in 1958. "I've always felt that if the Museum could, they would increase it and do the right thing by me. I hope I'm right. In the meantime I'd lead a pretty confined life on what I make."[177] In September 1963 she complained, "My work for the Museum and the Authors is suffering from the delay with my salary cheques ... if the spark has gone out of my work it is due to this uncalled for strain. I hope they will soon get it settled, because if they don't, I fear I shall be ill."[178] The changes of the mid-1960s eroded her sense of economic security even further. There was a difference of interpretation over how much money Creighton was owed, and delays in getting money out of Ottawa. The problem seems to have been connected with the upheavals at the museum; Roy, who did not see how the institution could honour a past director's oral promise that the museum would financially support Creighton's work while she was president of the CAA, believed that she herself was caught in a dilemma, responsible for living up to a budgetary commitment made by a departing director which she could not defend on the basis of the museum's criteria.[179] Resignations, Roy's own recurrent illnesses, and job redefinitions conspired to make the situation more difficult. Confusion reigned, and Creighton felt insecure. "I understand that from today my rate of pay has been raised from six to twenty dollars. I know they have been working on that, but has it gone through? And does it mean that I must wait until the end of October before any salary cheque comes in? It is a very fortunate thing for me that I've always managed to put a bit aside, but how desperate a situation this would be for a woman who had rent to pay and nothing coming in. It isn't that I can't wait, but the uncertainty that has clouded the past few months to such an extent that I came down with a very bad dose of influenza, and am now typing from my bed ... Nobody can do good work under these conditions."[180] Financial insecurity stalked her on the morrow of her cancer operation. "It is also unfortunate that on the eve of the horror that awaits me I have to be plagued as I was last year by difficulties with salary payments," she wrote with deep bitterness. "Never have I worked harder or deserved [the difficulties] less."[181] The following year, money still seemed to flow sluggishly out of Ottawa. "Years ago I taught school for six months in Mexico and at the end of every month I had to take a large square cloth to school for my salary which was paid in silver dollars," Creighton remarked acidly in a letter to Roy. "Perhaps that is how my two month's salary is coming from the Museum, for it hasn't appeared yet. Hope springs eternal, and perhaps the mail will have it on Monday."[182] The cheque arrived six days later, and Creighton remarked, "I will now go out and pay some bills."[183] A year later, her downstairs tenants had bought a house, and she was forced to contemplate selling her own.[184] Creighton nurtured a sense of grievance against the museum, and remarked in 1970 that the museum had never even asked her to give a talk in Ottawa, "which I think is dreadful."[185]

It would be simplistic to attempt to account for Creighton's growing rift with the museum and with Roy strictly in terms of an impersonal institution's exploitation of an industrious field worker. To some extent, Creighton withdrew herself; she had museum contracts lined up but accepted instead a Canada Council grant to write her memoirs, and she explained her feeling of being "cut off from the Museum" in 1968 by her need to finish *Bluenose Magic* and her autobiography.[186] If on one level the issues were strictly ones of budgetary cheese-paring and economic insecurity, the "money" issues surely condensed wider concerns and controversies about the contemporary relevance of the idea of the Folk. Roy and Creighton were pushing in opposite directions. Roy's consistent emphasis on asking for systematic research, contemporary relevance, and "science" drew on an anthropological tradition and had affinities with Barbeau's theme of cultural modernization; such rigour was an important aspect of an emergent professionalism. Creighton remained in her heart a storyteller: the "Lady of the Legends." Just as the story-reading "Aunt Helen" at the radio station CHNS had represented a role that both preserved and undermined traditional gender ideals, the public persona of Creighton in the 1950s and 1960s was that of the favourite Victorian aunt, an innocent enthusiast and amateur finding her way in a tough world. The image was well crafted and deceptive. Creighton knew what she wanted to be and the kind of message she wanted to convey. The impression left by her letters is that of a tough and talented organizer, a capable writer, and an engaging popularizer of the idea of the Folk.

With determination and flair, Creighton made herself into the master interpreter of Nova Scotia and the Canadian authority on all things "Bluenose." The reversal in her fortunes from her early disappointments in the 1930s to her fame in the 1970s was complete. The freelancer compelled to search high and low for sponsors in the 1930s had become a Folk hero, the best-known writer in the province. Honorary degrees, civic and provincial honours, and the Order of Canada all spoke of her success. Films, ballets, operas, and records all drew on the Creighton collection. Collected by Creighton in a small fishing cove on the eastern shore in 1933, the "Nova Scotia Song," popularly known as "Farewell to Nova Scotia," became the province's unofficial anthem. Creighton's collection had clearly come to define a certain idea of Nova Scotia's identity, and she exerted a degree of cultural influence approached by no other figure. It seems legitimate to speak of "the Creighton Phenomenon," for in two short decades her work came to be regarded as the true voice of the Folk, defining what was essential, unchanging, and enduringly valuable in the culture of Nova Scotia. Creighton may have lost the theoretical battles she waged privately in her letters with Roy in the 1960s; but she clearly won the war for popular influence in her own society, which, since 1928, she had fought with such determination and intelligence.

CREIGHTON'S FOLKLORE AS AN IDEOLOGICAL INTERVENTION

So persuasive and popular were Creighton's works, both in Nova Scotia and in Canada as a whole, that the picture they drew of Nova Scotia has come to seem part of common sense and popular tradition rather than the outcome of debatable assumptions and choices. Just as "her" song become the province's, so did "her" reading of social and political realities become, for many people, part of the taken for granted world. One woman's antimodernist outlook came to appear to be the natural, spontaneous voice of the Folk.

The most general assumption of all those who constructed the Folk was that there had once been a certain organic unity within society. Once, when society was whole, there had been folkways shared by all. Now, in the fallen modern world, this substratum of customs and beliefs was accessible only to certain gifted intellectuals. These hidden resources could in turn serve as mnemonic devices, allowing "us" to remember who "we" once had been before modernity had taken its toll. Returning to the Folk meant a collective return to essence, to spontaneous truth, and to a forgotten age of organic social unity. As a social concept, "Folk" worked in an entirely different way from "the people," the "working class," "fishermen and farmers," or "primary producers." The Folk were those who were uncontaminated by the influences of the modern world, who clung to the old ways and the traditional ballads in the face of industry and mass culture. Their essence was decency, deference, humility, modesty, and loyalty to family and kin.

In constructing this "Folk," Creighton was doing nothing unusual or improper. As David Whisnant discerningly remarks of the parallel Appalachian case,

Clearly, the work of a "mere" ballad collector has inescapably political dimensions. It involves presuppositions and judgments about the relative worth of disparate cultural systems; the selection of certain cultural items in preference to others – frequently in accordance with an unspoken theory of culture; the education (not to say manipulation or indoctrination) of a public regarding the worth (or worthlessness) of unfamiliar cultural forms or expressions; and the feeding back of approval-disapproval into the "subject" culture so as to affect the collective image and self-images (and therefore the survival potential) of its members.[187]

Creighton, like all collectors, was inevitably selective, creating out of the vast realm of popular cultural forms a "Folk culture" that conformed to assumptions appropriate for someone of her class, gender, and ethnicity. The debate that should occur over Creighton's immense cultural legacy is not over whether or not she deliberately "distorted" the cultural realities she described but rather about the implications of her essentialist editing of an idea of identity. Is this particular reading of identity still useful in a twentieth-century society? If so, for whom and in what way? Were there, and are there, alternatives?

   And if answering such questions means directing a critical light on Creighton, we must continually remind ourselves of the social context in which she worked, shaped as it was by gender, class, and ethnicity, and by an emergent ethos of professionalism through which her words came to be more authoritative than those of most other cultural producers. Moreover, her empirical work in collecting songs and other aspects of folklore has bequeathed to the future an immense collection of data, which can be, and now is, being "read against the grain" and incorporated into narratives and strategies quite different from those propounded by Creighton herself. The black community, for example, has found her work an invaluable source for the reclamation of history. Had hers been one of a dozen major cultural interpretations, her selectivity would not have had such a general impact. But for the reasons we explored in the first chapter, alternative voices – particularly those rooted in a counter-hegemonic working-class movement – had been stilled. Many of the problematical features of Creighton's intellectual work were further magnified by its elevation into semi-official status by the tourism state. In probing the ways in which this essentialist vocabulary of identity was constructed, we should not simplistically draw up a bill of indictment against Creighton. We should rather probe and evaluate the cultural logic of Innocence as a whole, and the ways in which Creighton's thought naturalized conservative assumptions about class, gender and sexuality, race and ethnicity, irrationalism, and local identity.

   Class is never addressed as such in Creighton's thought, but a universe of assumptions about class and cultural distinction is implied throughout. Creighton's assumption is that there is or should be organic unity within society. Society is not divided into groups with their own perspectives and conflicting interests, but shares an underlying core of traditions. Throughout Creighton's works the reader is constantly reminded, both overtly and subtly, that what he or she is reading has a bearing on all Nova Scotians, on "the people," past and present. Some of the best examples emerge from her work on superstition and magic and from her analyses of the cultural hold of the traditional ballad.

Thus, in *Bluenose Magic*, we are informed that what we are encountering is a unifying synthesis, "magic," which all Nova Scotians share, whether or not they are aware of it. "The fact that witchcraft is mentioned in the Bible justifies many practices in the minds of our people," Creighton remarks. "At the slightest raising of an eyebrow this fact is called to mind."[188] "Whether Captain Kidd, the English pirate, ever visited Nova Scotia is a debatable point and not too important for our study here. The main thing is that people think he did and that to this day they are looking for his treasure."[189] The book's jacket copy is completely faithful to its contents in this regard:

From the warm and colourful inhabitants of Nova Scotia come unique tales of witches and weather signs, hauntings and happenings, cures and curses all passed down through generations. Belief in the occult is still prevalent among Nova Scotians whose ancestors – largely English, Scottish and Irish – brought to North America a rich heritage of culture and folklore ... Have a wonderful time with BLUENOSE MAGIC. You will find yourself often in its pages.

And further: "Stories are presented in the narrators' own words and a running commentary attempts to explain why Nova Scotians interpret their beliefs as they do. Perhaps Nova Scotians are particularly sensitive to supernatural experiences because we are a sea-faring people or, if not, at least we have the sea all around us."

Bluenose Ghosts, for its part, introduces us to the peculiarities of "our country people."[190] This usage of the word "people," especially if prefaced by "our," condenses an entire ideology of an organic social order.

An organic vocabulary is also very active in Creighton's handling of Folk music. Folk essentialism postulated that underneath the buzzing factionalism of modern society, one could find an ur-text of constant Folk values. As Kittredge had explained, a ballad had no author; the teller of the story was unimportant. Grimm's "das Volk dichtet" conveyed a sense of the Folk speaking with one voice. This portrait of a simple society might stand as a plausible, if inevitably highly speculative, version of the pre-history of some tribe at some unspecified place and time. It was hopelessly unrealistic with regard to Nova Scotia. Dave Harker notes perceptively that a characteristic of the Folk tradition was that "popular" and "folk" were used interchangeably "with extreme vagueness," and "'the people' and 'the folk' likewise."[191]

According to Creighton, the "singers of songs and tellers of stories in this province" were characterized by a fierce fidelity to the *original* tale and the *original* ballad, and were loath to "deviate from the text by inventing something to fill in a space." This made them "excellent informants."[192] Yet surely there was a powerful contradiction in Creighton's thought about ballads, which could be saved only by dividing Nova Scotians into the "true" Folk and the "impure." Apart from the Child ballads, many of which had been quite considerably reworked in Nova Scotia, how could one so assuredly reconstruct the "original version"? And why should musical change be so conservatively equated with "deviation"? Certainly one is entitled to doubt whether many Nova Scotians ever conformed to Creighton's stereotypical notion of their true ballad-singing, fiercely traditional essence. Her impression of a ballad-singing rural society, as one of her more perceptive correspondents suggested, relied on a sort of "sampling error," because her interest in the rural areas around Halifax was greater and her contacts there much more accepting and accessible than in other parts of the province.[193] In this bias, Creighton was at one with an entire generation of Halifax middle-class cultural producers for whom one implicit requirement of the essential Nova Scotia – at Peggy's Cove, along the "Coast of Songs" – was that it be located within easy driving distance of their city. She also shared a pervasive sense of a dwindling, static, unrenewable resource that middle-class people must take steps to salvage. This was the logic, for example, of excluding Pete Seeger from the Miramichi Folk Festival for fear local singers would lose their musical virginity when they started to copy his style.[194] They could not be trusted with the treasure they unwittingly carried.

Perhaps the implications of an organic conception of society were nowhere more clearly brought out than in the work on Lunenburg County, which marked Creighton's initiation into the broader world of folklore. Amidst the miscellaneous detail of the monograph, Creighton ventures a social interpretation of the rural fishing communities she visited: "Lunenburg seamen are among the most expert in the world, which is remarkable as they were an inland people before migrating. As fishermen all share in the total catch they have a common interest in making it a good one, and labour troubles are practically unknown."[195] Written on the basis of just four weeks' field work carried out in 1944, this judgment was remarkable for its self-assurance, conservatism, and inaccuracy. For although the Lunenburg schooner fishery was widely hailed in right-wing thought as a model of a fairer, better capitalism, the selectiveness of this vision was extreme. The deaths of eighty-eight fishermen in the Lunenburg-based fleet in the August gale in 1927 were a dramatic reminder of the precariousness of the occupation. No matter how many works were written about their quaint ways and their friendly manner, the aftermath of the disaster was a bleak reminder of the low monetary value the state attached to the lives of these romanticized workers. Instead of responding to the crisis of safety in the offshore fishery (of which the deaths from the 1927 and 1928 gales were merely the most dramatic example), the state removed the fishermen from public workers' compensation. It did not insist that schooners carry survival suits or radios, both available items that could have saved many lives.[196] The supposed traditionalism of the fisherfolk (under the misleading ideology of the "co-adventurer") would be later invoked in denying them collective bargaining rights and in applying modernization schemes of destroying ("relocating") fishing communities without respecting the views of the people who lived in them.[197] In 1944 Creighton could easily have elicited memories of the disasters of the 1920s and their aftermath, and heard the echoes of the last great strike in 1937, in which Angus Walters of the *Bluenose* had played a role. Clearly, essentialist stereotypes of the hardy, independent fisherfolk, no matter how ostensibly flattering in their professed admiration for people living honest, natural lives, could be used to naturalize their poverty and suffering in one of the country's most difficult and complex industries. When a left-wing trade union tried to circumvent the propaganda of the National Sea Company in a bitter strike after the war, they took explicit aim at the myth of the fishermen as a "breed apart," hardy individuals who had no need of a union. ("Fishermen are not a peculiar breed," one prominent union leader proclaimed. "They are just people and workers with the same needs and desires that other workers have.")[198] The radical working-class movement seemed to have an acute awareness of the subtle danger posed by the web of myth and romance that had been woven around the fisherman's occupation.

As an analysis *researched* in 1944, Creighton's commentary on Lunenburg was selective; as an analysis *published* in 1950, after so many of the quaint "fisherfolk" had rallied to the cause of a radical union, only to have their struggle broken by the combined force of a luridly sensationalist media campaign, the intimidation of monopoly fish capital, the Nova Scotia government, and the courts, Creighton's notion of perpetual labour peace was misleading. A close parallel would be a Chicago-school sociologist venturing to Asbestos in 1945, and publishing in 1955 an account of the timeless Catholicism, organic social unity, and romantic Folk customs prevailing in that small, conservative Quebec town – drawing on Robert Redfield's work on the "little community" and the Folk, perhaps – oblivious to the labour wars that had erupted in the interim. The revealing difference between the two cases, however, was that Creighton, unlike the hypothetical academic from Chicago, claimed "insider" status, an intuitive knowledge of the Folk, whose essence she thought she had grasped.

For Creighton, Lunenburg County is a land of tales, and although there is the odd story of a drowning at sea, the world of work and wages rarely intrudes upon an idyllic portrait of a rural district. Only potently racist tales about native peoples remind us of the divisions within Nova Scotian society – and these are not framed by Creighton as tales about race or conflict. It is instructive to compare her description of the "old days" of the Lunenburg schooner fishery with the oral history compiled by Peter Barss. Barss is also somewhat romantic in his portraits of the men of Lunenburg; they emerge as plain-speaking folk, an interpretation intensified by his attempts to depict the dialect. Yet the most powerful images of his book, and the stories his respondents remember most vividly about the "good old days," are about grinding poverty, death, and exploitation. Trawlers lost a couple of men every summer, the working conditions on vessels were "inhuman" (according to one of the workers), the wages and hours far worse than North Americans had come to expect. As one fisherman recalls:

Dory fishin' was disgustin' – a disgustin' job. A fearful disgustin' job. To go down there in that hold with the frost hangin' down – icicles hangin' down o'erhead from the deck planks. Go down there to bait up five tubs of gear to a dory. And you stayed down there till you had it baited up – till the cook blowed the whistle for breakfast about half past two or three o'clock in the mornin'. Gettin' to the table was a race, like a race, you know, all a race – one feller tryin' to get ahead of the other ... The most time that I had to spend out was ... at one time ... was seventy-two hours wit'out a wink ... we was on our feet goin' right straight, goin' right straight – seventy-two hours. Lots o' fish, see. Never saw the bunk, you.[199]

Suddenly the image of the quaint, contented Folk seems less plausible. We recall a point well made by Raymond Williams: the myth of a "natural" or "moral" Folk economy, antedating capitalism, idealized a social order that was "as hard and as brutal as anything later experienced."[200] Nova Scotians fled the Lunenburg Banks fishery in droves in the 1920s and 1930s because, *pace* Creighton and dozens of other authorities on the Folk, they were not uncomplainingly resigned to the cruel sea, but were able to make a choice and vote with their feet against some of the worst working conditions known to North America.

The perspective that produced Creighton's particular reading of Lunenburg County was a complex form of paternalism. Creighton's blindness to certain facts stemmed from her class perspective as a whole. She believed, with Mackenzie, that there were havens of unspoiled folk in Nova Scotia, but they were fast disappearing – a useful argument in attempts to pry funds from reluctant benefactors, no doubt, but also a view that conveyed a sincere and apocalyptic perception of cultural decline. "The time is pressing, because life is changing and the radio is introducing new music into homes which only knew the old," Creighton wrote to a like-minded Marius Barbeau in 1947. "If we wish to retain our treasures, we must do so at once, or the opportunity will be gone."[201] Six months later, this alarmist impression of a drastic erosion in the standing of the ballad had been strengthened by Creighton's field work in southwestern Nova Scotia. Here, she told Barbeau, there were "pitifully few songs" (meaning, of course, "traditional" songs). "Between the old people having passed away, and the radio bringing a new form of entertainment, there is nothing left to get," she concluded gloomily. "Occasionally a singer would be found who might know a verse or two of a ballad, but a real old timer who can sing from dawn to dark and never repeat could not be found."[202]

Such a perception of change as decay and disintegration influenced Creighton's response to development in general. On those rare occasions on which she put her hopes and fears for the Folk into words, she expressed grave misgivings about the ways in which modernity, even better living standards, would undermine the innocence of "her" Folk. Her worries about economic development focused not upon the class injustices and inequalities it imposed in Nova Scotia, but on its threat to the Folk, whose quaint innocence might be lost. For once they were regularly employed in industrial occupations, the Folk would lose their defining characteristics. They would acquire ideas about social mobility. "There is a possibility of an extensive air force development not far from my district which may bring a new prosperity to my singers," Creighton wrote in 1937. "If that goes through their somewhat primitive outlook may give way to a social ambition which will rob them of all their charm."[203]

But how could an urban middle-class folklorist protect the innocence of the Folk? People who wanted to make their living out of folksong were caught in the classic dilemma of Innocence as a mythomoteur paradoxically fuelled by both liberalism and antimodernism. They were, in practice, the emissaries of the very modernism they were trying to escape in theory. Their tape recorders, their organized Folk events, and their records all shifted into the cash nexus forms that once were created spontaneously and without economic calculation. That which had had value only in use now came to have value in exchange. Antimodernists found themselves repeatedly in the position of promoting what they were ostensibly sworn to oppose.

One can observe Creighton wrestling with this ideological antinomy when she negotiated with "Folk performers" who were to sing on the CBC in 1938. "Take a deep breath now, because I have another nice shock for you," Creighton wrote to one. "The fee for each song you sing will be ten dollars. That is the same amount that trained singers get, and should be sufficient to pay any expenses met in going and coming, and still leave you a nice little sum in your pocket." Then she inserted a cautionary note:

Just one word of warning, if you don't mind. Don't take any advice from anybody on how to sing them, and don't change them one little bit from the way you sang them to Miss Senior and me. We want the story told as easily and naturally as you sang it to us in your own home. All you need to do is to know them thoroughly. I would suggest that you sing them over to yourself while you work and while you are alone with your family. Why not sing while you peel potatoes or scrub the floor? That will preserve the natural quality which is their greatest charm.

Yet, Creighton added, the performance should not be *too* spontaneous – it would not do, for example, for the performer to forget words (which often happened in impromptu social gatherings and which was part of the traditional dynamic between singer and audience). No, the songs must be rehearsed. "If you want the words of any of your songs let me know and I'll send them to you. In case you haven't got the Bold Pedlar I'll enclose a copy. Will you time the singing of it, and tell me exactly to the half minute how long it takes to do it?"[204] Staged authenticity, a rehearsed spontaneity, an oral tradition that one memorized from a folklorist's written text: all were practical contradictions traceable to the antinomies of Innocence as a modernizing antimodernism.

As far as possible, the Folk should be shielded from outside influences, and their music allowed to continue in its unadulterated purity. Creighton identified strongly with the purist ethic of Louise Manny's Northeast (Miramichi) Folk Festival, which started in 1958. Late in her career she took the time to explain this ethic to an official of Walt Disney World. "There were strict rules at the early Festivals that none but folk songs should be sung, and singers from other places were not invited to perform," she remembered. "In fact your own singer Pete Seeger told Dr Manny once that he would like to come to her festival. Her reply was, 'We'd love to have you Pete, but you can't sing.' He must have been taken aback, but she was right. Her local singers would copy his way of singing and the authenticity of Miramichi singing would be lost."[205]

This perception of Folk culture as a sort of delicate Elizabethan filigree, so fragile that it needed to be vacuum-sealed and guarded in a dark cabinet, left Creighton and other folklore experts in an odd position. Although middle-class and urban in their own backgrounds, and often lacking extensive knowledge of the communities they visited, they nonetheless functioned as arbitrators of authenticity, and wielded more authority on such matters than the working-class people who sang the songs and espoused the folk beliefs. Creighton in 1983 recalled the twenty-fifth anniversary of the Northeast Folklore Society, and remembered how rigorously she and Louise Manny had scrutinized the songs of the Folk for signs of potential contamination.

What an experiment that first festival was with the contestants largely lumbermen and fishermen who had never sung on a public stage before. We arrived early, and while we enjoyed the comfort of Louise Manny's sitting room she would answer her 'phone, turn to me and say, "So and So wants to sing Such and Such a song. Is it a folk song?" If we said no her reply would be, "No, you can't sing that. The judges (you [Sandy Ives] and I) say it's not a folk song." Perhaps without realizing it we were setting a standard for Miramichi festivals which resulted in singers recalling half-forgotten traditional songs and collecting others from friends; otherwise they would have been lost for all time."[206]

This was a cultural politics based on class and professionalism, a view of an embattled Folk who needed to be protected from themselves, tempted as they were by air bases, radios, and television, not to mention Pete Seeger. Creighton could exercise this power of cultural selection as an accredited professional, even though her knowledge of those she called the "very rough people" of the area was slight and she had little inclination to learn much more about them.[207]

Such class perspectives affected Creighton's handling of her informants as individuals. She was genuinely fond of the Folk, and she regarded certain of them with warm affection. (As she remarked of her informants in *Bluenose Magic*, "They are kind good people, serious one moment and at the next revealing a sense of fun and a quick humour.")[208] She also never forgot their intrinsic and irremediable inferiority. She believed in a beautiful relationship between rich and poor, an elegant symbiosis untinged by resentment or the desire for gain. Such a connection worked if both sides accepted the permanence of their social positions and their respective roles. "I always treated my informants with respect," she explained to a writer who had suggested that informants were interested in money. "We didn't call people by their first names in those days as we so often do to-day and it [made] them aware that they possessed something of importance. Visits were Occasions in his [the informant's] quiet life, and an evening session always ended by a family treat of a fruit drink and a little cake or cookies to which [I] would contribute ice cream or something to make it festive."[209]

Her gift-giving strategy was classic paternalism. Often Creighton would present her informant with a photograph, a gift that was "more personal" than money, and that invoked a gift-giving relationship of mutual reciprocity and personal understanding. Not everyone was delighted with the photographs: "Too bad your wasting good money having them developed. Please burn the negative," wrote Angelo Dornan, a critical and important informant.[210] A beautiful relationship between rich and poor was not one sealed with money, which would have been too explicit an objectification of that which had passed between them.

Between the middle-class visitor sweeping in to a coastal village with her car and her tape recorder and the people of the inshore fishing communities there was a considerable economic and cultural gap. As Jane C. Beck reminds us, this difference was expressed in the way Creighton dressed. "She was always very much the lady, believing 'that a collector should never dress down while working; the informants are flattered when you arrive clean and neatly dressed and are therefore more prone to make friends.'"[211] They were friends of a sort. In Creighton's folklore practice, her informants were not fellow citizens, but "the Folk," exotic Others, primitive but charmingly so. Thus, in her private correspondence Creighton felt free to describe the physical attributes of Ben Henneberry, whose songs provided her with her most precious treasures, in words one doubts she would have used in relation to her bridge companions at her elegant parties of the 1930s. "Comic songs, love songs, ballads long forgotten, many of them very rare – indeed whenever any other man sings for me I marvel yet again at the memory of my dear Mr Ben," she wrote to Howard Angus in describing her discovery of Devil's Island. "And such a [picturesque] figure he is, being so horribly ugly, poor thing. But with it all so very kind and obliging."[212] In *Maclean's*, Creighton emphasized the ironic contrast between Henneberry, the humble fisherman-singer, and the exalted cultural material in his repertoire: "It seems very strange that from the lips of this fisherman, words come forth which may have inspired men like Shakespeare."[213] It seems strange only within a preconceived hierarchy of culture, which places "Shakespeare" and a Nova Scotia fisherman at opposite poles. "I am enclosing a copy of a short article written for the *Dalhousie Review*," Creighton advised A.J. Campbell of the Bureau of Information. "Also a few pictures of Mr. Henneberry. Where he appears in collar and tie he is at my home where he had come to sing into the dictaphone. He is more picturesque in his oilskins."[214]

The pastoral perspective allowed the Folk to be picturesque and quaint exotics, not fellow participants shaping a common culture and political order. One is reminded of Raymond Williams's complaint about George Eliot's complacent success with formulaic descriptions of "the 'fine old,' 'dear old,' quaint-talking, honest-living country characters."[215] The criticism could be applied almost word for word to the Folk as imagined by Creighton. "These kindly folk were well worth studying, although on the other hand they were no study at all," she wrote after her first visit to Devil's Island.[216] Creighton described her "discovery" of Dennis Smith at East Chezzetcook in similar terms: "What a pleasant sight met my eyes, a dear old man sitting in a rocking chair with his gentle wife in a straight-backed chair beside him."[217] These are one-dimensional Folk, not complicated people with politics, histories, sexualities, hopes, despairs, and futures. Creighton's perception of many of her fellow Nova Scotians involved more than a little condescension.

As was typical with modernizing antimodernism, fondness for the Folk was combined with a hard language of objectification and calculation. Creighton very often spoke of the Folk not as people but as a kind of natural resource. The way she discussed the Folk in her correspondence crystallized the doubleness of Innocence, which simultaneously sought to conserve the supposed warmth and spontaneity of pre-modern cultures and to bring them to market as commodities. Part of her appeal to various potential promoters of folklore was that they had to act quickly lest the Folk product expire. The mines of authenticity might close down, the treasure, encased in its living shell of skin, might be dissipated. "One point ... must be kept in mind," she wrote to A.J. Campbell of the Bureau of Information, hoping to persuade him to back a film on the Folk. "The scenic effects can wait of [if] necessary until spring, but Mr Ben [Henneberry] must be captured immediately. His work is hazardous and he is growing old. Further research has shown me no singer to equal him in the province. He is unique. The island would lose most of its appeal without him, especially with Mr Faulkner already gone. Could it be done at once? This fall?"[218] Her warning to Charles L. Glett of Audio Productions of New York was no less direct: "Folk-singers today are old people and they are dying off quickly. If this picture is to be considered it must be done this spring or summer, or not at all."[219] Even more objectifying language was used in *Maclean's* in 1937: "The point is that Nova Scotia's wealth is not all wrapped up in material things. Her wealth of song is something that will grow in value as the years go by and none of the old singers are left."[220] As the folklorist Neil Rosenberg observes, to treat folklore as a natural resource, "something which is nonrenewable, is to view it as a static form, a survival," the "fossilized remains from earlier patterns of culture."[221]

Creighton was separated from those from whom she collected the songs by a wide gulf of class. Her possessions, her way of speaking, her ability to pursue the collection of folksongs without a secure guarantee of financial return set her far apart from the people who sang the songs. So far as one can tell, Creighton did not experience a shock of disorientation when she encountered people living in material circumstances she herself would never have had to endure. Instead, she merely applied to them the universal and timeless standards of propriety prevalent in Halifax society.

Yet she could hardly help but notice that parts of the rural Nova Scotia in which she collected her songs were wretchedly poor, stricken with disease and suffering. "We finished at Sherbrooke with three more Child ballads, ending a trip that was a mixture of ups and downs," she remembers in her memoirs. "We enjoyed the kind people who were pleased, as they said, to be of service, and the happy atmosphere of the MacNeill home, but the poverty and hopelessness of many farms where the soil seemed unyielding and the future unpromising was depressing."[222] She treated these harsh realities with a refined Victorian delicacy. Poverty was an embarrassment for both participants in the folklore encounter. There was compassion and caring, as well as condescension, in Creighton's view of the wretched social conditions she so frequently observed. She did not want anyone else to write from her folk collector's diary for fear they would be too candid in their description of rural wretchedness. "Here there are many intimate glimpses into the lives of the people who have sung for me and related their stories and beliefs," she said of her diary in a letter to the Centennial Commission appealing for their support for her autobiography. "I would not want anybody else to write of my work from that diary because it is not always complimentary where conditions have been distasteful. I do not intend to hurt any singer's feelings by dwelling on the hardships in any personal way. Yet they are many, but I feel I can point them out with discretion."[223] And she did. Her delicacy probably made sense for someone seeking a peaceful life in a small province, and suggested an honourable wish that her informants' feelings should not be heedlessly hurt.[224] This delicacy extended even to changing the words in songs. Creighton asked that "Hatfield Boys" be changed to the "Hanstead Boys," since she had lately met "some of the Hatfield family who are charming people. The song is not complimentary, and I should hate to hurt their feelings. The name Hanstead has the same number of letters, and would serve equally well."[225] Such delicacy did not make for a frank analysis of Maritime social problems.

Of course, class was not wholly evicted from the Creighton canon. One can find within Creighton's 1932 collection songs that speak of social conditions and conflicts in nineteenth-century Nova Scotia. "Guysboro Song," for instance, contains a pungent analysis of conformity in a rural setting: "In the county of Guysborough my first breath I drew / 'Twas in the poorest county that ever I knew / The people were poor, and I think they were proud / It is no harm to think if you don't think too loud." "Captain Conrod" is a critique of conditions at sea and of a Methodist captain who was "One of the stingiest old beggars that ever was seen / Salt cod and religion he gave us to eat / And then once a week one small chunk of meat."[226] But this is a "class analysis" that can be made only against the book's own ideology of the Golden Age and the miracle of the Child ballad.

Creighton saw the poverty of her Folk more as a personal impediment to her collection than an indictment of capitalism. The way of the ballad collector is hard, she observed in an article on Roy Mackenzie:

Many people think we spend our summers travelling over lovely byroads and sit by the hour listening to quaint old characters spinning yarns and singing songs. They also suppose our winters are spent in contemplation of the fun we had last summer in preparation for another jolly round of visits the following year. When you tell them that the harder you work in the summer the harder you must work all winter to transcribe your notes they look bewildered. We don't talk about the hardships, the over-night accommodation which in the old days could even be repulsive, the dirty kitchens in which you must often work, and the unpalatable food you are often obliged to eat, the danger of running into somebody with a mental aberration away off on a remote farm, the stuffy rooms which haven't been opened to the pure air for fifty years.[227]

Food posed some particularly difficult class dilemmas. Creighton worried about eating in houses that had not been properly aired, and mentally marked down as "fine day" houses those "forbidding" dwellings whose conditions promised to be too repulsive for a lady's luncheon. She learned to take her own sandwiches along and eat outside; one clearly did not want to break bread with the poorest of the Folk.[228] Mackenzie, in contrast, had learned to cast "false delicacy aside"; he consumed "boiled potatoes, mammoth slices of bread, and tea that had been boiled until a spoon would stand upright in it.")[229] Creighton seems never to have reflected critically on the economic and social conditions underlying the meagre diets and filthy kitchens she encountered. Her language was precisely Victorian in its emphasis on sanitary reform – impure air, personal cleanliness, distasteful food. If there was a considerable refinement and delicacy in Creighton's sense that she should not embarrass the folk by dwelling on their poverty, there was as well a certain lack of interest in understanding its political and social logic.

Thus, in spite of her impeccable local credentials, one would be hard pressed to distinguish many aspects of her portrait of the Nova Scotia fisherfolk from the most essentialist and stereotypical product of tourism promotion. "Quaint tales of a quaint district," is her summary of the folklore of St. Margaret's Bay. "Can you see in your mind's eye a picture of the little white houses dotted among the trees that line St. Margaret's Bay? Can you see the water never more blue than here, and the little waves that dance for very joy in the sunshine?" In the village of Hubbards, one found "homely fisherfolk" living "in quiet content, a whimsical sense of humor making them delightful conversationalists." The automobile and science counted for little here, and Folk superstitions were firmly held (although the fisherfolk might vainly try to deny it): "If one is able to penetrate their reserve a pretty tale of the supernatural results, and the nervous look of the eye and the credulous tone of the voice belie the statement that witches are believed in no longer."[230]

Gender joined class as an aspect of the gap between the "Lady of the Legends" and her Folk. Creighton's own self-definition was that of a "lady," a synthesis of gender and class ideals. She never forgot the gulf of gender and class that separated her from her informants. Creighton emphasized the culture of the men of the Folk. Only at Pubnico, she wrote, had she found women predominating among the singers.[231] Hers was a particular and historically specific reading of a world of masculinity and male occupations she had not explored at first hand.

Drink was the classic issue in which her ideals of class and gender converged. Roy Mackenzie and other male folklorists, she observed, liked to debate how best to approach an informant: whether to shake hands, whether to go straight to the point, or whether to beat around the bush. A woman lacked this flexibility, "for the sooner she explains what she is doing all alone in a distant fishing village, the better."[232] (The practical question of her physical safety, as well as her respectability, was of course a realistic thing for her to worry about, although she was likely at no more risk in fishing communities than in Dartmouth). A lady would never use drink as a way of loosening inhibitions and creating the convivial atmosphere in which certain songs were normally sung, a policy of temperance that went against the expectations of many thirsty members of the Folk. Providing drink for informants was countermanded on practical, aesthetic, and moral grounds. To provide drink for singers would constitute an expensive system of bribery, and a collector would face unending costs. Ironically, however, the end result of such expensive bribery would be muddled and incoherent songs. Finally, although a male collector might use liquor judiciously, a young woman would run the risk of creating the wrong impression. She would lose the respect of the fishermen.[233] A young woman, placed on a pedestal by the traditional fishermen, would lose her position if she began to dabble in drink.[234] Many men in rural Nova Scotia, and particularly on the South Shore, had developed a subculture of drinking; the bootlegger (an unofficial seller, rather than a manufacturer, of drink) is still a figure in many working-class and rural communities.[235] Elsewhere in the countryside there was a strong tradition of temperance. The centrality of drink in either case is an aspect of working-class masculinity that was firmly erased from Creighton's portrait of the Folk.

She was never more Victorian than when discussing this issue. Drink and folksong were notoriously connected. Mackenzie, for one, believed the relationship was intimate and enduring, and consequently did not hesitate to use scotch as a lubricant in his dealings with informants.[236] Creighton, however, viewed drink with alarm and distaste. On Devil's Island, she was frequently advised, "You ought to come at Christmas; that's when you'd get the songs. We dance in the lighthouse from Christmas to New Year." She emphatically declined the invitation. "I sensed there would be drinking which would mean muddled thinking and songs begun but never finished."[237] When she went to South East Passage,

The men kept hinting that I should have brought something along to loosen their throats, but I had concluded early that if a young woman couldn't get a man to sing without bribing him with drink she wasn't worth her salt. Those who drink will take all the free liquor you supply, and then their singing gets muddled ... A male collector might use liquor effectively, but he should have a limited amount; a woman, particularly a young one, would forfeit respect ... With our high spirits, a genuine liking for the people, and our objective always in mind, any further stimulant would have been redundant and material came in a constant stream.[238]

When she did confront some drinking singers, she found the songs were "not what we wanted."[239] "There is a big difference," Creighton reflected in 1987, "in the performance of a man who has been drinking, and one who is sober and proud of what he is doing."[240] The Folk, in their unlettered innocence, mingled drink, play, and song, but this was merely further evidence they harboured cultural treasures they scarcely understood. Although there were pragmatic considerations involved in the decision to collect only in "dry" settings, the strategy also functioned as a subtle editing mechanism, silencing those songs that might have emerged only once drink unleashed inhibitions. The temperate and careful strategy followed by Creighton, which often entailed collecting from the singer in the presence of the spouse, may also have militated against her recording such distinctively masculine forms as the "tall tale."[241]

Gender ideals also had a direct impact on the place of sexuality in Creighton's imagined Folk Nova Scotia. That place was barely discernible. In contrast to most Folk traditions described throughout the world, those of Nova Scotia were remarkably asexual. In this case, what we encounter in Creighton's work is not folksong and folktale as these were ordinarily put forward by actual men, but a sense of what folklore would be like if it were created by ideal men, men with control over their manners "I never told them I wasn't interested in bawdy songs," Creighton recalled of her sessions with the fisherfolk.

On the rare occasion when one was sung I would record it and then, when the singer wasn't looking I would quietly erase it from the tape. That happened one day when a group of men were singing in a fishing shack and a man from another village was brought in. As his song progressed the atmosphere became tense and as he went jauntily out I felt that the other men were embarrassed, until I remarked that I had erased that song from the tape. You wouldn't believe how relieved they looked. Fishermen may not be highly educated, but they are sensitive to what is fitting for an occasion.[242]

In her memoirs, a similar (or possibly the same) incident is placed in Little Harbour, on the Eastern Shore. This time the offending fisherman is portrayed as a Lunenburger who "came in and contributed a number that not only had no merit as a song, but was definitely vulgar."[243] It should be stressed that in deleting songs that offended her Victorian sense of propriety – for which she was well known among others interested in Folk culture – Creighton was acting in accordance with the practices of the largely middle-class world of Anglo-American folklore. Child may well have excluded certain ballads from his famous canon on the basis of sexual references; collectors such as Cecil Sharp "did not, and could not, publish the songs they collected without expurgating even mild sexual references."[244] Still, by the postwar period, when Creighton was most active in collecting beliefs and superstitions, puritanism had relaxed to the extent that a prominent authority was appealing to Canadian folklorists – and indirectly to a presumably unenthusiastic Creighton – for "bawdy" songs (such as the missing verses of such national treasures as "The Red Light Saloon" and "The Winnipeg Whore").[245] Most local "bawdy songs" were probably nipped in the bud by Creighton's demeanour and by her preference for conducting sessions in the presence of spouses and outside the workcamps where many folksong traditions had most strongly developed.[246] Edward Ives suggests in *Joe Scott: The Woodsman-Songmaker* that bawdy songs were present in the woods and that some woodsmen even specialized entirely in sexually explicit "blackguard songs," although he leaves open the question of how important such songs were within the traditions of Maine and New Brunswick. Conversely, perhaps the Child ballads were generally seen as belonging to the polite sphere of women's culture, often somewhat scorned by men ("Never cared much for that kind of song" ... "My poor old mother used to sing that."), whereas freshly written ballads, whether bawdy or not, and very often dealing with the "man/woman business" from a masculine point of view, were those that were most popular in the lumber camps where so many songs originated.[247] The Creighton collection suggests that men in the region did sometimes sing Child ballads, but they may not have sung them nearly to the extent that one would assume from the way the collection was edited for publication. *Ballads and Songs from Nova Scotia* does present some local material that might raise a few Victorian eyebrows – "Barrack Street," for example, is a song that cautions young men against the thievery of the Halifax prostitutes[248] – but it leaves us with a sense of a decorous Folk. As for superstitions and Folk beliefs, Creighton's Folk men must be unique in the entire world in lacking, in an otherwise remarkable repertoire of cures for witchcraft and liver ailments, any remedies with sexual connotations.[249]

On questions of race and ethnicity, a more complex assessment is demanded by Creighton's work. Her unreflecting use of the category "racial stock," with its implication that cultural traits are biological, must be considered problematical by contemporary standards, and congruent with the emphasis she always places on origins and essences. "Folk" and "race" have had a long, intricate relationship with each other as master-concepts of organic conservative ideology. In the absence of further explanation, Creighton's attachment of brief ethnic markers to aspects of folk belief implies that race (which would today be called ethnicity) alone is the governing influence over a given cultural behaviour. "As you know," Creighton explained to Roy in outlining some of the difficulties of categorizing superstitions and folk beliefs, "people in this province have all sorts of mixed racial backgrounds. The informant's name would mean nothing outside the province, so I have put after each item the name of the place where it was found and the racial origin. These could be abbreviated in publication to read E. for English; I for Irish; AC for Acadian French and so forth. I hope you will agree that this is a good idea.[250] (Creighton, following the practice of the census, relied upon the ethnicity of the father or the "head of the household" for her ethnic designations). Creighton's straightforward use of such markers begged many questions. One of its more curious results was the virtual disappearance of the Irish, whose specific cultural traditions were blended into the Anglo stew, even though many "English Canadian" songs are Irish in provenance.

As for people of colour, and notwithstanding her enduringly valuable role in preserving elements of minority traditions, Creighton's "essentialism" may be fairly described as placing both blacks and natives on the periphery. Stories of "Indian" barbarism and a story highlighting the ludicrous gullibility of blacks were told in *Bluenose*

Ghosts, which, in the absence of critical commentary or counterbalancing stories of similarly bloodthirsty or credulous whites from minority perspectives, gave a distinctly exoteric tone to the discussion of the province's visible racial minorities. Her handling of native issues in *Bluenose Magic* seems equally problematic. Native religious beliefs concerning creation are incongruously placed in the book, implicitly equated with tall tales and folk remedies. In contrast to her straightforwardly essentialist designation of other traditions as "Acadian" or "English," Creighton focused in this study on the scarcity of "pure-blood Micmac Indians," and remarked, "Consequently many old customs and beliefs have been forgotten and others have suffered from acculturation. Mixed up though they are, there is enough left to provide a worth-while study." Finally, as her historical authority on native culture she cited Thomas Raddall, whose novels tend to portray natives as bloodthirsty, tomahawk-wielding savages.[252]

Yet any evaluation of Creighton's handling of sensitive questions of race must place her work in its context. Throughout Canada, middle-class social thought on such questions emphasized "racial stock." Racism was endemic in the Nova Scotia of the 1930s and 1940s. Theatres were segregated, and some whites on occasion had responded with violence when blacks stepped over the unwritten but powerful boundaries restricting them from living in certain neighbourhoods.[253] In collecting songs from blacks, in studying black folklore during her time in Indiana, and in allowing that black Nova Scotians had a cultural identity worthy of preservation, Creighton was also helping to break some new and important ground in Nova Scotia.

I have found [Creighton informed the Rockefeller Foundation] that our negroes, always spoken of here as colored people, sing spirituals, adding verses of their own. This opens up an entirely new field. I have a date on with an old coachman for Monday morning. He is going to sing while he works in the garden of a friend of ours. These people are all near Dartmouth which is fortunate. I am eager to find out how good their material is. It seems incredible that I have lived here all these years and have never known that our local negroes were singers.[254]

Creighton did collect folksongs from blacks, but she felt uneasy in black communities. "The reason my work especially in the Preston area was limited was because it was definitely unsafe for me to collect there alone, or indeed even with a companion," she would later reflect. "Also this community lived too close to my home and if they were insisting on money which I didn't have, it could have been difficult."[255] Perhaps this is the context for her deceptively pluralist argument that black folklore should be collected by blacks themselves.[256]

Creighton found payment to be a "problem" with groups, like blacks and natives, who were firmly outside the boundaries of Innocence. In truth, both groups rather scared her. She was badly frightened by "menacing looks" at a Micmac funeral she was attempting to record. Ian Sclanders's famous article on Creighton in *Maclean's* described the folklorist as glancing up and seeing that "angry Indians were closing in on her from all sides. As she grabbed her recorder and fled there were mumbled threats, but she wasn't stopped."[257] (One wonders if Sclanders had been watching too many westerns.) As for collecting in the black community, Creighton flatly believed it to be dangerous for her. "I've done enough work among them to know that this is no place for a woman alone," she remarked to Carmen Roy in 1963.[258] She was similarly frightened away from a black community when she encountered evidence that a drinking party was in the works:

My last visit was on a beautiful summer day and I had two friends with me. To my delight Mr Riley was sitting in his doorway. This meant I could leave the converter and batteries in the car ... All went beautifully until a horse-drawn vehicle appeared and one of his sons got out. He said he didn't want his father to sing because it was bad for him, and that he could sing too but he wanted five dollars a song. This was so different from anything I had previously encountered that I was bewildered until it became evident that a party was about to begin and we were in the way. I was sorry to leave the old man because he enjoyed performing and in his later days there would not be many would appreciate his singing. Before I could work up enough enthusiasm to go back, Mr Riley died and I regret that so many of the words I had taken down before I had recording equipment are without music at all.[259]

"I packed up in a hurry, and was too discouraged to go back," she remembers in her memoirs.[260] Equally clear indications of pending parties had not kept her permanently away from the white fisherfolk.

Creighton's definition of the Folk thus did not easily extend to those who were of a different race. To the extent that certain songs and sayings from Creighton were written into the Folk canon, it is fair to say that these were ethnically narrowly defined. Nonetheless, her efforts to cross lines of ethnicity and race were unusual at the time. She maintained a constructive attitude towards efforts by blacks to do folklore research on their own traditions. Crossing lines of class and race was not something a gentlewoman from Greater Halifax did every day. Her efforts to do so, and the limits imposed by her social universe, are nicely encapsulated in a line from a letter she wrote to the eminent American folklorist Alan Lomax: "On the whole they are very nice people to work with. I've always liked our colored people here. We have often employed them in the house."[261]

These assumptions about class, gender, and ethnicity and race were buried in Creighton's working methods and her handling of other material. Creighton's fascination with the supernatural, by contrast, was an explicit theme that dominated much of her work of the 1950s and 1960s. (The three major titles are *Folklore of Lunenburg County*, *Bluenose Ghosts*, and *Bluenose Magic*). This supernatural research also carried a conservative ideological charge. In a sense, the spirit world she constructed in her books was an ultimate vision of transcendental Innocence and Otherness. Her work, her frequent public appearances, and the widespread use of her books in the school system gave pre-modern irrationalism a salience in the province it probably would otherwise have lacked. No doubt many Nova Scotians were and are superstitious, in company with many Canadians. Ghost stories and tales of witches are popular additions to a summer campfire. Some people, perhaps especially in the areas settled by German-speaking "foreign Protestants" in the eighteenth century, may have made witchcraft a more important part of their social identity than was the case elsewhere in Canada. How important it was, and for how many people, remains completely unknown.

As David Whisnant observes, ballad-collecting can be a circular process. Predisposed towards the older cultural forms, romantic folklorists understandably emphasize those particular aspects of the total cultural system. By doing so, they attract the attention of others similarly disposed.[262]

Superstition- and belief-hunting can be no less circular. Belief in the supernatural – in witches, ghosts, magic, forerunners – was probably not much more common in Nova Scotia than anywhere else sixty years ago, and one could grow up in the province without sustained exposure to the imagined supernatural. Creighton herself, who had not heard tales of the supernatural in her childhood, provided convincing evidence of this.[263] Yet she persistently claimed that superstition was a fundamental element of Maritime culture. Creighton introduces *Bluenose Ghosts* with the remark, "The diversity and extent of our people's belief will, I think, surprise you."[264] But, given that Creighton had become more and more immersed in the world of parapsychology and had been pursuing such tales for over two decades, her collecting focus may well have stimulated a rather skewed idea of the popularity of the occult in the province. The occult doubtless has devotées from St. John's to San Francisco. Whether a disproportionate number of them lived in Nova Scotia and claimed the occult as part of their ancestral essence has never been seriously investigated. Certainly belief in the occult cannot be taken as a proxy for "Folk" beliefs in a society in which so much information was conveyed by newspapers and magazines from across North America. One informant, who, like Creighton, had had no direct personal experience with witchcraft, did report a childhood memory of seeing a book on this subject in his house. It came from California.[265]

Since the massive popularization of Creighton's works on the occult, however, the supernatural has been represented as a key ingredient of the provincial identity. It has been promoted by the provincial tourism industry and by films put out by the provincial government. Creighton's writings on the occult have even been used in the province's school system. What earlier Nova Scotian intellectuals would certainly have regarded as insulting stereotypes questioning the rationality and progressiveness of their society have become part of the essence of a province as reimagined by twentieth-century Innocence. Tourism and travel writing now aggressively promote the image of superstitious Nova Scotians spinning ghostly tales by the sea. There is something odd about the prospect of schoolchildren, who will probably never learn anything much about the Presbyterian thought of Thomas McCulloch or of the Social Catholicism of the Antigonish Movement, emerging from the educational system with a firm grasp of 101 ways to ward off a witch in Lunenburg County, all as part of "their tradition."

The school system has been important in spreading what is literally a form of "magical thinking" about identity. Creighton provides us with an insight into how her own appearance in a classroom could validate the superstition of the "forerunner."

Last week I spoke to a school class of extra bright children, aged 12, and thoroughly enjoyed it. One girl startled me by stating that her father had looked up from his bed five days before his death and had seen the devil and was terrified. My immediate thought was, "What dreadful thing had he done?" That I will never know, and probably he hadn't done anything. But after I came home I recalled a singer telling me that if you see the devil in life you will never see him in death, so I asked the teacher if she would pass this information on as an old folk belief. The teacher was glad to do so because she said this is a nervous pupil who bites her nails a lot. A thing like that could be upsetting to a family, so I was thankful to have recalled that belief. [266]

Creighton was being considerate and kind. She was also placing her considerable cultural authority behind an impressionable child's belief in the occult.

The impact of Creighton's fascination with the occult went far beyond the school system. A large appreciative public loved her work on the supernatural. *Bluenose Ghosts* was a bestseller, and on economic grounds alone Creighton had every reason to promote her popular titles in the field. As she put it bluntly to Carmen Roy,

Song books published with the melody don't make much money. *Bluenose Ghosts* on the other hand is still doing well and sold 600 copies in the last six months. Some day I would like to add a scholars' appendix and make an index, but I will always be glad I wrote it as I did because it has got through to the people and teen-agers love it. In fact on Hallowe'en a girl of about fifteen came to my door looking for treats and realized suddenly where she was. She said, "Did you write Bluenose Ghosts? It's fabulous. Will you autograph my pillow case?" (She had brought one to carry home her treats.) There have also been many side benefits in royalties where stories have been used for many purposes. I am probably more surprised than anybody, and the royalties have made it possible for me to enjoy things that my Museum salary would never permit. [267]

Nothing made a more popular subject for the Canadian Authors' Association or for soirées in Greater Halifax. Creighton found she could attract a good audience for supernatural talks even during one of Halifax's legendary February storms. "I told them all the scary stories I could think of," she said of one such gathering. "They loved it and asked for more, and then the paper carried a write-up." [268]

There is room for much more research on the actual prevalence of occult beliefs in Nova Scotia, and the interaction of such beliefs with modernism. Scepticism is an appropriate response to the jacket copy of *Bluenose Magic*, which states that among the "warm and colourful inhabitants of Nova Scotia ... belief in the occult is still prevalent." It may well be that some people in the province, and throughout North America, felt a desperate yearning for authentic evidence of magic in the world. An even more sceptical interpretation would suggest that the occult, rather than representing a major element in the beliefs of most Nova Scotians ("the thinking of our own people," in Creighton's words) [269] was blown out of proportion by a folklorist who was a devout believer in the spirit world, a preoccupation that became more pronounced in later years. In 1960 she received a visit from the spirit of her father:

I had gone to a side wall in my sitting room where a picture of him is hanging, but he was far from my thoughts. I leaned over to place something on the floor and whether I heard a sound or what forced me to look up I can't say. Anyhow it was as though the electricity were switched on and I found myself looking straight at his picture, but it was framed in a filmy cloud about four or five inches thick and in an oval shape. Then as suddenly it was as if the switch had been turned off and everything was normal, but I felt I had made contact with my father. Funnily enough I tried to hold it off from me and yet cherished it. Enough unusual things have come to me personally to give me a sympathy with the subject and the maritimes are full of such experiences. There was nothing frightening about the one I have experienced, but so far I can see no reason for it happening. It was not something I imagined, but was as real as it was unexpected.[270]

For Creighton, tales of the supernatural confirmed her in her religious beliefs. Although she drew upon the "expertise" of the Parapsychology Foundation in New York, she felt their representative was misguidedly secular in thinking that evil was a human construct. The devil was literally an active and energetic presence in Creighton's world. Heavenly visions, described to Creighton by "good people who would never dream of making up such a story," may well have been intended to reassure people that "God and his angels are nearby."[271]

Although sceptical about accounts of the occult given her by drinkers and those raised in a "superstitious environment," Creighton was inclined to credit those that came to her from her social equals, especially middle-class persons of temperate habits. An account of a visitation by Christ to a man suffering from a disease is followed by the exclamation, "Think of it. A person like that does not make up such a story."[272] Why would "good people" make up such stories? she wondered, naively disregarding the ways in which such beliefs can surface in many people confronted with disease and death.

In addition to its general contribution to irrationalism, problematically construed as being an integral and near-universal aspect of Nova Scotians' "cultural heritage," Creighton's work on superstition, because it characteristically avoided providing analysis or context for the description of superstitions and legends, leaves behind a disturbing impression that it validated wounding stereotypes and prejudices. The witchcraft stories she collected reflect an unbridled misogyny, aimed particularly at old and poor women in rural areas. Controlling such "witches" entails elaborate strategies to starve them to nothing; if these remedies do not work, there are more violent measures in the repertoire. If such beliefs were commonly held in Lunenburg County, a thesis that has not yet been systematically explored by social historians, they surely came with a heavy burden of prejudice attached. It was valid to unearth and record such stories, but harmful, surely, not to contextualize them in ways that would bring out their function and importance in rural society. Otherwise, as tales of unremitting cruelty told to us by people who are, we are assured by Creighton, the kindly representatives of the Folk, they attain problematic credentials as part of the "cultural essence," particularly when imparted to children. If Creighton's reader was promised deeper knowledge of what was "for many of us ... part of our way of life," an insight into "how we think upon these subjects, and how we express our thoughts," that way of life and those thoughts were often about violence against old women.[273]

There are then two general problems to be raised about Creighton's handling of witchcraft and Folk belief. One is that by rendering such phenomena as colourful curiosities, Creighton "naturalized," as quaint aspects of Nova Scotia culture, practices and beliefs whose inner logic deserved both reconstruction and critique. (Lunenburg witchcraft was not merely quaint, as at least one trial for murder with overtones of witchcraft – subsequently popularized in a story by Thomas Raddall – eloquently testified.)[274] Once again, the problem was that of creating a strange and foreign "Other" within one's own society, for whom one had no responsibility and with whom one did not have to maintain a political or cultural dialogue. The second objection is that by so emphasizing, for her own biographical reasons, the survival of superstitions, Creighton surely misrepresented the culture of a province in which conventional institutional churches, and not witchcraft cults, had long set the tone of spiritual life. That some Nova Scotians believed in witches and magic is undoubtedly true, but whether an apparent Lunenburg pattern could be generalized across the province (or indeed be regarded as a general phenomenon in Lunenburg County itself) remains deeply problematic. Whether more Nova Scotians than Ontarians or residents of New York City believed (or presently believe) in witchcraft and the spirit world is an entirely open question. Yet in this case Creighton's "sampling error" created a sense, both outside the province and within it, of superstition as somehow constituting a major part of collective identity. Runaway bestsellers, Creighton's books on ghosts and magic created an image of the credulous, pre-scientific Nova Scotian folk, cowering terror-stricken in their storm-tossed, rock-bound hamlets. The historian Jackson Lears observes that the recourse among late Victorians to what could be called a "European folk mind, a realm of magic and myth preserved in popular tales and superstitions," and a growing fascination with spiritualism suggested a very common longing for intense feeling among those dissatisfied with the "spiritual blandness diffused by liberal Protestant culture."[275] Creighton's psychic enthusiasms were a literal echo of Vaughan Williams's belief that, in uncovering the old English music preserved unknowingly by the "more primitive people of England," he was actually seeing a kind of ghost in the manner of a psychic researcher.[276] Frank Parker Day's *Rockbound*, Will R. Bird's travel writings, and a host of other works have developed the sense of a Folk Nova Scotia that is essentially primitive and pre-modern in its superstitions.[277] It is an emphasis startlingly at odds with the turn-of-the-century local histories or Calkin's early study of folk beliefs.

Creighton's work implied, finally, a reactionary form of neo-nationalism. There was a fascinating irony here. In the 1930s, as someone who identified with the British orthodoxy and the Child canon, Creighton was obliged to marginalize locally composed songs, which were lumped into the "Other" category or not collected at all. Thus, although Creighton's immense reputation today rests very much on the idea of her steadfast commitment to local culture, her initial instinct was to marginalize local efforts in favour of locating the true gold of the Child ballads. If this was neo-nationalism, it was of a particularly Anglophile type. Although there were songs that could have given Creighton's neo-nationalist pride in Nova Scotia an oppositional edge – one thinks, for example, of the coal miners' "Arise Ye Nova Scotia Slaves" – these could obviously not be thought representative of the "essence" of the province as conceptualized within a conservative perspective. Creighton's conservative imagination had a far greater impact on Nova Scotia than that of other folklorists because she was not merely sojourning in the Maritimes to write a monograph or two, but was a permanent resident. As Tallman notes, "She lived here, knew and loved the people, and published a wide array of first-rate folklore collections out of this knowledge and love."[278] Creighton herself emphatically distinguished her epistemological position as an insider inseparably attached to the people about whom she wrote from that of an outsider who viewed them from a distance. Responding to Roy's critique of her manuscript on folk beliefs and superstitions, she eloquently championed her "insider's" intuitive insights.

I am not writing of Them, the People From Nova Scotia, but Us, We People of Nova Scotia ... After all, I am 6th generation on both sides of my family, and the beliefs I give as my own are not made up by me, but are part of my inheritance as a native of this province. This, I feel, takes this out of the realm of being just another compilation of beliefs and superstitions, but part of life shared by the collector. Why can I not serve the dual role of collector and informant when I have so much to offer? And why should my traditional beliefs not have their place as well as those of any other inhabitant? They cannot possibly detract from the book's scholarship and they certainly add to its authenticity and worth. That, at least, is my impression. Otherwise anybody could write the book providing they had a file of index cards. Take that away and you remove its soul.[279]

As a sixth-generation Nova Scotian, Creighton assumed she was deeply and intuitively linked to "the people" about whom she wrote. Although clearly separated from many of them by boundaries of colour, ethnicity, class, and gender, she claimed to share with them a deeper cultural essence transcending all such divisions, despite her own childhood, from which were absent the folksongs and traditions she was now treating as essential. This was the very nub of a pastoral politics that would construct through its selective mechanisms not evidence of cultural differences but rather a neo-nationalist vision of cultural unity.

The impact of this strong identification with place was highly conservative. So far as one can judge, Creighton never spoke out against economic or social injustices. She identified strongly with a standard romantic position on the massive outmigration of Nova Scotians from the province in search of economic opportunities denied them at home. Outmigration was not viewed as an example of the failure of a social order; it was romantically "naturalized" as the outcome of the seafarer's propensity to wander the globe in search of adventure. "I am a Nova Scotian with the vagrant gypsy blood / A-flowing and a-coursing through my veins," read a poem by the young Creighton.[280] Conservative neo-nationalism typically depicted outmigration as a kind of success story: "It is an actual fact," Creighton boasted, "that this province more than any other has contributed men to occupy high positions in the various cities of Canada."[281]

Now study your great seats of learning,
From where do your principals come?
How many bank presidents schooled in the east

Have now reached the ladder's top rung.
Professors and great theologians
Nova Scotia has born them and bred,
And where'er men have gone o'er the face of the globe
'Tis the Bluenose who always has led.[282]

So went Creighton's poetic response to the exodus. As R.B. Bennett
once put it, thinking no doubt of himself, the "large percentage of
great men" born in the Maritimes was due to the early privations of
their lives and the "heroic self-sacrifice of fathers and mothers in
providing education for their children." Their outmigration from the
region merely attested to their sterling qualities.[283] This common
theme in conservative regionalism meant that outmigration could be
redescribed both as an aspect of a romantic history – "gypsey blood"
– or as a story of upward mobility. Outmigration was thus safely and
hegemonically handled. One can describe this romance of the exodus
as a kind of vague "neo-nationalism" – it does praise the sterling
qualities of the group in question – but also as a response that makes
no political commitments. The neo-nationalism of Innocence was
peculiarly directionless. Unlike Quebec, where a stark contrast
between the Folk and modern times could inspire both conservative
and radical variants of nationalism, Nova Scotian neo-nationalism
looked back on vanished glories rather than anticipating a transformed future. (Perhaps the closest Creighton ever came to harnessing her music to an overtly political purpose was in 1971, when
she used a song called "The Hills and Glens" from her *Maritime Folk
Songs* for a song honouring the Conservative leader Robert Stanfield
– a "local son" who had won national prominence – as a revealing
gesture honouring his departure from Nova Scotia.)[284]

Neo-nationalism requires heroes, and in Creighton's reimagined
Nova Scotia this role was undoubtedly taken up by the fisherfolk.
Although Creighton ranged the Maritimes in search of song and
lore, the "canon" of core songs and beliefs came from the "Coast of
Songs," which extended about one hundred kilometres on either side
of Halifax. Creighton believed that more of the old songs had survived on this coast. Perhaps she was simply confirming a longstanding cultural pattern of urban cultural producers' developing
grand generalizations on the basis of short visits to the rural hinterland closest to them. (One could call this the "Peggy's Cove Syndrome," after the Halifax County fishing village that became the
province's key symbolic landscape in the 1930s.) Seafaring songs
predominated, partly because of this geographical focus and partly
because Creighton was well aware that songs of the sea had a

Canada-wide appeal. "There is no doubt that the traditional songs found among simple folk interest the average person, and when they can be linked up with the lives of sea-faring people, the story of their survival cannot help but have a very wide appeal."[285] The coal fields generated many songs of social protest, which historians have found useful. How many more might have been gathered in the 1930s? Yet they have never entered the canon of classic songs, the "folk music" which, tautologically but conclusively, defined the Folk. Even "The Honest Working Man," which has become a kind of popular anthem of Cape Breton, and which Creighton did record, did not attain the status of "The Nova Scotia Song," the very distillation of the theme of romantic exodus.[286] How many songs of protest and struggle were among those dismissed by Creighton in 1932: "Our trip to Cape Breton is over, and although we were only able to get a limited number of songs, we learned a great deal about the country. Gaelic is the language of old songs. There is practically nothing to be found in English except songs of very recent origin and little literary value"?[287] Songs from the Halifax County shores became central to identity; those from the Cape Breton mines, with their suggestion of a society divided, were marginalized.[288] As for "lore," no fewer than 113 items in *Bluenose Magic* concerned ships and the sea, the majority of which emanated from fishing communities; only 9 items referred to coal-mining.[289] Although Creighton was willing to assist in the collection of Cape Breton miners' lore and in the organization of the miners' choir, the Men of the Deeps, her published work suggested that the fisherfolk, although not nearly as numerous as the province's industrial workers, had become the true bearers of the Folk essence. The quaint fisherman in his sou'wester was what the public wanted to see, as Ryerson Press had divined when marketing Creighton's work on the supernatural. "The jacket is terrific, even to the drop of perspiration on the brow of the fisherman," Creighton wrote to Lorne Pierce after receiving *Bluenose Ghosts*. "And such eyes! The timid will be afraid to read the pages, but it should be an invitation to any stouter hearts."[290] Fisherfolk, with their co-adventurer ideology, could be imagined, if one did not enquire into their lives too closely, as an independent peasantry. The mining proletariat and the working class in general, although more numerous than the fisherfolk, were far less easily romanticized and therefore far less "essential."

The ambiguities of Creighton's neo-nationalism were evident in her uncritical acceptance of the Child canon well into the 1940s. The songs that counted were, to a disproportionate degree, the traditional British ballads collected by Child. Although Creighton evidenced a far greater interest in local songs than Mackenzie, and collected many more than he did, she did not present a proportionate number of the local songs in her published work.[291] She still tended to work within the "Child/Other" categories. The bias towards Child ballads influenced both the means through which songs were elicited and their subsequent chances of being preserved in print. "I never told a singer what I didn't want," Creighton recalled years later, "but kept conversation going on the line I wanted them to follow. 'Do you know [the] one about the milk white steed?' was a great help. Many songs, all ancient ballads, use that term but the singer isn't likely to know more than one. It also served to get their minds on older songs."[292] Creighton was very proud of having located, out of Child's 305 ballads 43 songs in the Maritimes that were clearly variants of them.[293] When she mailed her manuscript of *Traditional Songs of Nova Scotia* to Lorne Pierce in 1945, she noted proudly: "An American writer once wrote that sixteen ballads had been found in Canada. As you see, I have thirty-seven."[294] In 1947 the somewhat over-simplified dichotomy of "traditional" and "local" still helped her think about the songs she had found: "The Nova Scotia records contained some unusually beautiful music, culled from the fishing villages and outlying communities," she advised a Prince Edward Island correspondent in 1947. "The best of these are traditional and were brought over by early settlers who have been singing them ever since. Songs that deal with local events are interesting too, and should be preserved."[295]

This comment, like her later collecting strategy, suggested a significant broadening of Creighton's perspective on what should be included among the truly significant. One can hardly blame Creighton for having discovered folklore through Mackenzie, Child, and Cecil Sharp; the English influence was further strengthened through her associations with Karpeles and especially with Doreen Senior of the English Folk Song and Dance Society. Nor was Creighton unusual in her sense of being a Canadian provincial in a cultural world centred on London. "Tell me quite frankly what London thinks about the music," she asked her editor in 1933. "From a letter written by Mr Dent to my brother I am a bit at sea. I fancy, quite between ourselves, that they will think over there that as music it can't compare with the beautiful quality of the English songs. Well, that's all right. I got what the province had to offer, and that is the most I could do."[296] To her credit, Creighton would later regret not having collected the broadsides produced as recently as the First World War. (She remembered particularly a gruesome song, circulated on a broadsheet, commemorating the Halifax Explosion).[297] Her transition to a more inclusive North American concept of folklore seems to have been prompted by her trip to New York and her discovery of the scope of the emerging popular market for folklore. Adhering rigidly to the "Child/Other" schema would limit her access to this developing market. Creighton was also impressed by the commercial success of a popular collection of Newfoundland songs. When she wrote Doreen Senior about the collection in 1943, she seemed divided between her freelancer's sense of appealing to a booming market and her fiercely defended English traditionalism.

In Newfoundland there is a cheap paper covered volume [put] out by a commercial firm, devoted entirely to local songs. I believe it is selling like hot cakes. All the service people who are there now are interested because they have heard the fishermen singing them. Consequently this would be a good time for us to put a similar publication out here. I have written Mr Doyle to see if he would advise it, and to find out how many he has sold. I have over a hundred, but not nearly all of those have tunes. I think we might make some money there. Hope you have no objection. [298]

But although Creighton relaxed the "Child/Other" hierarchy, she never completely escaped it.

The "Child/Other" syndrome encapsulated an entropic sensibility. For Creighton, where the radio played, the ballad withered: the new methods of communication and the values spread by them were inimical to the Folk culture on which she had staked her career. The younger generation, too interested in the radio and phonograph, no longer had to create its own entertainment,[299] and one had to search in remote areas to find tunes with the "breadth and symmetry only found in the genuine expressions of an artistic folk," music that was "definitely good – traditional – unspoilt."[300] As a correspondent noted in 1951, "It is indeed amazing that you have been able to find so many of the really old songs. With such a wealth of Child ballads in front of you I can see why it is that you are so [disdainful] of any song which is obviously less than a hundred years old."[301] Creighton used radio, television, and modern publishing to make her vision of the Folk a popular one, all the while holding that the modernity that made this dissemination possible was wiping out Folk culture at its source.

Thus, thanks largely to Mackenzie and Creighton, the notion of Nova Scotia as a haven of singers of Elizabethan ballads, preserved from modernity by their conservatism and isolation, took hold. Creighton developed the theme in an article in Maclean's in 1937, which illustrated how powerfully the dichotomy between the "real" ballad and merely "local" songs worked in her thought. Explaining that Nova Scotia was especially blessed with "excellent songs," Creighton qualifies her statement by dividing the songs into two types.

There are two types of folk song in Nova Scotia, traditional and native. The latter we must dismiss with little comment. I wish I could state that Nova Scotia has given birth to songs of great lyrical beauty or stirring ballads of the sea, but such is not the case. For the most part, our local songs are only interesting locally.

However, there are exceptions. The sea epic, "The *Chesapeake* and the *Shannon*" is one. In this case, words written locally were adapted to a tune at least 500 years old. The story is familiar in Halifax, into the harbor of which city the *Shannon* towed her captured prize, to the delight of the people.

... Local songs were usually written by unlettered folk and set to familiar tunes; tunes which accompanied very much older songs. Interesting as some of these native songs are, it is those which were brought over by our early settlers and have remained in the memories of our people which are our greatest treasure. These are songs which the old man of today learned from his father, who learned them from his father, and so on until the origin of the songs is lost in antiquity. They have survived here in a remarkably well-preserved form.

... Our standard is that set by Mr Cecil Sharp, the great English collector, whose lovely songs taken down in England and in the Appalachian Mountains of America are the inspiration for all who have come to this work at a later date. Out of 190 songs which we noted this summer, we consider that sixty-two are comparable with the best folk songs ever discovered anywhere in the world. This is a good percentage, for often one must taken dozens of useless songs in order to get one worth saving.[302]

That Creighton should have attained the status of a major standard-bearer of Maritime and Nova Scotian culture is doubly ironic, given both her early identification with the Child-fixated English tradition and her related tendency to view many of the songs composed by rural Nova Scotians as "useless."

The survival of the Child ballad in North America *was* a fascinating cultural phenomenon. Nonetheless, one suspects that, as in the case of the occult, Creighton's strategy of selection transformed one small aspect of local culture into a defining aspect of provincial identity. As Laurel Doucette and Colin Quigley, two students of the Child ballad in Canada, note, Ben Henneberry supplied Creighton with 90 songs; only 9 of them were Child ballads. Angelo Dornan of Elgin, New Brunswick, brought her 135 songs, only three of which were

Child ballads. To emphasize Child was to de-emphasize most of the "Other" songs. Moreover, as the same authors suggest, it is quite possible that the image of the province as a special haven of the Child ballad was primarily an artifact of the folklore research itself, and not the result of the province's supposed "traditionalism." The "Old Favourites" column in the weekly *Family Herald* (later the *Family Herald and Weekly Star*) of Montreal printed a total of 22 ballad types in eighty-five printings between 1895 and 1968, suggesting their popularity across the country (and questioning as well the folklorists' preoccupation with the 'traditional' ways of learning the ballads, some of which the Folk may well have picked up from the newspaper). Many Child ballads were to be discovered in Ontario, where comparable investigations began only in the 1950s.[303] If the notion of Nova Scotia as the pre-modern haven of the true English and Scottish ballad meant that most of the folksongs rural people liked to sing were relegated to second place, it may also have meant that Innocence functioned as a self-fulfilling prophecy, constructing through selection that image of consistency and British traditionalism that it could then present as the province's true essence.

The key to the present difference in the ways Nova Scotia and Ontario are imagined and represented as communities may well reside in the precocious cultural modernity of the former, not the latter. That is, it was Nova Scotia that first experienced the folklorists' modernizing antimodernism, directly imported from the most developed centre of research in the United States. Nova Scotia's earlier and more developed articulation of a thoroughly twentieth-century culture of antimodernism created the preconditions for the image of a primitive province "full of songs." In fact, as both Mackenzie and Creighton pointed out in other contexts, twentieth-century Nova Scotia was light years removed from some "romantic" land of song. The vast majority of Nova Scotians never sang them, and they can therefore in no sense be taken as culturally representative. The assumption that the Child ballads were the common songs of "the community" before the advent of radio was wholly typical of the essentialism of Folk philosophy and wholly unsubstantiated. "Of the people who live in the various communities that I have ransacked, the great majority have neither heard of these ballads nor have ever suspected the hidden powers of the persons who sang them for me," Mackenzie wrote.[304] For Creighton, the folksong was remembered by a tiny, hidden minority. Yet the image of the singing Maritimes proved remarkably durable, and in time it became, with the revival of the 1960s, a kind of reality. "It begins to look as if the Maritime

Provinces of Canada will join the Appalachians as the two great regions of American folk song," Alan Lomax wrote to Creighton in 1957.[305]

Creighton's convictions – about class, propriety, drink, race, and the Nova Scotian identity in general – had a direct impact on the kind of folklore she created and her intellectual and cultural legacy to her society. Creighton was never a twentieth-century cultural relativist. She valued one culture above all – the English-speaking culture of Shakespeare, whose name figured throughout her writing as a kind of gold standard of cultural significance. Ballads and lore did not lead one to cultural difference – to any sense of how various groups might have distinctive cultures, or how different classes may have shaped language – but to cultural unity. The Folk were Other, not in the sense of having their own distinctive culture to explore and respect, but as charmingly primitive early drafts and relics of a common English-speaking tradition. This ancient and true culture worked, as it were, behind the backs of the Folk. That was why one needed folklorists: to release the gold of true culture from the dross of the people who were its temporary custodians.

Another approach to collecting would have constructed another Folk and a different lore. Even in Creighton's published work, one can sense a tension between some of the material presented and the framework within which it is assigned its meaning. For all that Creighton emphasized the isolation and traditionalism of the people of Devil's Island, the first folksong she collected on that island was a piece of local and thoroughly urban folklore – the sad story of the "Babes in the Woods."[306] Yet this "first" and very important song was ranked 135th in the 150 songs of *Songs and Ballads of Nova Scotia*. Her Devil's Island Folk loved the song "Mary L. McKay." This was not a "traditional" ballad, but a song commemorating an event in 1913 that had been published in *Canadian Fisherman* in 1914. As J. Murray Gibbon pointed out, it clearly was not a folksong. Nonetheless, the Folk, in their ignorance, were singing it with enthusiasm and conviction.[307] In both instances, the fisherfolk were not behaving like isolated islanders far removed from the world around them, but like people who learned songs published in fisheries publications and on urban legends circulating in Halifax. This was hardly surprising for people who routinely went in and out of the bustling twentieth-century city as a normal part of their working lives, and who were so familiar with modern radio broadcasting that they knew Creighton as "Aunt Helen" before she had stepped ashore on the island. "The essential conservatism of primitives was a truism in the thought of this period," Julian Stallabrass remarks on the "idea of the primitive."

"The construction of a complete network of convention guiding the artist's every move made primitive creation seem effortless ... credit for conscious activity was removed from the artist, and the primitive art work became essentially a product of nature."[308] Presenting the Folk as people who unreflectingly repeated the songs of the ages misrepresented the complexities of rural and urban cultural interplay and, perhaps, subtly devalued the individual creativity and originality of the singers themselves.

Creighton's assumptions and methods have been overtaken in folklore studies by ways of thinking that are diametrically opposed to her "salvage" sensibility. Creighton looked for the underlying unity of the Folk, that essence of the Nova Scotian in which she could share. Modern writing on folklore describes a multiplicity of folk groups, with overlapping boundaries, and defined in any number of ways (by ethnic group, occupation, family, religion, nationality). What defines them as "folk" groups, for some, is simply that they engage in artistic communication (most commonly oral) in small groups. The notion of the Folk as the isolated bearers of authentic culture has thus eroded: one can have a folklore of the photocopier room. The entropic equation of change with deterioration or catastrophe – the Folk are disappearing! the last stand of the Ballad! – has yielded to a sense that there is no bedrock essence of cultural changelessness that modern-day flux can place in jeopardy or, conversely, that modern-day folklore can resurrect. The stark dichotomies – traditional community/modern society, *gemeinschaft/gesellschaft*, Folk culture/mass culture – that guided so many Folk theorists for so long have gradually become museum-pieces in social theory. As Philip Bohlman, focusing specifically on the case of folk music scholarship, has observed, "Rather than expressing concern over the disappearance of folk music, it preferred to see change as normative and creative; rather than subscribing to restrictive categories that limited folk music to rural venues, it ascribed importance to place on the basis of community, the aggregate of individuals that interacts with its physical and cultural environment."[309] The conservative sense of a cultural catastrophe – the vibrant antimodernism that from Herder and the Grimms shaped the international discourse of the Folk, and which locally was echoed so clearly by Mackenzie and Creighton in their sense of disappearing cultural treasure – is no longer widely held to be a plausible account of how musical repertoires specifically, or cultures in general, have changed. As Bohlman remarks,

The spread of various forms of literacy throughout the world has not been the death knell of folk music that some scholars have alleged. It becomes increasingly necessary, in fact, to expand our understanding of the range spanned by such concepts as orality and literacy, especially when electronic and other media of transmission exert a growing influence on folk music.[310]

It is now generally accepted that ubiquitous culture contact has not caused the wholesale disappearance of cultural distinctiveness or the use of folk music to signify that distinctiveness. Contemporary theory asserts that the identity that shapes groups and generates folklore may be both shared and differential, that is, derived from both core and boundary, similarities and differences ... Such theory goes a long way to explain the complexity of ethnic groups in industrialized nations. When we go so far as to say "the term 'folk' can refer to any group of people whatsoever who share at least one common factor" ... we tender great latitude to the social basis of folklore.[311]

A significant aspect of the new thinking has been to describe the individual creativity of Folk artists in ways that bring out their individualism and ingenuity. The Folk performer no longer appears as the passive loudspeaker for the voice of the Folk. A small but telling gesture is the transformation in the concept of "authorship." Such contemporary works of regional folklore as John Shaw's edition of Joe Neil MacNeil's *Tales until Dawn: The World of a Cape Breton Gaelic Story-Teller* and Sandy Ives's various books place in the foreground the individuality and creativity of the individual telling the story or singing the song.[312] (Creighton's first work might well have borne the title *Songs of Ben Henneberry*, had this more respectful framework been in place in the 1930s.) This seemingly small alteration in the etiquette of authorship marks a profound change in conceptualization. From the blurred homogeneity of the Folk, often as seen from a great social distance, we move to the artistic choices and versatility of individuals whose cultural expression takes shape in a particular performative context. It is a move that, in robbing us of the comforting notion that there is in society a solid essence of Folk wisdom waiting to be discovered, pays us the dividend of a much more interesting and dynamic portrait of how cultural forms change and grow. If one no longer believes that the essence of folk tradition is repetition and changelessness, then the search for the true "origin" and all the byzantine discussions engendered by it come to be seen as rather arcane and pointless scholastic disputes. At the same time, one opens the fascinating and potentially illuminating problem of why cultural changes occur and what functions they serve. (On these issues academic folklorists in the region, centred at Memorial University, have made some major contributions.)[313] It is true, of course, that as these explorations continue, the very utility of the word "folk" grows ever more indistinct. If today "we are all the Folk," then what is gained by using so ideologically freighted a word?

In its unspoken arguments and key concepts, Creighton's immensely powerful and popular concept of the Folk, through which so many have grasped what they believe to be the enduring essence of a society, was very conservative. On the most general level it encouraged irrationalism by bestowing upon decontextualized superstitions and prejudices the status of cultural essence. On more specific points it has been shown to have been irrevocably tied to conservative conceptions of class, gender, race, and ethnicity. What made these eminently debatable positions seem so irrefutable was their seemingly spontaneous genesis from the Folk themselves. *Das Volk Dichtet*. And everything the Folk had to say, once their words and songs were filtered through a dense web of assumptions, was almost invariably a comfort to the established order.

THE LOGIC OF CULTURAL APPROPRIATION

Creighton left an immense intellectual and political legacy. In the most obvious sense that legacy is present in her collection of tapes and file cards, which remains an invaluable and underutilized source for regional scholarship.[314] Her publications are still widely read and songs from her collection have been widely heard. The Nova Scotia Department of Tourism and Culture, operating through its Cultural Affairs Division, has granted $50,000 to the Helen Creighton Foundation, which aspires to be "a facilitator and forum for folklife activity."[315] (This figure represents an unusually high level of provincial public funding for a non-commercial cultural activity.) In 1990 the first "Helen Creighton Festival" was described in the Halifax *Daily News* under the headline, "Celebrating Ourselves: The Helen Creighton Festival praises the spirit of Nova Scotia." "The collective memory of Nova Scotia is steeped in tradition – of pirates and rum runners, of Micmac legends, of fast schooners and the people who sailed them," Richard Lavangie wrote in his coverage of the festival, with the confidence of someone relating a widely shared commonsense. Creighton's influence, he added, was to be felt around the campfires of children at summer camp, in the songs sung in pubs, and in countless other ways.[316] It is a striking measure of Creighton's success in naturalizing certain highly conservative assumptions about the Folk, about Nova Scotian society, and about the moral order in general that her highly selective reading of the past should now seem part of a hegemonic interpretation of the essential Nova Scotia. It suggests how successfully an antimodernist canon has come to be identified with the intrinsic character of the province and recognized as such by an impressive range of opinion.

This recognition is the result of a politics of cultural selection through which certain sayings, stories, and songs of various members of the supposed Folk were appropriated, transformed, and then rebroadcast by other groups of professional urban cultural producers. The great attraction of the Folk for conservatives was that they were outsiders, and yet posed no challenge to the established order. They were Innocents in a drab world of calculation and modernity; their songs and sayings were produced without expectation of reward in quaint islands far removed from capitalism and modernity. Yet to "save" the culture guarded by these Folk meant to break down the isolation of the islands. The challenge was to remove the common-property resources of songs and sayings, which had hitherto had no market value, and to transform them into marketable commodities, to take that which had had value only in use and redeem and preserve it by giving it value in exchange. To preserve the idealized "culture" of the Folk was necessarily to commodify it. This was the contradictory logic of modernizing antimodernism.

Creighton was part of this larger pattern of cultural appropriation and commodification. The logics of antimodernism and class worked their way through a particular person, whose conservative outlook predisposed her towards certain established interpretive frameworks. And these frameworks were decisive. Their emergence determined what the facts of cultural difference would "mean." The Folk could have been made to speak many things within any number of enabling frameworks. In other places, and on rare occasions in Nova Scotia, the Folk may be heard to protest, to mobilize, to name enemies, to organize and reorganize old and new traditions in a dynamic and inclusive process. Elsewhere in North America, a very different Folk wisdom was "collected" in other social settings – in prisons and work-gangs, for example – than was "collected" in the fishing and farming villages of the Nova Scotia. What if Creighton had forsaken the fishing coves and gone to the prisons? Yet this was only a small part of the problem. A collector such as Creighton was also an editor, an animator, a producer, selecting certain informants, rewarding certain cultural acquisitions, marginalizing that which was not "of the Folk," indeed literally erasing (as we have seen) those ribald songs and sayings that true members of the Folk would regard as an embarrassment, as untruthful representations of who they really were. Creighton's labour of description and redescription constructed a particular kind of Folk in Nova Scotia: the Folk who were as unchanging and as natural as the rockbound shores surrounding them – and almost as politically and socially inert.

Creighton exemplified many of the problematic features of an entire group of cultural producers who created and naturalized Innocence. In some respects Creighton represented an extreme example of the construction of rural Folk within and for an urban gaze. The twentieth-century invention of the Folk required the emergence of specialized intellectuals who could marry international theories of folklore with a reconceptualization of local evidence. These semi-professionals slowly acquired a position of cultural authority. What they defined as folklore, filtered through a grid of middle-class aesthetics and political values, came to constitute a canon. The Folk were traditional, somewhat reclusive, relatively uninterested in protest or in politics, fiercely superstitious, family-centred and respectful of conventional moralities – all of these eternal attributes were contingent descriptions, created by particular people with particular values, selecting out of a vast universe of cultural phenomena those that suited their nostalgic conservative predilections. Creighton in particular exemplified a politics of cultural selection. The Folk that emerged from her work was, at least in part, an edited version of "the people," cleansed and essentialized. These are the Folk who have since become naturalized as representing "the" Nova Scotia tradition.

The Folk as evoked by Creighton represented a quaint survival. They spoke to an intrinsically conservative sense of identity. They were sturdy and self-reliant, defending in their dwindling enclaves of cultural authenticity the old oral and spontaneous cultures that everywhere else were succumbing to the sad plague of the newspaper, the radio, and all the mindless bustle of modernity. But in Nova Scotia the plague had not swept everything before it. In the fishing coves there was still a chance of experiencing an older and better way of life. Innocence found the steadfast heart of Nova Scotian culture in exactly those backward, isolated villages that an earlier Victorian generation had viewed as embarrassing deviations from the ideal of improvement. To do so, however, it had to incorporate these quaint hamlets into the twentieth-century culture industry. Songs, poems, sayings, and lore, once circulated without the expectation of direct monetary return as a common property resource over which an especially talented individual might establish certain limited use-rights, became private property, subject to royalties, appropriated in their own interests by those outside the Folk.

For the disciple of Child, and for modernizing antimodernists generally, there was good justification for appropriating and "salvaging" the songs by commodifying them. The songs taken from their present-day custodians, the Folk, did not really belong to them in the first place. Appropriation of Folk culture was never clearly defined as such, because this resource was never really conceptualized as belonging to the Folk. After all, some of these ballads had inspired Shakespeare; the very superstitions found in the ballad "The Cruel Mother" were also to be found in *Macbeth*. For Creighton, it was " these points that make ballads and folk-songs of tremendous interest and value.[317]

Appropriating the "resources" of the Folk could also be justified on the grounds that they were useful for the renewal of high culture. Initially Creighton had argued on behalf of leaving the songs as she had found them. She protested in 1932 when her publishers in London took "decided liberties" with her work by fitting the words more neatly to the music.[318] Gradually, however, she saw the "beauty of some of the tunes," and not the intrinsic interest in studying the words, as the greatest value of the music she collected. She wrote in 1945, "They could be used with excellent effect in moving pictures, and I believe this is what the film musicians want to do."[319] Creighton came more and more to see the folksongs as a kind of raw material for high culture, as unprocessed ore which a unified culture could refine and refashion. *Twelve Folk Songs from Nova Scotia* was clearly folklore of this type, in the "Greensleeves" tradition. The pianoforte accompaniments written by Doreen Senior were intended to be of assistance "to people who can only use the songs when arranged with accompaniments." Through such appropriation the folksong as a form was being redefined. Once sung by untrained voices often unaccompanied by any musical instrument, it came to be seen more abstractly, as a melody, accompanied by pianos or orchestras, a staple of the school curriculum and music festivals.[320]

When the journalist Ian Sclanders asked her what practical purposes were served by the songs she collected, Creighton considered his question answered, at least in part, by a CBC radio presentation of "Sam Slick" that used background music composed from her collection.[321] Her memoirs conclude with a proud list of the uses to which her songs had been put:

Now in 1975 I see our songs used in text books in Canada and abroad. Many have been arranged for solo and choral singing and appear in sheet music; others are combined with melodies from Newfoundland for orchestral playing. I am especially pleased that locally we have a band number composed by Kenneth Elloway, choral arrangements by Mona Maund, Eunice Sircom and others, and harp arrangements by Phyllis Ensher. We have two symphonies by Klaro Mizirit, conductor of the Atlantic Symphony Orchestra, and one by Alex Tilley as well as a mini-opera by Steven Freygood.[322]

As Richard Tallman remarks in his careful critique of Creighton, it was an approach that raised profound doubts in the minds of professional folklorists, because such "popularizing tends to misrepresent the folk culture to the general public. Inevitably, popularization focuses on the quaint, the romantic, and the curiously rustic. It draws upon the personal, elitist aesthetics of the collector and the popularizer without due concern for the aesthetic judgments of the folk from whom the lore has come in the first place."[323]

In addition to these formal problems, the process of appropriation raised some disturbing politico-ethical questions. To put it bluntly, who now remembers Benjamin Henneberry? Yet without his prodigious feats of memory and performance, "Creighton's" collection would never have achieved its national fame and fortune. In the emergent folklore of folklore, Henneberry's achievement was minuscule compared with the heroism of the person who "collected" him. His role in the evolving neo-nationalist narrative was that of a static treasure, not that of a living, breathing Folk musician. The aura of greatness and achievement attached not to Henneberry but to Creighton alone.[324] Not everyone meekly assented to relegation to the margins of the story. "If the aim of those singers was to mangle those old songs so that they would be completely unrecognizable they succeeded admirably," Angelo Dornan, one of Creighton's key informants, remarked in 1958.[325] His opinion of the transformation of the songs he knew well scarcely mattered. The songs were succeeding with the markets that did matter, and for them Creighton was the star. The "Folk" themselves tended to fade in the background.

The key to Creighton's career was the transformation of cultural items once held in common and created for use into privately owned commodities exchanged on the market for economic gain. Although the issue of "commercialization" has been dismissed by the historian R. Serge Denisoff as a "time-tested bugaboo of the Left,"[326] and many discussions of the issue do proceed from a paternalistic ethos of "guardianship" over the naive and humble Folk, the issue of economic rewards can surely be posed without creating a left version of essentialism in which the innocent Folk are robbed of their treasure by designing and exploitative outsiders. Creighton did not become a millionaire on the basis of her collecting. She was merely keen to reap the rewards to which she was entitled. She regarded the songs and the stories as resources. The metaphors of the "gold mine" and the "treasure," which recur again and again in Creighton's descriptions of her work, are metaphors that speak powerfully of the processes of appropriation and commodification. Of Ben Henneberry of Devil's Island, she writes: "It was here ... that I found my gold mine."[327] Collectors resisted sharing informants with others, she remarked in her autobiography, "in the same way that a person with a treasure map keeps the information, hoping that he will some day be able to find the place for himself."[328] Before it was mined and brought to market, the "treasure" had no commercial value. In some lumber camps and fishing communities the songs were thought to belong to the person who had introduced them to that setting. It was considered wrong to sing another person's songs in his absence, because they belonged to him.[329] They were held and enjoyed in common, but (in some social contexts, at least) placed in the special trusteeship of the individual who first sang them, in a flexible form of ownership of cultural property. These songs – a common-property resource, open to all – were then "given" away to collectors for free. Whoever "discovered" them could claim property rights over them and use them as raw materials for profitable books and records. The storms and controversies that swept Canadian folklore from the 1920s to the 1960s (and that went on in many other places as well) often centred on this tricky business of transforming use-values once held in common into commodities bought and sold in the North American cultural marketplace.

Three especially difficult issues arose in the conversion of songs held in common into commodities produced for private profit: territory, copyright, and state sponsorship. Territorial disputes among rival collectors were acrimonious because jurisdictional conventions were not clear. Collectors based their claim to "professional" status on knowing their territories, not on the mastery of difficult specialized techniques. There were few significant barriers of skill or capital to entry into the trade. Creighton defined her territory as all of Nova Scotia, minus the areas around Tatamagouche and River John colonized by Roy Mackenzie. Otherwise, Creighton claimed the whole province: "Since this is my specialty in Nova Scotia, the field is known only to me in its entirety."[330] In 1936, when she was about to embark on her journey to the United States, she asked that she be given some sort of official accreditation so that her audiences would know that the government was behind her. She reasoned that such government backing would ward off competing collectors. "If I go down there independently certain people in my audience are sure to ask me if there are more songs to be collected in Nova Scotia or if the field has been exhausted. I should have to tell them that there are quantities of songs although there is not likely to be a second

Mr Ben Henneberry. Then it is possible that a delegation with more enthusiasm than skill will come up here, a further [collection] made and the songs taken out of the province."[331] Creighton's argument was interesting. The songs were seen as a kind of "cultural property" that the state should protect from people outside the province, although Creighton herself, in publishing the songs in London, was somehow exempt from the charge of exporting them. Perhaps collecting in French-speaking areas by an outsider could be justified, but Creighton claimed the songs sung in English. (Creighton, who was not very fluent in French, nonetheless later advanced a claim to "my Acadian folk songs" as well.)[332] One reason for Creighton's strained relationship with Edith Fowke, another major Canadian folklorist of the mid-twentieth century, was the absence of any clear boundaries separating their areas of jurisdiction. Fowke, who defined her field as all of Canada, seems to have angered Creighton by not deferring to Creighton's claims to control of almost all Nova Scotian materials.[333]

If the territorial issues were complex, copyright questions were even more so. Could one copyright a folksong? How else could one transform it into private property? But then how did one distinguish one version from another? As early as 1929, as her collecting career was just beginning, Creighton identified the issue of copyright as the key to deriving a monetary reward from the folksong. She asked J. Murray Gibbon for his advice:

Then to grow very practical for a moment, how would you advise me to make a profit for myself? Being a collector yourself you know the work entailed, and as we have to drive some miles for some, and then add to our journey by a sea voyage for others, and as we can only then get a few in one visit, it not only takes much preparation, but a great deal of time as well. That we enjoy it thoroughly is one consideration. But on the other hand I should like to think that there would be some monetary reward forthcoming. Therefore should I copyright them, or what would you suggest? I am appealing to you because I know how deeply interested you are in this work.[334]

According to the conventional legal wisdom, original work done in the way of collecting folksongs gave the collector as strong a claim to copyright them as she would have enjoyed for her own compositions. However, there was nothing to prevent anyone else from going to the same source and collecting the same folk tunes – and the second person would receive a copyright as well. The advent of mass media made such questions more difficult. "The radio scrounges east and west and pays very little," Lorne Pierce of Ryerson Press complained. "Our history with the c.b.c. has been that while they may pay fancy salaries to their own staff they hope to get our most jealously guarded materials for little or nothing. After all your years of work you would be very foolish to be too generous. Words and songs are copyrighted and surely you should be entitled to the extra fees which the copyright should guarantee you."[335] Creighton, who had embarked on her American tour worried about attracting a crowd of interlopers, was made all the more apprehensive about her property rights by an American lawyer at one of her lectures. He cautioned Creighton "against giving away too much lest the field be taken from me," and thoughtfully offered to act as her attorney.[336] Whether or not the lawyer's advice was decisive, the Creighton papers after the 1930s bulge with copyright questions: with letters granting permission to use the songs on payment of a fee per song,[337] with questions over whether a given artist was using the "Creighton Version" of the "Farmers Curst Wife" or another,[338] Creighton's royalties on "The Nova Scotia Song (Farewell to Nova Scotia)" and so on. One of Creighton's reasons for trying to get Nova Scotian songs into print as soon as possible was that publication would confirm her claim to copyright. As she wrote in 1949, her unpublished songs were stranded in a kind of legal limbo, neither unequivocally her property nor a public resource. Would other entrepreneurs move in and take her possessions?

What a lot of troubles there are in life. There's Nina Finn now who must always seek the unattainable, no matter who gets hurt on the way. She is determined to sing my unpublished songs on her radio program; the only ones from which I hope ever to make any money. Unfortunately she knows many of them, and I took her to the singers and let her hear them. She has now convinced herself that it is quite ethical for her to sing them, although she knows how I feel about it. How far she'll go I don't know.[339]

Once Creighton entered the employ of the National Museum, she took care to establish that she had permission to adapt folksongs collected under the museum's auspices for broadcasting purposes. If the Canadian Broadcasting Corporation paid her for her songs, she was to pocket the proceeds. However, songs collected in the field by a folklorist employed by the government officially remained "the property of the Museum. Permission should be obtained whenever the folklorist wishes to use his material for ends other than those which the Museum patronizes."[340]

Creighton faced copyright questions with anxiety in 1949 and 1950. "Mainly, of course, we want the songs sung, and I would hate to be so grasping that nobody could afford to sing them," she explained to Frank Flemington at Ryerson Press.

On the other hand, a set rate should be charged anybody who makes a phonograph record for commercial use, as in the case of the song "Goodnight Irene" about which I wrote you. Listening to Mrs Fowke's program on Saturday afternoons where folk songs from all over the world are broadcast, I realize how low our stock is in Canada, and how greatly we need to increase it. I think you will find professional singers wanting to make that use of them ... Another source of revenue should be from films. The National Film Board has already used tunes from my Songs and Ballads from which they paid ten dollars a song which is probably a very low price for a moving picture company. In cases like this, I would pass some of the receipts over to the original folk singers, for I think they should have a share in them. However, that's just between them and me. Ben Henneberry, a fisherman, made forty dollars from one film which used four of his tunes. In that case I gave the whole of it to him, but I couldn't always afford to be so generous.[341]

Noblesse oblige: within a pastoral framework, the superior party retained the conditional privilege of bestowing favours and granting gifts. But why these songs were in Creighton's gift rather than Henneberry's can be answered not by attributing any unusual degree of acquisitiveness to Creighton – she had at best a very mild case of royalty fever – but by remembering the context of antimodernist commodification that structured Creighton's strategy of appropriation as much as she in turn constructed the Folk.

There was, finally, the explicitly political dimension of the transformation of common into private property. The state played a pivotal role in the making of a folklorist. The state could support folklorists directly by supplying them with employment (as the National Museum did with Marius Barbeau) and indirectly by drawing upon their skills in tourism promotion. Creighton needed little prompting to see the tourism potential in the Folk. "I would give a series of two or three lectures to be delivered to some six hundred people at a time," she proposed to the publicity bureau in 1936, hoping for support for her American tour. "Pamphlets of Nova Scotia could be dispersed at the door. The value in advertising to Nova Scotia would, of course, be very great."[342] Creighton's fervent support of tourism can be traced over fifty years, from articles boosting tuna-fishing as "Fishing Sea Lions" in the 1920s and 1930s to her serving as part of a travel awareness program in 1977.[343] The role of the state was also important in financing books. "I personally am of the opinion that fortunes of the manuscript [*Traditional Songs from Nova Scotia*] are bound up in your own ability to make friends and influence the right sort of people," Lorne Pierce of Ryerson Press told Creighton in 1949. "I would strongly urge you to write on your own behalf to the Premier, referring him to the correspondence and asking him to undertake it, to write the foreword or better yet permit you to dedicate it to him. Sometimes a politician cannot withstand that! This is not my day to be subtle!"[344] Creighton, who had long enjoyed a good relationship with the Liberal government – it had supplied her with a car and encouraged her American tour – duly obtained the foreword from Macdonald and a subsidy for the book's publication.[345] State sponsorship of folklore provided a relatively painless and inexpensive means of legitimation: it suggested that the state apparatus was open to the humble as it simultaneously undercut the significance of class division. In its cultural, economic, and political aspects, appropriation transformed what had once been non-commercialized activities and beliefs into commodities with value in exchange. The antimodernists who created the Folk thus served as the missionaries of the very modernity they were lamenting.

POLICING THE BOUNDARIES OF THE FOLK

The Creighton phenomenon, then, represented a politics of cultural selection, not the neutral registration of that which was obviously just there in Nova Scotia culture. Rather than focusing the cultural honour and fame on the figure of the middle-class collector, attention could have been focused on the persons who told the stories and sang the songs. They could have been represented not as members of some primitive chorus of organic unity, but as complex and contradictory creators in their own right, as working people wrestling with received artistic forms and performing in particular historical contexts. Such a reconceptualization of folklore would have meant jettisoning the very idea of "the Folk" as a supposedly simple people uncontaminated by the printed word and modern capitalism. In presenting the local traditions of stories and songs in this more realistic way, attentive to the reception as well as the delivery of the song, and refusing to separate the "lore" from the worlds of production and reproduction, cultural producers could have treated their informants with greater respect.

The political issues at stake in defining the Folk and the true Nova Scotian tradition as the unspoken assumptions of the entire enterprise were generally kept under the surface. But on one significant occasion Creighton was obliged to spell out, with unforgettable clarity, her social and political reading of the Folk. Perhaps the most revealing and important single document from Creighton's career as a definer of cultural commonsense was written as part of her intervention against leftist influences in folklore in 1960. Creighton attempted to have the RCMP investigate Pete Seeger, and expressed grave concerns about the political leanings of Edith Fowke, whom she sought to discredit.

Any dispute between two professionals in the same small field is, of course, susceptible to a variety of readings. One might, for example, emphasize personal rivalry. This was probably an element in the Creighton–Fowke controversy of 1960. Creighton's attitude towards Fowke was hardly warm by the late 1950s. Creighton and Fowke came from opposite ends of the country and had different ways of thinking about society. Fowke had grown up in Lumsden, Saskatchewan. She was not a Communist, but she did have an interest in the left, and had been involved in experiments in socialist education on the Prairies.[346] Unlike Creighton, she was interested in songs of industrial protest, which she thought were rather thin on the ground in Canada. Nonetheless she highlighted the extent to which traditional songs in Canada, including those of the east, raised social issues: "A Crowd of Bold Sharemen" was about fishermen who went fishing for cod and turned on their captain when he refused to share the cod livers; and Larry Gorman's famous songs were often (in her eyes) satirical attacks on employers.[347]

Creighton's hostility to Fowke could well have had both territorial and ideological dimensions. She was outraged when she heard one of her songs from the museum collection on Fowke's radio show.

I have been pacing the floor since I heard Rawhide play my unpublished song, "Phoebe" from the new Wm. MacCauley record. Do you know who allowed Edith Fowke to go through my Museum collection, both words and music? That she gave this beautiful song to Bill MacCauley without my permission or knowledge? That he wrote a commentary with the song that gives no intimation of who collected this particular variant, and then, instead of asking me for a song from Prince Edward Island, listed this as coming from that province? I'm sure there can be no mistake because I have checked words and music with my copies here, but before I write her I want confirmation from Ken Peacock. I can't feel that you knew anything about it, but who did? And if she would take one of my songs, what else might she have taken?

I have realized for some time that Edith is ambitious and craves publicity, but I never dreamed she was underhand or dishonest. Fortunately the Crawley Films sent me a copy, which they did with great pride, and I feel sorry Edith has got them in this mess. If Louis Applebaum or Neil Chotem were to go to the Museum I would want them to be shown the tunes Ken has done, but I wouldn't expect them to take anything without my permission. After all, these tunes are mine, paid for by the Canada Council. I want composers to use them, but with the proper credits such as you would expect from any honourable person. But this is beyond the pale. And then to take it out of this province and give it to p.e.i. Moreover she has seen at the end that the Waterloo Press is given credit for the songs taken from her "Folk Songs of Canada," but my poor Phoebe looks like a motherless child.[348]

Fowke had innocently and inadvertently offended Creighton by not deferring to her assumption that she enjoyed property rights over the songs in the museum's collection.[349] There was probably something more than heartfelt sympathy in Creighton's response to the news that Fowke's cbc show had been taken off the air, in which she wrote that the cbc's decision must have been "hard on her", but perhaps it would give her a chance "to think and to realize how much the cbc was responsible for her success. Actually she is a very good collector, but I think she needed a little set-back to get her values straight."[350] Creighton's misgivings may also have been intensified by Fowke's interest in the very type of bawdy song that Creighton so actively erased in her Nova Scotia collecting.[351]

However, one would do Creighton an injustice to characterize the Fowke–Creighton controversy of 1960 as a question principally of personal rivalry. Creighton was, for the most part, generous and fair in her dealings with her professional colleagues. If she appeared somewhat vengeful in her relations with Fowke, it should be noted that she later wrote on Fowke's behalf when the latter was nominated for the Order of Canada, and generally maintained friendly relations with her.[352] Personal differences, which did exist, should not be allowed to distract unfairly from the ethico-political seriousness of Creighton as a cultural producer.

The surfacing of Pete Seeger in Creighton's 1960 correspondence concerning Fowke suggests the much wider dimensions of her ideological program. Seeger was the bête noire of the American right.[353] The son of a concert violinist and an ethnomusicologist, Seeger had become identified in the 1950s as the leading exponent of a style of cultural politics diametrically opposed to Creighton's Folk conservatism. As early as 1941, right-wing American congressmen had targeted folksongs as a possible source of subversion; Seeger's refusal to answer questions and incriminate others in the McCarthy period clearly identified him as a leftist in their eyes. Because of his politics, Seeger would be blacklisted from prime-time television until his controversial appearance on the *Smothers Brothers Comedy Hour* in 1967. Seeger was a symbol of the attempt to tie a concept of the Folk and folksong to "progressive politics" through a politics of cultural selection quite different from (although no less essentialist than) that of Creighton.[354]

Creighton viewed radicalism, labour unions, and social protest with horror. She despised attempts to combine folklore with progressive politics. When she thought she had discerned such tendencies in Edith Fowke she was moved in March 1960 to write a rare manifesto setting out her views of the organic social order. The context of her remarkable letter, which deserves to be quoted in its entirety, was a recently published collection of folksongs concerning workers and their struggles which Fowke had sent to Creighton. Included in the book were a number of songs to which Creighton took violent exception. As she explained to Carmen Roy,

A few days ago I received a copy of Edith Fowke's new book, Songs of Work and Freedom. It is very well done, but what a subject, for these are communist songs. I am embarrassed to know how to thank her. She does this documentary type of study very well; I would say it is her forte. But why is it that people like Alan Lomax, Pete Seegar [Seeger], Peggy Seegar [Seeger], and now Edith, apply folk songs to communist propaganda? She doesn't call this book folk song, but it is her interest in folk songs that has led her along this path. I remember years ago recording the song Solidarity Forever from a very nice young professor, and it made me shiver. Evangelist songs stir people to good, but trade union songs stir people to hate and to seek their own advancement. I'm glad I don't have to review it, which would be hard to do as a friend.[355]

With commendable frankness Creighton then wrote to Fowke. In doing so she made what is perhaps the most striking, cogent, and articulate statement of her particular reading of the Folk:

Dear Edith,
    It was good of you to send me a copy of your new books, and I appreciate your thought. Knowing me as you do, I wonder how you expected me to react to such a subject as you have chosen. If this were a document on the type of song sung by a certain section of the people at a certain time in our

history, then I could find much to commend in it. But you encourage people here to sing these songs. I will never forget my feeling of horror when a young professor who had sung me Cape Breton songs asked if I would like to hear Solidarity Forever. He had heard it at a communist meeting during his college days in Toronto where he went in the process of growing up. As I listened I could understand what that song would do to a group of workers. I have always understood that this is a communist song, and that raises the question in my mind as it does in the minds of my friends – where do you stand in this? It looks as though you had lined yourself up on their side. If am wrong, and I sincerely hope I am, please wire me collect. It would be a great relief.

I'm afraid I don't share your sympathy with labour. At present we in Halifax have been working hard for tourist trade to [bolster] our economy, and had a lot of conventions booked. What has happened? A plasterers' strike, and possibility of a loss of a million dollars to the city. So selfish, so lacking in public [spirit]. As for myself, I have an enormous bill to pay for carpentry done on my house last fall. It was an excellent job and I couldn't have had nicer [workmen]. In fact when one of them blew off the roof in a gust of wind and was badly injured he looked up at me from his hospital bed and apologized for having given me so much trouble. I would like to engage them to do more work but they've priced themselves out of my budget. The house needs painting, but there too the cost is prohibitive. Where is it leading?

One song says, "when the earth is owned by labour and there's joy and peace for all." God forbid. In our day man has accomplished so much that he seems to think that he is God and that material betterment is all he needs. That's all very well when you're on the crest of the wave, but what is he going to do when automation puts him out of work – automation that has become necessary because labour's demands can't be met? Then he will realize that man alone is poor and helpless. Human nature being what it is, he will then blame God for his troubles.

I know nothing of your religious convictions – it is something we have never talked about. It is love we want in the world to-day above all else. Love for one another, but above all else love in Almighty God. We must also fear, worship, and serve Him, not being merely lip-service Christians, but honest practising ones. If labour would put half the fervour into their spiritual life that they give to their unions, their troubles would solve themselves, and instead of a lot of discontented persons stirring themselves up to protest their lot, they would be counting their blessings and helping one another. This is something the world must learn or we are doomed to extinction like other civilizations before us. It isn't easy, and takes tremendous faith and courage. We all rejoice to see the poor and oppressed raised to a better standard, but in my thinking they are not the ones I feel most sorry for. The people I pity are those who have never known God in their hearts, for it is only with Him that one can ever know that peace which passeth all understanding.

These things meaning a great deal to me, I don't usually let myself go like this. But you have shared your book with me and it is only right that you should know where I stand. Other people will deal with you more kindly. Or will they? What will the critics say? I hope you will forgive me for being so outspoken, but I would be a poor friend otherwise.

As ever ...[356]

This is a rich document indeed, a condensation of an entire anti-modernist view of an organic social order. It is a lament based on a pastoral vision, a sense of society in which Creighton and the injured workman are bound together by reciprocal obligation and custom. Creighton's profound insight was that "labour" and the Folk could not truly coexist as categories. To preserve the Folk, the labour movement, with its horrible songs of social disunity, must be symbolically (and perhaps literally) erased. To construe the Folk tradition as in any sense a "working-class" tradition (as Creighton believed Fowke, Seeger, and Lomax were apt to do) was to undermine the concept of the fundamental unity of social classes. Creighton's critique also suggested, that hers was a commercial antimodernism. She high-lighted the symbolic centrality of tourism as a "community enter-prise" she warmly supported and even identified as a necessary aspect of her own local patriotism, so clearly opposed to labour's selfish and destructive attempts at collective advancement. Creighton also raises high an evangelical standard of Christian revivalism against the menace of communism.

The letter reveals Creighton at her most limited and her most admirable. Here she has defended Innocence by demanding that it never be politicized, that the organic unity of society was something far above mere politics, mere class. She had followed the Quest of the Folk to its inevitably corporatist and conservative conclusions, and defended her view with cogency and intelligence.

Roy replied to Creighton's alarming critique of leftists in folklore on 31 March 1960. Her reply focused not on the issue of civil liberty but on her doubts about the factual accuracy of the case against Fowke and Seeger. She was not sure that Seeger was a Communist, and told Creighton that he had denied being one in a recent conver-sation. [357] Creighton was not reassured. On 2 April 1960 she replied to Roy's cautious bureaucratic response with a call for more drastic action.

I have been thinking about Pete Seegar [Seeger] and your doubts about whether I am right. I didn't know he wanted anything from the Museum,

so I would like to make a suggestion. It can do him no harm, and indeed
would be fairest to all of us, including yourself. It should be a simple matter
for the Museum to make a confidential inquiry through the RCMP and the
FBI, asking if he is known to have leanings towards the left, and what his
record is. I think you will find that he is on a list of people they keep their
eye on, but they must think he is keeping within the law because he seems
to move freely between the two countries. Others have asked him the same
question you have, and with the same result. I have met him only once, and
was sorry our time was so short. He struck me as something of an idealist,
and I should think he wants sincerely to help the oppressed. I found him
quite charming, but even in that short time he told me that his sister was
then behind the iron curtain. He must have an amazing way with a crowd,
and an ability to organize group singing, that is quite phenomenal. If you
could analyze his progress you would understand the use to which he puts
folk songs. However why not settle the matter and put us all at our ease as
I suggest?

To-day I had a librarian friend at the house who has lived in the USA and
knows Roosevelt University where Edith's book was published. She volun-
teered the information that this university has strong leftist inclinations.
Before acknowledging the book I took it to a friend who is in charge of
personnel in a big oil refinery and asked what he thought of it because,
goodness knows, I don't want to be unfair or hurt anyone unduly. He felt as
I did. I think I had better send you my copy and you can judge for yourself.[358]

Did the case go any further? It is difficult to say. Creighton was well
connected in Ottawa, and at least one RCMP inspector was known to
be active in the Canadian Folk Music Society.[359] It would have been
a simple matter to mention the matter to him. Fowke replied at once
to Creighton in a letter distancing herself from the left. Although it
is not possible to cite this letter directly,[360] its gist may be surmised
by a letter from Creighton to Carmen Roy of 4 April 1960, in which
she reported that Edith Fowke had written to reassure her about her
political beliefs. On the basis of this letter Creighton was prepared
to conclude that Fowke's "politics are sound and her motives right."[361]
A relieved Roy repeated this illuminating phrase in her reply of 12
April 1960, which evidently marked the end of this important
correspondence.[362]

Creighton's letters condense and make more precise the entire
politics of the Folk in the postwar period. They document the now
powerful material strength of an institution whose employees were
explicitly concerned with the soundness of the politics of those to
whom the state distributed its rewards. Moreover, they suggest that
the definition of the Folk and its true culture was a question of

political orthodoxy. Creighton was of course debating a much more important ethico-political issue than whether Fowke should receive museum contracts or Seeger be allowed to visit Canada. She was using the instruments made available by Cold War anti-Communism to defend her authoritative reading of the Folk. Thus her letters, although they might be read from a conventional standpoint as suggestive of one intellectual's moral choices in the Cold War, are more interestingly situated within the framework of Innocence, and suggest its unresolvable contradiction.

The contradiction was that Innocence upheld the pre-modern, quaint, therapeutic Otherness of a Folk it was simultaneously drawing inextricably into capitalist social relations and the modern liberal order. Mobilizing the state bureaucracy and the RCMP to create a certain kind of Folk, free from the taint of radicalism, was a way of sealing Folk discourses, of insulating society from whatever critique antimodernism might make of capitalism. The RCMP, the enormous new bureaucracies of tourism at the federal and provincial levels, the school system – these institutions were crucial to the maintenance of Innocence, and would work in various ways to make Innocence an authoritative way of seeing. And all were bound to entangle the antimodernist Quest of the Folk in antinomies. The folklorists' Quest of the Folk, that moment of 1920s romanticism, which in Creighton's case we traced to a romantic moment by a storm-tossed sea, ends here, with discussions about informing on dissidents to the police and about the division of patronage spoils in an impersonal state institution. There was a good deal about the twentieth century – prosperity, radio, politics, labour unions, "Solidarity Forever" – that Creighton persistently identified as adversaries of her project and possible contaminants of the organic unity of the *gemeinschaft*. She was responding to the spectre of social protest not from momentary fear but from her deeply conservative pastoral ideology of reciprocal and beautiful relations between rich and poor. With care and hard work, she had constructed the imagined world of the Folk with the conceptual tools at her disposal. Bringing the RCMP in to enforce its borders was the logical outcome of any serious effort to defend Innocence against the social unrest of the twentieth century. Creighton thus exemplified the common and painful dilemma of modernizing antimodernism: in struggling to protect her imagined Folk from radicalism, she inevitably politicized the very Innocence she was struggling to purify of politics.

3 Mary Black and the Invention of Handicrafts

> Nova Scotians are conscious of the value of handcrafts and it is
> difficult to keep up with their requests for instruction. It takes
> a little effort to sort out which of these are based on sincere
> rather than trivial interest and to train good technicians; but
> above all it will take time and more time to awaken our
> craftsmen to the fullness of the rich design forms which lie all
> about them but of which they are now largely unaware.
>
> Mary Black, "Improving Design in Handcrafts," 1952

THE ROLE OF HANDICRAFTS IN INNOCENCE

Helen Creighton successfully made a particular antimodernist reading
of Nova Scotia into something that seemed a simple matter of common
sense. She took an entropic conservative ideology and made it into
something that both Nova Scotian and Canadian nationalists could
see as speaking to their own sense of identity. But this elevation of
folklore to such a position of cultural prominence in twentieth-century
Nova Scotia only captures part of the Quest of the Folk in Nova Scotia.
In many respects, the handicrafts tradition was a more visible and
obvious indication of pre-modern Innocence than the emergence of
folklore. The casual tourist, who might never read a work of folklore
or listen to a folksong, would be unusual indeed if he or she were
not exposed to local handicrafts of one sort or another. The Folk and
handicrafts went together. Enthusiasm for things "of the Folk"
included admiration for the material objects the Folk were thought to
use in their daily lives. In Nova Scotia, as elsewhere, the Folk revival
entailed the redescription of the "arts and crafts" of the Folk as signifiers of essence. Creighton promoted handicrafts in her journalism,
as handicrafts proponents promoted the work of Creighton: Folk ways,
Folk arts and handicrafts can all be seen as part of Innocence, the
conscious elevation of pre-modern forms and antimodernist ideas to
symbolic primacy in a modern industrial society.

Yet the two projects faced dissimilar challenges. Creighton could select elements from an extensive and vigorous singing tradition in conformity with her conservative ideological perspective. The handicraft revival required different strategies. While Creighton could *select*, the handicraft revivalists felt obliged to *invent*; and while the state and the tourism industry figured in the background of folklore, primarily as influences on the market, they both necessarily had a much more direct and powerful structuring impact on the supply and demand of handicrafts. Folklorists had much more to work with than handicrafts revivalists: they could edit the repertoire of the countryside to produce an official version, whereas the handicrafts revivalists faced a society in which handicrafts were a dwindling resource. If the emergence of folklore was best captured in metaphors of mining, the invention of handicrafts required the language of technical training.

This chapter traces the invention of the handicrafts tradition in Nova Scotia, primarily through the prism of the career of Mary Black, the pre-eminent craft revivalist. It outlines the international context and describes local attempts at handcrafts revival before 1942. An examination of Mary Black's career as a bureaucrat and organizer is followed by an analysis of her implicit ideology, which combined an emphasis on state-directed commercialization with a philosophy of naturalism in which handicrafts were considered "authentic" insofar as they mirrored the natural world. Finally, it traces the impact of this ideology in action, and argues (by comparing two instances of invented handicrafts, Chéticamp carpets and the Nova Scotia tartan) that Black's model of state involvement gave the handicraft revival a legitimacy and power it otherwise would have lacked.

There was little original about Nova Scotia's twentieth-century craft revival in the international context. What is surprising is how late it was. Elsewhere, the stigma once attached to the handmade products of the home and workshop faded as they attained scarcity value at a time of mass production. From the mid-nineteenth century, arts and crafts movements in England and the United States had held up the ideal of traditional handicrafts as the authentic and pre-industrial antithesis of dehumanized factory labour. Important craft revivals commenced in the rural United States as early as the 1890s. They were as culturally complex as the antimodernism in which they had their roots. Such revivals represented in part the "revival" of old ways in the interests of sustaining rural communities and in part the invention of pseudo-traditions in the interests of satisfying a massive urban demand for things that seemed authentic, rustic, "of the Folk."[1]

In Canada as well as in the United States, the twentieth-century urban middle class eventually came to admire rather than scorn the "older ways" and look upon them with a fond nostalgia. In 1953 Helen Hutchinson noted in the *Family Herald and Weekly Star* that handicrafts had become extremely popular, having overcome the stigma once attached to things that were handmade.[2] As J. Murray Gibbon – who was as prominent in this sphere as he was in the folk revival – had noted a decade earlier, handicrafts were experiencing a continent-wide renaissance as interior decorators found forgotten treasure troves among the Pennsylvania Dutch, the mountain folk of the Appalachians, and the habitat of the southern highlanders.[3]

Handicrafts and an antimodern sensibility are obviously connected. As noted in a recent catalogue for an exhibition called "Older Ways: Traditional Nova Scotian Craftsmen," the present craft revival is fuelled by modern anxieties. "We live in disquieting times and we feel ill at ease with the products of our technology. The tendency is to look to the future for an answer to our nervousness. Perhaps it is important to pause for a moment and reflect on the past."[4] This "reflection" on the past is greatly assisted by handicrafts, which, when situated within a certain framework, allow one to imagine the simplicities and certainties of a less demanding age. From the perspective of early twentieth-century antimodernists, handicrafts spoke reassuringly of cultural continuity and of old traditions to an urban middle class unsettled by the pace of change. For every William Morris reclaiming lost traditions of craft in the name of socialism, there were a hundred middle-class men and women for whom handicrafts served, and still do serve, as mementos of an imagined past of authenticity. Less obvious, perhaps, is a second drive behind the handicrafts revival: tourism. Throughout the world, tourism has intensified and transformed the production and distribution of handicrafts, which have come to function as souvenirs. Tourism created a vocabulary in which the handicraft was a sign of true "authenticity." Since before the turn of the century, North American tourists have returned from their vacations with handicrafts, material proof of their encounter with something outside (or before) the everyday world of industrial capitalism. Additionally, a handcrafted and distinctive souvenir bears witness that the tourist has indeed made the journey, and it thus plays a role in authenticating his or her individual saga. One does not prove one has been to Tahiti, for example, by returning with articles that could as easily have been bought in North America – even if the "localization" of the article in question is achieved through standard techniques of "authentication" that vary remarkably little in their achievement of the handicraft effect from one place to another.[5]

On either count, the handicraft revival in Nova Scotia was entirely predictable. What is surprising is how late, and how difficult, this revival turned out to be. It took far more effort, against greater odds, to naturalize a description of Nova Scotia as a haven of handicrafts than it did to describe it as the sanctuary of the Child ballad. In 1943 it was a matter of common knowledge among those interested in sponsoring a craft revival that Nova Scotians lagged far behind the rest of North America in handicrafts. "In perhaps no part of this continent has there been such neglect of the native crafts as in Nova Scotia," argued the *Maritime Co-Operator* in 1943.[6] Jim Lotz, in *Head, Heart & Hands*, a history of crafts in Nova Scotia, remarked four decades later: "From being the orphan of the arts, crafts have become central to the province's identity."[7] Why did this transition occur and what did it suggest about the politics of cultural selection?

"Central" as handicrafts may be to identity today, they were almost invisible by the late 1910s and early 1920s. Many of the reasons for this trend were similar to those found throughout North America. Industrial capitalism marginalized many urban crafts; others it destroyed entirely. Some were undermined through the market competition of the factory, some by technological obsolesence, some through their inability to maintain their position in labour markets overstocked by underemployed rural producers. Thus Halifax sailmakers, bakers, printers, painters, coopers, and others, who once boasted impressive unions and workplace rules, confronted severe threats to their traditions and identities in the twentieth century. Some crafts were entirely destroyed, and others adapted to industrial capitalism as best they could.[8] The pattern of craft disorganization was probably no less pronounced in rural areas. High levels of out-migration, the extensive penetration of the countryside by urban manufactures and merchant credit, the gradual winding down of wooden shipbuilding, and the instability of occupational categories outside the cities meant that "old ways" of making things were under severe pressure from the mid-nineteenth century on. Doubtless some rural crafts survived without much transformation – the making of apple barrels, blacksmithing, boat-building – but not many. A second factor limiting the survival of crafts may well have been their relatively modest development, even before the advent of industrial capitalism, in the various parts of the province not dominated by agriculture. Although it was an idée fixe of romantic middle-class Haligonians and tourists that fishing villages, home of the hearty

and independent fisherfolk, must also be havens of domestic handicrafts (especially weaving, woodwork, and leatherwork), apparently
they rarely were. Rugged coastal areas were not well suited to the
development of the agricultural base such craft traditions normally
required. Some heavy sweaters, undergarments, and mitts might be
produced from the few sheep kept in such areas, but it made more
economic sense to obtain most woven articles through trade with
areas where sheep-rearing was more common.[9] The sturdy and independent fisherfolk consequently rather disappointed those who were
looking for memories of, or models for, rural self-sufficiency and
craftsmanship. In Cape Breton, for example, where Scots traditions
of weaving clothing, sheets, and blankets persisted, both carpets and
clouties (the local name for the Island's intricate and beautiful coverlets) had been imported from Scotland by emigrant professional
weavers. Such handicraft traditions had virtually disappeared by the
1930s and even the requisite raw materials for woollens were difficult
to obtain. When, in the 1940s, the time came to reinvent the Cape
Breton traditions of weaving, homespun yarns were nowhere to be
found.[10] Throughout the province old looms had been long abandoned, and many had been burned for firewood.[11] As craft revivalists
learned to their regret, the early twentieth-century Nova Scotia countryside was no tranquil haven of traditional crafts.

On the whole, it appears that "craft," both in the narrower sense
of bodies of people defending exclusive skill-based rights in the
labour market and in the broader sense of vigorous rural traditions
of making by hand articles for home use, was probably no more
developed in nineteenth-century Nova Scotia than elsewhere in
North America. By the twentieth century, craft had perhaps declined
further than elsewhere in a province where the heavy industries of
coal and steel and the rapid growth of transportation and secondary
manufacturing had changed so many aspects of economic life. The
crafts had declined through struggles over power, status, and trade
unionism, and through rural depopulation, the diffusion of waged
labour, and the rural impact of the urban consumer economy.

The stories of the craft workers – the Halifax boilermakers' resort
to industrial sabotage, the carpenters' full-hearted embrace of
Labourism, the economically indispensable domestic manufactures
of farm women – are rich in incident and character, but they have no
place in the history of crafts as developed as one aspect of Innocence
and retailed by a small army of craft revivalists. In this imagined
history, the crafts were once aspects of a rural economy of self-
sufficiency. The "old ways" of the country Folk were then "forgotten"
through some collective lapse of memory or through a mass outbreak

of laziness caused by modern conveniences. In truth, they vanished in a process of social change and struggle. In the cities, workers who had invested their lives in the "old ways" faced painful and difficult adjustments. In the countryside, domestic industries and handicrafts might be abandoned in favour of products from the catalogue, and the drudgery of housework mitigated (although only somewhat) by labour-saving devices. And if a powerful stigma was attached to the "old ways" by the 1930s, as revivalists would later claim, they might have noted that the coal miners whose skills could no longer guarantee economic security, the farm women who faced the endless tasks of sewing and mending clothes, the carpenters in the city who faced poverty after a lifetime of work had good reason to steer their dependents away from a life of working with one's hands. Entropic antimodernism registered the fact of the decline of handicrafts but, as usual, could only describe the change simplistically in terms of cultural degradation and erasure.

In this setting, the twentieth-century "revival" of handicrafts therefore entailed, at the very least, the reinvigoration of languishing crafts. It more often involved the wholesale invention of craft "traditions." Crafts in Nova Scotia were not so much the continuation of age-old traditions handed on through the generations as they were the products of a conscious state policy of meeting the expectations of tourists, who came to the province expecting to find quaint, handmade articles that were somehow "typical" of Nova Scotia.

Given the rather unpromising local materials, why did some middle-class cultural producers nonetheless feel that a revival of handicrafts was imperative? Much of the answer lies in the power of external examples, particularly those of Quebec and New Hampshire. The idea of reviving or inventing handicrafts as a solution to economic crisis seems to have been a common notion of the 1930s and early 1940s; and it is no surprise to find Marius Barbeau and J. Murray Gibbon as central developers of the idea. In Quebec the craft revival, promoted by both of them and by such corporate institutions as the Canadian Steamship Line and the Canadian Pacific Railway, took hold in the 1920s. For Gibbon, the president of the Handicrafts Guild (which had grown out of the Montreal Women's Art Association), the Canadian craft revival seemed to serve the larger purposes of dominion-wide unity almost as well as his numerous Folk festivals. He seems to have felt that the revival of needlecraft might take English- and French-speaking Canadians back to common Norman origins, not to mention providing a point of contact between the Canadian-born and the recent European immigrants.[12] The building-blocks of the Quebec revival were the Cercles de Fermières and the

Ecoles Ménagères. The Cercles de Fermières was founded in 1915 and represented small groups of rural women who met locally with the encouragement of the Department of Agriculture to develop gardening, poultry-raising, bee-keeping, the raising of sheep for wool, and the home manufacture of textiles. By the 1930s various handicrafts had been reshaped through the pressure of tourism: the "catalogne," for example, was transformed from a bed-covering to a floor-covering. The Beaupré coast had become a vast sales territory for blankets, coverlets, and rugs. Major hotels (including the Château Frontenac and the Manoir Richelieu) began to stock handmade items for the booming tourist trade. In the 1920s especially many tourists had started demanding the handmade article over something more polished.[13] The state became centrally involved in the Quebec revival in 1929, when, in connection with the back-to-the-land movement, the provincial government created a school of handicrafts in the Department of Agriculture. Inaugurated on 10 July 1930, the school helped train leaders who then went out into the countryside, teaching spinning, weaving, dyeing, and rug-making.[14] By the 1940s those who yearned for a revival of crafts in Nova Scotia could turn their eyes towards Quebec, where, Gibbon claimed, one found 60,000 looms and 100,000 spinning-wheels busy making fabrics, decorations, and ornaments for country and farm houses.[15] *The Hands Are Sure*, a National Film Board production about the Quebec craft revival, became part of the arsenal of local craft promoters.[16]

The craft revival had so completely succeeded in Quebec that by the 1940s it was making purists afraid that serious cultural damage was being done to crafts traditions. Marius Barbeau, one of the first Canadians to study carefully the tradition of hand-hooked rugs, considered the Quebec craft revival a mixed blessing because early craft forms were damaged by the pressures of the tourism marketplace and by the interventionist state. His language was that of an outraged entropic antimodernism:

Now most of the homespuns, hooked rugs and statuettes offered to tourists are vitiated by the undue haste that goes into their making or by the skimpy materials or poor models used. Teachers, preaching more rapid methods of production to the younger generation, periodicals, printing patterns for handicrafts, with such details as to leave no room for creative initiative; national and provincial exhibitions, placing emphasis on quantity and novelty: all these form part of the same upheaval.

In the last two decades, a well-meant but misleading educational effort has heavily contributed to demoralize handicrafts. Under its tutelage, talent among the weavers has been snuffed out; ancient patterns, in constantly renewing forms in weaving and hooking of rugs, have fallen into discredit; invention and self-reliance among the folk-workers have been branded as futile. In their place were substituted "cartons," patterns and instructions printed in various periodicals. And, as if to introduce a new system, there followed the sale of standard spinning wheels, looms, yarns, tools, manuals on dyes to the rural workers. A centralized control, through the agency of rural clubs, has proved efficient but deadly, in the twenty years of its activities.[17]

Nova Scotian craft revivalists attended not to Barbeau's dire warnings about cultural decay but to the Quebec evidence of economic growth. The centralized control and the tourism-oriented industry denounced by Barbeau were exactly what they were after. They gazed admiringly at the splendid success of Gaspé wood-carving and to the proliferating shops of the Beaupré coast. In the interests of the *bonne entente*, Quebec sent its emissaries to the rest of Canada to spread the good word of the craft revival. Oscar Bériau, the provincial handicrafts organizer, went so far as to foresee the "various races composing our great Dominion" pooling their contributions to create a "truly Canadian popular art" through handicrafts.[18]

New Hampshire was perhaps as influential a model as Quebec for Nova Scotians. There the inauguration of the "League of New Hampshire Arts and Handicrafts" was a direct inspiration for the provincial government's first measures in stimulating crafts. Enthusiasts (like Helen Jean Champion, a notable travel writer) looked to the New Hampshire model, where they found the state's comprehensive 1931 craft survey and its program of encouragement for handcrafts the "most comprehensive plan for the development of home arts and crafts."[19] This plan included the league of arts and crafts, sponsored by the state government, which provided qualified instructors, encouraged the use of local products, and marketed the output. Why not market Nova Scotia crafts the same way, craft enthusiasts asked, especially at a time when visitors were increasingly demanding homespun, woodwork, and iron and other metal work?[20]

Other forces in the handicrafts revival were of local genesis. Handicrafts made some economic sense in a deindustrializing province located at a distance from the most populous markets. As the male breadwinner economy went into a tailspin in the 1920s, women must have searched anxiously for some means of support. This was how the new emphasis on handicraft was remembered in Chéticamp, where the women turned to making carpets as other economic alternatives disappeared. The rise of a tourism economy meant that things that had been produced strictly for use within the household, such as hooked rugs, suddenly had a value in exchange. The emergence of a tourism state meant that promoters began to agitate for home-made souvenirs, lest the spinoff benefits from tourism flow directly out of the province.

The period from 1900 to 1940 should be seen as one in which the elements of the craft revival slowly took shape and began to cohere. Since the nineteenth century, natives in Nova Scotia and Maine had specialized in making splint-ash basketry and had sold such articles in urban markets and to visitors. (The anthropologist Harold Prins argues that this form was an invented tradition that cannot be traced back in the archaeological record to the period before natives made contact with whites, although it came later to be regarded as a quintessential aspect of "Indianness.")[21] Hooked rugs were sold in large numbers to tourists visiting fishing-coves from the 1920s on. It was only in the late 1930s, however, that the tourism-driven handcraft revival became a powerful cultural force. Three projects in particular commanded public attention: at Chéticamp and St. Ann's in Cape Breton, and Terence Bay in Halifax County.

The story of the Chéticamp rugs began in 1927, when an American designer reinvented a local rug-making tradition. At St. Ann's the key activists were A.W.R. Mackenzie, a Scottish-born Celtic reviv-alist, and his partner Angie Mackenzie, who were both seized by the idea that Cape Breton was the cradle of Celtic culture in North America. Their Gaelic College became the focus of annual Scottish mods, and one element within a general "tartanism" whereby a province, less than a third of whose population claimed Scottish origins, nonetheless became more and more Scottish with each passing year.[22] Part of this tartan wave was the Mackenzies' crusade to revive Scottish handicrafts and home industries in Cape Breton, which went under the slogan, "More sheep on every hill and a loom in every home!" This campaign had already borne fruit in 1939, with the founding of the Gaelic College at St. Ann's. The Dennis family, the owners of the Halifax *Herald*, and, despite their relatively recent arrival from England in the late nineteenth century, powerful shapers of neo-nationalist ideologies in interwar Nova Scotia, promoted the "Star of the Sea" experiment at Terence Bay. Thanks to the Halifax newspaper, this village had become a symbol of the disastrous impact of the Depression on fishing communities. The handicrafts revival here provided a testing-ground for theories of Catholic social activism. The Extension Department of St. Francis Xavier University and the Sisters of Charity helped launch a wide-ranging campaign of community uplift, including a house-to-house survey, shipments of fresh milk, the organization of community gardens, and the donation of hundreds of gallons of paint and one hundred barrels of lime for whitewash: the effect was to make the village look "trim, freshly painted and limed and neat in appearance."[23] A craft centre, devoted especially to weaving and woodwork, persisted from the 1930s on, under the aegis of the Star of the Sea Convent and with the backing of Senator W.H. Dennis, the proprietor of the *Herald*. The project waned during the war, when it became more profitable to fish than to make handicrafts, but was revived in following years. Some of its articles were even marketed through Eaton's and Simpson's department stores.[24]

These three "flagship" operations of the craft revival of the 1920s and 1930s were accompanied by other local efforts. Since the late nineteenth century, provincial exhibitions and agricultural fairs, funded in part by the provincial government, had encouraged Nova Scotians to display their "domestic manufactures": in 1880, for example, awards were given at the Provincial Exhibition for the best rag carpet, the best hearth rug, the best patchwork quilt. There were also separate categories for "Indian Work" and "Fine Arts and Ladies Work."[25] In Pubnico, local women were inspired by the exhibitions of the Canadian Handicrafts Guild to participate in newly commercialized craft activities.[26] By the 1940s certain Women's Institutes had already developed specialities; the institute in Belliveau's Cove, for instance, turned out well-known Evangeline Dolls.[27] Henrietta B. Andrews of Cape Breton produced tapestries. As she poignantly explained to the travel writer Clara Dennis in 1941, her reliance on handicrafts had already presented her with a dilemma. A man from Toronto, acting through a Sydney agent, had purchased five of her six tapestries. She had not wanted to sell the sixth, which depicted Ossian hiding in the Highlands of Scotland, with "the Fair Naomi Kneeling by his Side," because it meant so much to her. Still, she was poor, and there was a demand. Would Dennis agree to buy it? The money was urgently needed.[28]

Henrietta Andrews was not alone in seeking money from her humble home industry in a market in which she had precious little bargaining power. A touring public hungry for the crafts of the Folk began to sweep into the fishing villages and other rural hamlets late in the 1920s. The handicrafts of rural women made a tremendous difference as the economic crisis devastated the resource industries. As always with twentieth-century antimodernism, the paradoxes were fascinating. Hungrily searching for emblems of Folk authenticity and the last artifacts of the "dying ways," tourists served as the vanguard of the market. They also transformed the making of rugs from a minor sideline into a mainstay of some fishing families. What became known as "the hooked-mat mania" was an early sign of the potential power of the Nova Scotia handicraft in the urban market of the eastern seaboard and the speed with which local traditions could be swept up and transformed by the sudden fads in North American culture. The handicrafts revivalist Ramsay Traquair rather snobbishly described the organizers of this 1920s cyclone as "commercial dealers, of the lower sort"; the romantic poet Margaret Lathrop Law described them as "antique dealers, interior decorators, and summer cottagers from the States, all possessed of the hooked-mat mania," who, no longer content to wait for the rugmakers to come to them, descended upon the rural Nova Scotians in droves, buying up rugs everywhere, some of which could be "antiqued while you wait; simply plant them for a week or so on any grassy slope of Nova Scotia; sun and shower will do the rest."[29] In exchange for their "tradition," many rugmakers cashed in on a shining slice of modernity: a new piece of linoleum.[30] Hooked rugs became a mainstay not because of age-old tradition-alism but because impoverished people had to find some way to survive the crisis of modern capitalism. As one Chéticamp woman remembers the trade, it was hardly an arrangement between equals:

And there were some people going around with big trucks. They were giving oilcloth for the floor and they'd take the rugs. There was a woman at Point Cross – she was using her house for that. The fellow would come with a load of stuff and leave it there and she would collect the rugs. She would trade the value in rugs. And at last they were trading for clothes, under-clothes, coats for men and women – all traded for rag rugs ... There's a lot of people during the Depression who lived on the rag rugs. They had children and they could get clothes – even if their rugs were worth more. They couldn't sell them. There was nobody to buy rag rugs then. So they would trade for them.[31]

The unemployment of so many male breadwinners in the 1930s had transformed the craft work traditionally undertaken by these women from a supplementary craft into an activity some families required for survival. By 1929 Helen Creighton was praising the making of hooked rugs as "Nova Scotia's great home industry." In Nova Scotia, she remarked, "It is the hooked mat that swells the slender purses of the women who live in the country. In olden days there was little profit in the undertaking, for everybody could do the work, and there was nobody left to buy. It served then as a means of artistic and creative expression and gave a touch of warmth and brightness to the home. To-day, however, tourists clamor for it, and what at one time was merely a pleasant and utilitarian pastime has become a profitable profession."

According to Creighton, this home industry had first blossomed in St. Margaret's Bay, where one Mrs. Baker had sold a rug through a local business. The success of the venture led to a shop named (with due deference to the tourist's thirst for "tradition") "Ye Olde Tyme Hooked Rugs." "Now [in 1929] tourists scour the country to find the sort of mats they like," she remarked. One enterprising distributor had sold $4,000 worth in the past season alone. At Chester, a magnet for American summer visitors, one woman specialized in ship patterns; elsewhere women concentrated on such patterns as "the Boston sidewalk" and floral designs.[32] Many of these Nova Scotia rugs would find their way to the United States, where they would then often be redescribed as "traditional crafts of New England."

For handicrafts revivalists, the period from 1920 to 1940 was one of numerous promising beginnings and meagre conclusions. Towards the end of the period, handicrafts had already started to acquire a certain symbolic status in the definition of the Nova Scotian identity. When the Province of Nova Scotia took over the windows of the Star Building in Montreal for a promotional display in 1940, it took care to place a number of hooked rugs among the model schooners and Nova Scotia flags, and when Charles Mogull of Mogull Studios visited the province to make a scenic film of its leading sights, he was steered towards the craft workers of Chéticamp.[33] "Nova Scotia is famous for its beautiful hand-hooked rugs," provincial tourist propaganda claimed in 1940. "These, with such distinctive items as 'Evangeline' dolls, quaint leaden oxen, miniature eel and lobster traps, curious carved woods and hand-wrought iron novelties, make interesting souvenirs of your visit."[34] The Antigonish Movement (an important movement of Catholic social activism, whose key strategies were cooperatives and adult education) saw handicrafts as fitting within its grassroots vision of cooperative development. Having proclaimed the slogan, "Workers of the world, arise! You need not be proletarians!" they could hardly resist the lure of the craft revival, which seemed the very epitome of their vaunted "third path" between capitalism and socialism.[35]

Yet, for handicrafts revivalists, these were mere beginnings that, by the 1940s, seemed urgently in need of becoming something more than that. A 1942 conference in Antigonish was impressed not by the plans successfully launched but by opportunities missed. This Antigonish Conference, organized by the Extension Department at

St. Francis Xavier on 14 and 15 April 1942, was perhaps the equivalent of the Quebec Revival of 1929. Here, Frank W. Doyle explained in the *Herald*, was a "million-dollar industry awaiting development," one which wartime scarcities had made opportune and even necessary. A handicraft revival in the midst of war could draw upon the under-utilized labour of women and children, and that of men too old or otherwise unfitted for war service.[36] The very presence at the two-day conference of representatives from the Department of Hand-crafts, Quebec, the Department of Rural Reconstruction, Newfound-land, the Interdepartmental Committee of Canadian Handicrafts, and numerous Catholic agencies and movements testified to the province's relative slowness in responding to an idea that had already captivated numerous organizations and governments. The conference concluded with a call for greater state involvement and cries for a return to racial instincts of craft intrinsic to the Nova Scotian character. The instinct of craftsmanship was "in the blood," one speaker urged. Proof of this theory could be found in the United States, where Nova Scotian building contractors had succeeded beyond all expectation. Clearly, "every country boy is born into this world almost with a [jack knife] in his hand and a desire to build." Harnessing a similar racial instinct, Quebec had managed to build a great handicrafts industry. Nova Scotia need only follow its example.[37] Now it was time for the state to act, "so that handicrafts, home crafts and creative arts would in the future have a large and fully merited place in the scene of things in Nova Scotia."[38]

The state was more than happy to respond. Handicrafts repre-sented some very down-to-earth benefits for a government that was attempting to get re-elected. Supporting handicrafts was both pop-ular and inexpensive. By taking a few modestly encouraging steps, the government would win favourable editorials in the Halifax *Herald* and elsewhere.[39] Handicrafts also provided an inexpensive way for the Liberals to respond to some of the social issues raised by the left-wing Co-operative Commonwealth Federation, while simultane-ously appealing to a tourism industry central to its economic strategy. (The replacement of Angus L. Macdonald by A.S. MacMillan in 1940 did not change the government's focus on tourism.) There were votes, and possibly state revenues, to be gained from supporting the looms and lathes of the province. On 18 August 1942 Harold Connolly, the minister of industry and publicity and a tourism zealot, wrote to Mary Black, an expatriate Nova Scotian and authority on handicrafts: "It is important that we get our arts and crafts setup into operation immediately and for that reason it is imperative that we secure the services of a director at once."[40]

MARY BLACK: ''NEW WOMAN'' IN HANDICRAFTS

The recipient of this urgent message, Mary Ellouise Black (1895–1988), was a dynamic and idealistic professional occupational therapist. She is the most fascinating of the various cultural producers to have pursued the craft revival, partly because of her unique position within the state, and partly because she left behind an illuminating series of "diary notes," handwritten extracts from her personal journal that frankly describe the day-to-day decisions that went into the reinvention of the handcrafts of the Folk. Even in this presumably edited form, Black's candid comments on her contemporaries in the state and on the handicrafts revival make revealing reading.

Born on Nantucket Island, Massachusetts, raised in Wolfville, Nova Scotia, and a graduate of the Acadia Ladies' Seminary, Black had distinguished herself as a volunteer during the Great War (for which she was honoured with a life membership in the local Robert Borden Chapter of the IODE).[41] More than Creighton, Black was a "New Woman," a tough-minded, energetic professional. Having moved in American circles, she lacked Creighton's anglophilia and perhaps some of her elitism; her writings are far more down-to-earth and practical, with fewer romantic passages. Yet the two were similar figures, admired each other, and clearly identified each other as allies in a common cause.

Black began her career in Nova Scotia. In the 1920s, like so many other Nova Scotians of her generation, she was compelled to chose between unemployment or outmigration. From 1922 to 1939 she worked as an occupational therapist in a string of American hospitals from Boston to Milwaukee. In the late 1930s she realized a long-held dream and journeyed to rural Sweden, the promised land of the Folk and handicrafts revival.[42] Black made weaving her special area of expertise. Her standards were drawn not from traditions passed down in her own family, which were few, but from her knowledge of European handicrafts. Black would build on this early training to become a recognized international authority on weaving techniques.[43] By 1940 Black wanted to come home to Nova Scotia. Word of the movement to revive Nova Scotia's rural arts and crafts had reached her in Milwaukee, and she started to write letters to anyone in the province who might advance her interests. She took care to describe her connections to a rather generically described rural Folk – the "fishermen, farmers, guides, Indians etc." – she had met in her frequent vacations in the province. She also underlined her family's political credentials: her great-grandfather had been a circuit judge in Nova Scotia, her father had been Grand Master of the Masons, and her brother was employed by the Nova Scotia Liquor Commission in Kentville.[44] She was duly offered the position. By 12 February 1943, Black was on the civil service lists in the new position of Supervisor of Handcrafts in the Department of Industry and Publicity, at an annual salary of $2,800.[45] Black became the senior expert on handicrafts within the bureaucracy until her retirement as "Director of Handcrafts" in 1954.

By the time she arrived in Nova Scotia, Black had an almost utopian liberal vision of the redemptive power of craft in the modern world. She believed that occupational therapy was an excellent way, and frequently the only way, to establish rapport with the mentally ill. It provided the desperately needed bridge back to hopeful life for the returned soldier and the sanatorium patient. Crafts were valuable therapy for the wounded of the modern world. On a much larger scale, crafts could also heal the wounds of damaged regions.

The "craft revival," loosely defined, had been a feature of Nova Scotian life since the 1920s, but in Black's eyes the term, applied to the crafts she encountered on her return to Nova Scotia, would have been wildly inappropriate. The "revival" was merely a modest beginning. When she returned to Nova Scotia in 1943, Black did not find much to admire in the crafts she saw in the province. She explained the paucity of fine handicrafts in the utilitarian vocabulary she found congenial. The early Nova Scotians had simply been too concerned with material survival to worry much about gracious living, she reasoned, and therefore their crafts were unrefined and not very distinguished. 'Weaving in Nova Scotia never reached the refinement or beauty which it did in the United States,' she informed Charles Bruce, the novelist and poet.

There is no comparison between the weaving found in Nova Scotia and the beautiful weaving of the Penn. Dutch country, the deep South and the summer and winter weaves of the Swedish settlers of the Connecticut valley. Drawing my own conclusions from what I have found in N.S., I believe our early settlers were so concerned with keeping themselves clothed and warm that they had no time or means to develop beauty. Much of the weaving in the deep South was done by slaves; itinerant weavers travelled through the New England states and followed the settlers west. With a much more thickly populated country than our Atlantic Provinces money circulated more freely and better materials and cloth could be brought in from England and France. In all my travels in N.S. I have never been able to track down any but the simple tabby or twill blankets or linens ... The women were so tired of the everlasting spinning and weaving that they threw their looms away and welcomed the commercial weaving with open arms. Had it not been for those living in rural, inaccessible areas, hand weaving would have become a lost art.[46]

Even the "few overshot patterns" unearthed in Cape Breton (actually a large collection, which has excited other authorities of the history of weaving) did not impress Black. "I do not think there was very much weaving, other than homespun wool and linen and the mixture of the two done in Nova Scotia," she reflected in 1966. "Life here for the early settlers was pretty tough and they had little time for anything but bare necessities."[47] "By piecing together bits of information gathered from here and there," she wrote in 1951, "the historian concludes that the rigors, necessities, and limitations of this new land resulted in the production of only the most utilitarian types of weaving – the linsey-woolsey for everyday wear and the blankets for the beds, with the choice wool reserved for the family and the tags and rough bits spun and woven up for the doubtful comfort of the hired man and the itinerant traveller."[48] Like some of the romantic handicraft revivalists in David Whisnant's *All That Is Native and Fine*, Black seems to have viewed local weaving as uninteresting because it simply reproduced standard patterns and did not evoke the creativity of the individual craft worker.[49] (Here was a further contrast with the collectors of ballads, who preferred stable and "original" forms.) Black clearly believed that the history of handicraft in Nova Scotia provided, at best, a rather meagre legacy for the twentieth-century handicrafts revival. This conviction, founded as it was on her firm belief in her own high professional standards, gave her freedom to invent new craft traditions where the old ones had fallen short.

Distinctly unimpressed by the past record of handicrafts in Nova Scotia, Black viewed their present situation no more favourably. Her first impression of local crafts was obtained in a visit to the shops of Halifax in 1943, where she found a "few pieces of woodenware[,] unpainted furniture, and few pieces of pottery, but nothing of interest."[50] Of a handicraft class she observed later the same year at the Mount St. Bernard convent in Antigonish, she wrote tersely: "no originality, designs poor."[51] Native children at the residential school in Shubenacadie did pottery work that was "mechanically" good, "but every piece is [poured] into a mould made from a piece of commercial pottery."[52] Elsewhere in rural Nova Scotia, as she learned from L.A. DeWolfe, a leading provincial educational authority, teachers had no interest in crafts and were not encouraged to develop expertise in the field by their students' parents. Handicrafts were stigmatized. "One desire of parents is to get children educated and away from manual labor, any hand work is looked down upon," Black observed. Given this feeling against handicrafts in rural communities, she feared that any plans for a revival of crafts on a large scale might be unrealistic.[53] On 26 September 1944 she visited the Lunenburg County Fair. She wrote that she rather liked the "nice traditional + nicely hooked mats," then exclaimed, "but oh the needlework and crocheting!"[54] Mary Black had a vivid sense of starting almost from scratch. The Nova Scotia handicraft tradition had to be made, not found.

For a woman to undertake this project within a male bureaucracy proved difficult. Black and Creighton shared somewhat similar experiences in the new cultural sphere. Both of them were among the first women in the province to drive automobiles. Black took up driving so early, in fact, that she was required to paint on her own licence plate.[55] Whatever the uncertainties and difficulties Creighton faced as a consequence of her indirect relationship with the distant museum, Black's position as a rare woman bureaucrat within a traditional civil service was probably even less to be envied. It may be that this difference in institutional context goes some distance to explaining why Black reflected on gender politics so much more consistently than Creighton did.

Black's Handcrafts and Home Industries Division was the first branch of the government in which a majority of senior staff was female. Of the seven individuals in the division in 1948, six were women.[56] Black was aware of gender issues, and worked in a cultural field crisscrossed by gender lines. Metalwork and woodcarving were thought to be men's work, and Black's December 1947 report noted the need for an instructor "in metal and woodcarving (preferably a man)."[57] Black did not seem particularly concerned about dividing other crafts on the basis of their "appropriate" gender. While most of the numerous weavers' guilds were made up of women, one Glace Bay group, formed under the direction of Mrs Wilson Grant of the United Weavers' Guild, was made up of young married couples; "the husbands," Black reported admiringly, "actually taking more interest than their wives."[58] In the special class held for ten boys in the fishing community of Little Dover, weaving was seen as a means of correcting the seasonal variations of the inshore fishery: "Special instruction in weaving was given to ten boys at Little Dover in an effort to get them on a productive basis. These boys spend only two or three months a year at fishing and are idle the remaining months. The response of the group was very good."[59] Although the male weaver had been a common figure in nineteenth-century Nova

Scotia, particularly in Scottish areas, the activity had come to be identified as a women's domestic activity in the twentieth century.

No less than folklore, the new handicrafts program was ambiguous in its implications for gender relations. On the one hand it brought women into the state bureaucracy in unprecedented positions of authority, probably represented an opportunity for rural women to achieve a measure of financial independence, and ostensibly honoured and valued crafts which had come to be defined as "women's work" and which were now seen as crucial to the province's tourism effort. On the other hand it did not give women secure or very remunerative positions within the bureaucracy, nor did it change women's subordinate position in the household.

Black herself saw the handicrafts movement as something that fell far short of a breakthrough for women. She found wartime Halifax a difficult place for a woman, "pot black at night + no protection from police."[60] Her own department, variously named the Department of Industry and Publicity and the Department of Trade and Industry, was scarcely more congenial than the war-darkened city. Black was ground down by its entrenched sexism. "What a nasty sarcastic cuss!" she remarked of her deputy minister, who had lectured her about the need to commercialize crafts, but offered no concrete suggestions.[61] "A pr. [pair] of despicable males," she exclaimed, recalling a 1951 discussion with her minister and deputy minister regarding handicrafts. "They had nothing constructive to offer – chief interest was to criticize. Placing responsibility on me but no actual authority. No terms of reference. Do not even know what has been accomplished."[62] Black condemned the commanding officer of *HMCS Cornwallis*, the host of one of the "Craftsmen at Work" exhibitions, as a "four-flusher" for having shoved an important handicrafts exhibition into a filthy building, "full of mice and the downstairs rooms, [which] according to the noises that came from them all night might well be described as a w-house [whorehouse]! I complained about the dirt, mice + noise but got nowhere with Martin [the commanding officer] except to have him invite me to move to his home. Nothing doing, told him I'd prefer to stay with my own crowd."[63] It seemed sadly appropriate that, shortly before her retirement – which the province did virtually nothing to mark – Black spent her time at the office party fending off the unwelcome advances of a senior male in the bureaucracy, whom she described as "quite 'fresh' so much so I refused to dance with him."[64]

Inappropriate behaviour at office parties was the insult added to the chronic injury of an inadequate budget. Black's appointment and the handicrafts program in general smacked of tokenism. Giving even minor sums to worthy crafts producers seemed beyond the state's frugal budget. For example, the proprietor of a woollen mill, a "very delightful old craftsman," produced lovely wool, well suited to the production of tweed. Black's minister, Harold Connolly (who never seems to have supported the craft revival), refused him a grant of a mere $500. An exasperated Black found the Nova Scotia government guilty of a "stupidity" that was "shortsighted."[65]

When Mary Black left her post in December 1954, she had the sense that had she gone on for an indefinite period, nobody in the Department of Trade and Industry would have noticed. Not one word had been said to her about her going, nor about her successor.[66] She left thoroughly embittered with her experience in the Handcrafts Division. Her experience was not that unusual: the provincial government's cautious steps into the cultural sphere frequently took the form of well-intentioned experiments that inevitably shrivelled into underfunded corpses, and the few innovators who aimed at a new cultural role for the state worked without much support from the Liberal government. Black's ambitious program of craft development would have required far more than a division with only seven members in 1946 and ten in 1950.[67]

Black found the Department of Industry and Publicity an intensely frustrating place. Harold Connolly, the minister, gave her no terms of reference "nor any specific directions as to procedure," Black later recalled, "and altho [although] I outlined what I felt should be attempted little was said as to how to go about it or where to start. I had the distinct feeling that they could not care less whether or not N.S. had a Handcrafts program – and I found out later how right I was!"[68] Connolly distanced himself from handicrafts, and forbade Black to contact him directly.[69] Black never forgave Connolly for his indifference, even after he tried to make amends: "He had never been in sympathy with, nor interested in Hcfts [handicrafts] and on several occassions [occasions] was quite mean + nasty in his remarks + expressed dissatisfaction, yet would never state any terms of reference nor outline plan nor would discuss the program."[70] And when Connolly did pay close attention, Black suspected partisan motives. In May 1949 Harold Connolly's secretary telephoned Black with instructions to place a large order for mercury yarns. She was to reorder the yarns monthly through one Mervyn Johnson. This type of yarn was of little use to her. Nonetheless, possessed of a certain political instinct, she realized that she should submit the order, and did so. Was it merely a coincidence that Mervyn Johnson nominated Harold Connolly as the Halifax North Liberal candidate? Mary Black hinted that it was no coincidence by attaching the press clipping announcing the nomination to her complaints about the worthless yarns in her diary notes.[71] In her experience, the expanding "tourist state" was warrened with patronage appointments. In Amherst, a private gift shop complemented the Tourist Bureau. "It appears," Black remarked caustically, "this shop is 'let out' to favorite political workers regardless as to whether they have any knowledge of Hcfts [handicrafts] or not." Black obtained the gift shop for her own candidate, but she complained that it was later "given to 'political interests.'"[72]

All in all, Black perceived the department as a viper's nest. And the world outside was only slightly more receptive to her ideals. Black saw numerous competing and contradictory interests at play in the politics of the provincial "craft revival." Proponents of Antigonish cooperatives and adult education had an interest in any craft revival, and Black thought they eyed her suspiciously, fearing she might undermine their own programs of craft instruction. (They had good reason to distance themselves from Black, for she did not believe their techniques of craft instruction were sound).[73] The Department of Education, which did teach some handicrafts in its manual training program, had (according to Black) "rather ancient" ideas.[74] Black could hardly avoid intruding upon the turf claimed by provincial artists. A spokesperson for the Society of Fine Arts smugly advised her that she would get nowhere unless she worked under the society's guidance.[75] The Nova Scotia College of Art and Design wanted some sort of alliance, and Black discerned that Donald MacKay, the principal, did not like the idea of any other group handling handicrafts. Later she reflected that she and MacKay were always "poisonously polite to each other."[76] Other figures in the field seemed pathologically suspicious of her.[77] The world of Nova Scotia handicrafts was fragmented; how could it ever be turned to the interests of the state and raised to Black's artistic standards?

Black had two answers. One was to coordinate design and production so as to improve the quality and increase the quantity of craft commodities. The other was to reform and greatly extend the marketing of handicrafts. On the production side, Nova Scotians had to be taught to produce quality handicrafts. Only extensive technical training, expert assistance in design, and the competitive stimulus provided by exhibitions would enable the province to produce a range of attractive craft articles. On the marketing side, Nova Scotians had to learn how to sell their handicrafts more aggressively by placing them with such large department stores as Simpson's and Eaton's, or by developing their own gift shops for the expanding tourist trade.

In a "ten-point program" of 1944, Black developed her case for handicrafts on the utilitarian principle of "the greatest good for the greatest number." Handicrafts would improve living standards, provide employment for wounded veterans, and assist remote and undeveloped parts of the province (such as the troubled coalfields). Such social welfare objectives could best be met through "a central bureau for coordinated efforts and for the dissemination of information and exchange of ideas to those interested in Handcrafts, and to give instruction where needed." Exhibitions, both rural and urban, travelling exhibits, state-trained lecturers, official bibliographies, and lists of materials, equipment, and tools: these were to be coordinated by the central bureau. The bureau would standardize prices, dictate standards of design and workmanship, and inspect all articles made and offered for sale by groups or individuals under its sponsorship, which, if they met the provincial standard, would be awarded an official seal of approval. The state's role would also encompass experiments on native materials (such as shells, stones, and berries) and an experimental centre where novel handicrafts could be developed.[78] As the central architect of the craft revival in Nova Scotia, Black always insisted that the economic and cultural motivations for the movement had to be indissolubly linked.

Not much of this ten-point program was ever realized, yet Black's handicrafts revival cannot fairly be considered a failure. Her central bureaucratic achievement was to establish the Handcrafts Division as the Nova Scotia centre for crafts. She succeeded in bringing a wide range of international handicrafts information to the province. In 1945 exchange bulletins were received from Quebec, Vermont, Pennsylvania, and the American Craftsmen Co-operative Council of New York, all of which helped the centre instruct and guide Nova Scotians in the development of crafts.[79] In 1944 the department became a member of the Canadian Handicrafts Guild, which placed it in direct contact with "all current trends and developments on Canadian Handcrafts," and it reported extensive links with the American Craftsmen's Co-operative Council Inc., of New York City, with which it ultimately hoped to establish business contacts.[80] In May 1945 the department (in cooperation with the art college) brought the Canadian Handicrafts All Canada Needlework Exhibit to Zwicker's Art Gallery in Halifax. The exhibit (until it was hurriedly packed up and sent back to Montreal in response to the city's postwar riots) elicited a favourable response.[81] The department maintained a small library of international craft books which were loaned out to crafts enthusiasts. It also imported inspirational films on handicraft revivals.[82]

Black also succeeded in publicizing handicrafts. In her 1945 report she estimated that she had travelled 12,000 miles and spoken to 1,000 individuals in the previous year.[83] Perhaps her key pedagogical tool was the annual craft show – the "Craftsmen-at-Work" exhibits that became part of the annual provincial calendar. The first "Craftsmen-at-Work" exhibit took place at Simpson's department store in Halifax in 1945. It was a glowing success:

We worked all day Sunday and by night everything was up, the catalogue made up ready for the printers and all under control. Opened at 9 A.M. Had many very interested visitors, many of them like myself greatly surprised at the work being done by Nova Scotians. Mrs Manning Ells, of Port Williams loaned us a very large Cheticamp hooked rug (At least 12 × 18 Ft) which was made especially for the Ells home. This was the background the rest of the articles hung and grouped around this. With hundreds of service people at large in Halifax having nothing to do now the war was over, we had a much larger attendance than we would have had otherwise.[84]

After another successful craft exhibit in 1946, Black decided that the exhibition should be moved annually to a different locality in the interests of giving handicrafts maximum publicity. The exhibit moved to Sydney in 1947, to Amherst (1948), Yarmouth (1949), Truro (1950), Lunenburg (1951), Halifax (1952), Antigonish (1954), and *HMCS Cornwallis* (1955). Perhaps the most historically significant exhibit was not one of these annual exhibits, but a special show put on for the Nova Scotia Sheep Breeders' Association for their 1953 meeting in Truro.[85]

The division also promoted handicrafts through its own publications. In January 1943 it began to issue a quarterly bulletin, *Handcrafts*, which was sent to interested persons free of charge; its mailing list rose from 250 in 1945 to 9,000 in 1952. A handwritten report on the Handcrafts Program for the fiscal year ending in March 1952 noted 567 office interviews, 134 field interviews, the receipt of 2,975 letters, the loaning out of 495 books and 294 designs, and the annual rental of 24 looms per month.[86] "It is most interesting and gratifying to be able to report that there has been a spontaneous, whole hearted response to the Handcrafts and Home Industries program as inaugurated by the Provincial Government in February, 1943," Black wrote in her annual report for that year. "Contrary to expectations, individuals and groups have sought the services of the Department and no time or effort has been required to stimulate interest."[87]

Given Black's own interests, it was perhaps inevitable that weaving would dominate the handicrafts revival. Weaving was by far the most popular Nova Scotia craft. In 1947 no fewer than thirty-three groups were conducting classes.[88] In her 1947 report, Black singled out four outstanding groups: the "L'Artisan" group on the Clare Shore (who were finding "an excellent sale for well made articles of design and heritage native to their race"), active groups in Digby and Pictou, and the Gaelic Foundation tartan-weaving program at St. Ann's.[89]

There were more than twenty weaving groups (which often took the quaintly anti-modern name of "guild") with about four hundred members in the province in the mid-1940s. Many were active in communities devastated by the decline of coal: guilds could be found in Port Morien, Glace Bay, Reserve Mines, and New Waterford. Others were found in Canning, Halifax, and Beaver Bank.[90] The revival was particularly marked in Cape Breton. "At Ingonish Beach, one of Cape Breton's little east shore fishing villages, a group of ten women took a three week course at the looms under Elizabeth King of Annapolis Royal and then formed the 'Cape Smokey Weavers Guild' which meets to discuss techniques and designs for homespun clothes and materials which they hope to make for the winter." It was part of a more general pattern, noted the Halifax *Star* in an article entitled "Strides Taken by Handcraft Industry," of many new weavers' guilds and their gradual move onto the commercial field, "where they will offer only the best materials, produced from wool to wearer in the same locality."[91] Some groups, like the Halifax Weavers' Guild, which began with a nucleus of only 24 people on 11 February 1944 and quickly expanded, defined its aesthetic mission clearly: "to stimulate interest in the technical development of hand weaving, to encourage weavers in general to set the highest possible standards for their work, with emphasis on careful selection and suitability of materials, combination of colours and design, superiority of workmanship."[92] The division coordinated the ordering of looms from the Quebec manufacturers (the only Canadian sources of supply) for such groups.[93] Over one hundred such looms were in operation in 1948, according to the division's estimate, in addition to the two-hundred-odd placed through the Handcrafts program and its weaving classes.[94] In a climate of state encouragement and economic instability, the revival of weaving apparently held an economic appeal that extended to persons other than its middle-class organizers.

Other crafts were less important in the revival. Although leatherwork had received a tremendous stimulus in the war (as a "masculine" craft well suited to the purposes of rehabilitating military men), Mary Black was severely critical of both the quality and the exorbitant prices of the leather articles.[95] At Malagawatch and Marble Mountain, there were groups devoted to quilting, knitting, and rug-hooking;

rug-hooking predominated on the Western Shore, while at Central East Pubnico, groups turned to rug-hooking, quilting, and the making of stuffed toys. The formation of the Atlantic Woodcarvers' Group, which claimed a membership of fifty in 1945, also suggested the further development of local crafts.[96] Pottery activities (under the supervision of the Extension Department of the Nova Scotia Technical College) were also expanding, although Black was never very confident about the quality of local efforts in this area.[97]

Local leadership was important in the craft revival movement. In Shelburne the craft revival depended very much on Raymond Standefer, a navy veteran and woodcarver who held a major interest in a local tourist inn, which he had "localized" with decorative panels and figureheads. In 1946 he secured the active support of the town newspaper, the *Coast Guard*, in establishing a craft centre. From the start, the craft revival and tourism were linked; the centre was seen "as a measure to promote industry in the home and as a tourist attraction." High hopes were attached to the centre, which was visualized as serving all of Shelburne County. It was to serve two purposes. First, it was to "promote a new industry in which there is no limitation." Second, it was to "provide a drawing card for tourists who are interested in seeking articles, hand-made, of a high degree of skill at a localized centre." Here was "a measure to promote industry in the home. Its purpose will be to promote the skilled crafts and its arts and the sale of its resultant products." The *Coast Guard* proclaimed its firm support for the venture. "We wish to stress the fact that we, who are sponsoring the plan seek no profits; our aim is to create something worthwhile for the craftsmen of this country."[98]

Such local manifestations of the craft revival required the coordination, inspiration, and pedagogy of the state if they were ever to amount to a coherent plan of development. Leadership was to come from Halifax. In addition to the indispensable bureaucrats of the division, a newly coordinated and rationalized voluntary handcrafts sector began to play a role. Perhaps the most promising sign was the formation in 1945 of the Nova Scotia Handcrafts Guild, organized at the Lord Nelson Hotel as part of the Exhibition Week program.[99] In 1947, after meetings with the acting deputy minister of the department, the guild was given the green light for its legal incorporation.[100] Working craftspeople, hobbyists, gift shop managers, and any other interested parties were eligible for membership. It was a revealing way of defining the guild's constituency, which stressed economic considerations over those of aesthetics.

From 1939 to 1951 a craft revival, to which Black had made a central pedagogical and organizational contribution, had undoubtedly occurred, and an impressive network of handicraft groups and interests had emerged. There were the large guilds - the Nova Scotia Craftsmen's Guild and its affiliates, the Metal Arts and Potters' Guilds. There were weavers' guilds in Halifax and in Yarmouth. Numerous Women's Institutes were also enthusiastic about craft development. From the division's perspective, these local groups needed to be represented by one committee in order to create a craft centre that would standardize production methods, buy materials in bulk, and undertake to promote craft products. The state was required to help coordinate the development, for even if strong guilds and associations eventually grew up within the province, they would still require a government subsidy.[101]

The division's function in this craft movement was to inspire, to instruct, and, perhaps above all, to publicize – to make the craft movement come alive in the public media. It did so with flair. The craft revival was called into being, and its images were driven into public consciousness, through planted articles in *Saturday Night, Maclean's, Canadian Women's Journal, Family Herald and Weekly Star, House Beautiful*, and *Canadian Art*.[102] The department's own publication, *Handcrafts*, served to instruct local artisans and to publicize Nova Scotia as a craft centre. On 29 September 1945 a film on Nova Scotia handicrafts was given its first showing. Created by the provincial filmmaker Margaret Perry with the department's extensive cooperation, the film was received enthusiastically by Black, who pronounced the show "very good" and predicted that it would "aid our program immensely."[103] From 1947 on, *Where to Buy Handcrafts in Nova Scotia* promoted local craft outlets for the tourist trade.[104] Black also prepared publicity on provincial doll makers for broadcast on CBC shortwave to Europe.[105] Black even began to worry about over-publicizing the craft revival and creating expectations among tourists that the local crafts producers could not meet. "It has been more of a problem to keep publicity under control than to seek it," she observed in 1949, "as it has been felt that there are not enough articles being produced at the present time to warrant much advertising."[106] In New Brunswick, the pottery studio of Erica and Kjeld Deichmann, two emigrants from Denmark, was attracting so many tourists every day, thanks to the massive publicity bestowed on their enterprise by the National Film Board, *Maclean's, Weekend Magazine*, and the travel bureau, that a move to a new studio in Sussex seemed advisable by 1956.[107] In Nova Scotia, Scottish handcrafts at St. Ann's achieved a similar popularity.

HANDICRAFTS AS IDEOLOGY: UTILITARIAN PLANNING, NATURALIST ESSENTIALISM

The handicrafts revival both differed from and resembled the emergence of folklore. The hand of the state was everywhere in the handicrafts movement, as it was not in folklore, and the entire process seemed to require a level of "invention" that was foreign to the recovery and selection of folk music and lore. In both instances, however, cultural goods that had once been produced primarily for use were transformed into articles for exchange in a capitalist market. No less than the folksongs newly brought into the matrix of individual rights and royalties, handicrafts were revolutionized: once created at home on a largely non-commercial basis, or (to a much less extent) as survivals of an older urban economy rendered unprofitable by industrial capitalism, they were now fully integrated into possessive individualism and modern exchange relations. Like the folksong, the handcrafted article had a twofold significance: as a commodity in the market economy, and as a symbol of the Golden Age of the Folk.

Advertising innocence, marketing the "pre-industrial," bringing originality to a vast anonymous public starved for a particle of authenticity: this craft revival demonstrates, as clearly as any other mechanism of Innocence, the workings of its central logic – the commodification of forms considered pre-capitalist, folk, and "authentic," whose appeal lay precisely in the fact that they seemed to come from a time before twentieth-century capitalism. The invention of a "distinctively Nova Scotian" handicrafts tradition in the second quarter of the twentieth century was of a piece with so many other acts of retrieval and redescription: a Gemeinshaftlicht vocabulary of family, community, and intimacy made (through state policy and the conscious imposition of an ideology of absolute artistic standards) accessible to the Gesellschaft of modern capitalism, an innocence cancelled, preserved, and transformed in and through the market and the tourist gaze.

At the same time, noting a similarity between what was happening in folklore and handicrafts is not the same as arguing that the two processes followed identical paths. Black herself was an ideologically anomalous figure, and her craft revival a fascinatingly different process from Creighton's campaign for folklore. (Black, in contrast to Creighton, rarely wrote generally about her underlying perspective on her activities; therefore, our sense of her ideological position must be inferred from texts written for very different pragmatic purposes.)

Black confounds our expectations of what a craft revivalist should be about. With other inventors of traditions, a certain romanticism, however compromised by practical realities, prompted an ideal of finding in Nova Scotia a haven from the iron logic of modernity. This can certainly be seen in Creighton's impassioned conservatism, but it was not evident to any great extent in the thought of Mary Black. Others fled to culture from the market; her strategy was to bind the culture and the marketplace ever closer together. She was a pioneer of planned consumerism, a practical, pragmatic, liberal reformer for whom crafts were never some lost Atlantis of childlike spontaneity. In this she perhaps more closely personified the Scandinavian practice of enlisting craft knowledge for modern industrial design than an articulate Nova Scotian antimodernism. Crafts were socially therapeutic not because they were somehow outside the modern cash nexus, but precisely to the extent that they were embedded within it.

In her role as the publicist of the handicrafts revival, Mary Black understood that the appeal of the newly invented tradition of craft resided largely in an antimodern reverence for older and better ways. Mary Black could rise to the occasion and summon up the image of the unspoiled fisherfolk, whose primitive and innocent response to nature could be incorporated in modern handicraft designs.

It may be difficult for persons in contact with modern art in our nation's capital or larger cities to understand our approach here in Nova Scotia to the design problem, but once knowing and working with our craftsmen we come to understand their point of view. More than once at our annual Craftsmen-at-Work Exhibition have groups of trained craftsmen, graduates of schools and colleges in Canada, England, and the United States, [been] seen to listen spellbound while some woman from a remote farm or fishing village described her craft. The uncomplicated living and thinking which we need so desperately in our world today is expressed by these women who have experienced on the one hand the gentle restfulness of a smiling nature and on the other the sometimes desperate fight for survival against her cruel uncompromising rages. They have lived close to the soil, the sea, and the forest.[108]

In this passage Black demonstrates her mastery of the vocabulary of antimodernism. Contemporaries were certainly not slow to note the resemblance between her activities and Creighton's. The Kentville *Advertiser* remarked that one of Black's "abiding interests ... was to discover examples of craftspeople untouched by modern notions," just as Creighton had done.[109]

This was plausible, in a sense. The craft revival was about recovering something vaguely pre-modern, and it fit well within a general cultural pattern. Yet neither its commander-in-chief, Black, nor its foot soldiers, the craftspeople, seemed to have spent much time, as good antimodernists should have done, agonizing about the erosion of authenticity in modern society. Sometimes Black did hunt for "authentic craftspeople" and sought to promote them, in a Quest of the Folk parallel to Creighton's. She shared with Creighton a confident sense of being able to distinguish the genuine from the spurious on the basis of international standards. Yet whereas an entropic sensibility seems to have been very much part of Creighton's vision, it was not in evidence either in Black's writing or, more important, in her practice. For Black, in contrast to Creighton, authentic essence was not really there to be "discovered." *Authenticity had to be created.* The state, through its program of handicrafts, could teach its citizens how to be authentic Nova Scotian Folk – how, in particular, to respond correctly to the natural landscape around them.

Thus the irony was that, although Black's (successful) effort to establish a handicraft tradition in Nova Scotia fed directly into antimodernism (what better evidence could one have of the province's "older and better ways" than the presence of independent artisans happily pursuing their trades in defiance of mechanization and the twentieth century?), she was not herself an antimodernist. She was a liberal progressive professional, guided by ideals of efficiency, competitiveness, moral therapy, and commerce. In her vision, handicrafts were not in any sense to be seen as havens in a heartless commercial world. They were to be fully integrated into the market, and those that were not viable on those terms had no claims on public sympathy or support. Black was firmly attached to a professional, businesslike approach to handicrafts. She evinced remarkably little nostalgia for simpler days and older ways, many of which had produced work far beneath her aesthetic standards.

The tension between using supposedly age-old forms to slake the twentieth-century consumer's modern thirst for authenticity was nicely caught in the word "Handcrafts" itself. Black gave two reasons why "Handcrafts" (not "Handicrafts") was the keyword of her Nova Scotian career. One was an implicitly antimodernist argument. She and others in her division had simply liked the older form, "Handcraft," better – they preferred its archaic sound. The second, more substantial, and quite contradictory reason was that "Handcrafts" sounded "more like an industry," whereas "handicrafts" sounded "more like a 'side line.'"[110] The selection of the old word was thus linked, through a peculiar logic, to the new industrial purposes the crafts were supposed to fill.

This is both familiar and very different ground. It is familiar because we are once again dealing with the marketing of authentic essence. It is different because Black believed that this essence had to be created, virtually ex nihilo, through a process of state-directed professional development. To produce *Nova Scotian* handicrafts (as opposed to the actually existing handicrafts produced for generations by rural people in Nova Scotia) required state cultural intervention. Nova Scotians could not learn how to be Nova Scotians in the world of handicrafts by themselves, which is why so much of Black's energy would be spent on importing, and then keeping, European handicraft producers in Nova Scotia. The Europeans held the keys to Nature which untrained Nova Scotians themselves were unlikely to find on their own.

At what goal did the provincial handicraft revival aim? As an occupational therapist, Black formulated her purpose in therapeutic terms: Nova Scotians needed handicrafts because they had a "distinct group problem to be dealt with – a problem of inadequacy and defeatism." Handicrafts were a kind of social therapy. They would rescue individuals and groups from the maw of neurosis, despair, and maladjustment. In a 1938 article on "The Therapeutics of Weaving," Black, then an occupational therapist at the State Hospital in Ypsilanti, Michigan, had argued that weaving could help the retarded, patients with destructive tendencies, and patients who were overactive, restless, elated, or otherwise maladjusted.[111] Could one not apply the same idea to a much larger group – the historically defeated Nova Scotians? Yes, Black reported, in an enthusiastic letter to the *American Journal of Occupational Therapy*: "A program that seemed comparatively simple at first glance, in its concept of commercialism and culture, began to take on a deeper meaning as the large group broke up into smaller groups and small groups of people who became individuals – individuals with problems as acute as those suffered by many hospitalized persons." She reported that one "self-centred, definitely psycho-neurotic individual" in Nova Scotia had, through the building up of home industry, "become a most successful business woman. The latent talents that laid undeveloped for years have been given an outlet that has completely changed her whole personality." Another Nova Scotian woman had been saved from chronic alcoholism. In contrast with her American work in the hospitals, here in Nova Scotia the quality of the product was a primary consideration: and the social problems of "inadequacy and defeatism" were to be rectified when high-quality articles found a ready sale. Commerce in handicrafts was thus a form of regional therapy.[112] "I have always had a firm conviction that our ultimate salvation, both National and individual in [is] through the constructive use of our two good God given hands," Mary Black had written to the president of St. Francis Xavier in 1942[113] – but on the basis of this "firm conviction" Black proceeded not to a romance of the simple life, but to a fervent belief in the redemptive powers of the market.

The core of Black's craft ideology was a combination of professionalism and liberal individualism. She shared with Creighton, and virtually all the interwar antimodernists, a very low opinion of collectivism in general and labour in particular. In May 1945 Black reported on a visit to Cape Breton: "Talked with group in Glace Bay re. starting some classes. Made arrangements to give 2 weaving classes. Mrs Wilson Grant was one of the organizers. My first experience with coal miners families. I got to know a number of them quite well. They felt it was always their 'right' and never a privilece [privilege] to have things."[114]

Four years later she detected a defective individualism in fishing communities. Although the fisherfolk had long occupied a central position in middle-class dreams of the craft revival, Black reported that "our experience has been people won't show interest if effort made to make them do it. Groups who apply are far superior we have as many groups applying as we can handle."[115] For Black, the invention of crafts should benefit those who organized themselves to take advantage of them. This was emphatically not a social welfare program. She observed in 1949 that those who were unsuccessful in the marketplace "usually had an inferior product, wanted too high a price, had made no attempt to contact markets, or were uncertain or late with deliveries."[116] For the liberal progressive, it was up to the individual to help him- or herself. The state would provide resources and assist in marketing. It would insist on quality control through moral suasion. Ideally, it would back up this moral suasion with surveillance and discipline. Rather than entrust quality control to the craft workers or the somewhat undiscriminating market, Black anticipated a state inspection program, and looked for her model of handicraft "panopticism" not to the prison-towers of Jeremy Bentham (which Michel Foucault has made so famous), but the more commercialized, gender-specific, and probably more pervasive capitalist model of the Duncan Hines restaurant inspectors. "The Duncan Hines inspectors are never known. They visit eating places and report back directly to the association which in turn advises the eating place that they are eligible for listing in 'Good Eating.'"[117] We are light years away, in this admiration of surveillance, from any nostalgic notion of restoring the freedom, spontaneity, and domesticity of the "older ways."

Black's new handicrafts were to be, first and foremost, business enterprises. Their cultural value was realized in business success. "The progress has been most gratifying," Harold Connolly, Black's minister, reported in 1945. (One suspects the deeply sceptical Connolly was merely echoing Black.) "Old arts and crafts have been revived and the progress made to date will doubtless continue. In this revival we are aiming at quality. Our first thought is to make the crafts commercially worthwhile to the people of the rural districts. If we can succeed in improving their revenues we can then proceed to the cultural, upon which emphasis is laid in some quarters."[118] If Black was not literally the author of his words, she might as well have been. Unless Nova Scotian craftspeople assured merchants of a steady stream of good souvenirs, the shelves would be filled with Asian-made products, some of them stamped "Made in Nova Scotia." "The apathy and inertia on the part of some individuals and groups in grasping the opportunities offered them is, at times, most discouraging," Black complained.[119] Throughout her career in Nova Scotia she encouraged craft producers to assist the workings of the market mechanism, to guarantee the smooth flow of craft products from the artisan to the merchant. She diagnosed the problem as one of inexperience. The "apparent lack of co-operation" between the "producing craftsmen" and the "retail outlets" could not be blamed, she reasoned in 1949, on either group:

There is still much to be desired and worked for in the establishing of better understanding between the producing craftsmen and the retail outlets. Blame for this apparent lack of co-operation cannot be laid at the door of either group. Both are new in the business, many of the shops are endeavouring to operate without capital and with little knowledge of marketing and the craftsmen, on their part, have not fully realized the necessity of filling orders accurately and on time. It is felt also that they do not fully realize the extent of the potential markets open to them. The craftsman producing a well styled, well executed article had difficulty in keeping his orders filled.[120]

From her perspective, "the marketing of the craftsmen's products" was the "most serious problem with which the Division is concerned."[121]

Her market assumptions were written into her specific prescriptions for policy. Romantics had seen (and still do see) one of the great attractions of craft production as being the integration of workplace and home, work and recreation, the public and the private realms. In contrast to the alienated wage worker who had to abandon his or her home and family for hours on end, the artisan (as wistfully imagined by the urban romantic) was a person for whom the pace of work was determined by the nature of the task at hand, and who worked within the warm and friendly confusion of the household or workshop where rigid lines between home and work were not drawn. Whatever the plausibility of this vision of "pre-industrial labour" – which unrealistically forgets the role of the market economy in enforcing deadlines and exerting pressures – it left Black cold. Crafts-people selling from the home, or guilds selling from their centres of production, should, she argued (in a programmatic statement of the 1940s) sell their products in the antiseptic settings twentieth-century consumers demanded:

1. A special room or building with an entrance directly from the street should be set up and retained for the sale of handcrafts;

2. There should be no visible signs of living in the room or building nor sight of household activities being carried on through open doors;

3. There should not be any mingling of animals [or] children with customers. Premise and goods must be clean and goods attractively displayed, preferably in cases.

4. Sale of goods should be restricted to own products of which a fair size stock must be carried at such times as the outlet is advertised as being open.[122]

Such modern marketing methods effectively cleansed the craft product of the taint of humble labour. The product's beauty could be appreciated abstractly, without the distraction of its real conditions of production in a (household or workshop) labour process. It could become a purer, better commodity if it were decontextualized, freed from the burden of its history. Crafts could be relieved of their (unacknowledged) collective history and be reborn as instances of romantic individualism: as isolated, spontaneous acts of individual creativity. "Myth," wrote Roland Barthes, "deprives the object of which it speaks of all history. All that is left for one to do is to enjoy this beautiful object without wondering where it came from."[123] And around these purified and beautiful commodities would grow up a scientific technology of marketing, a "system ... whereby definite orders will be placed and a steady market assured," a memorandum from the branch urged in 1951.[124]

Of course, these imagined breakthroughs to the full marketing of spontaneity and authenticity were not uniquely Black's. She had been influenced by Scandinavian and other foreign models, in which a strong Handcrafts Association maintained large wholesale warehouses and retail shops, supplied designs and materials, and paid the worker upon the satisfactory completion of the order.[125] For Black, the purpose of any handicrafts program was to make it possible for an industrious individual to earn a comfortable living. This was quite feasible, she wrote in 1956, provided that "he or she is willing to work as hard at production as though employed in any other activity. Production must be set up on a systematic basis however, and the craftsman must possess natural talent, good technical ability, and an understanding of design and marketing in order to succeed."[126]

This doctrine of professionalism extended beyond marketing to the manufacture of the products themselves. Black did not hesitate to pronounce a decisive and revealing word: "technicians." The idealized actors in her ideal handicraft program would be the *craft technicians*, producing only so many "individualized" and "unique" items as the market demanded. And Black understood that this market was a tourism-driven market. The tourists, ultimately, determined the nature of "handcraft authenticity." The tourists' market preferences would determine which crafts were to survive and which were to sink. Thus the tourists were to be the ultimate arbiters of authenticity, for they constituted the market, and the market, redemptive and sovereign, is (or should be) fully in command, dictating what crafts were produced and where they were sold.

What the tourists demanded, and gift shops required, were crafts "with a Nova Scotian flavour." In 1947 it was found that these had "sold immediately."[127] Mary Black underlined this point in "Handcrafts in Nova Scotia":

The Government is particularly interested in helping groups and individuals develop their crafts to the point where they will be readily saleable because they are cleverly designed and styled. The day of the poorly made, [stereotyped], [drab] bit of handicraft has passed. Articles of this nature have sold simply because there was nothing else to buy ... Tourists who will visit Nova Scotia in the future will look for interesting craft products of materials and designs really belonging to the Province.[128]

There were other, more abstract, arguments for the creation of new, distinctively Nova Scotian handicraft traditions. In a 1952 article in *Canadian Art*, Black borrowed the nationalist arguments of the recent Report of the Royal Commission on National Development in the Arts, Letters and Sciences (the Massey Report) in urging Canadians "to develop our own national culture free from an excess of American,

British, or foreign influences." Yet she made this appeal to patriotism after an extended discussion of the tourist market:

A great many of the people who purchase Nova Scotia handcrafts are tourists who come from central Canada or from the United States. They seek articles the designs and materials of which will be evocative of this province. Therefore in planning our programme it is necessary to promote designs which are related to the environment in which they originate. We must, at the same time, strive to produce enough variety in product and pattern to attract the attention of both the discriminating purchaser and the souvenir hunter. And good taste is essential in both types of product.[129]

There was remarkably little pretence in Black's programmatic writings of trying to present craft workers as autonomous artists, or to suggest that artistic self-expression ranked anywhere near the top of the handicraft agenda. Crafts were indeed therapeutic, but only insofar as they reflected market mechanisms. The division's 1949 report stated, "Tourists are asking for articles with a Nova Scotian feeling, so every effort is constantly being made to urge producing craftsmen to use designs of this nature."[130] Better yet, they were willing to pay more if they were assured that the products were well made "with a Nova Scotia design if they really wanted them."[131]

But in this seemingly universal ideology of the liberal marketplace, how could one attain such a Nova Scotia design? One commonsense answer could be ruled out from the beginning: not by building on handicrafts traditions as they actually existed in the present-day province or had existed in its past. Black never seems to have doubted that there were absolute standards for handicrafts, according to which Nova Scotian crafts were inferior. She had been a student at a Swedish craft school in 1937 and was always inclined to look to Europe for her examples of "excellence" in craft.[132] Public taste in home furnishings in Canada was "very bad," she argued, and there was, in contrast with Sweden and other Scandinavian countries, "little or no heritage of a National handcraft."[133] In 1953 she and an associate went to judge handicrafts (mainly weaving) at the Hants County Exhibition: "We ... gave *very low* marks, authorities didn't like this but we explained we had certain standards to uphold + none of their articles met these. We'd be glad to give assistance with classes. Guess we'll never be asked again!"[134] Leatherwork in the province was equally deserving of censure. Remarking on the work of one Mr Bourke, who brought in leather samples, Black wrote, "Good workmanship but poor design. Same old story no idea of design and most unwilling to learn."[135] She was no more impressed by the hooked rugs which, by the late 1930s, had become the province's most famous handicraft. For the most part, Black shared the opinion of Auville Eager, a New York stockbroker and frequent correspondent of Premier Angus L. Macdonald, who lamented the failure of Nova Scotian producers to achieve international standards in their products:

It is pitiful to me to examine the hooked rugs of Nova Scotia offered for sale, which represent so much effort on the part of some women, probably very much in need of funds, which remain unsold. In my opinion, a number of such unsold rugs do not attract the buyer because of unacceptable pattern or unsatisfactory combination of colors, even though the workmanship is perfect. In other cases I see sales deterred by poor workmanship, yet with simple instructions I believe that the average rug hooker could be easily shown the type of work that is desired and is saleable. [136]

His does not seem to have been an isolated reaction. Lilian Burke, an American entrepreneur, tried to market the hooked rugs of Baddeck on the American eastern seaboard. According to Père Anselme Chiasson, she blamed her disappointing sales on the "unpolished" nature of the colours and designs and the "mediocre" quality of the work. When the women of Baddeck resisted changes in their traditional designs and bright colours, Burke turned her attention in 1927 to the community of Chéticamp. [137] Black believed that some of the hooked rugs were of acceptable quality, and were probably "the best examples we have of pure Nova Scotia traditional design," but she was distinctly unenthusiastic about most of them, and urged upon the government the need for a well-trained instructor to raise the standard of the craft. [138] There was a "definite lack of understanding of the modern use of design and colour" in rug-hooking, Black complained in 1949. This aesthetic failure had resulted in poor sales. [139] It would never have occurred to her that the use of colours might legitimately vary from one cultural group to another, and that there was no a priori reason why bright colours were not a defensible, and indeed traditional, choice in rural Nova Scotia. [140] In this and other instances Black was not just the proponent of the new and invented handicraft traditions, but the active critic of the old and superseded. Even such traditional farm activities as knitting mittens and socks were not exempt from her international handicraft standards. In 1944 she wrote of the individuals on isolated farms who made such humble articles, "It has been necessary to send special instructions to these individuals, as the grade of articles they were producing was not suitable for sale. It is at times difficult to introduce new patterns and designs where the original one has been considered 'good enough for fifty years.'"[141] Fifty years of falling short of timeless and universal standards clearly did not a valid tradition make.

One could hardly create a vibrant tourism-oriented handicrafts sector on the basis of such mediocrity. For a progressive like Black, organizing for the craft revival could best be accomplished through the state's encouragement of radically new designs and methods. Because "tourists who will visit Nova Scotia in the future will look for interesting craft products of materials and designs really belonging to the Province," the Handcrafts branch should "aid those who cannot create their own designs or style their own articles," free of charge.[142]

The most radical organizational consequences of this notion would be a provincial structure in which the state agency hired skilled designers to produce designs "indigenous to the province," which would then be circulated to local workers, who would work from them. (Better, Black wrote with an almost brutal candour, that rural craftspeople work from "a good design created by someone else" than "a bad design of their own.")[143] Had this strategy matured, it would have entailed an official reinvention of outwork. "Authenticity" would be planned in the city and executed in the countryside. The nostalgic and liberal image of the individual craft worker's artistic creativity would be preserved and marketed. This image would be constructed through the institution of tightly centralized, state-supervised, scientific controls over the labour process. Handicrafts were too important to be left to craft workers.

If the state was seen as one vital nucleus of change in this progressive ideology of handicrafts, its agents on the ground were to be craftspeople who had received professional training that reflected European standards. In fact, it would probably be for the best if Nova Scotian crafts were made by Europeans. They, far better than the aesthetically misguided Folk of the mining towns, farms, and fishing communities, could root "good design" in the unforgivingly provincial soil. "European techniques, practically unknown or seldom used in Canada, when combined with Nova Scotia design ... will result in interesting fresh new handcrafts that will bring satisfaction to both the creator and the user," Black argued.[144] There was no comparison between their heritage of handicrafts and the Canadian. And although Black did not make this argument explicitly, the need to appeal to the important American market for Nova Scotian handicrafts suggested the value of importing European experts. The revival of "folk" arts and crafts in the United States had involved the direct imposition of European (particularly Danish) forms, which then came to set the accepted standards for "genuine American handcrafts."[145]

A true Nova Scotian handicraft tradition would not arise, then, from the Nova Scotians themselves, many of whom lacked even the rudiments of craft training, and were apt, even if given competent designs, to resort to unsuitable and garish colours. In 1943 Black viewed ceramics in the province as something which possessed "limited markets + no future." Only under the guidance of the "right person" with an outlook for the artistic as well as the functional would it ever be otherwise.[146] Notwithstanding its name, even the weaving of "homespun" could not be safely entrusted to the unsupervised home. It had to be approached in a disciplined and systematic manner if it was to become "a lucrative profession" in the mid-twentieth century world.[147]

Yet Black cautioned the handicrafts professionals against too rapid or drastic an imposition of European standards on rank-and-file Nova Scotians. In encouraging producers to use designs they might not understand or particularly like, the pedagogic state was required to move cautiously. Serious handicrafts were only just beginning to be created in the province. "The one thing that we must remember and continually hold before us is that we are young in our handcrafts," Black wrote in 1952, "that we have a long way to go, and that we must proceed slowly."[148] State-trained "good technicians" held the key to this cultural metamorphosis. Through scholarships and other programs, these technicians would transmit their skills to subsequent generations, thereby creating a specialized knowledge and a "tradition of fine crafts in Nova Scotia."[149] "The services of a Designer are ... badly needed," Black remarked in 1943, "to produce designs with a true Nova Scotian flavour and to help raise, in general, the standard of design and colouring among craft workers."[150]

How could these craft technicians, some from Europe and others professionally trained by the local state in European handicraft traditions, be sure they had captured the essence of Nova Scotia so demanded by tourists? Black arrived at a doctrine of handicrafts as the mirror of nature. Nova Scotian handicrafts could attain their inner truth only by the direct incorporation of natural forms. Crafts were to be direct representations of nature, virtual byproducts of the Nova Scotian land and skies. "Designs must be made up of forms with which we come in daily contact, – a flying gull, a native flower or a fish from the sea," Black urged (although, in common with most Nova Scotians, Black would also have come into more frequent contact with automobiles, paved streets, and radios). "We must be capable of understanding them and they must be of the common denominator of our lives." She thought "craftsmen" were already responding directly to nature: "The rough bark of a tree suggests to them place mats in handspun linen; the piles of an old wharf suggest a design for weaving or a block print, as does the shadow of a gull on a sandy beach. The 'V' formation of Canada wild geese in flight repeated over its surface is perfect for an unusual tweed."[151]

The state handicrafts revival thus had a critical pedagogical role in teaching Nova Scotians how to look at nature, and, more specifically, how to see the true forms they had for centuries somehow missed. If for Mackenzie and Creighton the mission was to arouse interest in traditional ballads that the vast majority of Nova Scotians had never heard, Black's mission was to teach the vast majority of Nova Scotians to see patterns in nature they had never before discerned. "Proceeding from the premise that good design in handcrafts is based on the orderly arrangement of the forms we see around us, we must first of all teach people to see the beauty inherent in these forms," Black argued. Slowly, the state would "awaken producing craftsmen to the innate beauty of his material, with stress on form and finish, design and mass rather than on ornamentation." An unhappy Nova Scotian tendency to Victorian overdecoration would be replaced with a pleasing "simplicity of line and colour." As well-trained technicians, the Nova Scotian handicrafts producers would eventually awaken "to the fullness of the rich design forms which lie all about them but of which they are now largely unaware."[152]

And here, in a progressive thinker attuned to bureaucratic control and discipline, we find a clearly marked, practical path back to anti-modernism and to the Folk. That the Folk were closer to nature, and that their songs were in a sense the songs of Nature, had been a staple theme of romantic theories of the *Volk* since the early nineteenth century. In Black's emphatically essentialist philosophy of craft, true Nova Scotians, attuned to nature, would almost inevitably be insulated from the diseases of modernism that were sweeping the artistic world of the 1950s. (On this point Black was not wholly consistent: Nova Scotians must have been at least potentially suscep-tible to the menace of modern art and aesthetic relativism, or why would she have felt the need to polemicize against it?) It was difficult, she argued, for big-city people to understand the Nova Scotian "approach to the design problem," because they lived far away from the natural world from which the simpler Nova Scotians drew their direct inspiration.[153] "We in Nova Scotia, except for the occasional visit to the big city, are dependent on reports in handcraft and allied magazines for our knowledge of what is new, acceptable and considered prize-worthy in the field of handcrafts," this full-time resident of a suburb of a major Canadian city remarked in *Handcrafts* in 1956. She defended absolute standards of handicrafts against the first stirrings of handicraft modernism:

Perhaps it is because we are so far removed from the centres where all this happens that our values are quite different, but frankly we cannot see merit in a lopsided vase; a contorted figure; a flaunting of technically incorrect craftsmanship flippantly labeled "a modern interpretation." In this little sea-girt province of ours we are conscious of an inherited sense-of-values which gives us courage to face up squarely to our problems; to meet and face a changing world with the best ideas and mechanical skill of which we are capable.[154]

In this passage, aimed at a broad public, Black ironically pays homage to a "inherited sense of values" as the guardian of good taste, presumably the same local taste she spent so much time privately denouncing.

By and large, for Black, the authenticity of handicrafts emerged primarily not from historically existing traditions or inherited values but from isolation in the natural "sea-girt" setting. Such a vigorous naturalism would give the invented handicrafts a guarantee of authenticity that history evidently could never provide. Slowly, surely, true forms would emerge. Romanticism was thus brought into the vision of the progressive reformer. The vision of a direct, virtually unmediated response to nature drew upon the romantic landscape tradition, with its emphasis on *plein air* naturalism, immediacy, and spontaneity. And the handicraft was to be something it had never been before: not a collective response to social life, enforced by collective standards and shared traditions, but (at least in form) an individual, artistic response to the natural world and an attempt to distil its essence. "The work of Nova Scotia craftsmen improves yearly," Black reported in 1950. "It is becoming distinctive of the province in design and the use of native materials."[155]

AN IDEOLOGY IN ACTION

It was one thing to work out this ideology of handicrafts, with its rhetorical conjugation of "tradition" and "progress," and another to influence the actual course of events.[156] Mary Black set the tone for handicrafts from 1943 to 1955. She established training programs, publicized crafts through annual exhibitions, imported European craft traditions, and helped invent and popularize new forms. She was a part of the emergence of a new idiom of handicraft. It might well have emerged without her, but not as such a powerful, widely diffused, and "natural" commonsense.

Training was the most practical and direct way in which a progressive reformer could transform provincial handicrafts. Black was deeply convinced that handicrafts could and should be a profession; weaving, for example, should be governed by accreditation procedures. The Handcrafts Division's standard course in weaving was accordingly designed to prepare the student to complete the requirements for basic and intermediate standing in the Guild of Canadian Weavers.[157]

The practical dilemma that confronted Black was that of creating a training tradition that met her standards. She had little confidence in the existing centres of craft training. In 1946, as a means of discovering "competent handcraft teachers," the department announced scholarships for a summer course in handicrafts at some approved centre or school, with the initial intention of sending students to Mount Allison University in Sackville, New Brunswick, for a summer term. After a "thorough investigation" of Mount Allison's program, Black decided to give the students a "stiff orientation course" herself.[158] "There does not appear to be any organization interested in training young people for this new and interesting field of activity," Black remarked of handicraft education in 1948,[159] an observation that implicitly condemned the efforts of convents, the local technical school, voluntary groups, and cooperatives.[160] Plans for setting up a more professional training centre would immediately encounter "many problems – one of the most acute being the securing of properly trained personnel to direct its activities. In all likelihood these teachers will have to be brought in from outside the Province."[161] By the late 1940s Black could not find anyone to teach "advanced craft techniques," and she complained that many of the students were now ready for advanced training which her present instructors were not equipped to give them.[162] Although veterans from the Mount Allison program and the Newfoundland Handcrafts Centre in St. John's could fill this gap to some extent, Black was convinced that only Europeans would be able to teach handicrafts at an advanced level and introduce more sophisticated concepts of design.[163] It was necessary to have "well trained instructors" if the problem of design in the handicrafts program was to be dealt with, wrote Black, but this was "a problem in itself as many of our craftsmen have advanced to a point where their knowledge is comparable to that of our junior instructors. We are attempting to meet this problem through special refresher courses, scholarships for

advanced training, and trips for our instructors; through the employment of guest instructors with specialized training in one or more
crafts; and by utilizing the services of well trained European
craftsmen now living in Canada."[164]

In the Handcrafts Centre, which opened in the Cathedral Barracks
in Halifax in 1948, Nova Scotians could learn how to produce designs
"typical of Nova Scotia." The centre was to make craft training available upon request and without charge to all adult Nova Scotians over
sixteen years of age who were willing to come to Halifax. Those who
could not visit Halifax could obtain sample articles of the "distinctive"
handicrafts, and "full directions for the making will accompany each
article."[165] Based in Halifax, instructors from the centre would range
through the countryside, bringing the new craft techniques to a wide
audience.

Evaluating the success or failure of any training program is difficult. From Black's highly critical point of view, her centre failed utterly
in pottery, which from the start she had considered a highly problematic craft in Nova Scotia. Beginners who had worked through two
or three sessions were still beginners, and their further development
was hobbled by a scarcity of qualified teachers and by inadequate
teaching facilities and equipment.[166] Despite a "special effort ... to
close the gap between Nova Scotian pottery and the ceramic craft of
the rest of Canada" and to develop the Danish styles that had worked
so well in New Brunswick, the pottery gap remained.[167] By contrast,
weaving, Black's home ground, became the triumphant success story
of the division.

The crucial problem in handicrafts training was a shortage of
skilled technicians. Black's strategy of professional development
called for the importation of European techniques and, where possible, actual Europeans. She intensified rather than initiated the
"Europeanizing" trend.[168] The division was "attempting to meet" the
problem of a shortage of handicraft skills through special refresher
courses, scholarships for advanced training, and trips for our instructors; through the employment of guest instructors with specialized
training in one or more crafts; and by utilizing the services of well
trained European craftsmen now living in Canada." Black was optimistic about these Europeans.

Once the language difficulty has been overcome these craftsmen have much
to offer. There is no comparison between their heritage of handcrafts and
ours. We are missing a great opportunity if we do not utilize their knowledge.
European techniques, practically unknown or seldom used in Canada, when
combined with Nova Scotia design, after the craftsman has once understood

the feeling of this new country, will result in interesting fresh new handcrafts that will bring satisfaction to both the creator and the user.[169]

The same wartime conditions that had protected local handicrafts from European competition provided an opportunity to recruit skilled European refugees.

It was easier said than done. Black was frustrated by the low federal and provincial priority given to this issue. When in 1948 the Nova Scotia government refused to give assistance to a group of displaced Estonian leather workers, Black remarked, "This was only one example of N.S. government stupidity which was shortsighted as they were very talented fine people + something could have been worked out for them."[170] Two Polish emigrés, Krystyna and Konrad Sadowski, represented Black's greatest disappointment in recruiting foreign talent. According to the Sadowskis themselves, they had been invited, "as a potter and weaver artist team, to leave our work in Brazil and come to this Country to work in the development of and appreciation for handcrafts in Canada."[171] According to Black, Mr Sadowski had been attached to the Polish division of the Royal Air Force in England; she does not mention having invited them.[172] Whether invited or not, the Sadowskis represented Black's ideal of European handicraft culture, for between them they could make both Gobelin-style tapestries and elegant ceramics.[173] Although their uncertain grasp of English prevented them from communicating readily with students, Black considered the Sadowskis excellent designers. After two years, however, relations had soured. "They feel very superior to rest of staff," Black complained in April, 1951, " + should have much higher salaries. Cannot get point they can't be given preference over Nova Scotians also even tho they have very good training + talent + experience their language is not too understandable."[174] There were other problems. Settled with state assistance in a Halifax County fishing village, the Sadowskis operated away from Black's supervision. When their uninsured studio burned down, the Handcrafts Division lost one of its looms and some pottery equipment, and Simpson's department store lost the supplies it had loaned to Konrad Sadowski in preparation for a pottery exhibition at the store.[175] The affair of the Sadowskis is discussed in many indignant entries in Black's diary notes.

Other European recruits adapted more smoothly. Danish "craft technicians" (such as Mrs Valborg Pedersen, "a graduate of the outstanding Kage Technical School of Denmark," who had operated her own studio in Copenhagen just prior to the war) came to be influential. "Mrs Pedersen is now conducting classes in weaving," Black reported in

1946, "but will later concentrate on the creation of designs and hand-craft samples with a true Nova Scotian flavour."[176] Undoubtedly Black's finest catch was not a recent immigrant, but an Englishwoman who had been resident in Canada since 1938: Bessie Rosemary Murray, born in Crewe, trained at the College of Art, Lancaster, and a designer of garments.[177] More than any of the other Europeans, Murray – who first met Black on 16 March 1943, having been referred to her by Harold Connolly[178] – would fulfil Black's dream of naturalizing European craft traditions in the province. By the 1950s the world of handicrafts in Nova Scotia and the region in general had been trans-formed by new European craftspeople, whose work came to dominate representations of the region's handicrafts.[179]

Black's progressive handicrafts ideology was thus partially suc-cessful in transforming craft training. It was much less effective in transforming marketing structures. Throughout the period, mass-produced foreign-manufactured items dominated the local souvenir market. Securing a stable portion of the vast souvenir market for local producers remained difficult. In 1943 Black visited the Zeller's store to discuss souvenirs. Although she found their shoddy souve-nirs "poor [in] both design and workmanship," she did not feel "we could produce in quantity at price they would be willing to pay."[180] Large merchandising organizations such as department stores would be unable to promote their own sales as long as many handicrafts remained spare-time activities, with irregular and uncertain output. Furthermore, local handcrafted articles were not price-competitive, "since normal retail mark-ups on the price the craftsman requires to make production worth his time, frequently place the price to the consumers out of competition with factory-made goods. Part of this difficulty arises because the craftsman, buying his materials in rela-tively small quantities, has usually had to pay retail prices, which are reflected in his cost structure."[181]

It was a painful dilemma. There was little point in attracting thousands of tourists if the economic benefits to Nova Scotians were minimal. Moreover, flogging inferior goods to tourists might have a discouraging effect on the trade itself, and Black, like Creighton, seems to have linked support for tourism with patriotism. Black agreed with the Canadian Travel Bureau in its condemnation of the imported "atrocities" scattered as souvenirs on the shelves of the large shops, and with the Halifax *Chronicle-Herald*, which complained that

Goods of the most gaudy and cheapest manufacture were crowding Nova Scotian products into the background, sometimes because they were lower in price or perhaps because they offered dealers greater margins of profit.

Little consideration was given, apparently, to the fact that a permanent business was being destroyed by "hit and run" sales of baubles that could be bought as cheaply south of the border. "Souvenir of Nova Scotia," the label borne by some products, meant merely that the article had been purchased here – not that it was native to the province, a product of Nova Scotian hands or that it had anything to do with this part of Canada.[182]

Yet what could be done? In her years as Handcrafts Director, Black was "continually hearing criticism of our Nova Scotia, as well as of all Canadian, craftsmen for not producing attractive handcrafted souvenirs, on a mass production level, at a price that the tourist was willing to pay." From Black's perspective, the criticisms were misplaced. Asking the "artist-craftsman, regardless of his media, to personally mass produce his creation is, to me, a gross fallacy and impossibility," Black remarked to Mrs Angus L. Macdonald. "The endless repetition of one article would destroy all creativeness and even at best the working hours and stamina of one man or woman could never be geared to meet the demands for a mass produced souvenir."[183]

Perhaps firmer state control over supplies and production, and the creation of a marketing board would enable local craft workers to compete with the manufacturers of cheap souvenirs? Throughout her directorship, Black and her staff thought about solutions that would give the state such a central role. They had encouraged local sheep breeders to produce wool, and had publicized their materials in *Handcrafts*.[184] But they also dreamed of a public handicrafts centre that would buy all materials wholesale, operate a large warehouse, and sell only to the handicraft industry. They had attempted through education to bring handicrafts up to a European level. Through small loans, they had sought to make looms and other equipment available to a broader population on a rental-purchase basis. However, perhaps the time had come to coordinate the efforts of individual craftspeople, each of whom could work on a portion of a larger project determined in the public centre and designed by professional designers (an interesting state coordinated proposal for re-establishing "manufacture"), with the centre allocating the supplies and setting firm deadlines for delivery.[185] They had attempted to expand the marketing of handicrafts through a booklet, *Handcrafts in Nova Scotia*, 25,000 copies of which were distributed in 1956 alone through gift shops, hotels, and tourist information bureaus. They had encouraged the emergence of five semi-private gift shops affiliated with travel bureaus. Perhaps the time had come for the state to exert a more direct control over its own shops, with tighter leasing arrangements and 50 per cent quotas for Nova Scotia handicrafts, 20 per cent for other Maritime products, and 5 per cent for the works of Nova Scotian authors (specifying, in particular, the works of Helen Creighton) and artists.[186]

In short, Black and her colleagues pressed for a progressive state regulation of handicrafts, to shore up professionalism, extend market share, and even turn handicrafts into a quasi-industry. They were frustrated at every turn. The Handcrafts Division, whose formation may have been primarily a Liberal sop to the Antigonish Movement and the CCF, commanded little respect within the state, not even from the minister responsible. Black was advised that "government regulations" forbade both the purchase of materials on a wholesale level for resale to craftspeople and the state's direct involvement in marketing their wares.[187] Elaborate plans for gift shops foundered on well-established traditions of political patronage.[188] Without a reform of marketing, handicrafts continued to be sold as they had been before: many were sold directly from the home, a few were directly commissioned by merchants, and many others were sold on consignment.

Black had greater success in determining what was sold. Her central mission was the invention of "typically Nova Scotian" handicrafts for the tourist market. "Tourists are asking for articles with a Nova Scotian feeling so every effort is constantly being made to urge producing craftsmen to use designs of this nature," Black noted in 1949.[189] Expatriate Nova Scotians, such as those grouped in the Nova Scotia Societies in the west, were particularly susceptible to the appeal of such articles.[190]

How could a Europeanized craft tradition produce articles with a "Nova Scotian feeling"? By grasping the essence of nature, by mirroring key natural forms and colours, local handicrafts, even if entirely European in their approach to design, would be "essentially Nova Scotian" in their content. Essentialism was never taken more literally than in the ensuing search for natural essences. Dyes squeezed from berries, for example, were thought to signify a deeper, more authentic truth than ordinary dyes for those who shaped the province's handicrafts image. "It may seem somewhat contrived to you," wrote Judith Crawley apologetically, appealing for help with a film about Canadian handicrafts she was making for the British American Oil Company, "but in order to keep some unity in the film we are trying to stick to crafts which are related in some way to nature. I realize that with weaving this is difficult but if you can suggested any good Maritime weaver who uses vegetable dyes we would be delighted. Or perhaps there is a weaver who uses traditional patterns related to pioneer days or to nature in some way."[191] The more "natural" and rooted to the soil, the better the handicraft. Over two decades the division left few stones unturned (or bayberries unsqueezed) in its arduous search for "natural" dyes in what was an attempt to derive a "truly natural" Nova Scotian essence.[192]

Craftspeople who wanted to prosper and win the division's support were well advised to take such essentialism as seriously as the division did. Woodcarvers who had fallen under "the influence of carvings from other Provinces" (presumably Quebec) were told to steer clear of such outside influences – advice that was wonderfully inconsistent, given the enthusiasm with which European design was promoted.[193] "Character dolls" that supposedly depicted typical Nova Scotian folk in their native dress were showered with official approval. Souvenir dolls dressed as Evangeline and la femme de Clare apparently originated with Helen J. Macdougall, superintendent of the Women's Institutes for Nova Scotia; Marguerite Gates was to win renown for her dolls dressed as Scottish Highlanders, Evangeline, and Fishermen at the Canadian National Exhibition.[194] The most famous of all the character doll-makers, however, was Rosamond Pipes, who was strategically positioned in the tourist market at Amherst (and was the sometime proprietor of the Wind-A-Mere Gift Shop). She created not only "Folk Dolls" but also dolls that represented specific characters from Nova Scotia's real or imagined past: Sam Slick, the Giant MacAskill, and the Giantess Ann Swann.[195]

Maritimicity – that special *bricolage* of stuffed lobsters, brass bric-a-brac, lobster traps, and "crafts of the sea" – became a leading motif of the newly invented crafts of the Folk. Craftspeople working in this field had a difficult time meeting the demand for mermaids, fishermen, and fish, not to mention the stuffed lobsters, which apparently entered the arsenal of provincial tourism circa 1949.[196] Seashells at Digby were revisualized as ashtrays, and by the 1940s the model lobster trap had become the indispensable piece of evidence that the tourist had indeed made an authentic journey to the Atlantic Coast.[197] Even someone like Mary Black, normally so attuned to the international standard, was influenced by the new orthodoxy. Although she had at times expressed her sense of unease about the aesthetics of the hooked rugs of the fisherfolk, she nonetheless insisted in 1952 on their cultural significance. Such traditional artifacts expressed "things that have been in the bone and mind of Nova Scotians ever since the Province was settled."[198]

Black failed in her short-term project of making handicrafts a major practical concern of the provincial state. In 1954 one embittered worker, whose resignation Black had recently requested, taunted her former supervisor with her failure over the eleven years of the program: "You seem to have worked yourself into a corner and for my part I don't see much future for handcrafts." At that moment, Black later remembered, she did not see much of a future either.[199] When she retired a year later, she did so with a sense of bitterness and failure. The program was allowed to deteriorate. The Handcraft staff was down to four by June 1958, with five vacancies.[200] Those who remained in the division felt frustrated that, despite the demand for crafts across the country, they could not effectively respond. They feared that Nova Scotia was losing whatever advantage it had gained in the 1940s: "As an economic factor of growing importance, the gift market has been valued at 12 million dollars for Canada as a whole – Nova Scotia is still a major producer of craft items although other provinces are increasing at such a rate and particularly in contrast to the general slowing down of production in Nova Scotia, that the initial leading position of this Province is rapidly becoming a thing of the past. The conclusion is that leadership in the craft field, once carried by this Division, has been weakened by those factors which have crippled its operations."[201] By 1960 only a director and clerical staff were left. At the end of July the weaving and silver instructors had resigned, and the division was absorbed by the Department of Education.[202] The goal of a handicrafts policy that was centralized and coordinated by the state had disappeared. As Jim Lotz notes, in the 1960s and early 1970s "no single individual had overall responsibility for encouraging and directing crafts in Nova Scotia as Mary Black had between 1943 and 1955. The Handcraft Centre in the Department of Education had few resources, and most craftspeople wished to have as little as possible to do with the government."[203] When Black walked out of her office at 1 p.m. on 30 December 1955, she was saying goodbye to her progressive dream.

Yet the disappearance of handicrafts as a visible state policy did not mean the erasure of the changes wrought by Black as the practical philosopher of the crafts revival. To a remarkable degree, state-orchestrated publicity had made it seem a matter of simple common sense that handicrafts were an intrinsic part of the Nova Scotian tradition. It went without saying that handicrafts represented the province more authentically than any of the products of local factories or mines (even if some of those industries could claim a century's lead time over some of the new "traditional" crafts). This publicity campaign apparently worked, both outside the province and within it. Outside Nova Scotia, the province Black had dismissed as a handicrafts backwater in 1942 was hailed as a haven of handicrafts by the *New York Times* just sixteen years later.[204] The more specialized *Cross-Country Craftsman* of Washington urged "leaders of the craft movement who believe that state guilds merit the support of their state governments" to give serious study to the handicraft program in Nova Scotia, and praised the government's handicraft directory.[205] The Nova Scotian Societies in the west, with their large and growing membership of expatriate Nova Scotians, were particularly interested in distinctive provincial handicrafts as icons of identity.[206] The idea that Nova Scotia was "naturally" a centre for handicrafts also had a strong constituency in the province. Lorna S. Grayston, organizer for the Nova Scotia Summer Festival of the Arts at Tatamagouche, believed that "there is probably more native ability in the arts and crafts per square mile in this small area than anywhere else in Canada."[207] (One can only imagine how Black would have responded to that claim.) Florence Mackley established the Museum of Cape Breton Heritage in North East Margaree to highlight what had come to be one commonsense view of Cape Breton history: that its essence was to be found not in industries, but in homemade household items. (The museum housed the largest collection of drafts for coverlets in Canada, although in comparison with other parts of North America, as Mackley honestly pointed out, Cape Breton had only a very small number of overshot coverlet drafts, and those were simpler patterns than could be found elsewhere.)[208] Perhaps the firmest evidence of the new position of handicrafts as symbols of the province came with the royal visit to Nova Scotia in October 1951. "It was the desire of the cabinet that the gifts should be so distinctively Nova Scotian that there should be no question of their having originated elsewhere," Black reported. "To this end they should be as far as possible be made of materials indigenous to the Province, should be the products of the minds and hearts and hands of Nova Scotia's craftsmen and women; and should be presented as gifts to the people of the Province to their future Queen and her family."[209] Princess Elizabeth and Prince Philip were to be given agate jewellery; Prince Charles was to receive a model of the *Bluenose*; and Princess Anne was to receive a doll from Rosamond Pipes. They were all to receive copies of *Lure of the Sea*, a book of Wallace R. MacAskill's haunting photographs of the sea, specially bound in sailcloth.[210] The gifts suggested how thoroughly provincial identity had been redescribed by the twentieth-century vocabulary of Innocence, and how well the revival of handicrafts fit within a more general antimodernist myth-symbol complex.

FROM CHÉTICAMP TO HALIFAX: THE SIGNIFICANCE OF MARY BLACK

Mary Black's significance was that she contributed to the cultural redescription, and in a special way. The presence of the state was not

Cover of "Craftsmen at Work" Exhibition at *HCMS Cornwallis*, 1955. Mary Black Papers, MG 1, vol. 2144, no. 1, PANS, N-6345. Inset, promotional stamp advertising Nova Scotia handcrafts.

as marginal as its subsequent disappearance from the field of handcrafts might lead one to suppose. As was the case with other invented traditions of the period, state power *generalized* and *institutionalized* new traditions that might otherwise have been more limited in place and episodic in impact. This argument can be illustrated by a closer examination of the two most successful invented handicraft traditions of the period from 1929 to 1954: Chéticamp rugs and the Nova Scotia tartan.

Young Mary Black as a nurse. PANS N-7148.

The mature Mary Black as an authority on weaving. PANS N-7147.

A resident of one of the interesting Acadian villages of Nova Scotia with her old French spinning wheel

Although the Folk formula was extended to cover the other "white races" of Nova Scotia, the Acadians – whose costume and handicrafts did lend themselves to it – were the first to be extensively framed in this manner. This photograph probably comes from Clare. From *Nova Scotia, the Ocean Playground* (1930), 30.

The Piper at the border, clad in the Nova Scotia tartan. Nova Scotia Information Service. PANS 27226.

That the urban appropriation and, where necessary, the invention of rural folkways and handicrafts would have proceeded without Black and the provincial state can be shown by the case of Chéticamp, one of the starkest instances of the urban rearrangement of rural crafts. Chéticamp, a French-speaking community on the west coast of Cape Breton Island, has been renowned since the 1930s for its rugs: resembling tapestries, ranging in size from massive carpets to delicate coasters for coffee mugs, the product is instantly recognizable by its muted colours and floral patterns. For many visitors to Nova Scotia, Chéticamp rugs are their most prized souvenirs.

Before 1927 the women of Chéticamp had made hooked rugs in much the same way as the women of other coastal villages. Using chicken-feed sacks and red tobacco bags (which were useful for depicting the brilliant leaves of autumn), the women made bright, vibrant rugs depicting scenes from daily life.[211] One woman and her daughter hooked a rug ten feet square, with a dazzling lobster depicted in the centre; it sold for $100.[212] Women organized these efforts themselves, without the formalized hierarchies of factory labour.

In the 1930s the women of Chéticamp were taught another way of working and another way of seeing. Capitalist social relations emerged. The wife of the Chéticamp plaster-mine manager commissioned a large number of carpets, for which she engaged a variety of women at fifty cents per day, working them from eight in the morning until five at night. The decisive turning-point in the history of Chéticamp was the arrival of Miss Lilian Burke, "une grande artiste de New York," who, after unsuccessfully attempting to convert the women of Baddeck to her vision of a new handicraft tradition, arrived in Chéticamp in 1927.[213] Of Irish and Polish descent, Burke was a friend of the Alexander Graham Bell family and a visitor to their summer estate at Baddeck, Cape Breton. The Bell family had a strong interest in handicrafts and had tried to teach lace-making to local women in Baddeck. An occupational therapist like Mary Black, Burke returned to Cape Breton after the war and undertook craft revival work in earnest.[214] A Catholic who could handle a conversation in French, she was able to make herself understood in Acadian Chéticamp.

Burke showed the women of Chéticamp new techniques for treating their cloth. She proposed sulfuric acid instead of vinegar as a fixative for the colours. Her biggest changes were in designs and colour schemes. Instead of using bright primary colours, the women were taught to mix their colours to produce pastel tints. Their rugs were transformed from brightly coloured and locally designed products carrying images of fishing life to soft, pale, understated symbols of Victorian formality and refinement.[215] As the *National Geographic* put it, "Under the guidance of Miss Lillian Burke, a New York designer ... [g]arish, hard colors have been replaced with soft-toned pastels; stark, angular designs exchanged for graceful antique motifs of flowers, animals, and birds, or classic patterns."[216] A style of rug-making appropriate for a fishing family's cottage had been transformed into a style suitable for the homes of the wealthy in the eastern United States.

Miss Burke and her partner offered the transformed rugs for sale at their boutique in Baddeck. Any unsold carpets were to be returned to their owners. Whatever lingering doubts about Burke's scheme may have existed in the community were dispelled when the first Chéticamp carpets sold quickly in 1927. In 1928 two hundred carpets were shipped to Baddeck, and yet another adventure in reinventing cultural tradition was underway.

Everything about Chéticamp rug-making was transformed. The labour process was completely redesigned as Burke gradually increased the size of the carpets. A carpet of hundreds of square feet would occupy ten women working for weeks or even months on end. As was so often the outcome of the scientific redesign of work, conception and execution were separated: conception of the carpets took place in New York, while the rugs were executed in Chéticamp. Burke would send precise design instructions from her New York gallery, leaving nothing to accident or to the untutored aesthetic choices of her workers. (Burke knew rather little about the actual techniques of making the carpets.) If, having seen finished carpet on the floor, Burke was displeased with some nuance, even one she herself had earlier desired, the colouring would have to be redone. As Anselme Chiasson notes in his fascinating study of the process, Burke would stand on a chair to acquire a good view of the large carpets together, and, indicating a particular person and a particular carpet, would remark, "A little more pinkish there" or "a little more yellowish here." To make a carpet a "little more pinkish" meant an immense amount of work: it had to be replaced in the frames, the wool with the unsatisfactory tint had to be removed, and other wool had to be tinted to the desired colour and crocheted once again back into the carpet. Small wonder that the exasperated craftswomen would, after Burke had left the room, mock her with their own versions of "A little more pinkish there," "Yellowish here and there."[217]

Here was exactly the kind of craft revolution Mary Black would look for a decade later: a planned attack on a large urban market, backed up by professional design and a disciplined and efficient labour force. This was a reinvention of the craft-based manufactory, a way to have both the aura of authenticity of hand production and the division of labour of modern industry. And it meant the imposition of aesthetic and economic discipline on a once independent form. Workers came to fear Burke's visits. They also felt restricted in their options at a time when the Great Depression had wiped out economic alternatives. Workers in Chéticamp would wait as long as six months for word on their carpets. In 1938–9, they would be paid between seventy-five and eighty cents per square foot.

Jim Lotz, a historian of Nova Scotia handicrafts, rather romantically depicts Lilian Burke as a joyful woman "who sowed lupin seeds along the sides of the road as she travelled from Baddeck to Chéticamp."[218] Burke had a great deal to be joyful about in the deal she had struck with the simple folk in Chéticamp. The workers took most of the risks and worked for a pittance; Burke took virtually no risks and sold the carpets at enormous profits. In 1936 and 1937 a movement of resistance, centred in the local cooperative, fought for the re-establishment of a payment rate of one dollar per square foot. Burke took the agitators to court on the ground that the Chéticamp carpets were now her artistic property, and that consequently the cooperators had been guilty of a kind of aesthetic misappropriation.[219] (Like Creighton's folksongs, the new "folk art" of Chéticamp was awkwardly positioned between use value and exchange value.) What Chéticamp historians refer to as "La fameuse crise de 1936–1937" broke Burke's lucrative monopoly, although for some time she continued in the business (and, in response to the competing buyers of labour, even raised her scale for piecework). Long after her removal from Chéticamp in 1939, Burke's influence would be felt. By transforming a disorganized rural handicraft into a coordinated manufactory dominated by a trans-Atlantic notion of the beautiful, she had made the carpets of Chéticamp a feature of great houses in many cities in the eastern United States.

Burke's local success represented what Black was attempting to accomplish more generally in all of the province's handicrafts. It suggested that there was a general cultural logic at work, through which local crafts that evoked a lost age of Innocence would be invented by middle-class designers for sale to urban consumers, often through the direct imposition of new traditions and modes of organization on the countryside. This does not mean that the state reorganization of the craft revival was an insignificant development. Lotz's comment that handicrafts have become intrinsic to Nova Scotia's identity suggests something important about the particular way a handicrafts tradition, considered by revivalists to be virtually a nullity in the 1930s, became so potent an element of Nova Scotia. Only the state could successfully generalize a local reorganization such as that witnessed at Chéticamp to make it apply to the province as a whole. It required state power to make a contingent, contested reading of the true craft of the Folk into a commonsense – to naturalize it. The significance of state intervention emerges when we contrast the case of the private and local redescription of one form at Chéticamp with the most successful single transformation effected through Black's strategy, the Nova Scotia tartan.

The notion that Nova Scotia was in some essential sense Scottish attained great influence in the second quarter of the twentieth century. Angus L. Macdonald, the most influential premier of the period, was committed both to tourism and to a particularly romantic reading of Scottish history. Under his leadership, provincial funds were given to the Gaelic College (headed by a man who could not speak Gaelic), key provincial tourism sites were "tartaned" with Scottish names, and a brawny Scots piper was stationed at the Nova Scotia border. "Tartanism" – the reading of Nova Scotia as a sort of "Scott-land" across the waves – triumphed as a way of thinking about the Scottish essence (or the "Highland Heart") of Nova Scotia, and was accepted even by Nova Scotians who did not claim Scottish descent.[220] The actual "tartan" at the centre of tartanism, however, was the achievement not of this labour of ethnic redescription but of the handicrafts revival. The Nova Scotia tartan was invented by an Englishwoman in 1953. It originated in Mary Black's division and represented its moment of triumph.

Although the Nova Scotia Sheep Breeders' Association was not renowned as a force for radical cultural change in the province, it was the association's desire to mount an exhibition devoted to the uses of local wool that made the Nova Scotia tartan possible. The Handcrafts Division was invited to organize a special display as part of the exhibition. Black decided on a panel depicting "archetypal Nova Scotians" amid the changing seasons. Work began on 9 June 1953. Few problems were posed by the Acadian girl "in traditional dress" or by the United Empire Loyalist surrounded by "his wife and child, a hen and pet cat." Then came the Autumn panel of the mural, and with it a serious difficulty. A kilted Scottish shepherd was minding his sheep, duly assisted by his sheepdog, with the lone shieling in the background. (This was a deft way of tying in Scots romanticism with handicrafts: a simulated "lone shieling," a humble shepherd's lodge commemorated in a famous poem expressing nostalgic longing for the Hebrides, had recently been reconstructed in Cape Breton.) Obviously a Scottish shepherd lolling about in front

The wool mural depicting the history of sheep in Nova Scotia, commissioned by the Nova Scotia Sheep Breeders' Association. The Nova Scotia tartan was used for the first time on the small kilted figure to the left of the pine tree on the far right of the photograph. It is now in the Old Woolen Mill, Barrington, Nova Scotia, which is part of the Nova Scotia Museum. Nova Scotia Museum Photograph.

of a lone shieling in Cape Breton had to wear a tartaned kilt (although it was doubtful if a Cape Breton shepherd ever had). Which clan tartan should he wear? Confronted with this same dilemma in Cape Breton Highlands National Park, Premier Angus L. Macdonald had inclined towards the Macdonald tartan. For the Halifax craft revivalists, however, the question seemed more difficult to resolve. It was a knotty problem, and neither tradition nor present practice offered many solutions. There simply was not much of a tradition of tartan-weaving in Nova Scotia. As Florence Mackley notes in *Handweaving in Cape Breton*, although one "would probably expect to find many of the old tartan setts in Cape Breton homes," this was simply not so. Most of the early settlers were not accustomed to tartan-weaving.[221]

Part of the handicraft revival was the establishment by the Gaelic College at St. Ann's of a handicraft centre that emphasized weaving, which officially was opened by Premier A.S. MacMillan in July 1944. Mary Black had taught at the college in the summers of 1943, 1944, and 1945. She was, characteristically, a tough critic. "Mrs M. [Mackenzie?] keeps F. busy – no chance to weave; her own weaving a farce – not careful – breaks threads etc. + complains of loom not working well etc," Black complained in her diary.[222] By the end of the summer of 1943 she was somewhat more optimistic about tartan weaving at St. Ann's, but it was clearly a rather new skill for everyone. The tartan output received mixed reviews. Angus L. Macdonald, who had received a Clan Ranald couch-throw with the compliments of the craft centre, gave the local product a glowing report.[223] Those more expert in the field were somewhat less generous. An expert Scotswoman visiting the province informed Black that the colours were "rather garish."[224] Yet the tourists loved them, garish or not. As early as 1947 demand far exceeded supply,[225] and by the mid-1950s, thanks to extensive state financial assistance and Black's sponsorship of the project, the weavers at St. Ann's were turning out tartan by the ton.

The growth of tartan production at St. Ann's did not clarify the knotty problem of which clan tartan the fancifully conceived Scottish shepherd should wear. It fell to Bessie Murray, an English embroiderer from Crewe, to tackle the issue. In a manner that was characteristic of the entire craft revival, she found the answer not in any history of Nova Scotia or Cape Breton, but in nature.

Innocence was, in large measure, a Greater Halifax production, and small rural communities on the outskirts of the capital played a disproportionate role in its history. If Helen Creighton's path of destiny had opened out at Eastern Passage on the coastline just east of Halifax, Bessie Murray's led on from Terence Bay just west of the city. The Nova Scotia tartan, as she conceived it, was to be the direct imprint of the Terence Bay landscape, with its deep-blue lake set in a circle of bleached white granite. It would be Scottish in form but natural in essence, its authenticity founded on the rockbound coast. As one account explains:

Ah! Now things began to fall into place for her [Murray]. The blue of that water was the blue of the sea and the sky, with the [autumnal] softness about it to suggest the name "October blue" and the beautiful clear blue of the cross on the Nova Scotia flag. And there were also the dark and light greens, for the evergreen and deciduous trees characteristic of the province by the sea. The white of the rocks was in the flag too, as background, and in the surf that pounds the Nova Scotia coastline on all its sides except for a narrow band of land that binds it to the rest of Canada. It remained only to add the gold to represent Nova Scotia's Royal character and the red to symbolize the lion rampant on the Nova Scotia crest on the flag.[226]

This historical account by Marjorie Major of Murray's ecstatic vision on the road to Innocence is itself an interesting attempt to create a romantic notion of romantic individualism and a moment of artistic inspiration. Whether it happened in just this visionary way is doubtful. Black thought that Murray had had some sort of "Nova Scotia tartan" design in her mind some time before the project came up, and Major herself notes the extensive book study of tartans the English embroiderer undertook in order to produce the tartan in time for the display.[227] Neither the English-born Murray nor the American-born Black was in any sense an expert on Scottish tartans.[228]

What is more important, the "Eureka!" version of the history of the Nova Scotia tartan understates how deeply structured this happy accident was. Had it occurred in another context (say, in a private workshop in Chéticamp or a purely commercial setting such as Eaton's), the tartan would never have been "naturalized" as a symbol of all Nova Scotia. But this invention occurred within (and by means of) a division of the state, which had been preoccupied for over a decade with creating an "authentic" Nova Scotian handicraft tradition, one that would be simultaneously natural and commercial. The tartan was the precise exemplification of the ideals of handicraft development Black had developed since the 1940s. It was professionally designed, European in its origins and structure, supposedly a direct reflection of nature, and devoid of even the slightest connection with Nova Scotian history. Bessie Murray, in a heartfelt thanks to Black for her support, wrote in 1961: "I want you to know that I shall always feel that you were the real one who started the tartan."[229] This modest acknowledgment of her friend's assistance contained a real insight: without Black and the state presence in the Handcrafts Division, this invented tradition probably never would have emerged in the first place.

Nor would it have ever been naturalized except in a tourism state that wanted to mobilize Scottish forms for the purposes of promotion. Although the shepherd's costume occupied only a minuscule portion of a very large mural, the tartan stole the show in 1953. By the time of the "Craftsmen-at-Work" exhibition in Antigonish in July 1954, the division had prepared enough tartan material to dress models in the material: soon there were requests for curling skirts and slippers. Black and Murray repaired to the office of Premier Macdonald. The premier, also known as the Grand Noble Chief of the Clans of Nova Scotia, was, unsurprisingly, very sympathetic to the idea of a Nova Scotia tartan. The Tartan Question – should this tartan receive state recognition? – went to the provincial cabinet. After due deliberation, the idea was favourably referred to the Lord Lyon, King of Arms, the Scottish official in charge of such matters. The Lord Lyon found the idea rather unusual. Tartans were not supposed to stand for political units but for clans, and a tartan for a province was a novelty. It was all rather perplexing, but in the end he approved the tartan, with the quaint proviso that a "Governmentally-sponsored tartan should not come into conflict with the clan system and sentiment." The anxious lord was reassured that none of the supposed Nova Scotia "clans" would be compelled to wear the tartan at pistol-point. The tartan was duly registered. A symbol supposedly confined to pre-industrial clans had now been appropriated by a modern state.[230] Over the next forty years, provinces, cities, and even Queen's University would be clamouring for the honour of their own recently invented tartans, all as an indirect result of the small division headed by Mary Black.

In the summer of 1954, less than a year after the little tartan patch had appeared on the tiny figure of the Cape Breton shepherd in the sheep breeders' mural, the Nova Scotia tartan was draped over the six-foot-four-inch body of the brawny Scots piper who piped tourists across the New Brunswick–Nova Scotia border. For Mary Black, the sight was a revelation: "When you first saw the piper at a distance his kilt and plaidie blended into a lovely soft blue-grey but as your car came up the slope the blue brightened and all the greens took on their own individual values and then the colours in the smaller units came into focus and there was the much-discussed new Nova Scotia Tartan."[231]

Although there was an element of serendipity in the emergence of this particular tartan at this particular time, there was nothing accidental about the existence of a state, oriented to tourism, that was willing and able to redefine the meaning of the tartan. It had the means and the will to make the Nova Scotia tartan more official than any number of floral designs in Chéticamp, and went so far as to incorporate the tartan into the province's armorial bearings in 1964. (The tartan can now be used only with the province's permission.) And it had the means and the will to broadcast news of the tartan far and wide. The Handcrafts Bureau fed articles to the CBC almost immediately, to the *Family Herald and Weekly Star*, and to *Newsweek;* it adopted the tartan for its own July 1954 issue of *Handcrafts*. Soon the tartan was everywhere – on books, on bulletins of the Board of Trade, on the provincial *Journal of Education*, on the jackets of the Tourist Bureau staff, on a new set of contour maps put out by the mapping division of the Department of Mines. When the Liberal member for Pictou West entered the Legislature in 1955, on St. Patrick's Day, he took care to wear the Nova Scotia tartan before launching an appeal for an "authentic Scottish, or Hebridean village" in Pictou County. The tartan's commercial success was assured: the division was soon fielding requests to use the tartan from an English playing-card company and a Manhattan manufacturer of bathrobes. Its political success was no less dramatic. When the Liberals met to select a successor to Angus L. Macdonald, they requested a piece of tartan for the centre table at their banquet. Political acceptance could go no further.[232]

The business response was no less enthusiastic. Eaton's department store helped transport the yarn to Terence Bay for the first consignment of men's tartan ties; it marketed tartan clothing aggressively.[233] The Nova Scotia Tartan Limited was formed on 6 August 1954, with Bessie Murray as president and holder of a controlling interest in the stock. By 1955 the new company was in business, and employed about forty-five people in manufacturing, supervising, selling, and bookkeeping. Eventually the operation moved to Yarmouth, where it was eventually absorbed by Bonda Textiles Ltd. In 1964 a new "dress tartan" was introduced by the company and officially registered in Canada, Great Britain, the United States, West Germany, and elsewhere.[234] The tartan had cash value. In 1973 Bessie Murray rejected Bonda Textiles' offer to pay the annual registration fee for Nova Scotia Tartan Limited in return for an option to purchase the name. "I have ascertained from several sources that the tax loss is worth a minimum of $5,000.00 and that the name itself is worth a considerable amount. It has been suggested that a reasonable amount would be the equivalent of the tax loss making a total of $10,000."[235] This was a tidy sum for a piece of "cultural property" and a "name" that had been developed with public money and under state guidance. As so often in the land of Innocence, the state had smoothed the path to profits and hastened the pace of commodification.

Here was Chéticamp commercialization writ large, a tribute to Mary Black and the cultural power of the twentieth-century tourism state. In both cases traditions had been invented that marginalized older forms in the interests of commercialization and in the name of "recovering" a lost handicraft essence. As had been the case in Chéticamp, the new form encountered resistance. The Nova Scotia Association of Scottish Societies withdrew its recognition of the tartan, and the senior Scottish society in the province, the Antigonish Highland Society, expressed its disapproval at a meeting on St. Andrew's night in 1954:

A warm discussion arose over the merits of the new Nova Scotia tartan. Most members disapproved of the tartan as an innovation too likely to spread and be abused. They felt that if a Nova Scotia tartan could be arranged, then why not a New Glasgow tartan or an Antigonish tartan or a Halifax tartan.

Some also frowned on the marketing of the tartan as being too monopolistic. The tartan can only be obtained from one source, while older and authorized clan tartans could be manufactured by any number of firms ... One member gained much support when he protested the clothing of the piper at the N.S. border in the new tartan. The incoming president, Rod C. Chisholm, stated his opposition to the tartan on the grounds that anyone in the province could wear it, whether of Scots descent or not.

This by no means exhausted the objections – economic, political, aesthetic – of the Antigonish society.[236]

The members of the Highland Society had grasped a key point: the tartan no longer signified anything about the Scottish traditions to which the society was attached. They glimpsed what full commodification would do to something they, as cultural conservatives, cared about. But their words were easily forgotten and marginalized in a wave of favourable, state-orchestrated publicity. Their purely local voice could merely protest ineffectually against that which a more powerful network of the state could make a sort of truth.

Since the society's protest, resistance to the commercialization of handicraft traditions has perceptibly waned. The tartan is now an uncontroversial (if not quite the ultimate) signifier of Nova Scotia, and it has been copied far and wide, throughout Canada, within competing regional vocabularies of tourism. Freed from its (tenuous) moorings in the clan and redescribed as a mirror of the province's (newly) archetypal rockbound coast, the tartan has been fully commodified and is now far beyond the reach of those for whom tartans once meant something specific. It has become a key element in the imagined Nova Scotia that the tourism state has called into being.

Increasingly, critics of the process of appropriation and commodification of the Folk and its forms could stand on no sure ground – not history or commonsense, perceptions of nature, because all of these were being colonized, and consequently redescribed, by tourism and by the state. One of the great paradoxes of intervention-induced cultural change, David Whisnant argues suggestively, "is its very durability and the degree to which imported forms and styles are accepted and defended by local people whose actual cultural traditions they altered or displaced."[237] So it was with the Nova Scotia tartan, which became a fully accepted symbol of the province's imagined Scottish essence and its thriving handicraft tradition. Oppositionists, those who defended a "subjugated knowledge" within this new cultural politics, were left with the bleak consolation of opposition and cynicism.

For all her impatience with the pace of change within the state and for all her liberal progressivism, Mary Black should be listed among the primary architects of the Folk. Through her the new handicraft traditions of Nova Scotia became part of the provincial identity. As the *Chronicle-Herald* observed on the occasion of Black's retirement, "The displays of hooked rugs, pottery and other handcrafts that can be found along the tourist-travelled highways each summer are monuments to her endeavor – the kind of monuments she would prefer."[238] If Helen Creighton had done more than anyone to naturalize the category of "the Folk," Black had made the category "real" by making it physically tangible, by transforming an abstraction into something that could be physically touched through newly invented arts and crafts. Handicrafts became the indispensable means of authenticating a visit to the province. Black brought the newly invented arts of the Folk to the market. There was now honour to be gained, not to mention money to be made, by setting out one's stall of folklore and crafts on a much-travelled Road to Innocence.

4 "O, So True & Real Like the Sea & the Rocks": The Folk and the Pursuit of the Simple Life

They are a numerous company, these pretenders to simplicity.
Raymond Williams, *The Country and the City*, 1973

If we are concerned with fishermen, it is not at all the type of fishing which is shown; but rather, drowned in a garish sunset and eternalized, a romantic essence of the fisherman, presented not as a workman dependent by his technique and his gains on a definite society, but rather as the theme of an eternal condition, in which man is far away and exposed to the perils of the sea, and woman weeping and praying at home.
Roland Barthes, *Mythologies*, 1972

INSIDERS, OUTSIDERS, AND THE LURE OF THE "SIMPLE LIFE"

Both folklore and handicrafts naturalized a certain reading of some Nova Scotians as Folk. Both of them were essentialist, even if their metaphors and strategies – selective preservation in one case, technical training in the other – were dissimilar. Helen Creighton and Mary Black, working in different ways in different fields, converged in naturalizing a sense of the Folk. Both of them lent credence to the notion of an organic community united around certain key values and traditions. But how much importance should be attached to the ways in which they imagined Nova Scotia? Was it the case that they were merely two cultural figures in a province in which such a rhetoric of the "Folk" was generally uninfluential? Or, to ask the question in the language of the new cultural history, whose discourse was this? Did any of it make any difference to the larger population outside the restricted circles of those seriously interested in folklore and handicrafts?

It is rarely possible to prove the impact of an ideology, a myth-symbol complex, or a mythomoteur. The positive methods of social history do not illuminate such questions very fully: we cannot retrospectively poll Nova Scotians on their underlying attitudes. Neither the traditional toolkit of the neo-Marxist cultural historian ("ideology," "class consciousness," "hegemony") nor the new improved linguistic toolkit of the new cultural history ("text," "interpellation," "subject-position") – not to mention bold Freudian generalizations on the basis of a few individuals in a society – conclusively resolve the vexed question of how to assess the impact of a given cultural practice. The best that is generally feasible in either the "old" or the "new" cultural history seems to be the drawing of plausible inferences from evidence suggestive of changes in words and in things. Even the most sophisticated analysis of the "subject position" from which a text may be read unproblematically cannot provide us with any guarantees that everyone will infer the same "subject position" in the given text, or that such "subject positions" were "fully inhabited."[1] Few historians would deny that liberal notions of the individual have been important to most North Americans, but this remains a plausible inference based on a wide range of evidence. What is true of so "obvious" a generalization is doubly true when we try to explore less explicit questions of national and regional identification. No conceptual breakthrough has occurred in the methods of cultural history, at least so far as I know, that would provide me with any certainty as I extend my analysis of the Quest of the Folk beyond Creighton and Black (whose assumptions can be thoroughly documented) to a much wider range of words and things concerned with Nova Scotia. My guess that Innocence provided a new "commonsense" about the Nova Scotia's identity derives from a process of examining the assumptions that were necessarily in place in order that certain positions could be advanced: in this way we can plausibly read a certain "organicism" into Creighton's work, for example, even if she never used the word. But such "reading in" becomes more and more problematic as the analysis becomes more general. Even if we can document the proliferation of antimodernism and the Folk motif through a wide spectrum of cultural practices – and we can – two hard questions remain: How representative was this vocal antimodernism of cultural attitudes in general? How important was this antimodernism in the lives of those who articulated such positions? In other words, did the new official "commonsense" of the province's pre-modern essence ever become the way most people viewed themselves? Did most people share the "new way of seeing"? In the present state of general knowledge, these questions cannot be definitively answered. Even with what we now know about cultural life in the post-1945 period, however, it would be a mistake to minimize the presence of other "commonsenses" (such as the belief in progress, as suggested by the popular reception of many development schemes)[2] or to overlook the ways in which, within the general framework of liberal hegemony, antimodernism could be combined with seemingly contradictory elements. It was and is possible to believe on one level in the golden age, the simple life, and the stolid Folk while extolling the virtues of progress, urban sophistication, and the risk-taking entrepreneur. In the present state of the historiography, it would be a mistake to claim to know more about the overall cultural patterns than we do. This chapter tracks the existence of the Folk motif in a wide range of cultural practices in twentieth-century Nova Scotia – from the writing of novels to the construction of tourist attractions – and makes the claim that, at least for a significant number of cultural producers, the idea of the Folk was of central significance.

There was no one organization that cultural producers had to join, and developing a general sense of those concerned with the Folk entails a certain degree of arbitrariness. Nonetheless, a plausible short list of cultural producers who worked with and on the Folk can be drawn up, and it includes many figures generally considered highly significant in the region. In addition to Creighton and Black, the list includes the creative writers Frank Parker Day, Andrew Merkel (with the "Song Fishermen" group around him), Thomas Raddall, Hugh MacLennan, and Ernest Buckler; the painter Marsden Hartley and the photographer Wallace MacAskill; the travel writers Clara Dennis, George Matthew Adams, Dorothy Duncan, and Will R. Bird; and finally the polemicists D.J. Rankin, Thomas Fraser, and R.V. Sharp. This is by no means a comprehensive list of the cultural producers susceptible to the appeal of antimodernism and the Folk. It merely names those who made glaring and obvious use of the idea of the Folk and expressed a strong support for their "simple life." Although many of these people were connected to each other by informal social ties or through such bodies as the Canadian Authors' Association, they were not in any real sense a cohesive "school." Some of these people were antimodernists through and through; others seem to have been dabblers who sensed that the Folk were in style. Some of these figures were born outside Nova Scotia (Duncan, Adams, Hartley, Raddall) or lived part of their adult lives outside it (MacLennan, Day). Of these "outsiders," however, the locally born Mac-Lennan and Day considered themselves Nova Scotians and returned frequently to the province; the English-born Raddall spent virtually all his life in the province; Duncan, an American from Illinois, based her "insights" into the Nova Scotia character on information supplied by her husband, Hugh MacLennan; and Adams, an American, came to Nova Scotia every summer for over two decades. The remainder were "local," but here again the category is not airtight. Some (like MacAskill, Raddall, Buckler, MacLennan) developed national and even international reputations, while others (Rankin, Dennis, Sharp) did not. This cluster of cultural producers is heavily weighted towards males, which more accurately reflects the subordinate position of women in the province than do the careers of Creighton and Black.

The good question feminist historians often ask – "Whose discourse?" – is therefore not easily answered in terms of dichotomies between insiders and outsiders, intuitions and stereotypes, Self and Other. The notion that celebrating the Folk and the simple life was merely a ploy on the part of the tourism industry and a foible of a few American travellers is untenable. Most of the outsiders, when inspected more closely, had strong local connections. But the insiders were a complicated lot as well. The majority lived in cities (although Raddall and Buckler both lived in small towns), and no fewer than five were residents of Greater Halifax. The insiders were therefore not really insiders in any meaningful social sense: they admired the simple lives of the Folk from a safe distance. Except for Hartley, who lived with the family he portrayed in his paintings, only Rankin, a priest in Cape Breton, had practical reasons to have day-to-day working contact with anyone remotely resembling the Folk. Despite their revealingly insistent presentations of themselves as "true Nova Scotians," most of these cultural producers were far more immersed in an international urban world of culture and perception than they were in the lived experiences of the rural Nova Scotians whose essence they described so confidently. Their links to the outside world, their striving to meet international standards, and their extra-regional reputations all directly contradicted the very image of premodern insularity they were often so intent on developing.

The ambiguous identity of so many of these cultural producers, as both insiders claiming special, intuitive knowledge of the Folk (as natives or residents) and outsiders far removed from the Folk (Haligonians, bourgeois, and actual or prospective emigrés) was important in setting the tone of Innocence. The Folk were not "us" but "them," not people with whom one shared a common polity and society but an element set apart, even within a shared Nova Scotia. Any attempt to make a neat division – between the "crude stereotypes" of tourists as opposed to the "sincere" products of the locals, or between "fake" nostalgia of emigrants as opposed to the "rooted" antimodernism of Nova Scotians – founders on three problems: often the same people were creating works of both types; the same concepts and visual images were being used across the two supposedly distinct fields; and the ideology of the simple Folk appears to have been much the same whether created by a Nova Scotian with a supposedly deep insight into "Our Ain Folk" or a New Yorker gathering impressions on a two-week vacation. Both outsiders and insiders presented a premodern world in which the Folk lived the simple life, and they did so as part of a general pattern in interwar North America, which affected everything from a drive to preserve and reconstruct old buildings to the cult of the suntan. Given that middle-class people in Nova Scotia were exposed to many of the same aspects of the culture of consumption as their counterparts across North America, this pattern is not surprising.[3]

What middle-class people often admired about the Folk, and loved about handicrafts, was the authenticity and calm they seemed to invoke at a time when social conditions were in an uproar and many testified to feelings of weightlessness and inauthenticity. The "simple life" was the phrase that best captured the personal side of antimodernism, the ideal for which one hungered if one devoured folklore and lusted after handicrafts. In interwar North America, as David Shi has shown, the urban middle class in many areas embraced the "simple life" and "plain living" with enthusiasm, and projected onto the screen of rural people they scarcely knew the utopian happiness of a stress-free existence. Hostility toward luxury and a suspicion of riches, reverence for nature and the rustic, admiration for self-reliance and frugality, nostalgia for the past, scepticism about progress, and an aesthetic taste for the plain and the functional: all were aspects of the search for the simple life.[4] For some, following in the illustrious footsteps of Thoreau and Tolstoy, the simple life should be the outcome of a profound choice within a rigorous ethic of individualist nonconformity. For others, the ideal of simplicity was a fad encountered in the *Ladies' Home Journal*, one aspect of an all-embracing therapeutic practice that stemmed from consumerism. Both the new therapies of the self and new lifestyles of simplicity promised to resolve the crisis of authenticity so many people seem to have experienced in turn-of-the-century North America. The simple life was not ideologically uniform. Progressives, for example, could combine an ideal of rustic simplicity with attacks on the "tyranny of things." (Even Frank Lloyd Wright can be seen as someone yearning for a version of a new organic simplicity.) The simple life as a style of the period between the 1890s and the 1930s ranged in its visible impact from the streamlining of art nouveau appliances to the cult of Riviera tourism (initially focused on the supposed natural simplicity of the Mediterranean peasant, who was said to be "as beautiful as the land.")[5] The popularization of the simple life in all these areas was a kind of applied, muffled antimodernism, an antimodernism safely adapted for consumer capitalism and turned into a lifestyle. The Folk were those who lived the simple life, and one could embrace their quaint ways and crafts with enthusiasm without making any risky commitments.

For many of the cultural producers in Nova Scotia, the Folk and the simple life were more serious terms. For outsiders who wanted to be insiders, for Nova Scotians torn between leaving and staying, the Folk offered a way of conceptualizing identity and dealing with the painful uncertainties of modernity. The overlapping and to some extent conflicting identities of the local cultural producers can be illustrated by considering the case of Hugh MacLennan, Canada's most gifted nationalist novelist of the 1940s and 1950s. It is often forgotten that MacLennan, one of most powerful imaginers of Canada as a national community, began his career as a convinced Nova Scotian neo-nationalist and antimodernist. Before becoming the intellectual who helped Canadians imagine themselves to be tied together by deep (if paradoxical) bonds of solitude and love, MacLennan served his apprenticeship in imagining a very different and separate Nova Scotia. (He may indeed have been a quasi-separatist.)[6] In his own mind, as a young expatriate, MacLennan was "of the Folk," a Nova Scotian to the bone. He was consequently painfully out of place in the modern world. Dorothy Duncan, his wife, describes the impact of New York and modern life on her husband during his visit in 1933:

It was painful to see this country of mine having a physical as well as an emotional effect on him ... the world this grown-up boy had always known was like a large and tolerant family, in which it was taken for granted that all its members were men of good will ... Automats appalled him and cafeterias made him furious; they were uncivilized, he assured me, and he'd starve before he set foot in one again. People who shoved things in his face and asked him to buy, people who prided themselves on making smart deals at someone else's expense, people who gambled large sums of money on watered stocks they knew nothing about and then shot themselves when they were cleaned, were suddenly become monstrous to me as seen through his eyes, though subconsciously I still accepted them as natural phenomena. That simply happened to be the way of the world I had always known.[7]

Even though the young MacLennan (as described by Duncan) had been toughened by the realities of his professional prospects in the

Depression, "he was still a Nova Scotian with a Highland lilt in his voice, a belief in the essential worth of human life, and an insatiable sense of wonderment."[8] One has a vivid sense of an Innocent abroad, a man from a distant time and shore suddenly dazzled with the modern world.

MacLennan's own account of what it meant to be Nova Scotian pushed this emphasis on his own personal premodernity even further. The "atmosphere of Homer" was "all around me in Nova Scotia when I was young," he recalled.

There, as in Ancient Greece, the people lived in small communities within sight and sound of the sea. Their ears and eyes were nourished by sea-sounds and sea-images. Homer's rose-fingered dawn rising over the loud-sounding sea, his men in small boats backing water in the fog as they listened to the tell-tale roar of breakers on a leeward shore, his helmsmen on clear nights taking their course from Arcturus or the stormy rise of Orion, Scylla diving for prey from the cliff, Charybdis sucking down small boats into her whirlpool and spewing them up again in a welter of boiling sand, the bones of the drowned rolling for ages through the depths of the sea – these images and countless others from the old poetic literature of Greece seemed to describe the environment of Nova Scotia more accurately than anything written since the birth of Christ.[9]

Insular, raised in an atmosphere more like that of ancient Greece than modern North America, fiercely opposed to progress and to Canada, MacLennan was from another time, another world. He was an innocent member of a Folk, abroad in a fast-changing world his childhood in Nova Scotia had not prepared him to understand.

Or so one might believe if one took these passages at face value rather than regarding them as descriptions of an imagined childhood in an imagined Nova Scotia. Hugh MacLennan, who developed these views of the "essentially Nova Scotian" at such universities as Oxford and Princeton, had grown up as a doctor's son in the coal-mining town of Glace Bay in the heart of industrial Cape Breton. His parents' home was located some distance outside the mining town, perhaps because they wished to shield their son from the vulgar influence of the workers. Their concern to keep their social distance from the miners was such that Dr MacLennan's outer clothing was strung on a clothesline far into the woods behind the house on his return from his medical rounds, "so that no risk of infection would arise."[10] After moving to Halifax in 1915, when Hugh was eight, the MacLennan family lived in a large Victorian house in the city's prosperous South End, within walking distance of the movie houses, restaurants, taverns, and office towers of the largest Maritimes city.

Here was someone, then, who had not spent a Homeric childhood gamboling about the rugged cliffs and spying sails on the horizon, but who had grown up in the industrial coalfields and in the fashionable district of a major Canadian city. His life had been shaped in an industrial and urban environment, not by the rugged simplicities of the sea and the fisherfolk. Yet when MacLennan came to imagine the community to which he belonged and which he wanted others far away to appreciate, he turned not to the scenes of his actual childhood but to the images of the primeval Folk braving the rigours of the sea.

MacLennan's case alerts us to the dangers of underestimating the "Folk" as a subject-position (that space summoned up by a discourse from which it can be read unproblematically). There was much more to his working out of a sense of identity than any crass interest in exploiting the Nova Scotia Folk for commercial gain. For MacLennan, and for most of the local cultural producers we are discussing, defining the Folk was part of defining oneself within a wider world, of answering a question sharply posed by the neo-nationalist journalist R.V. Sharp: "Do you know who we are?"[11] Many Nova Scotians in the interwar period were asking that question. Some would eventually answer it as MacLennan did. He decided finally to transfer his loyalties to Canada as an imagined community, and the issue of the separate Nova Scotian identity receded. But those who stayed, or who did not wish to lose their primary identification with Nova Scotia, faced a more difficult problem. What did it mean to be Nova Scotian? Here Innocence suggested a subject-position: that of the pre-modern Folk. To be Nova Scotian did not mean identifying with the working class (MacLennan, like almost all antimodernists, was quite clear on that score), although it could mean having distinct reservations about big foreign-controlled business, if not about capitalism. Many of the cultural producers were caught "in between," neither wholly admiring big business nor able to make a complete identification with labour. What it meant to be Nova Scotian in terms of an older sense of British nationality and the emergent notion of Canada as a national community was equally ambiguous. For many, including MacLennan, an intensified sense of Scottish ethnicity allowed one to be both passionately British and attached to one's native soil. Yet the waning of the British Empire, which had claimed the first loyalty of so many, and the narrowness and exclusiveness of central Canadian nationalism, within which Nova Scotia and its traditions counted for little, placed local cultural producers "in between" once again. A romantically reimagined Nova Scotia Folk could answer at once to their sense of class displacement, their local neo-nationalism, and their diffuse modern sense of anxiety and rootlessness. Perhaps no one speaks more fervently of the depth and the vitality of his or her roots than the person who suspects such roots are no longer securely grounded in anything.

Nothing, then, could have been more genuine – in the sense of answering perceived social and cultural needs – than MacLennan's subjective identification with an image of the pre-modern Folk, no matter how strange it appears in the context of the facts of his biography. At the same time, the boundary between the imagined "inside" of a community thought to be an integral whole (and therefore susceptible to authoritative urban interpretation) and the exploitation of the Folk as a set of sensations and sights for the tourist was an extremely porous one. Even people like MacLennan needed to make a living, and would turn to retailing images of Folk Nova Scotia in magazines like *Holiday* to do so. The stereotype of the slow-talking, unimaginative, placid and contented Nova Scotia Folk was not something invented by contemptuous outsiders. It answered local needs. The rural Folk, with their unreflecting sense of belonging, their unproblematic family lives, and their comfortable settled state, existed mainly in the imaginations of the urban cultural producers. But that is not to say that they did not play an important function there. These people "in between" could find in the Folk two great qualities: an authentic and primitive Otherness, which could speak to their own North American middle-class sense of inauthenticity and besieged cultural authority, and an eminently practical way of marketing their work in the cultural marketplaces of Canada and North America. Parallels could be drawn to the experiences of southern intellectuals in the United States. The "Nashville agrarians," for example, fashioned a fierce regionalist critique in which an idealized southern past was constructed as a rebuke to the ugliness and chaos of twentieth-century urbanism, industrialism, and secularism.[12] There were also significant parallels with social thought in Quebec.[13] In both places, as urban life came to be seen as more stressful and difficult, rural life (subordinate to and dependent upon the dominant term of the rural–urban polarity) came to be represented as more and more tranquil and idyllic; and in both places antimodernism deeply influenced the ways in which regional and national identities were conceptualized.

In some respects, Thomas Raddall, arguably the most influential twentieth-century novelist in Nova Scotia, seems to be the antithesis of MacLennan. He was born in England, came to Nova Scotia as a child, and worked for a time as a bookkeeper in the small town of Liverpool. Whereas MacLennan's twentieth-century Nova Scotia was still essentially pre-modern – even his imagined Cape Breton coal miners are brutish primitives more haunted by the ghost of Calvin than by the problems of modern industry or their grasping employers – Raddall's more completely developed fictional history placed twentieth-century Nova Scotia at the decadent end of an entropic historical process whose "Golden Years" are suggested but, curiously, never fully realized in any of his many novels.[14] Raddall and Mac-Lennan imagined two quite different Nova Scotias, and two quite different types of Folk. MacLennan's Nova Scotia was intrinsically Scottish and Calvinist, and his Folk were often fisherfolk; Raddall's was essentially English (or Yankee) and pragmatic, and his imagined Folk were often seafarers and others shaped by the golden age of sail. Despite these marked differences, both authors relied on the Folk as a yardstick of cultural entropy. In one famous story, "Blind McNair," Raddall developed the images of the South Shore community of "Shardstown" – the name itself, with its reference to the "shards" left over from the Golden Age, was a succinct reference to an entropic vision – and of the tragic ballad singer, a refugee from another age.

In Shardstown they sing ballads no more. Nor will you hear a chantey, for the chanteymen have vanished and the tall grass shines where once the shipyards lay under a snow of chips and shavings.

It is a village enchanted. There is the yellow dust of the street, the procession of dwellings down to the broad sheltered bay, where a fleet could anchor and only the lone fishing boat flashes a riding sail; and there is the little church and the store and the dry-rotten fish wharf asleep in the sun, all still as death. Half the houses are empty, with blinds drawn and faded and forgotten, and grass in the kitchen path ...

Before Shardstown became enchanted, the village stood pretty much as it stands now, but alive, with a smell of new-sawed wood in the air, and the sounds of hammer and adze, and the clack-clack of calking mallets. They built good ships in Shardstown then.[15]

It was a haunting story that deeply impressed older Nova Scotians who had heard old ballads in childhood and were delighted to be reminded of them.[16] Raddall's eloquent story spoke, and still speaks, to an entrenched local sense of Nova Scotian history as the story of a mysterious and tragic fall.[17]

As a long-time resident of Liverpool who had gone to sea and lived on Sable Island, Raddall was much less inclined than the Halifax cultural producers to a completely sentimental wind-and-water romanticism. Raddall prided himself on his factual realism: "Blind McNair" was prompted directly by Roy Mackenize's collection of ballads, songs which Raddall had heard sung in Liverpool, and by his discovery of notebooks containing annotations on nineteenth-century sea songs.[18] Raddall also knew the market for tales of the Folk and idyllic images of rural life. His introduction to MacAskill's photographic collection, *Lure of the Sea*, was a classic statement of the theme of the racial memories of the coastal Folk. Raddall urged the reader to turn the book's pages and "see what makes the dwellers of the coast a race apart, what puts the strength and kindness in the faces of old men, what makes young men see visions and go out to find if dreams come true. Turn them, old shipmate, and see the face of your own youth."[19]

For all this vintage antimodernism, Raddall was torn on the question of progress. His most striking attempt to wrestle with industrial capitalism and its cultural implications can be found in his oddest novel, *The Wings of Night*. Here he seems to break decisively with the tradition of the regional idyll by setting his romance in a pulp town and establishing a thoroughly peculiar romantic theme – the Quest of the Pulp Mill, in which our hero struggles to procure investment dollars for his underdeveloped community. Despite this seeming modernity, however, the Folk are nonetheless everywhere in the novel as graphic markers of cultural entropy. In the industrial town, the bleached faces of the industrial workers suggest that they have been weakened – "emasculated" – by progress gone wrong. The only hope in this desolate industrial universe lies far up the back roads in a tranquil rural community. Here we find, in the home of one of the Folk,

a sedate little chamber with linoleum on the floor, a set of armchairs and a sofa badly gone in the springs but bright with chintz, and a small foot-tread harmonium with yellow ivory stops and keys that looked like a second- or third-hand relic of the prosperous 1870s, broken-winded now probably but kept because it gave the room a tone at once religious and "nice" ... A small round table under the window held a big family Bible with brass clasps, and I knew without looking inside that the flyleaves were inscribed with the names of Bob Predergrass and his wife, the name of the minister, and after these in regular succession the names and birth dates of the children. The atomic age didn't mean much on the Back Road. The old-fashioned habit of life remained with these people as a sort of anchor, inherited and still useful in a world that began to change its winds for the worse in 1914.[20]

"Maybe," concludes Raddall's hero, "you have to go up the Old Back Roads to find people who still have the secret of tranquillity."[21]

The antimodern chord struck by MacLennan and Raddall represented something relatively new in writing about Nova Scotia. Nineteenth-century social thought had registered the existence of rural Nova Scotia. From T.C. Haliburton and Thomas McCulloch on, many descriptions of rural stagnation can be drawn.[22] Setting aside the questionable accuracy of these descriptions, we are struck by their perspective. When nineteenth-century authors, clerics, and politicians wrote about rural backwardness, they viewed the people of the rural areas as potential souls to save, subjects to sway ideologically, recruits for future plans. Part of the strategy of depicting their backwardness in the starkest possible light (as one finds especially in the hectoring satires of the good Reverend McCulloch) was to shock rural people into action by painting an unflattering portrait of their own weaknesses. These organic intellectuals of an emergent capitalism were engaged with the rural producers dialectically, in a process that involved the exploration of both differences and similarities, and whose intended outcome was a convergence of outlook and a common program of "improvement." The matter is quite different when this sense of dialectical engagement is lost. In the twentieth century, after rural citizens were described as the Folk, they became, at least in the words and things representing them, objects of contemplation. Like Helen Creighton, one felt fond of the Folk with all their idiosyncracies, not outraged by their irreligion or their backwardness. This is one (and perhaps the most important) difference between Joseph Howe, Thomas McCulloch, and T.C. Haliburton on the one hand and Wallace MacAskill, Hugh MacLennan, and Helen Creighton on the other.

And it is an epistemological divide far more profound than any that can be located between twentieth-century insiders and outsiders. By the twentieth century, the urban eye, whether it belonged to an American or a Haligonian, saw what it wanted to see in rural areas. An apt parallel is suggested by Maryon McDonald's analysis of tourism in Brittany. Before "rural tourism" became high fashion in Europe, "travellers, men of letters, and administrators regularly saw in the French peasantry, not a charmingly unspoilt naturality, but a backward, curious, illiterate mob in need of schooling."[23] In twentieth-century tourist literature, however, Brittany is required to be a world of unspoiled charm and tradition – of cheerful Folk customs and a quaint language. Tourists who encounter high-tech farming techniques can dismiss such evidence of modernity as some sad imposition, extraneous to the "'real' Brittany that is expected and that will be found." The image of Brittany (which appeals to the modern urban tourist "in search of all that urbanity, modernity and progress are not") can triumph over numerous discrepancies, because tourists can discount them as some kind of "misleading superficiality, an external imposition, a foreign influence, an intrusion of the 'system,' and so on."[24] In short, no countervailing evidence need disrupt the smooth working of the categorical polarity (modernity–simplicity) that tourists bring to their experience of Brittany. The parallel with Nova Scotia is uncanny.

Apart from a few interesting exceptions – such as Frederic Cozzens's whimsically romantic depiction of the interior of a fisherman's cottage in *Acadia, or, A Month with the Blue Noses*[25] and a number of romantic engravings – nineteenth-century representations of Nova Scotia were remarkably blind to those who are now considered the province's most interesting and archetypal inhabitants, its fisherfolk. Primitive conditions in rural areas were not admired but condemned, and because the fisherfolk frequently lived in poor hamlets without the benefit of those material comforts Victorians held dear, they were not seen as living the simple life, but as poor and unlettered people, suitable objects of the attentions of missionaries and charitable institutes.

When the twentieth-century intellectuals, by contrast, described rural backwardness, they did so with the effusive fondness of grown-ups describing a childlike world they had already left far behind. When they looked upon a fishing family's humble abode, they saw not rural poverty but the simple life. They rarely distinguished between a voluntarily chosen simplicity and that which the rural poor were compelled to adopt because they lacked the money to live in any other way. For all their efforts to see the Folk "as they really were," we find the twentieth-century antimodernists playing out cultural tendencies international in scope and not much changed by their application to a particular local scene. It would be far too simple to suggest that local cultural producers either merely reproduced or were entirely separate from the touristic stereotypes of Nova Scotia. Yet, with very few exceptions, an interest in defining the Nova Scotian identity (what we have called neo-nationalism) was intertwined with a tendency to define every aspect of the Folk as "picturesque" and "quaint." If, as E.R. Forbes cogently argues, contemporary Maritimers must challenge regional stereotypes of conservatism and backwardness, perhaps the first step is to acknowledge that many of these regional stereotypes have been invented not by prejudiced politicians in the rest of Canada, or by superficial tourists, but by Maritimers themselves.[26]

The Folk and their lore, handicrafts, the simple life: these were mainly local products, but their construction followed international rules. The market relations that secured this correspondence between the local and the international can often be seen to work with disarming directness. They included the responses to cultural products from the international cultural marketplace, which determined which local books would become famous and which handicrafts would sell. Responses to their products mattered to local cultural producers, who, in the absence of a large, stable Canadian market for their goods, turned to American pulp magazines and publishers. From the 1920s on, across one cultural field after another, the American (and British) literary markets indicated an overwhelming preference for romantic tales of the sea, portrayals of salt-of-the-earth Folk living quiet lives in traditional peasant villages, and nostalgic images of the Golden Age. To ignore these preferences was to be as perverse and strange as the tourist who insisted on noticing the tractors in Brittany.

Mediating between this international framework and local society were the cultural producers, many of whom were loosely linked in a network, but not as members of a coherent school. The only really organized movement seems to have been the evocatively named "Song Fishermen" of Halifax. This was more a light-hearted, whimsical South End literary salon than a disciplined movement. The Song Fishermen circle centred on Andrew Merkel, a Halifax poet who also worked for the Canadian Press. Merkel was an important cultural organizer. A key proponent of historical reconstruction, an important force in the immensely popular cult of the schooner *Bluenose*, and (with his wife Tully) the focus of a literary salon in his fashionable South End home, he helped shape Innocence as a mythomoteur in the 1920s and 1930s. *The Song Fishermen's Song Sheets* was published between 1928 and 1930. The turn to the Folk was made obvious by the title of their publication and in their literary strategy of antimodernism. As the literary scholar Gwen Davies notes, although as "attuned to the developments in modern poetry as were their colleagues in London, Paris, New York or Montreal, the Song Fishermen nonetheless turned to traditional ballads, old sea chanteys, and even Gaelic literary forms in an attempt to evoke what they saw as the essence of Nova Scotia – to convey in the language of the lyric and the ballad their affinity for the sea and their joy in the simple comradeship of the Song Fishermen coterie."[27] This conscious antimodernism inspired numerous poems in honour of dulse, the reprinting of old songs, and homages to the Giant McAskill, the Folk hero of

Cape Breton.[28] Like Helen Creighton, the group was particularly drawn to the fishing communities of Halifax County: they were especially intrigued by Peggy's Cove and the other fishing hamlets on the Atlantic coast south of the city.[29] "By October of 1928," Davies notes, "the group had evolved a dramatic image of themselves as 'Fishers of Song,' a loosely-connected fellowship of literary fisherfolk who culled from the wind, the sea, and the traditional life style of Nova Scotia the poetic catches that defined their province."[30] In "Nova Scotia Catches," a collection of broadsheets, and in *The Song Fishermen's Song Sheets* the group used traditional songs and marine images to create a sense of the true Nova Scotia. The headnote, entitled "Come All Ye," signified the poets' determination to reflect the province's folksongs (so recently brought to public notice by Mackenzie's recent collection) and perhaps to become honourary members of the Folk themselves.

Merkel, like MacLennan, was a city man who imagined himself to be subjectively attuned to the Folk. As a South End Halifax journalist, an employee of the Canadian Press, and the organizer of an urban literary salon, he was a man of the twentieth century. But his subject-position was that of someone from an earlier day, one of the simpler, plainer Folk from Down East:

We are rather isolated down here in Nova Scotia. The material and commercial centre of gravity is distant from us, and has drawn many of our people away. The march of progress goes by us on the other side of the hill. It is a march which leaves little time for playing or singing.

There is always plenty of time here, and it is when time is on your hands that you will sing. Ross Bishop, the clock-maker of Bridgetown, locks his shop, hangs a sign on the door, "Gone Fishing," and goes. You cannot do that in Toronto or New York. Ross has plenty of time on his hands. He plays five or six instruments of music. He studies geology. He is an inventor. He loves to sit quiet in the woods and listen to nothing in particular for no definite length of time. The windows of his soul are open. He does a certain amount of mending clocks, but he does not have to punch them as he did that time he worked up in Waltham.

Let us not get too ambitious. Keep your eyes free from the glare of big cities and big reputations. Keep your mind free from the contemporary illusion which names every new thing a good thing, and turns its back on old things which have been proved in many thousand years of human blood and tears. An instance is the Gaelic tongue, an instrument of spiritual and lyric expression welded through untold centuries by a poetic people, living right here in our midst and allowed by our educational authorities to wither and die for lack of literary development in our schools.[31]

As was so often the case, these joys of the simple life were best savoured from a South End Halifax living-room. How else can one explain why Merkel did not immediately abandon the bustle of a modern Canadian city for a rural community?

The Song Fishermen's most ambitious attempt to invent tradition and honour the Folk was an elaborate poetry contest and marine excursion held in September 1929. The two-day event began in Halifax with sea shantys and a lecture on Nova Scotia poetry. Then the Fishermen set off in a schooner for East Dover, a fishing village southwest of Halifax. The event culminated with the crowning (with a diadem of dulse) of the King of the Song Fishermen. By including Gaelic recitations and Highland dancing, the Song Fishermen combined Scottish Romance with the cult of the fisherfolk.[32]

More significant as a coordinator of antimodernism than any autonomous group of cultural producers was the local tourism state. Before state coordination of tourism, the emergence of the Folk as a tourist attraction can be traced back to the mid-nineteenth century, although only in a localized and decidedly idiosyncratic development. Since the 1847 publication of Henry Wadsworth Longfellow's *Evangeline*, an epic poem on the Acadian expulsion, Americans began to arrive in Nova Scotia to seek out the landscapes evoked by the poem. (That Longfellow had not set eyes on Nova Scotia when he wrote the work did not detract from the hold his imagined Acadia exercised on his readers.) As one might expect from a poet who drew directly on Swedish and German sources for his sense of Folk life, Longfellow's Acadian peasants seemed remarkably like Europeans. Americans longing for both European civilization and premodern innocence were intrigued. Readers were aided in the development of a romantic image of Nova Scotia by numerous prints. *The Home of Evangeline*, the 1864 Currier and Ives effort, was a fine example of cultural selection. Here was a land of half-timbered, vaguely Tudor manor-houses, lovely orchards, flowing honey, majestic oaks, and shady sycamores: Acadia was clearly a pseudo-European Arcadia, bathed in a warm pastoral glow and a suitable setting for one of Grimm's fairy tales. It was this imagined landscape that American tourists, their romantic imaginations fired by the poem, wanted to see for themselves. This required even more heroic editing efforts than eliminating the tractors of Brittany, but evidently it could be done. The Americans arrived, full of that sweet melancholic nostalgia for times past that some locals called the "Longfellow sentiment."[33] Nova Scotia attracted them as a place where one could experience "the sad and sweet memories of Evangeline and the pleasant land of Grand Pré."[34]

In the 1920s this European Folk formula was generalized to the rest of Nova Scotia through the publicity of the local government. A "Folk Nova Scotia" arose in the 1920s in a rush of purple prose, syrupy sentimentality, and trite cliché, much of it coordinated by the new government tourism agencies. Nova Scotia became an "an old-world land that civilization has not yet robbed of its charm," as one travel writer wrote in 1925: "True, you will hear the roar of trains, you will see the scurrying of automobiles. But still the ox carts creep along the roads, the great patient beasts plodding as in a dream, and by their side go weather-beaten old men who look with annoyance and disdain on the conveyances of modern life."[35]

As McDonald said of Brittany, a determined tourist could erase inconsistencies as so many extraneous impositions on the Folk essence. Why, one wonders – at least, if one is not inclined to essentialism – does the roar of trains and the scurrying of automobiles count for so little and the ox-driven carts for so much? The question can also be asked of Andrew H. Brown's article entitled, "Salty Nova Scotia: In Friendly New Scotland Gaelic Songs Still Answer the Skirling Bagpipes," which appeared in the *National Geographic* in 1940. By this point, the quaint drowsiness of the Folk celebrated fifteen years earlier has reached a dangerous point of narcolepsy: the pace of the oxen is now so leisurely "that drivers sometimes fall back asleep into the sweet-scented hay."[36] In Brown's imagined Nova Scotia, the twentieth century was at most a distant rumour. Of the thirteen landscape photographs that accompanied the article, four were of the picturesque fishing villages of the South Shore. Other photographs showed an old fisherman of Blue Rocks playing the organ for his wife in their humble cottage parlour; the *Bluenose;* cod-drying; a net-mending fisherman; and several Highland flings.

By the 1930s the Folk were no longer necessarily Acadian. They could be members of any ethnic group (significantly excluding, for the most part, natives and blacks). The archetypal members of the Folk in the tourist imagination were undoubtedly the fisherfolk – the one major social group commonly designated as "folk" in the collective noun applied to them. The fisherfolk were unquestionably the key Nova Scotians in the tourist gaze. The provincial publication of 1928 makes no bones about it: "A Nova Scotia Type" is the caption accompanying a photograph of a fisherman mending his net.[37] "In the scenic land of Longfellow's Evangeline, the haven of Grand Banks fishermen, the home of heroes, you'll find a friendly remoteness from the confusions of the world," readers of *Holiday* were told in 1953.[38] "The people themselves seem to have a different and more old-fashioned outlook on life than their fellow countrymen," reported the travel writer Frank Oliver Call. "An old fisherman, who sat basking in the sun while mending his nets, looked at us curiously, and we stopped to converse with him. He told us of the life of the fishermen and their families, of the great fire which years before swept over that part of the coast."[39] A photograph in the *National Home Monthly* showed "a typical Nova Scotia fisherman taking farewell of his wife before rowing out to his fishing vessel."[40] The examples could be multiplied ad infinitum.

Why visit the fisherfolk? They were fascinatingly quaint sights. They also provided rewarding social sites wherein middle-class visitors could re-enact an imagined pastoral history of deep interpersonal bonds across class lines. By visiting Nova Scotia one could recover a lost Golden Age of class harmony. "Visitors soon know all the folks about," said the official government publication in 1950, "and accept easily the deference given summer people."[41] In 1932 George Matthew Adams, a naturalist and syndicated columnist for newspapers across North America, and (thanks to the prompting of the Halifax *Herald*) an indefatigable booster of the province as a summer rest-cure for the beleaguered business classes of the eastern seaboard, assured prospective visitors in an official pamphlet that their "pedigree" would not matter among these down-to-earth Folk.

The people of this Province are weathered human souls. They have known all the privations, and their pioneers and forefathers bequeathed to them bravery and hardihood ... Sturdy, honest and humanly fine are the fisher folk who have been born and bred for decade upon decade upon the rocky shores of this Province by the sea. Their attractive homes are places of neatness and they are lovers of beauty. Their children have been educated and made fit for usefulness in the world.

These simple Folk boasted of no skyscrapers: "Theirs is a content and happiness near to the earth. The natural beauty of their sea, their rockbound coast, their lakes, rivers, forests, and peaceful farming communities, mean more to them than 'coronets' or heralded boasts of bigness."[42] And they were both friendly and deferential. The moneyed visitor need not fear that his or her social eminence would lead to unpleasant scenes. "I have especially loved the fisher folk," Adams exclaimed. So would his readers, should they pay them a visit: "You love their simple and honest ways, their straightforward manner and genial consideration for you."[43]

One might write off this peculiar production as typical of an ignorant outsider, but how then would one explain virtually the same tone in the travel books of Will R. Bird, the Nova Scotian author of wildly popular novels and one of the province's leading public historians? (Bird's after-dinner speeches to service clubs across Canada did much to shape impressions of Nova Scotia.) Any attempt to attribute Folk stereotypes to insensitive outsiders must founder when it comes to Bird's books – *This Is Nova Scotia, Off-Trail in Nova Scotia,* and *These Are the Maritimes* – all of which sold extremely well, and were as well received in Nova Scotia as throughout Canada. The antimodernist appeal of the Folk goes a long way to explaining the extraordinary success of Bird's travel books. In Nova Scotia, writes Bird, "Daily existence seems to have a different tempo from the rest of Canada, and there is that inexplicable strength of character that comes to those who live largely by themselves."[44] In Parrsboro the visitor could meet old-timers who still cherished the ballads of the "good old days."[45] In the Annapolis Valley, the travellers meet an old woman with blue-veined hands who holds a bowl of berries: "There weren't cars in my day," she drawls (drowsily, no doubt) "and I'm just as glad there weren't. We'd no need of them. Times change mighty fast."[46]

Local he undoubtedly was, but Bird nonetheless represented the voice of the Folk with a tourist's emphatic sense of their primitive Otherness. An "oldster" trades tales of the Micmacs with Bird, spitting and wiping his chin: "The lazy intonation of his voice seemed as physical as the touch of his hand, but when he paused, now and then, his mouth had the immobility of lips that can guard secrets ... His eyes brightened as he talked until it seemed that his shrivelled body was like a leathery coat of flesh and bones covering the spirit of a venturesome youngster." Without warning, the oldster breaks into song, and concludes his visit with Bird by saying, "Don't go thinkin' I'm crazy."[47] Elsewhere (even, improbably, in thoroughly industrial Sydney) the Folk spend their time sitting around their general stores and by their fireplaces, trading tales of witches and ghosts, of cruel natives abducting innocent white children and of blacks (in the appropriate dialect) much the worse for liquor.[48] The ethnic "Othering" we discerned in folklore was clearly operational in the wider setting of tourism promotion. They are a slow-moving Folk, these Nova Scotians, living in a drowsy, dreamlike land:

We entered the town [Lawrencetown] slowly and saw that the elms were as lovely as elms can be. It was drowsy and peaceful, and some small knots of people were gathered by the few stores and garages. We slowed and stopped, thinking that from the time we had entered the province at Amherst we had not seen a dozen persons who acted as if they were in a hurry ... Through the country districts one sees the old folk in doorways or in chairs under shade trees. There are mothers out with the children. Fathers standing together and exchanging small talk. Strangers must feel that here is a place where life is good, a grand country in which to retire.[49]

Such pre-modern Folk needed no coercive state to discipline them or order their affairs. Adams reported that he had seen but one jail in the entire Province. "Perhaps there are more," he added jauntily, "I have not enquired; besides, I am not interested in jails."[50] Bird took equal delight in reporting that there were no police officers, jails, unemployed, poor relief, or divorces in Pubnico.[51] Bird's imagined Pubnico was made up exclusively of a contented people, so calm and relaxed that, incredibly, they had no ailments. There was, moreover, no class distinction; thrift and careful living were respected by all; and everybody was well educated.[52] When, on infrequent occasions, Bird does notice poverty and hunger, these unsettling bits of realism are promptly whisked away. "There were many cars in Inverness [a Cape Breton coal town] but we found no old-timer with a tall tale or history," he writes (usefully documenting just how he selected his leading voices of the Folk). "Instead, we were told about closed mines and hardship and lack of co-operation by authorities and hard times and some families with little to eat. But the youngsters we saw looked happy enough and hardy enough and we hoped that some day coal mining would start again."[53]

This is only the tip of an iceberg of commentary on the Nova Scotia Folk, much of which, by the 1950s, had started to repeat itself. There was a developed rhetoric of the Folk that writers could call upon as the occasion demanded. Warm-hearted descriptions of quaint hamlet X could be easily used for portraits of charming harbour Y. Bird, for example, started to run short of phrases for the quaint fisherfolk, and took to surreptitiously borrowing those developed by J.F.B. Livesay: Livesay's description of Peggy's Cove was adapted to describe another community altogether.[54] And his description of the egalitarianism of the primitive Folk was suspiciously close to Adams's: "Here we saw how a proportion of our Nova Scotians lived. It is a region where pedigree doesn't matter, and the people are weathered human souls. Where families have learned from generation to generation to make a little go a long way. Where there are rough exteriors but kind hearts and true. Where there are those who lack money and education and background, and good luck, but who are the salt of the earth."[55]

His journey, concluded Bird, had given him "a stronger belief in that which has been said many times, that Nova Scotia is a place where beauty has had time to grow, where memories have gathered, giving depth and meaning to the lives of a people who always have leisure to be kind."[56] For his more alert readers, such a borrowing of bon mots from other authors might have prompted the cynical reflection that by the 1950s, drowsy as this quaint land of tranquil fisherfolk might be, its hyperactive publicists lacked the time to be original.

From 1920 to 1960 the imagined Folk were omnipresent in the works of the cultural producers we have selected for analysis. Four particular emphases can be drawn out of this vast literature: Cape Breton as the homeland of the Folk, the "fisherfolk" as bearers of cultural essence, the importance of the Folk to conservative gender ideals, and finally the broader use of the Folk idea within neo-nationalism in the province.

"OUR AIN FOLK" IN CAPE BRETON

By the 1930s, thanks to Innocence as a new way of imagining the true Nova Scotians, one no longer had to be Acadian to be one of the Folk. Now this privilege was extended to all people throughout the province who appeared to be picturesquely removed from the twentieth-century mainstream. Two groups, rural Cape Bretoners and the fisherfolk, occupied a place of special prominence.

Cape Breton's Folk were of special interest to those who wanted to intensify Nova Scotia's sense of Scottishness. It was easy to view "Cape Breton" as exotic, for it was in fact an island set apart, with a visible Scottish presence, many remote rural communities, and its own accent.

The Song Fishermen, some of whom had a serious if unrealistic interest in reviving Gaelic, once spoken widely on the island, merged the motif of the Folk and Scottishness by adopting the poet and writer James D. Gillis of Inverness. The Fishermen paid homage to Gillis's literary gifts and placed him in judgment over their poems. But he was unmistakably the living embodiment of the Folk in their eyes, a living, breathing primitive. His droll sayings and his quaint naiveté were savoured by a Halifax hungry for authenticity. Gillis even became a national figure of sorts, after William Arthur Deacon, the cultural broker and critic, included him in *The Four Jameses*, a fond, humorous study of rough-hewn literary figures in Canada.[57]

Gillis as seen in Halifax and Gillis as seen by certain Cape Bretoners were two different phenomena. In his own eyes and in the interpretation of some commentators in Inverness, Gillis was to be taken seriously as a writer. In "James D. Gillis Teacher and Author, An Appreciation of his literary and poetic genius," John G. Mac-

James D. Gillis. PANS N-6344.

Pherson told readers of the *Inverness and Victoria Bulletin* that Gillis was a "gentleman of high scholastic attainments, a brilliant and authoritative writer, and a poet of no ordinary ability ... I have heard it said – by men in whose knowledge I place reliance – that Mr Gillis is not only a great writer, but one of the greatest. Certainly few, if any, among the writers of modern times, surpass him in force of imagination, vivacity of allusion, or beauty and elegance of diction."[58] D.J. Rankin, writing as a conservative Catholic interpreter of the Folk, noted in *Our Ain Folk* (1930) the cultural freight carried by Gillis. In Rankin's novel, a young man, the recent product of a great university, had become fond of alluding jocosely to the book lately published on the Cape Breton Giant (Gillis's most famous effort). "Such an attitude towards the endeavours of an author who had gone to considerable pains and expense in an effort to perpetuate the memory of an outstanding figure in the community was deserving of censure," Rankin remarked (speaking through the mouths of various characters: his work is so didactic that every positively portrayed character can be safely viewed as his personal mouthpiece).

He could not understand why people supposed to be intellectual were addicted to the habit of throwing cold water on the literary efforts of men who were only trying to benefit their fellow men, by preserving traditions and memories, and by inspiring people to emulate the good example of those who have passed on ... If Robbie Burns had tried to write his verse in the manner and form, and using the expressions of Oxford University, would his poems have touched the hearts of the world? So why shrug our shoulders at a man who writes in the language of his own people hereabouts?[59]

Because, briefly, urban middle-class people were predisposed to seek out and relish rustic simplicity, and they wielded the cultural power in this situation. Gillis was generally depicted in tourism promotion of the day, and is represented now, as a quaint, droll figure of the backwoods.[60] For Deacon and for the Song Fishermen, Gillis was less a fellow poet and more a specimen. Gillis was enlisted by the Song Fishermen to judge poems on the theme of the Giant McAskill, and his idiosyncratic comments were lovingly preserved in their songsheet. Certain Gillicisms have become well known. The most famous is his comment in a prefatory "Brief Sketch" to *The Cape Breton Giant*: "I was twice to the United States; I do not say so for the sake of boast." Deacon found his delight in another Gillis passage: "The breath of St. Ann's cemetery is as fragrant and sweet as that of a flower garden. As one walks along he is apt to imagine that a costly deodorant has been sprinkled about a few minutes ago."[61] Gillis reached for dramatic effects and then unintentionally undercut them with a naive or prosaic word. To the modern middle-class ear, he was delightfully comic.

In taking up Gillis, the Halifax cultural producers were not engaged in an effort to understand someone from a different place and culture. They never showed the slightest interest in understanding how he functioned in his community or in placing him in his cultural context. The logic behind Gillis's use of language – whether, for instance, his diction was the result of Gaelic culture – interested them not at all. South End Halifax was content to pat the head of a decontextualized Cape Breton barbarian. The novelist Thomas Raddall recalled welcoming Gillis to Halifax for an appearance in the 1940s.

He got off the train with little baggage other than his fiddle and bagpipes, wearing a shabby suit of hand-me-downs, a greasy cap, and an ancient coat made from the pelt of a buffalo obviously afflicted with mange ... Our first job was to provide the visitor with a better outfit of clothes – shirts, underwear, socks and so on. For footwear he chose a pair of seamen's boots, calf-high, which would be "useful on the hills back home" ...

He was eccentric but not the self-important half-wit that some mistaken people thought he was. His indifference to soap and water was apparent, but his bald head was noble, the brow full, the eyebrows thick and black, his eyes a dark brown that glowed whenever he warmed to his subject, the eyes of a poet and philosopher. A grey moustache covered his upper lip and drooped at the mouth corners. He must have stood six feet in youth but hunched his shoulders now, and he walked with the long loose stride of a man of the hills. In Cape Breton, where he and many other people still spoke Gaelic, he was known as Sheamus Dhu (Black James) to distinguish him from other Jameses in the numerous Gillis family.[62]

Soon, Raddall continues, "all Halifax" knew "the famous James D. was in town." He was brought to the radio station and talked about Cape Breton traditions. He was invited by the millionaire F.B. McCurdy to Emscote, the family mansion on the Northwest Arm. "Sheamus Dhu," who is described as someone who ate mostly with his hands, complained to Raddall afterwards (with an accent alleged to be characteristic of Cape Breton) "I wass full before supper wass half over." Then, "after 'supper,' to bring luck to the house in the old Highland fashion, Sheamus marched from cellar to garret playing his pipes, followed in procession by the McCurdy family and all their servants. For a good job of luck the pipes had to be played in every chamber and closet. Sheamus told us later, 'That house is ass bigg ass a university!'"[63]

It is interesting that the version of Raddall's memoir in the contemporary local reprint of *The Cape Breton Giant* mitigated Raddall's "Othering" of Gillis by removing his attempt to capture Gillis's accent.[64] What remains unsoftened is the patronizing cultural politics of the entire phenomenon. Displaying Gillis in this manner without attempting to place him in his tradition (or, as some implied at the time, in the context of his psychological problems) was a sort of cultural cruelty, an abuse of symbolic power.

Had Gillis not existed, it would have been necessary for Halifax to invent him. And in a sense he *was* invented: the complex individual person was redescribed as the hilarious, quaint, unwashed, reassuringly tractable Cape Breton barbarian, a stereotype that seemed to fill a deep urban hunger for a childlike (not to mention kilted) savage. Halifax's homage to Gillis's literary gifts was a tainted tribute: his fame was that of the charmed child, the innocent abroad, the fondly patronized primitive. The Folk were "not us"; and Gillis was defined as "not us" by his quaint speech, his table manners, his Gaelic inflections, and most of all by his innocence. Raddall captured something of the cultural process involved when he referred to Gillis as a "sort of mascot" of the Halifax crowd (although his own ensuing description was no less patronizing and objectifying).[65] In Gillis, Halifax had found the living embodiment of the charms of a pre-modern time – and a stimulus for something close to camp humour.

If Gillis suggested the way the Cape Breton Folk could become a popular hit in Halifax, D.J. Rankin, a Cape Breton priest and a fierce conservative, suggested how Innocence might be set to work very differently in the interpretation of Cape Breton for Cape Bretoners themselves, as well as for outsiders. Rankin sought to rescue Gillis from the laughter of Halifax and literate Canada in general, because he was concerned to present the Cape Breton Folk in their true character, free from the misrepresentations and misunderstandings of outsiders. Rankin set out to present the first accurate portrait in print of the "true Cape Bretoner." He strongly objected not only to the ridiculing of Gillis but also to the nineteenth-century traditions of rural caricature. He found the results of this early literature dismal; they had "never amounted to anything more than apologetic caricatures, or else merciless travesties of the Cape Bretoners."[66] He took particular aim at Charles Dudley Warner's *Baddeck, and That Sort of Thing* – an early classic in American humour, in which the humour is mainly at the expense of the rural Scots of Cape Breton, who are depicted as unlettered, ignorant, and self-important. Rankin condemned the book as the work of a traveller who, once having enjoyed the hospitality and friendship of a people, proceeded to expose "to the gaze of future generations skeletons that would have been better off untouched."[67]

Rankin had an acute grasp of the politics of cultural selection, and developed a critique of how this selection had worked on Cape Bretoners. His polemical work is evidence that insiders were not securely insulated from the belittling words of outsiders. He was also the most political of the inventors of the Folk. His two key books – *Our Ain Folk and Others* and *On This Rock*, both published in 1930 – were unusually explicit in drawing out the conservative organic ideology of the Folk which other writers left as an unstated assumption in their work. Yet the paradox of Innocence remains. Rankin's locally constructed Folk were as much externally generated as those of the satirists he criticized.

For all his local credentials, Rankin constructed his Cape Breton Folk using materials borrowed from *Maria Chapdelaine* (the classic agrarian novel depicting a Folk Quebec) and various papal encyclicals. For Rankin, the fisherfolk of Cape Breton embodied the Catholic agrarian ideal, and he never deviated from his central didactic purpose of upholding the Catholic cause against its foes. *Our Ain Folk* follows the lives of the fisherfolk Charles Townsend, his son Harry Townsend, and his friend and confidante John Stacy. They are not so much characters as personified ideologies. In Rankin's imagined Cape Breton, local people like to walk about the countryside quoting papal encyclicals, delivering speeches to each other on the simple life, and "indulging in a flow of philosophy concerning the happiness of the poor."[68] That the poor can be happy and that relations between rich and poor can be beautiful are the two great pillars of Rankin's social thought. His rural characters were unsophisticated, he argued, but they could teach lessons to their urban counterparts about simple, good lives.

These hard-working, humble, honest fisherfolk and small farmers are in a certain sense more highly educated concerning the things of life that really matter, than are the majority of our college graduates of the present day. These farmers and fishermen, coming as they do into constant contact with the manifold works of Nature, have a better opportunity for studying the scheme of Life than their sophisticated brothers of the larger centres of population. Their slower-moving mode of existence affords them ampler scope for meditation and mental development, and therefore they must needs possess a deeper knowledge of the philosophy of life.[69]

A frantic modern world could learn from those who were living the life God had originally intended for mankind: tilling the soil, tending the flocks, and fishing the oceans. Rankin read a religious and philosophical importance into the "slower pace of life" so often eulogized in travel accounts. Good living and right thinking flourished where the pace was slower. These provincial virtues could provide inspiration for "those who are out in the more thickly populated centres of the Battlefield of Life," for "down here in Cape Breton, where life flows on more calm and serene than in many another place, we are accustomed to think more deeply. Perhaps we can view life down here from a truer angle. Is it not possible that we are nearer to the solution of the Riddle of Life, that we have secured a greater measure of happiness and contentment, simply because we are just a little bit slower-moving than our brethren of the big cities?"[70]

Besides affording proximity to the solution of the "Riddle of Life," living in tranquil Cape Breton provides the supplementary benefits of family values and the Christian tradition of mutual aid. As Charles Townsend and John Stacy debate whether to leave their fishing village, both "wisely appreciated the fact that, everything considered, the little village held out many inducements for the correct raising of a family."[71] In the organic Folk community, the spirit of true Christian charity is constantly practised. "If anyone in the neighbourhood suffered a loss, all helped to repair it. If a boat were wrecked, or nets destroyed, if a dwelling-house or barn was burned down, or if a domestic animal died, a collection was immediately begun for the unfortunate sufferer."[72] The Cape Breton Folk are, in sum, "the best and dearest people on earth."[73]

Rankin's Cape Breton Folk nonetheless face challenges in a changing world, some of which are more easily met than others. Seasonal unemployment and poverty, for example, haunt the fishing villages, but the main responsibility for poverty lies with the individual fisherman, who is thought to be unprepared, untrained, and unknowledgeable about his trade. But poverty is scarcely a major consideration in *Our Ain Folk*: "On rich and poor alike the good God has showered manifold blessings. The contemplation and the appreciation of these manifold blessings bring peace and happiness, regardless of one's richness or poorness."[74] Encounters with other classes in the rural community pose another challenge. Will children acquire ideas above their station in life from rich tourists? Perhaps, but mixing with people of the moneyed classes would do the children of the Folk good, for the rich Americans would broaden their minds and prepare them for a changing world.[75] The same pastoral vision pervades even the discussion of foreign bosses in the (thinly fictionalized) Sydney steel mill. Rather than resenting the foreign domination of the management of the local industries, the local Folk come to realize that they should be grateful to the foreigners for the benefit of their brains and experience.[76]

Underlying the questioning of the bosses of the steel mill and the menace of radicalism is an even deeper challenge faced by Rankin's Folk: the threat of a secular order. Throughout both his books the university, which teaches a crass materialism, is identified as a potential menace, luring the young Folk away from their true roots. Evolution was a cult that was spreading from the universities to engulf even the local upper middle class: Huxley, Darwin, Marx, and "other European scientists of this brand" had "wrought much havoc even in this faraway corner of civilization."[77] Even local social workers (presumably Rankin was referring to the Antigonish Movement) posed a threat by suggesting that poverty was a great evil. It had never occurred to these misguided secularists that "people may be poor in a worldly way and yet be richer than the richest millionaire in virtue."[78]

How should the Folk respond to these enemies within? "Work or starve" was a useful general answer to the demands of trade unions, Rankin felt, but the deeper problems required a renewed Catholicism. *On This Rock* concludes with a lengthy sermon from a visiting Mission Father on the subject of social peace, preached in the middle of a dramatic strike. (How such labour turmoil could be reconciled with a sense of Cape Breton as a haven from modernity remains puzzling.) The Mission Father reminds the workers that in the community, as in the home, the golden rule must be observed. A wise community was animated by a spirit of give-and-take between capitalist and labourer, for only cooperation between the two classes could produce social peace, efficiency, and prosperity.[79] Chastened labourers return to work, and peace returns to a Folk wise enough to listen to the Church.

It does not seem likely that Canadian labour historians will be tempted to abandon their neo-Marxist work on the class wars in Cape Breton in favour of Rankin's contemporary corporatist interpretation. Those familiar with this historiography will appreciate just how extravagantly the priest edited the social crisis in the coalfields to suit his own purpose and create an image of the Folk. (One may merely mention that the implication that foreigners were the backbone of radicalism overlooks how many Cape Breton-born miners were radicals in the 1920s.) Rankin's redescription of class-divided Cape Breton is less persuasive as an account of events than it is as a working model of how useful the Folk could be in ideological struggles over the meaning of modernity and development. Rankin was, of course, an unusual intellectual, and undertook a particular project: the defence of a specifically Catholic corporatist philosophy in the area of Canada that most closely approximated a battlefield of class against class in the 1920s. Nonetheless, it would be a mistake not to notice how closely Rankin's view of Cape Breton resembles so many other interwar redescriptions of Nova Scotia, even in its conscious echoing of *Maria Chapdelaine*. Having set out a static, timeless notion of Folk values and traditions as an absolute standard by which the evils of modernity can be judged, Rankin is drawn logically into a strategy of protecting the eternal Folk against radical contamination, in a way that vividly reminds us of Helen Creighton's own response to labour and modernity in general. And, as with Creighton, the antimodernist contradiction is palpable: defending an organic, oral, "natural" society, Rankin resorted to the instruments of propaganda and the public press. The only way to battle modernity, it seems, was to pick up its weapons.

AMONG THE FISHERFOLK

Even in Cape Breton, Rankin's archetypal Folk are not farmers but fishermen. For Creighton, the truest of the Folk lived along her "Coast of Songs." They were the "fisherfolk," a designation that has since fallen into disuse, but which was common currency in the interwar period. The fisherfolk had even less claim to be considered the archetypal Nova Scotians than had the Scots. In selecting the fisherfolk as the archetypal "Bluenoses," the middle-class cultural producers selected an occupational group that in the 1920s represented slightly over 8 per cent of the full- and part-time waged workforce. The fishermen were far outnumbered by industrial workers in every decade after 1900. The "typical Nova Scotian" adult was more likely to be a coal miner or an urban wage earner than one of the fisherfolk. For the middle-class people constructing the Folk, however, industrial or modern figures would hardly do as exemplars of the Nova Scotian people. They were patently not living the simple life; they were not as distinctive, and hence not as noteworthy.

A major reason for selecting the fisherfolk perhaps lies in another element of interwar culture: the rise of Canadian nationalism. At the same time as the region passed into deep crisis, Canadian nationalism was developing its key myths and iconic landscapes. The local cultural producers were left to find things about their region that both fit into this nationalism and suggested at the same time the distinctive contribution that their region made to the supposed Canadian whole. Although both farmers and fishermen were of the Folk, only the fisherfolk could be seen as being even somewhat distinctive in the Canadian setting. They became the archetypal Nova Scotians in the interwar period. Even in so urban a novel as Hugh MacLennan's *Barometer Rising*, the fisherfolk are definitional for Nova Scotia; they are the core of Innocence ruined by the calculations of the ruthless capitalists of the city.[80]

Among the novelists, no one captured the fisherfolk with greater apparent naturalism and intensity than Frank Parker Day (1881–1950). Like Mary Black's handicrafts, his fisherfolk are virtual mirrors of nature, "embodiments" of the rock and the sea. As with so many of the regional antimodernists, Day had one foot inside the region and one foot out. He was a Nova Scotia-born and Oxford-educated academic. In 1928, when *Rockbound* was published, he was the president of Union College in Schenectady.

Day's imagined Nova Scotia is a pre-modern world of rugged islands. ("Rockbound" is a thinly fictionalized Ironbound, and the "Outpost Islands" are the Tancook Islands; both are set in the Atlantic Ocean off the South Shore of Nova Scotia). Day's Folk Nova Scotia is no pastoral haven. *Rockbound* graphically describes the backbreaking labour of fishing and fish-handling, the raw viciousness of familial politics on an island presided over by a grasping patriarch, and the horrors of an offshore marine disaster. As Gwen Davies has shown, Day's gripping description of a great storm at sea was inspired directly by press accounts of the August gales of 1926, which killed many fishermen on the Banks. Other realistic details in the novel are drawn from the prewar period.[81] Day was attempting to marry realistic descriptions of the harsh realities faced by fishermen to a conventional regional romance. His detailed look at the work of the inshore and Grand Banks fishermen and his sense of the bitter familial conflicts in small communities set the novel refreshingly apart from the portrayals of tidy, idyllic fishing villages in other accounts. "Dem poets is de bunk … Dere ain't no magic nur enchanted islands!" exclaims the hero of the novel in a down-to-earth critique of Shakespeare's *The Tempest*.[82]

Day's novel of the fisherfolk thus had the substantial claims to truth of on-the-spot investigation. He had visited these islands, researched their geography and their folkways, and then presented his findings in thinly fictionalized form. One scholar has concluded that *Rockbound* offers readers an ethnographic insight into local culture and traditions, an "insider's perception of a particular group" and "a holistic picture of the folk heritage that guides the lives of the Rockbound fishermen."[83] Janice Kulyk Keefer, one of the leading critics of Maritime literature, considers *Rockbound* the one regional novel "which significantly comprehends – and demystifies – a 'sense of the sea' … Through a skilful use of dialect and descriptive prose, Day conveys to us the very taste and grain of a fisherman's life."[84] The eminent critic and author Archibald MacMechan had much the same reaction six decades earlier: he congratulated Day for bringing "realism into Canadian fiction," adding, "You have given us life, in the raw actuality. Motivation, character, thought, outlook are all true. Your people are alive."[85]

These readings are naive. If one can understand the response of the incorrigibly romantic MacMechan, one finds far less comprehensible the response of the post-structuralist Keefer, who might have interrogated more closely her own essentialist rhetoric of "the very taste and grain." *Rockbound* is of a piece with the entire Quest of the Folk. The novel is less a realistic description of the coastal community than an attempt to distil its Folk essence and thereby man's inherent nature. It is not an exception to antimodern naturalism and essentialism, but rather, in many respects, its most perfect regional expression. Paradoxically, by inserting into his description of this way of life a complacent portrayal of its drawbacks, Day strengthens the hold of a essentialist romanticism.[86] The incompleteness of Day's realism stems from his inability to avoid three fundamental tensions. The first, as noted by the astute contemporary critic Dr Eliza Ritchie, was the tension between social realism and *Rockbound*'s faithful adherence to the conventions of romance, exemplified by its papier-mâché heroine and its contrived and sudden happy ending. The second problem was more basic. Day's *Rockbound* represents Nature as all-powerful and determining. His characters are little more than pawns of Nature. As Leo Lowenthal noted of Knut Hamsun, "In this new ideology, which seeks to transfigure helplessness and subjection, the individual lays down his arms before a higher power in seemingly free volition. Man must expect the terrors of a meaningless life unless he obediently accepts as his own what may be called the alien of nature."[87] Although Day's right-wing proclivities led him not to Hamsun's fascism but to the quieter waters of the Conservative party, where he achieved minor prominence, he resembled Hamsun in his conviction that he could grasp the Rockbounders' inner truth – that they are driven by natural rhythms – and that their hunger, sexuality, and greed are simply forces of nature. He has a Spencerian sense of the "survival of the fittest."

Rockbound tells us almost nothing about the culture of these island primitives. They are always framed ("essentialized") throughout the book by opening quotations from Chaucer, which make an implicit case for the timelessness of human nature. Day had grasped the fisherfolk's inner truth of primitive animality before he considered any of the particulars in which this essence was expressed. Holding that man is essentially an animal dependent on the rhythms of nature, Day presents the fishermen as men reduced to their "primitive essentials" in their struggles to survive in a harsh natural setting. The island setting is isolated and stripped of all civilization. David, the hero, is less an individual person than a naive and questing Everyman in a Sou'Wester. Driven by a kind of reductionist passion, Day opens the novel on the isolated rocky island of Rockbound, and proceeds on to the even more isolated, stark, tempest-tossed Barren Island, a "gaunt plateau," where "life was stripped of all its shams."[88] This radical naturalism places *Rockbound* in a highly ambiguous position with respect to those very fisherfolk for whom such deep admiration is expressed. Day has believable villains but no believable heroes. The fisherfolk who perform this function are not really heroes but overgrown children – captives of a perpetual Innocence. They are great "overgrown boys" who experience love and companionship as a sort of "dog-like affection." Their musings on the universe are so vague and dim – "dim" is a persistent word in Day's characterization of the mental processes of the Folk – that the author must frequently intrude upon their primitive philosophizings to bring out what he feels is their universal significance. As with the prominent novelist F.W. Wallace, who referred to the "simple-minded Canadian fishermen,"[89] and whose books on the Banks fishermen suggest certain parallels with Day's work, it was a short step from admiration for the fisherfolk's simplicity to contempt for their mental capacity. The representation of dialect is an important indication of the cultural politics entailed in this book (as it was in the case of Gillis): whether in nineteenth-century habitant poems or in the representation of aboriginal speech in westerns, dialect provides an economical way of "Othering" the Folk primitive by establishing through language a sense of cultural strangeness and difference that is not otherwise argued for. The scenes in *Rockbound* in which the kind-hearted schoolteacher patiently strives to correct the hero's South Shore pronunciation ("wid" and "dat" to "this" and "that"), and then awards her pupil with a copy of Shakespeare's *The Tempest*, are patently an English professor's patronizing pastoral fantasy of relations with picturesque island folk. In *Rockbound* the dialect of the Folk is a grunting, primitive Other side of complex speech, perhaps all that the childlike, primitive fishermen, with their reckless sexuality, drinking bouts, and stripped-down emotions, really need. Day's handling of dialect serves to convey a sense of the childlike simplicity of the fisherfolk without any concessions to the complexity and intricacy of their actual speech. His fisherfolk indeed remain "rockbound," inarticulate human figures locked in an all-determining landscape of coastal rock and sea.

Day, it has been said, is a realist, and the proof of the ethnographic realism of *Rockbound* lies in the painstaking research he carried out on Ironbound Island in 1926 before he wrote his novel. It is certainly true that Day's summer of research was comparable to the time invested by a folklorist such as Creighton in investigating her own communities of the Folk. But the politics of cultural selection worked as powerfully in Day's case as in anyone else's. For someone who claimed deep insight into the innermost souls of the islanders about whom he wrote, Day did not stay very long. Nor is one persuaded by the realism of his portayal of the islanders' utter isolation. The Folk surely must market their fish somewhere; they probably are affiliated with province-wide churches; and their lighthouse keeper is probably a civil servant – all aspects of life that compromised their supposed isolation from the twentieth century.

The strongest critique of Day's realism was presented by a number of citizens of Ironbound Island themselves, in a rare instance of working people rejecting their representation as Folk in literary culture. The islanders' sense of betrayal stemmed from the friendly interactions they had established with Day. These interactions, insofar as we have evidence of them, do not suggest that the actual people of the island were particularly primitive. (It is revealing, for example, that Day loaned the lighthouse keeper on Tancook a copy of H.G. Wells's *The Outline of History*, a book that suggests a rather different grasp on reality than that of his fictional lighthouse keepers, who are predictably fixated on the supernatural.)[90] The islanders were upset about being regarded as so much cultural fodder. Day had not been candid with them about the purpose of his note-taking. He collected his notes on the sly (pretending on at least one occasion that he was preparing a lecture on Shakespeare). Like so many other cultural producers, he seems to have regarded the islanders as so much material to write up, and some of those written up did not like what they read. The "Offended Citizens of Rockbound" published a letter in the Lunenburg *Progress-Enterprise* contesting the novel's portrait of "us humble inhabitants" as "ignorant, immoral and superstitious." With a simple but not inaccurate insight into the economics of cultural appropriation, they speculated that Day might "accumulate quite a bit of money" from his enterprise.[91] Day immediately resorted to the nearest available alibi: *Rockbound* was based on stories he had heard as a child, not on any actual present-day community. The islanders' construction as primitive fisherfolk had occurred behind their backs, and for a cultural marketplace they could not influence. Protest all they want and use as many references as they might to suggest their familiarity with western culture, the fisherfolk simply had no influence over the ways in which they were represented within Innocence and marketed as the Folk Other.[92]

Far from demystifying the "sense of the sea," *Rockbound* exemplifies the enduring attractions to urban middle-class writers of an essentialist myth of nature and natural Folk. In the *Rockbound* debate, the construction of an ethnographic interpretation of the folk based upon a reductionist understanding of the environment was challenged by some of the informants themselves. Here were the seeds of a creative dialogue over the limits and ethics (in this particular society) of cultural selection, over the lines that divided legitimate if inevitably partial interpretation from the abuse of cultural power. One could imagine a society in which such a mutual exchange of insights would have made complex, subtle, and rich interpretations possible as the outcome of an extended if painful dialogue. But this would presuppose a deeper connection between the intellectual and the non-intellectual, a reciprocal sense of sharing in something of the same cultural project, and an entirely different type of cultural hegemony – not the interwar model of the Folk as a natural resource. Within a liberal order that was turning increasingly to tourism, such a reciprocal dialogue was unlikely to occur: appropriating and commodifying a culture seen as "Other" had become a mainstay of middle-class cultural and economic life.

The figure who presents the most problems for the thesis of this book is not Frank Parker Day but the American painter Marsden Hartley, whose search for a haven of authenticity and happiness in Nova Scotia had a heartbreaking intensity that commands respect. From him, in letters and documents not published in his lifetime, we get a different measure of Innocence, not as the calculated mythomoteur of distanced intellectuals, but as something close to a secular religion. Of the fisherfolk, Hartley would write, ecstatically, "these people are like deep, flowing rivers, oceans, of lovingkindness and all so still & quiet … It has been a sweet revelation to be among these completely humble people, and I wish I could do something for them such as play a guitar & sing for they never have anything of that kind. O, so true & real like the sea & the rocks."[93]

Hartley was writing to a friend in a private letter, not publicly marketing "authenticity," which makes his Quest of the Folk all the more poignant and troubling. He was a major figure in the development of artistic modernism in the United States, and he tried to assimilate European avant-gardism while remaining staunchly American. He was eminently a man of modernity in his restless wandering: he crisscrossed the Atlantic through much of his adult life, and rarely lived in one place for more than ten months.[94] When he arrived in Nova Scotia in 1935, he was still searching for bedrock in a shifting world.

Hartley stayed with a family called the Masons in their island home at Eastern Points, near Blue Rocks, Lunenburg County. The fisherfolk of the rockbound coasts presented him with an image of life as it should be lived. Hartley wrote in September 1936 to his friend Adelaide Kuntz, regarding the senior members of the Mason family: "They are so utterly & completely free of neuroses of any sort, and maintain an enviable balance between the material & the spiritual worlds that they symbolize for me the term, ideal. They love each other & you feel they were sent to each other from the beginning ... Every one of 'em like rocks from which fresh springs flow without hindrance."[95]

Back in the United States, Hartley worked on his memories of the Masons, distilling their Folk essence. Like Longfellow's Acadians, they became more and more "Norman" and medieval. He imagined them as personifications of a religious ideal, people who unquestioningly accepted the spiritual dimension of life. The reimagined fisherfolk lived happily and spontaneously in their immediate surroundings; and nature, though sometimes a cruel taskmaster, had given them strength, Christian fortitude, and beauty.

In one respect there was no comparison between Hartley and other admirers of the fisherfolk: his sense of the danger and hardship of their lives came from his personal identification with particular men. That Hartley so deeply admired and loved the Masons makes his case all the more haunting, for as much as any of the others, he developed a strong sense of the eternal essence of the Folk. When he came to write of the Masons, he too turned to *Maria Chapdelaine*, and went so far as to give the entire family names drawn from that book.

These were merely some of the most powerful of the literary figures who turned the fisherfolk from marginal figures into epic, essential characters. There was a generalized cult of the fisherfolk in the early twentieth century to which dozens of writers contributed. For some, it seemed to provide a vacation from modernity. Norman Duncan, the Ontario-born editor of the Saturday supplement of the New York *Evening Post*, and the author of gripping exposés of the urban squalor of that city's ethnic ghettoes, was seized in 1900 by the desire to write about the sea. He spent three summers in Newfoundland. The result was *The Way of the Sea* (1903), which was widely praised as a realistic account of life on the bleak Newfoundland coast.[96] Mazo de la Roche, the author of the highly romantic Jalna series, found herself so charmed by Thomas Raddall's tales of Nova Scotia that she asked him to find her a secluded cottage on the seashore, somewhere near Liverpool. She was very specific in her requirements: "It was important that the cottage be near (but not in) a small fishing village where she could talk to the people and see how they lived and worked. It must be comfortably furnished, with two bedrooms, a living room, a well-equipped bathroom and kitchen, and, of course, electrical connections. Also, there must be no other summer cottages or visitors nearby."[97] *Near* but not *in*, civilized but remote from other visitors from civilization: the ideal fishing cove (which Mazo de la Roche did not find in Nova Scotia) exemplified a strategy of amateur salvage ethnography which, in countless different poems, novels, stories, paintings and photographs, was to make the fisherfolk the archetypal Nova Scotians, the bearers of the province's true soul.

The images of the fisherfolk produced by apparently more rooted writers and artists were just as selective as portraits drawn by outsiders. Dorothy Duncan, the travel writer, provides a fascinating case in point. Her *Bluenose: A Portrait of Nova Scotia* is a book that has long been fiercely criticized in Nova Scotia for its free and easy relationship with historical facts. (At one time, even the card identifying the book in the card catalogue of the Public Archives warned prospective readers of the book's inaccuracies.) Although written by an outsider, the book relies upon Hugh MacLennan, the author's husband, as its authority on things Nova Scotian. *Bluenose* is inventively constructed as a dialogue between insider and outsider, with Duncan's stereotypical misunderstandings and confusions gently corrected by the more knowledgeable and rooted MacLennan. What emerged from this collaboration was a view of the fisherfolk that was if anything more patronizing and essentialist than that found in conventional tourist literature. Whatever the hardships of their simple seafaring lives, Duncan writes, the fishermen "loved every minute of it and wouldn't have traded places with one of my Illinois farmers for anything on earth."[98] (If this was so, why did so many of them leave to find better-paying and less dangerous jobs?) Her vision of Lunenburg County complements that of Creighton in stressing the county's stolid, unimaginative, peasant characteristics. "Politics and social affairs, except local events within their own community, hold no interest for them whatsoever. Thus they have produced no statesmen or intellectuals."[99] (Yet what about the academics and politicians who came from Lunenburg County? And how could anyone who has seen Lunenburg's astonishing domestic architecture, that exuberant carnival of Victorian ornamentation, be satisfied with so limiting a notion of isolated primitive Folk, when the townscape evinces such unrestrained enthusiasm for Victorian ideals of civilization?) Given their peasant stolidity and conservatism, it was all the more noteworthy for Duncan that the Lunenburgers had turned to the Grand Banks fishery and made such a success of it: "That they succeeded so well is not surprising as much as it is exemplary, for remember–these people have always been unimaginative."[100] These Folk were so stolid that they did absolutely nothing in the face of economic crisis but quietly accept whatever fate doled out to them. "On the farms as well as among the fishermen there had always been a tendency – racial as much as anything else – to accept bad times and do nothing about it."[101] (What about the union struggles?) Earlier, local histories of Lunenburg had stressed progressiveness – the chemistry laboratory in the school, the fine new public buildings.[102] Now, guided by the insider Mac-Lennan, Duncan was defining the essence of the town and the county as complete isolation from the twentieth century.

They were isolated, quaint Folk, these Nova Scotians imagined by Duncan. Their physiognomy was, like the new handicrafts, a mirror of nature, their folds and creases capturing the image of the granite cliffs that surrounded them. Their lives were insular but comfortable, light years removed from the pressures and complexities of twentieth-century modernity. Duncan's imagined Lunenburg is a staid, quiet island, a haven from the storms of the twentieth century. And insular and stolid as Duncan's imagined South Shore Folk generally are, the fisherfolk of the offshore islands are even more colourful and exciting.

Today it is only on the dots of rocky islands sprinkled along the South Shore that real outports survive. On nearly every large island large enough to maintain human life there are small, isolated communities of descendants of shipwrecks ... Some of the inhabitants of these islands have never seen a city or a motorcar, never seen an electric light except on a passing steamer; and certainly some have never seen a dollar bill. How they manage to live is a matter of wonder, since their relation to the rest of the world is practically nonexistent. But the color they lend to the Nova Scotian scene is unquestionable in the eyes of the outsider, once he hears about them.[103]

They are indeed wonderful, these stout-hearted Crusoes described by Duncan, whose isolation and purity transcends even that described in Frank Parker Day's *Rockbound* fisherfolk (who were at least depicted as being only too capitalistic) in their complete rejection of a cash economy. (One final interjection: if these Crusoes were so isolated, their diets must have consisted entirely of potatoes, berries, and a fabulous number of fish – which must have been difficult indeed to catch without purchasing fishing gear now and again.) Duncan joins a company of middle-class romantics, photographers, painters, and novelists who gloried in the pre-modern life of the rockbound coast and the elemental northern beauty of its granite bedrock. Certainly her fisherfolk of the remote islands are emanations of their landscape, echoing the bedrock simplicity of their surroundings, and just as surely they must have been endowed with some elements of Creighton's Bluenose magic – for they had somehow managed to bewitch Dorothy Duncan with their quaintness and charm without her ever having laid an eye on a single one of them.

GENDER IDEALS AND THE FOLK

One of the most important elements in Innocence was a claim that Nova Scotia, as a pre-modern society, was characterized by traditional "family values" and gender ideals. Here again there was a shift, though not a complete one, from nineteenth-century expectations. Nineteenth-century travel writings, generally masculine in perspective, had freely commented on the physical appearance of local women, but they had developed such commentaries within a grid of aesthetic assumptions that both the colony and the metropolis were thought to hold in common. Within Innocence, however, gender ideals were subjected to the same essentialist logic as everything else: one attraction of Nova Scotia as a therapeutic space for anti-modernists was its supposedly natural and traditional gender relations at a time when these were elsewhere subject to great questioning.

Throughout much of North America, as John D'Emilio and Estelle Freedman have observed, the dominant meaning of sexuality was changing from a primary association with reproduction in families to a primary association with emotional intimacy and physical pleasure for individuals. "In the colonial era," they argue, "the dominant language of sexuality was reproductive, and the appropriate locus for sexual activity was in courtship or marriage. In the nineteenth century, an emergent middle class emphasized sexuality as a means to personal intimacy, at the same time that it reduced sharply its rate of reproduction ... By the twentieth century, when the individual had replaced the family as the primary economic unit, the tie between sexuality and reproduction weakened further. Influenced by psychology as well as by the growing power of the media, both men and women began to adopt personal happiness as a primary goal of sexual relations."[104] We lack local accounts of the decline of the "reproductive matrix," but there is sufficient evidence to suggest that these general patterns did not pass Nova Scotia by. The weakening link between marriage and sexuality was heatedly and candidly discussed in a debate over free love in the daily press in 1920.[105] Nova Scotia was not culturally isolated from modern North America, and changes in mores in the United States and in the rest of Canada impinged upon Nova Scotians.[106] Innocence as a gendered ideological formation meant a politics of cultural selection that emphasized those aspects of gender and sexuality which set Nova Scotia apart from a fast-changing North American world. Sometimes, especially for men, Innocence entailed a claim that Nova Scotians, as natural people, lived according to a freer sexual code. More commonly, Innocence entailed a claim that "traditional" family life was thriving among the Nova Scotia Folk in a way it no longer was in the wider world.

Innocence sometimes took the form of a radical masculinization in representations of the Folk. Highly masculine imagery spoke to an international marketplace of cultural consumers, for whom Nova Scotia came to be seen as a place where the beleaguered men of modernity could recover their manliness through vigorous sports and a return to nature, and where they could delight in the availability and deference of attractive women. At the same time, as a modern province undergoing a twentieth-century transition to the service economy, and with less and less employment to offer men who had grown up working with their hands, Nova Scotian society itself was producing abundant materials for its own, home-grown "crisis of masculinity."[107]

Folk was a gendered concept. Men and women, "stripped of all their shams," as Frank Parker Day liked to say, had certain inalienable and fundamental attributes that defined their essences. Men and women of the Folk were close to nature, and did what came naturally. The overcivilized and denatured men of the modern city could recover some of their own essence by getting in touch with them. The irony of much of this symbolic remasculinization was that it was effected by people who themselves were evidence that some prominent Nova Scotians had departed from such traditional gender roles. Helen Creighton and Mary Black, in their different ways, both contributed powerfully to the idea that Nova Scotians were still traditional in their attitudes towards the family and sexuality, yet they were both career women who had pursued lives outside the confines of the reproductive matrix. This contradiction also worked in reverse. Capturing true manliness in novels, paintings, and photographs drew the men engaged in the symbolic labour of masculinization into cultural spheres traditionally considered feminine. Male cultural producers thus blurred in their lives the absolute "traditional" gender boundaries they celebrated in their works. Ironically, while they constructed a Nova Scotia in which men were men and women were women, the inventors of Innocence found themselves dealing with a modern world in which gender ideals and roles were confusingly blurred. Whether male or female, they were caught in the classic contradiction of celebrating the types of pre-modern man and woman that they themselves were not.

We have seen both Creighton and Black wrestling with this dilemma, Creighton defensively justifying her single status with reference to her ill health, and Black struggling determinedly against the entrenched sexism of the bureaucracy. Men wrestled with the new gender politics in different ways. Roy Mackenzie described his folklore in the vocabulary of hunting and seduction. He was just one man among many who reasserted in his rhetoric a vigorous prowess that was understated in his quiet life as a cultural figure. Male romantic painters took risks along the rockbound cliffs, pitting their easels and paintbrushes against the raging sea.[108] Thomas Raddall, who focused with a particular intensity on questions of sexuality and the Folk, was in his maturity a deskbound modern man who made his living as a bookkeeper and subsequently as a novelist. Yet in the edited version of himself he presents to the world, he conveys the sense of a man who knows the mean streets, and who, thanks to his seafaring days, understands the seamy side of Halifax, "of which the office and shop workers and churchgoers of the port knew nothing whatever." He had talked to the people of the waterfront – the "stevedores, wharfingers, junkshop keepers, bootleggers, whores, thieves, old seamen down on their luck, boardinghouse keepers – in fact, all of the human medley to be found only on Water Street."[109] (Thus he was not, despite appearances, "really" a small-town bookkeeper. He was, like Roy Mackenzie, a man of the world.) And in Raddall's memoirs and novels, the essence of Man is physicality and sexual drive.

The same "essential" men are to be found in the travel literature. As Hugh MacLennan exclaimed in Dorothy Duncan's *Bluenose* of some muscle-bound Lunenburg men, "Look at the muscles on those fellows straightening out the tackle over there. Some people in Nova Scotia say none of us should be called Bluenose but those fishermen. That's nonsense, of course. But these people are certainly more colorful than any of the rest of us."[110] Renewed interest in the legacy of the Giant McAskill as a tourist attraction (which offended some of the Folk hero's descendants, because it seemed to imply McAskill lacked proportion and intelligence) fit into this same identification of the Maritime man with muscularity.[111]

If urban male cultural producers often described themselves as tough men of the Folk and the archetypal Nova Scotians as the muscle-bound hardy men of the sea, they were also sometimes concerned to develop the theme of sexual "primitivism," to interpret sexual relations among the Nova Scotia Folk as somehow more natural and basic than they were elsewhere. Quite often "primitivism" in anthropology entailed the idea of a sexual life freer and less inhibited because it had developed in a "state of nature."[112] Sexual ideologies were changing rapidly in the interwar period, and those questions of sexuality which Creighton had excised from the record of the Folk were emphasized by certain male authors, possibly with one eye fixed on the market, but also with a utopian longing for a less inhibited society.

An emphasis on primitive sexuality and the Folk was most evident in the works of Frank Parker Day, for whom it followed logically on from his essentialist naturalism. In *Rockbound*, casual sex is seen as part of the daily life of at least some of the islanders. "Fanny was certainly a fine creature," writes Day of one Island woman, "but her morals were those of the birds ... She was great-hearted and could never refuse a strong fisherman half-crazed with lonely passion."[113] The New York *Herald-Tribune* publicized this aspect of Day's interpretation of sexuality when it noted, in its review of the book, "It is true that there are people of rabbit morals living on the outer islands of Maine and Canada."[114] One suspects it was the sex issue that particularly outraged the vocal citizens of Ironbound. They retaliated against Day by impugning both his morals and those of the "three women and two other men" who had accompanied him. No one "but an atheist would have written and given the public a book which is unfit for the reading of any one with pure thoughts and high ideals in life," they declared.[115] Although it was rare for Nova Scotians to protest the terms of their representation so vigorously, there are two other instances of controversies sparked by a visitor's amateur Folk ethnography, and both raised issues relating to sex.[116]

The more common theme in Innocence was not sexual freedom but the manly strength and energy of the men of the Folk. The masculinization of the Folk can be observed most clearly in the brilliant romantic photographs of Wallace MacAskill. MacAskill's photographs, still among the most widely distributed and most powerful visual images of the province, are representations of an imagined single-sex community. Not a single woman appears in the 108 classic "MacAskills" assembled in *MacAskill: Seascapes and Sailing Ships*, a collection of his most famous and powerful photographs. Rugged, hardy men of the Folk are everywhere: braving the sea, clamping down picturesquely on their pipes, instructing their sons in nautical lore, building their wooden ships, marching with oxen, unloading fishing vessels. The fisherfolk are at the core of MacAskill's most popular photographs. *Son of the Sea* (1921) is a stereotypical portrait of a grizzled Nova Scotia fisherman with a sou'wester and a pipe; *Toilers of the Sea* (1928) shows two men in a small boat with fishing-nets, but derives its elegance and drama from the lovely lines traced in the water; *Saga of the Sea* (1936) depicts male bonding, as a fisherman tells a sea tale to a boy who holds a model vessel. Women are nowhere to be seen.[117]

Others represent the gender ideal of separate spheres in a more subtle manner. Ernest Buckler, whose *Mountain and the Valley* and *The Cruelest Month* are among the greatest works of Maritime antimodernism, envisions any blurring of gender divisions as a sign of moral decay and urbanism. Indeed, Buckler's special target is the city, a malign, feminizing force that drains the men of the Folk of their vital substance and bodily fluids. As one father reflects, after learning that his son would like to live in the city:

The stone houses [in the city] were alike, and the days were alike, and never till they died could the people lie in bed at night and listen to rain on the corn after a long heat. They had nothing to breathe but their own tired breaths. I remember their faces. There was stone in them, too. They were all alike. They looked as if they never awoke from their tired dreams of the night. Their minds kept turning in their own tracks, like the weary wheels that could find no rest on the pavements. The soft-fingered, women-faced men lived in houses, and the house-smell clung to everything they said or did when they went outside. When they talked, it was empty, because their eyes saw nothing but the stone things that their hands had not built ... and none of them had anything to say that could not be said with words. It was very lonely there. They laughed too much.[118]

Thomas Raddall's gendered antimodernism is similar. His imagined Halifax is an obscene stew of machines and bodies, a "compost of soot and sweat and gasoline, of cloth and scent and paper, of hot food and warm flesh and stale human breath which hung in the streets and poured from the doorways of shops and offices." When Isobel, the heroine of *The Nymph and the Lamp*, slams the door on this urban nightmare, she is rejecting the city's soft, sensual pleasures (the "frantic pleasures that could not give content ... the flickering Californications that were not drama") for the simple life with Matthew, a vulnerable man whose own crisis of masculinity entails the loss of his skilled trade and his eyesight.[119]

The antimodernist explorers of an idealized masculinity developed a clear and dichotomous categorization through which the real men of the Folk could be separated from (and seen as superior to) the false, pale-faced, emasculated men of the modern city. Marsden Hartley, who was a homosexual, was the most taken with this ideal of the essential men of the Folk. When he came to Nova Scotia in the mid-1930s to find a "truer" version of his native Maine, Hartley was also searching for a "truer" version of men and of gender relations. He found his time with the Masons, near the community of Blue Rocks in Lunenburg County, to be "the richest experience of my life."[120]

What was so poignantly special for Hartley was the experience of being fully accepted within a family, of finding the sense of belonging he had never enjoyed as a child. (He was deserted by his father at an early age.) Once more, in the privacy of his prose poem about his adopted Nova Scotia family, *Cleophas and His Own: A North Atlantic Tragedy*, published long after his death, Hartley suggested how deeply Innocence could penetrate an individual's way of seeing. The poem describes the warm and loving family into which Hartley had been welcomed and the plain-spoken spirituality of the fisherfolk. At its core is the death of the two sons of the family, based on the actual drowning of the two Mason boys with whom Hartley was staying and whom he loved. It is a passionate evocation of personal loss. Hartley's intense grief and his sincerity place both his paintings and his elegy in a different ethical category from the common objectifying and distanced stance assumed by other cultural tourists.

Yet what is striking, despite Hartley's sexual orientation and despite his emotional ties to the fisherfolk, is that, no less than the heterosexual Raddall, he was deeply committed to an antimodernist concept of masculinity. The Masons were the true family Hartley had longed for, and their physical attributes were at one with the landscape: "It is a salt of the earth country & so good to get down to earth and its true values again – very primitive of course ... Men are all husky & handsome – women husky & not handsome, but they do hard work. Men all fishermen & look so contented, [to be] home off the Banks and safe in their own snug harbours."[121] Transforming the Masons into allegorical Christian figures, Hartley also turned them into essential women and men. Thus Hartley wrote of "Marie Sainte Esprit," the mother-figure of his narrative, in the essentialist manner that Roland Barthes pillories in the passage from *Mythologies* quoted at the head of this chapter:

The mystical splendour of this woman was of an entirely practical quality, she did everything right because form is an inspiring thing in itself ...

She was appointed Mother of us all ...

Down they go over the rocks, the women watching their men go off to the high seas, to the terrible Banks, not knowing whether they will return – some never do.

They snigger as they stand a while as if salt tears were of any avail, they shed them – picking up their pails where they left them, smile a little and wave hard-worked hands, pick a wild rose or two smell them urgently, perhaps eat a strip of salt cod on the way back, the evening light still warm on them.[122]

For Hartley, the woman was an exemplar of a pre-modern "Gothic" beauty. "Her face looked as if she had spent her entire life in the soft gleam of ancient stained glass windows, lighted by the western sun, for every smile seemed to have clear light in it, and every silence a warm glow of faith."[123] It is the natural light of a rural woman who has accepted her lot in a world in which there was no end to women's work, "but all of it [was] done with a kind of song in the throat and the soul filled with doing and not with raving about heaven or the Lord."[124] There is one (alienated) woman in this imagined Folk family who does not live in easy communion with her gendered essence. We are not surprised to learn that she works at a desk in a great city, and has been rejected by her family.

Hartley's representation (in both his "factual" letters and his "fictional" poems) of the male Masons – the father, whom he renamed Cleophas, and Alton and Donny, whom he redescribed as the "giant sons" Alphonse Adelard and Etienne – resembles Frank Parker Day's description of essential men in *Rockbound*. "God what men & the women suited to them," Hartley exclaimed to a friend in November 1935. "When I came up last week for the day to see the speedboat the two giant sons are building I was swept away by the tidal forces of their humanism, and the two boys nearly devoured me with affectionate devotion."[125]

Leander Knickle says that Alty (Alton Mason) is 'dead gone on me' which is cute, and I haven't heard that phrase since I was a kid myself and used it. Well I love both Alty & Donny, & if I were a woman I'd have a time choosing – for Alty is wild and all flair, all demonstrative. Donny is shy as a thrush and never ventures out of the deep forests of his being until he is sure he is safe – but being a man I have them both in the ways men have of being for each other, & it's all lovely, & I assure you, if I did murals, I'd do one of the family at supper or noon meal.[126]

These natural men, one lyrical and shy and the other tempestuous and impulsive, whose only vice is the minor one of occasion drunkenness, enliven the coastline with their giddy spirits. Theirs is an unsullied "childish innocence."[127] For Hartley, the "boys" (who in another vocabulary might have been described as two grown men, twenty-eight and thirty-one years old respectively) were the "quintessence of manly beauty & strength and joy. Never have I known anyone like them. Never a mean thought or act, drunk or sober, & their only fault was drinking now & then. They were fond of me &d I loved them."[128]

Hartley's two innocents, and especially "Adelard," are huge, muscular, elemental. Adelard is like some "devouring beast," all of whose thoughts are "emotionalized and dramatized by magnificent, opulent, voluminous body action." Tall (indeed, giantesque) Adelard is a striking figure, with smoke-black hair that stands six inches above his low forehead, and eyes that have the famished look of a ravenous wolf,

sniffing at the mouth of dungeons, or at the edges of forest fires, loving the pungence of the burning vegetation, sniffing it all in with lustful eagerness, for Adelard, life must literally burn to mean anything at all.

He lives utterly for the consummate satisfaction of the flesh, the kind of flesh making no difference.

Wrists thick as the butt end of an ox-yoke and for whatever it takes two to tear or lift, he says "nonsense – give it to me" and if it is a rock out comes half of the world with it, the entrails of the earth lie bare, and beneath all his strength lies a heart as tender and as beautiful as that of a young girl ...

He has no common codes, no inhibitions – he will give as much love to a man as to a woman. He was totally loved by all of them up and down the coast, and because he was thrown over by the first woman, I think he has transferred his affections to his men friends, for he loves them and will do anything for them, and with this comes no mercy, love for him being the outpouring of his devastating energy – all flame, smoke, fire, steam and animal hissing, he is thunder and lightning in one, and loves when he strikes. [129]

A passionate man living in sexual freedom outside the codes of bourgeois society: it is an image that pops up in odd places in the surprisingly numerous mid-twentieth-century evocations of true Nova Scotian masculinity, and Hartley has simply transposed it into a homoerotic key. In doing so, he has radically masculinized the fishermen he met in Lunenburg County. As Ronald Paulson suggests, the extent to which Hartley transformed the fishermen into icons of masculinity can be observed in the contrast between their images in photographs and those presented in Hartley's paintings. [130] The photographs that C. Alton Mason, the prototype of the animalistic Adelard, circulated were of himself as an urbane-looking gentleman, wearing a suit and a natty bow tie. Hartley's representation of Alton (or "Alton-as-Adelard") in "Adelard the Drowned, Master of the Phantom," imagines the same person as an immense, muscular, hairy-chested giant, with huge ape-like hands. Even in the sincere eloquence of his grief, which indisputably places his art and writing in a more admirable ethico-political position than that of most of the

"Adelard the Drowned, Master of the Phantom," 1938–39. Oil on board, 28" × 22", University Art Museum, University of Minnesota, Minneapolis. Bequest of Hudson Walker, from the Ione and Hudson Walker Collection. Plate 2 from Gerald Ferguson, ed., *Marsden Hartley and Nova Scotia* (Halifax: Mount Saint Vincent Art Gallery, 1987), 18.

C. Alton Mason, c. 1935, photo by Knickle
Studio, Lunenburg. Collection of Richard Mason.
From Gerald Ferguson, ed., *Marsden Hartley and
Nova Scotia* (Halifax: Mount Saint Vincent Art
Gallery, 1987), 50. Alton was the fisherman
Hartley reimagined as "Adelard."

other celebrators of the fisherfolk, Hartley still works within a conventional vocabulary of masculinity not very different, in its essentialism, from that of far more superficial writers.

Where did this masculinization of the Folk leave women? Innocence entailed a concept of natural gender roles. Women's natural
role was in the home. Although the actual conditions of the North
Atlantic fishing economy required many women not only to attend
to the household but also to prepare the fish for market, in the
imagined Nova Scotia of the Folk women were assigned only the
supporting roles of waiting for their hardy men and uncomplainingly
attending to their needs.

It would be difficult to say that the new tourism economy and
its associated cultural activities created no new opportunities for
such middle-class women as Helen Creighton and Mary Black. Yet

the opportunities were mainly those of sustaining the same sexist assumptions and ideologies of separate spheres that men promoted. In contrast with an earlier generation of women represented in politics, social reform, and literature – such as the first bestselling woman writer in the region, Marshall Saunders, whose romantic novel *House of Armour* (1897) is an implicitly political novel about a heroic female charity worker in Halifax – many of the most prominent women cultural producers of interwar Nova Scotia did not raise gender questions overtly. Women such as Black and Creighton, as well as the writers Evelyn Richardson and Clara Dennis and the filmmaker Margaret Perry, had created a new sense of the career possibilities open to women, sometimes against male opposition. (Black's struggle to have handicrafts taken seriously was paralleled by Margaret Perry's difficulties in serving as "Film Officer" for the Nova Scotia government. When filming a documentary on fishing techniques, she discovered that it was apparently "against the rules ... for a woman photographer to go to sea on a trawler.")[131] Ironically, the Innocence they were collectively helping to construct was ideologically hostile to any notion of equality for women. Political discourse in Nova Scotia before the Great War had been very much affected by feminism, which was a powerful presence in Halifax.[132] By the 1950s, however, some outside observers could not find prominent women anywhere in Nova Scotia except in the arts.[133] Whether the relentless masculinization of representations of identity actually worsened the position of women is difficult to say, but it is difficult to believe that it could have provided them with many inspirational images.

Although masculinization meant that real women were no longer to be seen in the Nova Scotia as imagined by Innocence, mythical images of virginal Folk women were allowed in the canon. Some of these could be traced back to the mid-nineteenth century. Evangeline is nothing if she is not a heroine of a Folk romance, the icon of a pure, chaste, and subservient womanhood. Young Acadian women were scrutinized eagerly by American tourists, who pronounced their eyes "lustrous," their teeth "white," their cheeks "rich with brown and blush," and "the mouth and chin ... more delicate ... than in the ideal Evangeline."[134] The image did not remain entirely static. Evangeline become somewhat more medieval in dress as antimodernism took hold. She seemed to afford even non-Catholic travellers a chance to indulge in some safe medievalism, a recreational cult of the Virgin for the holidaying Protestant. The most widely reproduced representation of Evangeline – the commemorative statue at the Memorial Park in Grand Pré – suggests not a forceful woman enduring persecution and suffering (which might have been one reading of the

Acadian experience), but a wistful, even rather coquettish, girl. She does not frontally confront us, in a gesture which might lead us to recollect the Deportation or consider her as a figure endowed with human agency, but rather turns her head modestly away. She is not a subject in her own right, but a presence for the (male) gaze. From Evangeline to Anne of Green Gables, virginal young girls have been extensively used as icons in regional Innocence, as reminders of the older and better ways supposedly characteristic of the region, yet perhaps also suggesting a certain tempting if ambiguous accessibility to the eyes of men.

Through Evangeline, the cult of pure womanhood pervaded not just tourism promotion but local festivals and events, from the crowning of Evangeline and Gabriel as part of contemporary Acadian festivals to the Apple Blossom Festival, with its annual parade of white-frocked maidens. This Romantic ideal has persisted to the present day: "traditional Acadian Sweethearts" (the no-name version of Evangeline and Gabriel, reduced to this generic version because of the declining popularity of Longfellow) "pledge their love in front of the memorial chapel" at Grand Pré on the cover of the 1990 official provincial tourist guide.[135]

The fisherfolk, unsurprisingly, were the special bearers of traditional gender ideals. Even the radical poet Kenneth Leslie, who broke ranks with Innocence and his fellow Song Fishermen on some issues, celebrated the domesticity of the fishing cove in his ode to the cliffs of Peggy's Point, guardians of the kettle and the cradle in Peggy's Cove.[136] The legions of Sunday painters who descended upon the fishing villages and made Peggy's Cove a byword for the picturesque were very interested in capturing the essence of the warm, happy families in the little communities. "Far removed from the neon lights and noise of the city," remarked L.J. Zwicker introducing his painting *Cape Breton*, "life on Isle Madame seems serene and self-sufficient. The importance of the Church, farming and fishing are so obvious they were stressed in the painting."[137] In contrast with the harried life of the urban dwellers, the fisherfolk, in this picturesque vision, lived in tranquil harmony with nature. "The painting of these two fishermen," explained the artist Robert Annand when he exhibited his genre painting in 1953, "is an attempt to show the strange unreal feeling the sea, and the men that fish, have for me ... The men are part of the sea and reflect its life."[138]

Antimodernism applied to gender had worked so successfully that even on the slightest and most indirect evidence, interpreters were prepared to find domestic happiness and tranquillity among Nova Scotian families. A few domestic details – laundry on a line, children at the blacksmith's – sent George Matthew Adams into paroxysms of nostalgic familialism:

We drove to West Arichat, and then came back and went as far as we could in the other direction along the beach. We got out and talked with the simple, hospitable people – mostly French – who live in Petit de Grat. Fish were drying in the sun. We took our camera, and children and folk flocked to "have their picture took." Mothers with babies in their arms and little tots, just entering walking-hood, joined the group. There were women at the tub, and before the stove. Clothes hung upon the lines in the rocky yards ...

... I walked into the old blacksmith shop and cast rather loving eyes at the old anvil and forge. I saw a barefoot boy again, watching the strong arm of the village blacksmith, pulling away at bellows and hammering the sparks from the newly curved horse-shoe.[139]

Nova Scotia was all the more a land of Innocence and happy childhoods for those who had left. Wistful nostalgia for a lost youth was sharpened among Maritime exiles by the experience of outmigration. As Thomas Fraser observed in his essay "The Spirit of the Maritimes," those who had "their faces set towards a far land" suddenly transformed "the well down by the willow tree with its age-old collection of hatchets, tin dippers, accidents among the smaller rodents and others of the animal kingdom, straw-hats, and general unsanitary debris" into a "spring of nectar."[140] Among such emigrants, the best images of home were those which conveyed the lost splendours of childhood. In MacAskill's photographs, so often included in the baggage of exile, not only the many children but also the delicate, wistful tints added to the black-and-white prints conveyed the attraction of old childhood memories. Exiles would often make just one simple demand of the province they had left behind them: that it remain forever the land of their childhood innocence.

All of this – the ruggedly virile men, the virginal but accessible women, the romantic courtships, the happy families – constituted a very selective way of reading gender relations in Nova Scotia. The fisherman with tuberculosis (a disease considered to be rife along the "Coast of Songs"), the hard-pressed women who did at least half the work of the fishing economy, the unhappy families, the abused children – these anomalies were ignored. We do not yet have much in the way of detailed monographs to set against this Norman Rockwell version of family life in Nova Scotia, but there are many grounds for scepticism about the actual existence of any "Golden Age" of the Nova Scotian family. There probably was never one single sexual code in the province. High levels of prostitution in Halifax coexisted

with the stern respectability of its middle class; the province's
Canada-wide reputation for high illegitimacy rates and relatively liberal divorce laws coexisted with an official ideology that esteemed
reproduction within marriage.[141] Nova Scotians debated sexuality
and the decline of the reproductive matrix as energetically as other
Canadians. We know that women often turned to infanticide and
sometimes to abortion to save their reputations or their jobs in Nova
Scotia before the 1920s. Judith Fingard's work has documented the
prevalence of violence against women in nineteenth-century Halifax
families, and although the rural case studies have not been done,
Karen Dubinsky's work on sexual crime in Ontario in the same period
would make one hesitate to assume that the rural and urban worlds
were poles apart in the dangers they presented for women.[142] A
process of cultural selection that edits out these complex, if only
partially explored, realities tidies away the pain and incidentally con-
tributes to the entropic sense of catastrophe that pervades discussions
of gender and sexuality today. The Golden Age, not just of sail but
of the family and "traditional values", seems durably installed as a
warm and vivid memory of a time that never existed. The notion
that once upon a time men were men and women were women in
the Maritimes, and that around the hearths of the simple folk gathered large and contented families, still makes the idea of the "Folk"
deeply attractive to anyone with an interest in evading the twentieth
century's difficult politics of gender.

"DO YOU KNOW WHO WE ARE?"
THE FOLK AND NOVA SCOTIAN IDENTITY

It remains, finally, to consider how aspects of the idea of the Folk
impinged upon local neo-nationalism. At a time of unprecedented
socio-economic crisis for Nova Scotians, many regional writers found
their greatest inspiration in the idea of the Folk, which answered an
urgent need to articulate a workable sense of Nova Scotian, and
sometimes Maritime, identity. This process of identity formation was
simultaneously dependent and unique. Innocence was dependent
because many of its elements were drawn from a much wider phenomenon of antimodernism, and unique because it emphasized those
elements of the Nova Scotian reality that seemed wholly and completely distinctive.

In some respects it is hardly surprising that middle-class Nova
Scotians turned so emphatically to the Folk in the interwar period.
Progressivism's belief in a regulated, scientific, and efficient capi-
talism seemed undermined by the troubles of the region's industries.

Middle-class people, worried not just by the economic crisis but by the Cape Breton labour wars and the challenge of Communism, had good reason to want to escape to an earlier and simpler time. The concept of the Folk, and of the province as essentially a Folk society – intrinsically rural, traditional, and conservative – gradually became a new matter of common sense, promulgated by cultural producers with both symbolic and economic interests in the success of this new vocabulary. It could, and eventually did, work as a way of creating a new subject-position: that of the "worker" seemed to evaporate, and that of the "Folk" took its place. In Halifax, for example, using elements from an older labourist ideological formation – such as the notion of the moral superiority of all those who worked with their hands (an idea that could be potentially aimed squarely at managers and owners), or notions of "manliness" that assumed the position of the male breadwinner as head of the family – cultural producers rearticulated these elements in their new myth-symbol complex. They created a new category, the Folk, and a new way of handling economic collapse and political decline, which were redescribed as the pursuit of a simpler and more colourful traditional way of life. New organic vocabularies of Maritime Rights and Nova Scotian patriotism marginalized middle-class progressivism and labour radicalism alike, in a process that combined coercion (the aggressive use of the military to break strikes in Cape Breton and elsewhere) and consent (the simultaneous appeal to workers and others to rally to the cross-class, regionalist banner of Maritime Rights).[143]

Canadian nationalism posed a particular problem. There were two strains of radical environmentalism at work in Canadian nationalist ideology of the 1930s and 1940s. One responded to the rocks of the Canadian shield, observed the age-old trading patterns of the St Lawrence River System, and concluded that the emergence of the Dominion of Canada was sanctioned by Providence; or one turned to the North American myth of the frontier wherein democracy, egalitarianism, innovativeness, and virility were seen to be derived from the forests, the unsettled wilderness, and particularly from the prairie west and the Canadian north. Whatever their many differences, "frontierism" and "metropolitanism" had something in common: they both implied a dismal marginality for the Maritimes in Canada. (Much more promising for Maritimers would have been an emphasis on Canada's "essentially" maritime nature, as part of a North Atlantic triangle. This idea has always had a limited appeal in the empire of the St Lawrence.) Both of the leading Canadian essentialisms marginalized the Maritimes, in a language that was often powerfully gendered.

fisherman in his sou'wester is from a photograph by MacAskill, as are most of the others in the publication. The "Hanoverians" mentioned in the text are the "Foreign Protestants" who settled in the Lunenburg area; they were not in fact from Hanover, but assumed the identity during the Great War (when it was not popular to be "German").

How could Nova Scotians respond to these redefinitions of the country, in which they were reduced to residual categories? One strategy was to insist upon the virility and raw courage of the Nova Scotians themselves. Facing the waves of the North Atlantic was something that real men did. (This was very much the tone of the cult of the schooner *Bluenose*.) Alternatively, there was the related strategy of the Folk. Nova Scotians *were* different, and that was a blessing. Nova Scotians were Folk, people who were true to their ancestral roots. One accepted the description of the quiet, stagnant east, but placed it under a positive sign. It was true that real Nova Scotians were slower and more traditional (although surely not more effete) than westerners, but they were at least the well-made, indi-

"Typical Nova Scotian fishing village." From *Nova Scotia, Canada's Ocean Playground* (1932), 32. This type of scenery became very popular in the 1920s.

Descousse on Isle Madame, Richmond County, a charming Acadian village, commands a wide sweep of splendid shore scenery. Reached from Grand Anse station on the Canadian National Railway or via Highway Route 4

D'Escousse (here spelled Descousse) and Ile Madame generally became a popular site for Folk commentary: Adams's eulogy to the happy Folk family, Silver Donald Cameron's views on "country cunning," and various paintings of the picturesque land of the Folk are associated with this part of Cape Breton. From *Nova Scotia, Canada's Ocean Playground* (1930).

vidualized results of a slow, sure process, not the raw, sadly homogenized products of the western melting-pot.

In "Do You Know Who We Are?" (originally published in the *Sydney Record* and reprinted in the *Busy East*) R.V. Sharp, an important figure in both Maritime rights and tourism promotion, shaped a notion of the Folk that depended on the concept of racial types.

For many commentators and for the shapers of the province's tourist image, the oxen were potent signifiers of unspoiled rusticity. From *Nova Scotia, Canada's Ocean Playground* (1932), 26.

He set out to explain why, in Canada, "East is east and west is west, and while Scotchmen become western Canadians, it seems that eastern Canadians frequently persist in remaining Scotchmen – or Irishmen or Frenchmen or whatever their fathers were."

East and west are intrinsically different, different in antecedents, different in style, manners and ambitions, different in the past, the present and the future. It is time the east sat up and began to pick its own clothes instead of trying to slide along on western cast-offs. The Maritime Provinces have gloried long enough in our great Canadian types – manufactured west of the St. Lawrence river. The east has smiled in the reflected glory of western boom sufficiently long. Let us pause and consider if in the Maritimes there are not also a few Canadians with a private glory of their own.

Canada west of Montreal was a sort of "melting pot" wherein "Scotchmen and Irishmen and Englishmen and Greeks and Scandinavians and Germans and Austrians and Italians and it may be even Jugo Slavs, have and do become Canadians in the course of a few years." Things worked very differently in the Maritimes. Rarely could one find a city or town "where more than five or ten per cent of the influential population have ever been 'melted.' The great bulk is native ore." Indeed, said Sharp, citing a comment made recently by an American theatrical producer, the Maritimes was full of "types."

"Types" – that is the word – English, Irish, Scotch, French, – types every one of them. Go into the country in the winter time and drop into the village

The marketing of Evangeline and the Nova Scotia Apple Blossom Festival. From *Nova Scotia, Canada's Ocean Playground* (1936), 39. The vaguely Norman design of the chapel, while hardly in keeping with Acadian traditions, does correspond rather well to Long-fellow's poem and to nineteenth-century representations of the Land of Evangeline.

store for a glance at the council round the stove. Run into any Maritime rural smithy and it is ten to one you will find the village "Uncle Ben" sitting by the fire conversing with the smith. Inside of ten minutes he will know the history of your past life and if any of your ancestors were ever hung, he will know that too. "Uncle Ben" is the living history of the village, he is acquainted with everyone in it, is related to half the people, and went to school with three quarters of the denizens of the graveyard on the hill. Types? – Go into a fishing village and ask one of the heavy-booted slow-moving old men to show you his boat. He will row out to it in a dory and leap aboard like a cat while you crawl fearfully up with the memory of your past sins looking at you from the water beneath ... The Maritime Provinces are full of types ... but they are not such as are cast from a melting pot. They are such as nature makes by the slow hard moulding of years acting upon generation after generation born and raised in one spot.

Maidens in white before Annapolis Valley trees, from *Nova Scotia, Canada's Ocean Playground* (1932), inside back cover.

The people of the east were therefore a special kind of Canadian – "Maritimers" – whose natural simplicity, rootedness, and traditional ways set them apart. They were, in a word, Folk. "When factories thunder in every city and town and skyscrapers touch the heavens, men will still be found in these provinces by the sea, eating their beans on Saturday night," Sharp concluded.[144] Here was a heroic feat of cultural selection, written by a man living in industrial Sydney, where the steel mill thundered loud enough for most people, including hundreds of immigrants from Europe.

Sharp's was a dependent neo-nationalism, constructed against (but also using the categories of) an opposed pan-Canadianism. Its political upshot was paradoxical. He combined a classically anti-modernist statement on the Folk with a stereotypically "progressive" strategy of reindustrialization through state promotion of secondary manufacturing. In 1919 progressivism and antimodernism coexisted uneasily in the same programmatic statement. For Sharp, the achievement of a true Maritime identity meant, paradoxically, the elimination of the prior conditions of the Maritime identity.

Thomas Fraser, another important writer on the theme of regional essence, agreed with Sharp's notion of the "old stock." In the east, one found people of steady ways. One did not expect either rapid improvement or dire poverty in the Maritimes. It was a region, Fraser explained, where times were never very bad.

There are no bumper crops of wheat to make a farmer independent in a single season; but on the other hand, there are no absolute crop failures, followed by pathetic appeals to the Government for seed wheat. There are good seasons, and bad seasons, for farmers and fishermen, lumbermen and miners. Sometimes the Lunenburg fleet comes back from the Banks almost empty; sometimes, such as last spring, for example, each man's share on the "v'y'ge" will run up to fifteen or sixteen hundred dollars, which, with board, is not bad for two or three months' work. Outside of the few cities in the Maritime Provinces, there are no very wealthy men; the average man works pretty hard and seldom gets more than a very comfortable living; but they are content, and I will go so far as to say that they are godly; and "Godliness with contentment is great gain."

The region's people matched this notion of slow growth. They were all "old stock," meaning French and Scottish. (The numerous but somehow stigmatized Irish and the invisible English always seemed to lose their places at the table in these discussions of ethnic essence.) This made Maritimers very much like the French of Quebec, "the products of strong racial characteristics, which are to-day in many respects as strongly accentuated as they ever were." The blood was strong, the heart was Highland (or French), and the consequences were wonderful. The true Nova Scotian was not, like so many thousands of people in the coalfields, a recent emigrant, but could claim (like Helen Creighton) six or seven generations in the province. "I doubt," wrote Fraser, concluding his case for a region innocent of ethnic impurities, "if there is a Doukhober, or a case of trachoma ... in the country east of Quebec."[145]

The image of an antique Nova Scotia made up of slow-moving and slow-talking Folk resistant to change has been popular as an explanation, in Ontario at least, of why the local economy has not grown and why Nova Scotians nurse grievances against Toronto. The brash, energetic (or, more crudely, intelligent) Maritimers get out, leaving behind the timid, the overly cautious, and the stupid. Underdevelopment is thus a consequence of a quaint Folk mentality. Such offensive stereotyping has been the bane of regionalist movements of reform throughout the twentieth century. But reactionary and pseudo-racist as it is, it cannot be said to be the invention of the insensitive, ignorant central Canadians. This representation of Folk essence was constructed from within far more than it was imposed from without, and many of the key architects of this interpretation have been local cultural producers.

The stereotypical Nova Scotian was a slow, deliberate man, beyond the reach of rash political ideologies. He was a conservative, and he steadfastly rejected any hint of radicalism. D.J. Rankin, for example, expressed with a clear and vibrant eloquence the anti-labour ideas implicit in virtually all versions of Nova Scotians as Folk. In his work, it is the Cape Breton worker who is Other, subverted by an incomprehensible "foreign element" glimpsed gabbling on street corners and perpetually making trouble. In Cape Breton, many workers are not of the Folk. Their strikes are a menace to the organic ties of community. Behind the strike are many of the "foreign element," needlessly importing conflicts from the central European states. The victims of the radical workers' crazed demands will be the poor shareholders of the steel and coal company, the provincial treasury, the employees deprived of their means of livelihood, their wives and children, and the storekeepers and the farmers of Cape Breton. Behind the menace of the working-class Other in Rankin's Cape Breton were insidious intellectual influences. Working-class organizers were merely Soviet agents, who urged their "sullen-faced" men to insane acts of violence, such as burning down the steel works and flooding the mines, "while Soviet money jingled in their pockets."[146] The labourite Mayor of Rington is an extortionist who is cheating the relief fund. Atheistic, socialistic Belgian miners constitute a graver menace to the Folk than even the Yellow Peril. By "taking charge of the workingmen," Sovietism was undermining the organic unity of the Folk.[147] Rankin made explicit the politics that others implied, whether through offhand comments or through the implicit politics of cultural selection.

By the 1930s and 1940s the Folk were numerous indeed in the imagined Nova Scotia constructed in books, articles, tourism promotion, painting, music, and handicrafts. That much we have established. This was no foible of a few folklorists or myopic tourists, but a new and powerful way of seeing among the cultural producers who specialized in representing the Nova Scotian identity. What sort of place is this? they often asked. And they would answer, drawing on selective readings of their own experience and the international literature on the Folk: this is a primitive place of simple Folk. Sometimes they would answer this way even if they lived in Nova Scotian cities and worked most of the time in Nova Scotian office buildings.

The category "Folk" was, from the start, commodified. From the beginning we find people looking for the marketable story, the money-making song, the winning image. And yet the cultural producers were also playing brilliantly to a local audience in search of identity, in search of something to be proud of. They produced myths that still seem powerful today, even if a precise measurement of their impact will probably never be within our grasp. In defining the provincial essence, in struggling to define for all time the core traditions and unchanging values of the true Nova Scotian Folk, the cultural producers were responding to the vagaries of international fashions and the fluctuations of the international market. They were never more the troubled children of a troubled century than when they sought solace from it in antimodern images of the Folk and their simple life in Nova Scotia.

5 The Folk under Conditions of Postmodernity

There never were any "folk," except in the minds of the
bourgeoisie.
The entire field is a grim fairy tale.

> Charles Keil, "Who Needs 'the Folk'?," 1973

The new cyberpunk youth countercultures of the nineties are
already being constructed out of the folklore of technology and
not, as was the case in the sixties, out of the technology of
folklore. Not out of Orientalist fantasies and agrarianist
nostalgia, or from the faded wardrobes of preindustrial
laborers, gypsies, or peasants, but rather, out of the postpunk
landscapes of the new science fiction, the vestigial romances of
the hacker ethic, and the fluid, makeshift vitality of fanzine
culture and electronic bulletin boards.

> Andrew Ross, "Defenders of the Faith and the New Class," 1990

BECOMING MORE ITSELF IN EVERY DECADE

"Nova Scotia," Kildare Dobbs wrote in a publication for tourists in
1986, "is a province that becomes more itself in every decade." None
of his readers could doubt that this peculiar procedure of becoming
"more itself" meant becoming the promised land of the Folk, handicrafts, and the simple life. Grizzled captains chat to small boys on
sunlit wharves, lazy rivers meander through lush fields on their way
to the sparkling sea, stately mansions glory in their Victorian gin-
gerbread: by becoming "more itself," Dobbs's Nova Scotia has
cleansed itself of the twentieth century. Handicrafts are everywhere.
"Visitors and tourists in any country love to shop for souvenirs and
gifts, often with an eye for a bargain, but also for the fun of dealing
with the locals and carrying things home to talk about," writes Dobbs.
"Since almost every small town and village in Nova Scotia has its
craft-shops that sell local products the province is exceptionally well
equipped to cater to this demand." There is not a smokestack or mine
or factory to be seen in a land where "Traditional skills can be found
almost everywhere."[1] By becoming "more itself in every decade" Nova

Scotia apparently has embarked on a project of eliminating every visible sign of its being a twentieth-century society. The essentialism of all this is hardly surprising, even if one rarely encounters so disarmingly frank an expression of it. The Quest of the Folk continues, even in a late twentieth-century landscape dotted with factories and warehouses, shopping malls and fast-food franchises. Dobbs's pamphlet edits out these alien forms, just as tourists to Brittany edited out the tractors.

As I have argued in the preceding chapters, social relations and ways of seeing, not intrinsic properties, determined who (or more commonly, which forms and traditions) were called Folk. City-dwellers, and for the most part the middle-class cultural producers of Halifax, were those who first "discovered" (that is, constructed) the Folk and then used the advanced means of communication open to them to popularize their "discovery." The Nova Scotia Folk were from the beginning an urban invention. The very category "Folk" suggested a way of defining a set of people who were somehow different (variously simpler, kinder, slower, and more rural – more innocent, in a word) than those who were categorizing them.

We have noted five characteristics of the Folk "formula" as applied to Nova Scotia:

1 It was incessantly preoccupied with essence – with locating the genuine wisdom, the true and original ballads, the cultural bloodstream uncontaminated by the virus of modernity, the fixed and final forms of culture.

2 The Folk were incarnations of a Golden Age, exemplars of an older and better time, bearers of ancient ways. An entropic conservatism esteemed their culture above that of others and struggled to preserve it. Guardians of the Folk often saw themselves as conducting a last-minute salvage operation to garner their cultural treasures before the Folk disappeared forever.

3 Both the techniques through which the Folk were produced and what they were made to say bore witness to the truth of the pastoral ideal, that of a beautiful relation between rich and poor that transcended the temporary, superficial, and divisive misunderstandings of class.

4 The Folk bore witness to the ethnic unity of the Nova Scotians. In some visions the Folk, speaking the language of the Elizabethans and singing the ballads of Renaissance England, bore eloquent witness to the ties of blood and language binding the English-speaking world together. In others, which responded to the obvious fact of a plurality of ethnic groups and hence a variety of

"Folks" in Nova Scotia, the idea of the Folk was a starting-point for Nova Scotian neo-nationalism, permitting the hope that there was a deeper and more fundamental unity underlying such ethnic divisions.

5 Finally, the Quest for the Folk was simultaneously a search for profits. The Folk were produced for and in a booming international market for things primitive in the interwar period. After the Second World War, the Canadian Folk revival was on in earnest, fanned by tourism, promoted by the CBC, and funded by the National Museum. The formula was international, the raw materials and cultural entrepreneurs local.

This Folk formula, already reduced to repeating itself in Will R. Bird's writings of the 1950s, has not waned in the years since. But there are strange forces at work in late twentieth-century cultural life, and the Folk concept is likely to be affected by them.

This chapter ventures a speculative and tentative survey of the "postmodern" Folk. Its key argument is somewhat paradoxical. On the one hand, the concept of the Folk has succeeded far more completely and thoroughly than anyone could have imagined in the 1930s. Nowadays, as Dobbs's little pamphlet suggests, evidence of a Folk society is everywhere. Three post-1970 developments in particular – "postmodernity" as a widespread cultural phenomenon, the intensification of the tourist gaze, and the arrival of thousands of immigrants in search of the simple life in Nova Scotia – gave the idea of the Folk a salience it lacked even in the 1950s. Nonetheless, there are some significant countervailing tendencies. A limited but important democratization of cultural life has loosened the grip of the market on representations of the province, and in this freer cultural environment some of those who grew up in rural Nova Scotia have begun to talk about their experiences in ways that undermine a Folk romanticism. Moreover, the overextension and commercialization of Folk forms has attenuated their aura, and the potential exists for alternative ways of seeing. Reflecting on the three theoretical currents that have structured this study – Marxian political economy, contemporary cultural studies, and neo-Gramscian theories that attempt to synthesize them both in a new understanding of how modern culture works – I conclude this book by showing how the crisis of the concept of the Folk represents some surprising opportunities for progressive cultural change.

In a now classic (if still controversial) 1984 article, the literary critic Frederic Jameson made the important suggestion that postmodernism represents the cultural logic of late capitalism. (I would amend this to read "postmodernity," to distinguish between the philosophical position and the lived experience.) Aesthetic production today, Jameson argued, has been integrated into commodity production generally: "The frantic economic urgency of producing fresh waves of ever more novel-seeming goods (from clothing to airplanes), at ever greater rates of turnover, now assigns an increasingly essential structural function and position to aesthetic innovation and experimentation."[2] As Jameson suggests, the culture of consumption, far from being inconsistent with Marx's analysis of nineteenth-century capitalism, in fact constitutes the purest form of capital yet to have emerged, "a prodigious expansion of capital into hitherto uncommodified areas," particularly Nature and the unconscious. For the cultural logic of this epoch he reserves Plato's conception of the "simulacrum" – the identical copy for which no original has ever existed. The "culture of the simulacrum" comes to life, writes Jameson, "in a society where exchange-value has been generalized to the point at which the very memory of use-value is effaced," and the image itself becomes the final form of commodity reification.[3]

Following Jameson, one can define postmodernity as the cultural force-field of late twentieth-century capitalist societies. Its attributes include scepticism about the great metanarratives of social theory and religion; the acceptance of fragmentation and the celebration of ephemerality and discontinuity; the loss of a sense of historical continuity in values and beliefs, and consequently in the possibility of "historical subjects"; and a reading of "reality" as a series of texts intersecting with other texts and producing yet more texts.[4] If modernity can be distilled as a new experience of time and space created by global capitalism and the new means of communication it has made possible, postmodernity is the intensification of that modernity, the experience of a radical simultaneity that, in undoing the effects of time and space, has changed perceptions of historicity and of language.

As was the case with antimodernism, Nova Scotia has hardly lagged behind the rest of Canada in being affected by this new cultural matrix. Postmodern architecture has redesigned much of urban Halifax, and the city's waterfront has become a curious approximation of a theme park, wherein a vague "pastness" is conjured up by cunningly placed nautical props. The pillaging of older historical forms has proceeded in earnest, as old buildings (and, in Dartmouth, an entire downtown district) have been "heritaged" to convey a vague, stereotypical "1860s-ness." New buildings, such as a sparkling Sheraton hotel, exploit the idea of plain early nineteenth-century styles to highlight the brass and chrome opulence of the hallways and boutiques within. (These boutiques sell, by the gross, photographs of quaint fishing-coves and authentic handicrafts). To walk through modern Halifax is to confront a battery of aesthetic signs, a pastiche of pseudo-nineteenth century images and effects, which, for all their ostensible historicism, testify to nothing other than the waning of any effective sense of living history. Outside the capital there is further evidence of the new style in a theme park at Upper Clements, which allows visitors to experience a simulated village, watch underpaid university students pretend to be happy nineteenth-century craft workers,[5] and play miniature golf on a course in the shape of Nova Scotia.

If, as Jameson and others urge, postmodernity is a more fundamental cultural condition than the passing fashions in "post" theories suggest, the insight that the taken-for-granted world is largely constructed through a socio-political process will not be readily unlearned. New ways of seeing, decisively influenced by television, have transformed not just the things people do for recreation but their entire sense of living in a constructed world.

What is the impact of this (probably enduring) condition of postmodernity on the concept of the Folk in all its guises? It intensifies and multiplies the demand for Folk images, for rustic hideaways, for rural authenticity. Postmodernity intensifies what Lears called the crisis of selfhood and jeopardizes the very concept of authenticity; it induces a kind of cultural panic and enhances the attraction of old, traditional forms, as modern advertising, with its cynical emphasis on traditional ideals of gender and community, clearly realizes. In the postmodern field of force, the pull of authenticity is considerable, but so too is the inherent tendency to enhance a market by producing simulacra. In this world, amateur ethnography among the Folk – the earlier middle-class solution – is simply not very credible any more. Under conditions of postmodernity there is a haunting suspicion that there is no longer a "backstage," a level of authenticity above or beyond the casual consumer encounter. (One may, at the gift shop at Peggy's Cove, buy a hundred mementoes of the fisherfolk, but with the chill realization that not one was made by, or is being sold by, the Folk, however defined.). The "Folk" motif will probably become more and more important as the cultural contradictions of late capitalism intensify; yet, as Walter Benjamin once observed, "that which withers in the age of mechanical reproduction is the aura of the work of art," an insight that applies also to representations that are coded "Folk" in today's consumer economy.[6]

One sphere in which the Folk motif has been worked to the point of exhaustion is in the promotion of business. As early as 1920 the

Halifax *Herald* was advertising itself and Nova Scotia as an "Eldorado for Advertisers" on the strength of the innocent simplicity of Nova Scotians.

> They are strong of body, direct of speech and straightforward in their dealings with their fellowman ... They indulge in no illusions. Wealth does not awe them nor are they greatly disturbed by the lack of it ...
>
> And they have a profound respect for the printed word. Nowhere else on this continent do the words, "I see by the paper," carry so much weight ...
>
> To attempt to paint a composite picture of the Nova Scotian is neither necessary nor wise ... But ... certain characteristics stand out ...
>
> (1) Honesty
> (2) Simplicity
> (3) Straightforwardness
> (4) Thrift ...

"This may sound old fashioned these days," remarked the author of a publication called *Nova Scotia's Profit Formula*, published about four decades later, "but evidently Nova Scotian workers still cling to many old-time values. It's part of the intrinsic charm of the place."[7] The Folk formula has been exploited brilliantly by regional businesses hoping to enhance their local market share by making it appear that consumption of a given product connects the consumer to a premodern Nova Scotian tradition. The ironies can be stunning. Although some of the province's industrial bread-making firms are directly descended from the nineteenth-century industrial concerns which helped wipe out the city's artisanal bakehouses, they nonetheless cheerfully advertise their completely industrial products as part of a longstanding tradition of craft pride. From ale to windows, the products of modern industry are sold in the region as the products of craft. The slogans of Sobey's grocery stores ("The Home Stores," "Friendly, That's Us," "Proud to Be Maritimers") have made a special point in recent years of emphasizing down-home connections with plain-spoken Folk. Similarly, business biographies, notably those written by Harry Bruce, routinely depict a captain of industry as integrally tied to the colourful Folk around him. Suggesting that regional capitalists are "of the Folk" takes precedence over realistic assessments of how their money was made.[8]

When every mass-production industry, from beer to automobiles, shamelessly markets its product by draping it in the images of the craft legacies that mass production helped extinguish, the aura of the craft ideal is diminished through overexposure. When the decontextualized art of the Folk becomes standard fare at museum after museum – as in the Canadian Museum of Civilization – it gradually comes to seem like one more decorating detail. When every craft fair comes to look suspiciously like the other, and when some "authentic" crafts are in effect generated through a division of labour, we find it more and more difficult to generate the illusion of escape to community. It is revealing to see how many of the "crafts" for sale are toys, those poignant emblems of an Innocence, a first-order experience, that yearning will never recapture.

Tourism also exploits the Folk past the point of credibility. It does so by radically cancelling the effects of time and space and by requiring the host society to adopt the techniques of mass marketing in order to succeed in this most global of all possible markets.[9] Paradoxically, a globalized postmodern tourism industry means even more Folk essentialism, because as each society submits to the standardization and homogenization of the tourist gaze, it also requires a brand name and some degree of customer recognition to enjoy any success as a tourist commodity. It logically turns to the task of becoming "more itself in every decade" as tourists become the vanguard of a world army of semioticians, reading everything as signs and looking everywhere for essences:

The tourist is interested in everything as a sign of itself, an instance of a cultural practice: a Frenchman is an example of a Frenchman, a restaurant on the Left Bank is an example of a Left-Bank-Restaurant: it signifies "Left-Bank-Restaurantness." All over the world the unsung armies of semiotics, the tourists, are fanning out in search of the signs of Frenchness, typical Italian behavior, exemplary Oriental scenes, typical American thruways, traditional English pubs; and, deaf to the natives' explanations that thruways are just the most efficient way to get from one place to another, or that pubs are just convenient places to meet your friends and have a drink, or that gondolas are the natural way to get around in a city full of canals, tourists persist in regarding these objects and practices as cultural signs.[10]

Such tourists often come to Nova Scotia in Quest of the Folk, and the province has increasingly promoted itself by means of Folk festivals and handicrafts. In 1989 the Department of Tourism and Culture mounted a promotion on the theme of the "Year of the Quilt," which included displays in its new Mary Black Gallery. In 1991 Nova Scotians experienced the "Year of the Basket." In the late 1980s Halifax built its tourism efforts around an "International Street Performers Festival" (the Buskers' Festival, for short) which has become one of the major events of its tourist season; it drew 400,000 people in 1987. In 1988 the Buskers' Festival was promoted by the minister of tourism and culture as part of the province's longstanding Folk customs: "Our Province and our people have much in common with the traditions of the Buskers. We share an appreciation for music and singing and dancing for its own sake, and as part of a community experience. The Buskers establish a very personal relationship with their audience – to the point where the audience becomes part of the performance. It's the same spirit you'll find at a genuine Cape Breton ceilidh."[11]

The Buskers' Festival serves as an excellent example of the postmodern adaptation of the idea of the Folk. Vaguely "Folk-like" and pre-industrial in its revival of an old European form, it actually has nothing to do with traditions distinctive to Nova Scotia. It is, in fact, pure spectacle, organized by private enterprise with state support. All that is historical about this phenomenon is that it turns to the purposes of the tourist state an activity that had been spontaneous and unorganized: at other times and in other parts of the city, busking is discouraged.

Tourists looking for the "Nova Scotianness" they have been trained by the tourism state to expect will see what they are primed to see: quaint fishing-coves and signs of the Folk (festivals, handicrafts, premodern rituals, and so on). As tourism has become a powerful cultural force, organizing the summer calendar of the misnamed "community events" and requiring a host of invented traditions, it has emphasized more and more the notion of a Nova Scotian Folk essence. In a sense, this is the same old antimodernist Innocence, given a new polish by the new and prodigious image-generating capabilities of capital and the state. It is also something different: a spectacle without the aura of the original and the authentic. Surely no one who attends the Buskers' Festival or visits the Upper Clements theme park is under the illusion that what she is seeing has any autonomous existence outside the brave new world of tourism. No one taking part in today's "festivals" and "clan gatherings" and "craft fairs" can be blind to the directly commercial role played by such staged events. Pointing out the "inauthenticity" of much of what passes for the Folk and its culture under conditions of postmodernity is unlikely to cause anyone to raise an eyebrow. Unlike so many earnest pilgrims to the fisherfolk of the 1930s, postmodern tourists no longer expect authenticity. True postmoderns accept the fragmented, the spectacular, and the contrived as aspects of contemporary cultural experience. In postmodernity, the Folk have lost their depth. No longer will the Folk essence be revealed only to intrepid ethnographers exploring the fishing-coves of Halifax County. Now it can be requisitioned by any casual visitor to the Halifax International

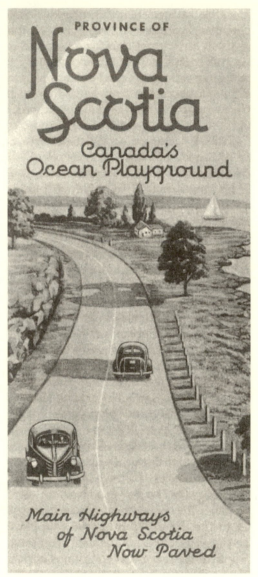

An early use of "Folk Art" on the official highway
map distributed free to summer visitors for the 1945
season: note the way in which the dimensions of the
seaside cottage are represented and its dollhouse
size.

The uses of the Folk in advertising: a promotional campaign launched by United Distillers Limited uses the images of the oxen, rockbound coastal views, and a fisherman contentedly working on a model vessel. Angus L. Macdonald Papers, MG 2, vol. 907, file 37A, PANS.

Airport. If it was always difficult to distinguish the "stereotypes" of outsiders from the "essentialism" of insiders, the very categories of "outsiders" and "insiders" have now been subverted. Postmodernity erodes the distinction between inside and outside, host and guest, the original and the copy, the spurious and the real. Is a bird painted on a rock from near Tantallon a "real" Nova Scotian handicraft – if the painting has been done in Latin America, reimported into Nova Scotia, and glued to a piece of "Nova Scotia" driftwood? Why not? Why should this be considered any less "real" than the buskers or the park at Upper Clements or a hundred other Folk phenomena under conditions of postmodernity?

Just as those who ostensibly rejected the stresses of modernity were often in the vanguard of modern market relations, so too have those who reject consumer capitalism often wound up as pioneers of Folk postmodernism. Prominent in what might be called the "second Folk revival" have been back-to-the-landers from the United States and Canada who came to Nova Scotia in the 1970s in search of honest Folk, the simple life, cheap land, and (often) a certain tactical distance from the American military. Meeting hostility and resistance in some places, these neo-pioneers (to use Eric Ross's splendid word)[12] undoubtedly left a distinctive mark on cultural and

Acadian Sweethearts on the cover of the province's official 1990 tourist guidebook:
"Nova Scotia celebrates its culture, history and heritage each year with pageants,
fairs, re-enactments and celebrations," the guidebook explains. "At Grand Pré,
traditional Acadian sweethearts pledge their love in front of the memorial chapel."
In the background is the ersatz Acadian chapel erected at Grand Pré, on the
grounds of the park created by the Dominion Atlantic Railway.

political life. Environmental movements in particular have benefited from their arrival. Their antimodernist ethic has interacted with local discontent over large, failed modernization schemes. Even in the absence of a good regional monograph on the neo-pioneers, one can observe some parallels and contrasts with the earlier antimodernist wave of the 1920s and 1930s. Like the first antimodernists, the neo-pioneers were part of an international movement: they were part of a trend that swept the industrial world in the 1960s and 1970s and resulted in the emergence of communes around the world. They also shared an earlier generation's belief in an unspoiled rural Nova Scotia Folk. But the revived antimodernism of the 1960s and 1970s was rather different in form from that of three decades earlier. It involved the actual rural settlement of antimodernists equipped with a vigorous if inchoate theory of what was wrong with the industrial world. Armed with the *Whole Earth Catalogue*, a collection of Folkways records, copies of *Harrowsmith*, and other weapons in their struggle for the simple life, the neo-pioneers were far more thoroughgoing and articulate in their antimodernism than their predecessors. An earlier generation had *sought* the "Folk"; many of the neo-pioneers were struggling to *become* them.

Eric Ross's gently ironic description of the cultural politics on modern Pictou Island conveys the dynamics of separateness and imitation in the neo-pioneers' history in one corner of the province. Perhaps the first visible indication of the back-to-the-landers' presence were the renovations in once decrepit farmhouses: "Sagging roofs were straightened, aluminum doors were discarded, beams were exposed, old brick, tiny window-panes and barn-boards were added, and old, dessicated furniture was stripped bare. Such dwellings reflected the newcomers' fantasy of the local way of life, a way of life they were soon striving to preserve from the pressures of government, developers and, indeed, from the locals themselves."[13] Arriving in the early 1970s, Pictou Island's neo-pioneers sparked early resentment against themselves and the people who had sold them their land. They gradually won acceptance as workers on the fishing boats and as neighbours who were willing to help repair tractors, do haying, and even dig graves. As the communal structure of the neo-pioneers' first settlement gradually drew closer to a more conventional, private-property model, they became more and more like the islanders who were there before them.

One difference between the antimodernism of the 1920s and that of the 1970s was the kind of Folk held up for esteem. Helen Creighton's Folk were kindly, God-fearing, law-abiding, and decorous, rather like her; the Folk imagined by the neo-pioneers were happy-go-lucky,

Cover of the Buskers' Official Program, 1988. The performances of the buskers drew a wide range of corporate sponsorships: local Ford dealers sponsored the People's Choice Award, Dynamic Funds Management Limited presented an award for the Most Dynamic Busker, Hostess Food Products Limited sponsored the performance of a juggler from Massachusetts, and so on.

hedonistic, and anarchistic, rather like them. Silver Donald Cameron's Folk, for example, came very close to exemplifying the hippie ideal. He rather incongruously placed his evocation of the happy, simple peasants of Richmond County in a book about the tumultous events of 1970–71 in Nova Scotia, when fishermen once more sought to organize under the auspices of a left-wing union. Although he might plausibly have placed this story in the context of the province's working-class history, Cameron elected to discuss an imagined Nova Scotia "peasantry." Cameron loves the local colour and peasant guile of the Folk. In an essay entitled "Country Cunning and Unofficial Life," he explains that as a resident of five years' duration he has come to understand certain deep truths about the peasants among whom he is living. These happy-go-lucky peasants drive when they're "paralyzed drunk," play hooky from their factory work to go off and make love in the woods, and have a wonderful code of "Country Cunning" that involves deceiving police officers and other authorities. Cameron loves his neighbours (to whom the chapter is addressed in the form of a letter) because they're not the polite, dutiful people who inhabit Creighton's books. No, they are full of the raucous, vulgar, Rabelaisian vitality that is the stuff of real life (at least as interpreted in the 1970s, from a perspective still discernibly warmed by 1968 and the afterglow of the Summer of Love). Echoing an old idea of Raddall's and Buckler's, Cameron contrasts the walking corpses of the city (now updated to the suburbs) to the warm-blooded people of the country. Here, even in the late twentieth century, the Nova Scotian peasants enjoy lives that are amazingly like those of Europeans 150 years earlier.

Another thing: peasants have a code of ethics which shifts according to the situation – but it's always based on loyalty to one's own people and suspicion of the squire and all his works. Acadian Fisheries is the squire, the government is among his works. When the squire and his toadies look at the peasants, they see lazy, shiftless liars. Thieves. Con artists. Poachers. Smugglers and bootleggers and drunks. Parents of illegitimate children. Truants from school. You name it: companies and governments want us to lead orderly lives, but peasants' lives aren't orderly.

But when the peasant looks at his friends and neighbours and relatives – the very same people – he sees generous and friendly folks who know how to have a good time, who are realists about sex and death, who don't get all hung up over laws and regulations, who rather enjoy winkling a few extras out of the squire, by fair means or foul. People who don't reckon that a lot of the foolishness that passes for education is really all that important. People who understand that when you have to protect yourself against power it pays not to be *too* candid. People you can trust.[14]

Thus Helen Creighton's imagined Nova Scotia is completely upended. The *real* Nova Scotians are now Cameron's devil-may-care hedonists, cheerfully thumbing their noses at authority. Here was a decidedly (stereotypically) west coast version of an east coast labour war: it was a little like *The Beachcombers Do Harlan County.*

Where Cameron romanticized, other neo-pioneers denounced. Believers in rural Innocence were often abruptly relieved of their illusions. Leslie Choyce has peopled much of his imagined Eastern Shore with childlike antiprogressives and crudely avaricious developers; Janice Kulyk Keefer's controversial postmodern version of the landscape of Clare is an alienated hell dominated mainly by ghetto blasters, used condoms, dune buggies, dish antennae, and a large cast of unappetizing primitives; the chapters of Humphrey Carver's memoirs that reflect on "saving" Nova Scotia's shoreline include this astonishing sentence: "In truth, it is the native Maritimer who has turned his back on his own land, and others have adopted it, with love and admiration."[15] Dualism is still at work in these evaluations, but now the Folk Other is placed under a negative sign. Once bearers of the truth of Innocence, the Nova Scotia Folk came to be seen by jaundiced neo-pioneers (and other disgruntled newcomers) as a decultured, deracinated residuum – a backward rural lumpenproletariat.[16] With their habits of hunting down furry animals (not to mention clubbing baby seals) and jaunting about the countryside in tasteless all-terrain vehicles, they were unworthy vessels of the hopes and dreams of those urban immigrants who had arrived loving them so much.

The impact of the neo-pioneers on handicrafts and "Folk art" has been immense. A large percentage of Nova Scotia's small army of handicrafts producers arrived in the province in the 1970s and 1980s. Two decades after Mary Black had planned to recruit craftspeople from Europe, sophisticated, university-trained craftspeople who would fulfil her vision of a technocratic craft élite gathered from all across the United States, Canada, and England. For many, handicrafts were secondary sources of income for their marginal farms. Candlemakers, leatherworkers, stained-glass artists, and weavers congregated in various parts of rural Nova Scotia (Bear River is one noteworthy centre). Gradually, inevitably perhaps, they began to band together in order to rationalize marketing and to secure state funding. One-person workshops began to hire apprentices. They began to rationalize production methods and coordinate the efforts of separate craft workers under one roof, unwittingly but faithfully re-enacting the script of Marx's *Capital*, volume one.

The most graphic instance of craft capitalism was Suttles and Seawinds, the commercial project of Vicki Crowe, a graduate of the New York School of Interior Design and a former staff member of *American Home* magazine. Influenced by a West Virginia model of craft development, Crowe returned to Nova Scotia in 1972 and began to explore ways of making crafts pay on the South Shore. A $20,000 loan from Industrial Estates Limited (the provincial industrial development branch), a large order from Abercrombie & Fitch, a feature article in *American Home*, and Suttles and Seawinds was up and away, producing craft products that ranged from expensive quilts to tea cosies. By 1979 the company had twenty-five full-time staff working in an old apple warehouse in New Germany and two hundred part-time sewers who produced a wide range of articles from ten-dollar tea cosies to thousand-dollar quilts. According to Jim Lotz, between 1978 and 1984 company sales grew tenfold. In 1984 sales exceeded $1.5 million, and the number of full-time staff had increased to fifty.[17]

However much they may have been initially inspired by William Morris, the new craft entrepreneurs were being drawn into the very culture of consumerism they had come to Nova Scotia to avoid. The marketing of crafts is now highly commercialized. The Halifax Christmas craft shows – distant descendants of Mary Black's "Craftsmen at Work" exhibitions – began in 1972 with a small ten-person effort at Dalhousie University; by the middle of the decade the Christmas Craft Market had about a hundred booths, and by 1985 the four Christmas craft markets in Greater Halifax were thought to generate about $2 million dollars in sales. Implicit in the neo-pioneers' craft revival was a new insistence on professionalism and "standards," through which strict aesthetic controls could be exerted. An association formed in 1974 representing "craftspeople" grew into the Nova Scotia Designer Crafts Council, which functioned something like a state-supported licensing body. (Work judged inferior by a standards committee would not be shown at the council's craft markets.) State support increased dramatically through the Department of Tourism, Recreation and Culture.[18]

In a book and several articles, Jim Lotz has argued that Nova Scotians should look to the "crafty entrepreneurs" for a way out of their economic difficulties. He tellingly compares the track record of the new crafts with that of Sysco, the Sydney steel-making facility.

In April 1988, the Nova Scotia Designer Crafts Council issued a review of production crafts in the province. It estimated that 287 craft ventures employed 3,720 people, full-time or significantly part-time, and generated sales of $10.4 million in 1983. In that year, the province spent $362,000 to support crafts, an amount repaid in sales tax revenue alone. By comparison, various levels of government have spent $1.5 billion on the Sydney Steel plant since its nationalization in 1967. When its latest modernization phase is completed, Sysco will employ only 700 workers. Meanwhile, craft production in the province has been growing by 15 per cent a year since 1983, and sales are expected to reach $25 million in 1989.[19]

Lotz's argument deserves consideration. Nova Scotia is far from its producers' major markets, and transportation costs are high. (These problems are more consequences than causes of underdevelopment, but it is not meaningful at this late stage to separate the two.) A progressive local state committed to an alternative to dependency and transfer payments might well look at those spheres, including handicrafts, in which distance from markets is counterbalanced by a high ratio of value to volume. The other side of this approach, however, is that industrial jobs are often unionized, well-paying, and theoretically open to people with a relatively low level of education, whereas the standard handicrafts jobs are generally non-unionized and often highly exploitative. Lotz rather understates the limited potential of any "small-is-beautiful" strategy in the absence of an alternative economic order centred on public planning. What besides sentiment would stop a really successful privately owned handicrafts business from relocating nearer its principal markets if, having expanded on the basis of the usual generous grants and forgivable loans, it had captured a large market share with its product?

Lotz, functioning as an organic intellectual of the new craft capitalism, echoes the commercial pragmatism of Mary Black, to whose memory his book is dedicated. In the second-wave handcrafts revival he celebrates, there is even less concern than in the first for handicrafts as expressions of an alternative aesthetic. According to Lotz, handicrafts should be supported because they generate employment and income with very little capital investment, create high-tech skills and production processes, establish decentralized factories, generate income for women and an outlet for female entrepreneurship, and integrate residents and newcomers in small communities in mutually beneficial ways. Only after listing these pragmatic objectives does Lotz note that crafts will also strengthen local and provincial pride and identity and preserve "traditional knowledge, designs and skills." One suspects that Mary Black would have agreed with Lotz in placing these two non-commercial objectives last in a list of seven.

The path that began with a rejection of materialism in the early 1970s ends in Lotz's book with a hymn of praise to Thomas Peter, whose *Search for Excellence* was, for a short time, the cult book of middle-class entrepreneurialism. As Sheri Aikenhead explained to the doubtless appreciative readers of the *Commercial News*, it has all become a matter of "making a buck on beauty." Thanks to the second-wave craft revival and the opening of shops that carried no foreign commercialized souvenirs, "buyers can get a piece of True Atlantic culture without the risk of imitation."[20]

To enter a Christmas craft fair in Halifax today is to enter into postmodern Folk rhetoric, an immense system of signs drawn from an imagined and placeless Folk past. The crafts on display are international, the styles from anywhere and everywhere. Everywhere there is "authenticity," warm fabrics, glistening wood, the promise of older ways and traditions – and it is all a thin veneer, as traditional as a Visa card and as warm and spontaneous as a television commercial. Even the supposed Folk art has the look of something mass-produced to order, the appearance of a mechanical spontaneity, something that duly repeats a formula known to work in an urban market. Those unable to make it to the craft fair may now do their shopping via the *Nova Scotia Crafts Catalogue*, produced for the Nova Scotia Designer Crafts Council by Eclectic Marketing. The various handicrafts are depicted in full colour, but apart from one vague reference to Nova Scotia's richness of history and tradition, no effort is made to "naturalize" the craft forms by placing them in a local context. From the toll-free number (operating seven days a week) and the possibility of ordering standardized craft forms on Visa and Mastercard, one concludes that one can gain access to handicraft authenticity without going to Nova Scotia at all.[21] Somewhere in heaven, Mary Black is smiling.

If the second-wave handicrafts revival completed the program contemplated by the first, the invention of Folk art has ushered into being a new category and a new matrix of theory and evidence. The theory is necessarily complicated and vague, because no one has ever succeeded in clarifying the fatally confused category of "Folk art." Folk art seems to mean anything a curator or collector wants it to mean. The art historian J. Russell Harper vainly sought relief from the intractable difficulties of the concept by multiplying adjectives: the art in question was variously called "people's," "naive," "provincial," "primitive," and "folk." Underneath these confusing labels, Harper's analysis rested on a simple dualism.

There are two kinds of paintings. One is created by artists as their vocation; they have trained themselves for it, and they see the results of their work taken up by connoisseurs and displayed in formal settings. The second kind has its source in a desire for personal expression and is intended largely for the enjoyment of ordinary folk; lacking in artistic suavity it may be, but it is a source of delight simply because its subject-matter is plain, its expression is honest, and its air is unpretentious. It is a reflection, direct and unhampered, of life as it is seen and felt by people immersed in a variety of work and leisure.[22]

This ingenious formulation succeeds in recapitulating an entire romance of the unreflective, honest, plain, and unpretentious Folk while also conveniently exalting the credentials of the professionally trained artist. The survival of the Folk in adjectival form – in Folk art – allowed for the retention of an unargued concept of the primitive, of an art that supposedly inhered in materials and in people enjoying an unmediated relationship with nature and an unproblematic, "fresh," "spontaneous" relation between conception and execution.[23] Of course, only trained people of discernment and taste can truly appreciate the primitive art of the simple Folk. (Presumably this means that the Folk themselves do not really know the value of what they are producing; like children, they produce a charmingly innocent beauty they cannot understand.) No matter: after the 1970s, crowds of neo-pioneers were ready to adopt primitivism as a style. Folk art, like baked brie, became a badge of membership in the urban cognoscenti. Primitive art in the living room suggested that the occupant was no mere suburban professional with a mortgage and a dental plan, but someone in touch with the deeper (yet simpler) things of life. The bright colours of Folk art, which Lilian Burke had once countermanded as inappropriately garish, complemented the white-on-white decorating schemes preferred by so many late-twentieth century postmodern urbanites. The extremely rapid "discovery," emergent popularity, official acceptance, and touristic commercialization of Folk art combined to make the phenomenon a fast-forward replay of earlier events in folklore.

Folk art themes have been present in tourism promotion from the 1940s: the covers of provincial highway maps included polished landscapes with trees, roads, and cars in proportion, but with tiny, anomalous fisherfolk cottages whose dimensions and proportions were drawn as though by a child. But it was only in the 1970s and 1980s that this wholly nebulous category came to be seen as an aspect of provincial identity. Much of the fascination with the form was associated with American expatriates. From the vast celebratory archive of local Folk art commentary, Charles Huntington's account of Charlie Tanner stands out as a classic of the genre. Huntington, an antique dealer, and his wife moved to Nova Scotia in 1974 from Maine "to get away from it all."[24] Like the Americans who "discovered" hooked rugs in the 1920s, the couple found an unappreciated and underexploited cultural resource in Nova Scotia: Folk art. They came to realize that

> we were living amidst a rich, untapped resource of creative productivity and imaginative potential. Of course, we did not know very much about our adopted environs; but in hindsight, we were, no doubt, the right people at the right place and time. It did not matter that we knew little of Nova Scotia's cultural history. What was important was that we quickly came to embrace and help document the flowering of a localized artistic impulse. One could not say that we witnessed or partook in a renaissance, because practically no artistic tradition had existed here ...
>
> The "art" of it [Folk art] is largely a subconscious, rather than conscious, expression. That is to say the people who made and still make folk art, by and large, only think of themselves as artists after years of our insisting that is what they are. Their initial motives come entirely from within themselves and these motives alter with a growing audience for the work.[25]

Perpetually on the point of disappearing, always already sinking beneath the waves of modernity – Roy Mackenzie was complaining about being "too late" in 1909 – the Folk Other has proved surprisingly resilient. Even in the mid-1980s, when telephones and televisions could be found in the smallest rural communities, the Other was evidently still there, painting in unharried innocence, guided not by his or her market (much of it now located in metropolitan Toronto), not by the surrounding culture, but by subconscious and spontaneous thought processes. Still, Innocence cannot function without its organic intellectuals. Just as folklore required the trained ear and the entrepreneurship of the folklorist, appreciating the work of the painting Crusoes of the coast requires the trained eye of the urban intellectual, as Huntington explains:

> One of the most challenging aspects of folk art is that art generally grows as much from other art as it does from life; but, for the folk artist, there is no art bank for him to draw upon for ideas, and few models to imitate. The folk artist is, by his or her naivete, spared traditional conventions. Folk art's common denominator is its freshness. If one seeks for some profound depth in Charlie's [Charles Tanner's] work, he will not find it. But, that is not to say that it isn't fairly rich in its own right. The final test of any work is whether it commands the attention of informed, receptive viewers.

This salute to Innocence is followed by an illuminating interview with the late artist, reported in the obligatory dialect:

C. Huntington. Do they [the artist's carvings] amuse you, do you find them funny?

C. Tanner. Ha Ha Ha Ha. Start swearing sometimes. No, I don't really think much about it; I just keep settin' and whittlin', carvin' them out the best way you can.

Tanner's work, according to Huntington, is confined by, but also somehow transcends, his "handicaps" – limited education and experience, ill health, even "restrictions in god-given skills" – and yet it "has its own life, its own mystery and that is why we thank Charlie for being what he was and doing what he did."[26] By virtue of his professional training, the intellectual has rescued for our gaze the safe otherness of the innocent Folk, whose work is simultaneously esteemed for its absence of metropolitan sophistication ("freshness") and subtly disparaged as something that requires special pleading. The aesthetic object thus framed is ambiguous, Art and "not-really-Art"; and the author's generosity in permitting. it within the field of high art is qualified by his understanding that he is being, in his own mind, so very nice and folksy and down home about all of this.

Folk art cannot evade the theoretical significance of the Folk category. The most important recent exhibition on the subject (which carries the vintage essentialist title, *Spirit of Nova Scotia*) is remarkable for the vigour with which the old techniques of "Folk construction" continue to be applied. Once the geographical provenance of an anonymous Folk object is known, one authority suggests, its decorative treatment must reflect "the ethnic heritage of both the community or county where it was found, and the ethnic background of its maker," a classic example of the ecological fallacy, ethnic reductionism, and the fallacious if truly venerable belief that individual creativity is reserved for practitioners of high art.[27]

We somehow expect to find the idea of the Folk thriving among the tourists, the back-to-the-landers, and certain collectors of art. Yet, far from being the harmless foible of a few marginal eccentrics, an unexamined notion of the Folk surfaces in such unlikely bodies as the federal Department of Fisheries. One study has demonstrated that federal fisheries bureaucrats made frequent use of stereotypical images of fisherfolk in their representations of their department's mission. Such state planners found the idea of the Folk a congenial one, because it allowed them to design their schemes for modernization without the inconvenience of consulting the people most affected. If the fisherfolk were indeed a race apart, admirable in their individualism but hopelessly primitive in their responses to the modern world, then it followed that they were the last people who should be consulted in any scientific program of fisheries management. The department spewed out a series of images of fishers as quaint, hairy, masculine characters while, in the privacy of internal memoranda, bureaucrats waxed eloquent about a "primeval economy" in which "people are obviously happy in peace and ignorance."[28] Resettlement of the Newfoundland outports – a fine example of technocratic social engineering – was justified (and critiqued) partly on the basis of just such simplistic dualisms. Similarly, a mythified view of the Folk and the Commons was used to sustain a view of what would happen if the state failed to evolve a complex web of bureaucracy and regulation around the "open-access" resource of the North Atlantic fishery. What would happen, planners argued, was that fishers, following the alleged example of African herdsmen, would rush to exploit the resource, hastening its exhaustion. A (grossly oversimplified and distorted) history of the Folk and the Commons in pre-industrial England was called upon to justify policy-making in mid-twentieth-century Canada.[29]

WHY GO BEYOND THE FOLK?

The only reasons to stop talking and thinking as if there were a distinct subset in society – the Folk – with their own customs, art, and songs, are in the end political and ethical. There is nothing wrong with the widespread use of the Folk motif in regional advertising, in the thinking of the Department of Fisheries, or in regional culture generally, if one accepts the premise that there is nothing wrong about the structure of power. At least for those not excluded from the Folk at the outset, the subject-position does "work" to construct a sense of identity. There is no reason to go beyond it if one believes that Nova Scotian history has concluded with the Nova Scotia Folk enjoying a relaxed and friendly way of life. One would attempt to dislodge the concept only if one were also anxious to contest the relations of power it helps to secure. It is only for the "left" – that is, that broad array of people and organizations politically committed to a society of equals – that such a project of ideological critique makes any sense. Why go beyond the Folk? Because, the left must reply, the category emerged from and continues to naturalize a form of applied social analysis that blocks any radical democratic alternative. For the left, the problem with Innocence and with the Folk is that they establish a political and social "commonsense," based on a commandeering of history and identity, which excludes at the outset a critical dialogue with the past and a realistic grasp of the present. There are no progressive items in this powerful language of the Folk that racial and sexual minorities, women and workers, or any other subaltern groups could requisition as a means of understanding and countering the daily injustices they confront.

A concrete example of the selectiveness and pervasiveness of the Folk framework may help to clarify this point. To say that it was in their early twentieth-century labour wars that modern Nova Scotians achieved their identity and purpose is to go up against a "commonsense" that has firmly relegated such events in workers' history to the periphery. They are, symbolically, nonexistent in the imagined Nova Scotia people see represented around them every day. Nonetheless, to question the centrality of the schooner *Bluenose* (which was indirectly very much the invention of the Halifax *Herald*) as a transcendental signifier of the Nova Scotian is to mock the central truth of a secular religion. Why? An untutored visitor might well believe that events in which thousands of people fought brave battles and made tremendous sacrifices were at least as important as a promotional sporting event launched by the local newspaper. But that visitor would be naively reckoning without the power of a myth-symbol complex underwritten by liberal ideology. The *Bluenose*, the fishing-cove photographs of MacAskill (and his numerous followers), folklore and handicrafts – all obviously speak to a core of values, a stable set of ideas, which is confirmed every day in a hundred venues. This set of ideas is not the natural reflection of a pre-existing reality, but constitutes a highly selective cultural framework within which some ideas are thinkable and sayable and some are not.

The ideas that are unthinkable are exactly those which the left, a virtually negligible presence after the 1920s, has to make a rival "commonsense." Instead of the Folk as a static and passive resource, the left requires the subaltern groups as creative and dynamic forces; instead of pastoral images of harmony between rich and poor, the left needs the memories of the struggles of the oppressed. Innocence is a sealed and deeply conservative ideological universe. The imagined Nova Scotia it has made so powerful a presence has been, and always will be, a hostile terrain for any conceivable left.

How could this conservative and complacently successful mythomoteur then ever be shut down? I would like to suggest two inevitably tentative approaches to this, corresponding to two contrasting positions in cultural studies. The position from which I have written this study, and which commends itself to me as the most promising for future academic and political work, represents an attempt to reconcile these two positions – Marxian political economy and Foucauldian genealogy – by combining their strengths in a third, neo-Gramscian framework. I have used this neo-Gramscian framework throughout this book. It might prove useful in other attempts to think through alternatives to the present conservative status quo. I use "might" advisedly, because (as Stuart Hall has remarked) "the purpose of theorizing is not to enhance one's intellectual or academic reputation but to enable us to grasp, understand, and explain – to produce a more adequate knowledge of – this historical world and its processes; and thereby to inform our practice so that we may transform it."[30]

Over the past two decades the Marxian approach has made tremendous gains in its analysis of the Maritimes, and it seems unlikely that a genuinely counter-hegemonic reorganization of regional culture could avoid drawing heavily on this body of theory and evidence. Within this perspective, "ideology" is traditionally a negative term – a word that designates a systematic distortion of reality that strengthens the ruling class by confirming its economic and political privileges. This is surely part of what is going on in Innocence, which has enriched a legion of gift-shop owners, advertisers, and tourism developers. And Innocence has also proved helpful in legitimating the social and cultural leadership of these businesspeople. It was invaluable in the 1930s and 1940s, for example, when, by appealing to the essential nature of the fisherman as a co-adventurer, businessmen were able to defeat radicals who defined him primarily as a worker. This political economy approach is far from exhausted, and needs to be extended. (It needs, too, to become much more historical.) It would be invaluable to have a more detailed and sophisticated historiography on the fishing communities, for example, so that data on life expectancy, standards of living, class formation, and so on are available to counterbalance the romantic images of the fisherfolk.

Typically, the left contrasts the saccharine images of the Folk with the harshness of the lives of working people. This strategy suggests the superficiality and distortion of the ideological works being criticized. As David Whisnant remarks of the parallel Appalachian case, "'Rescuing' or 'preserving' or 'reviving' a sanitized version of culture frequently makes for rather shallow liberal commitment: it allows a prepared consensus on the 'value' of preservation or revival; its affirmations lie comfortably within the bounds of conventional secular piety; it makes minimal demands upon financial (or other) resources; and it involves little risk of opposition from vested economic or political interests. It is, in a word, the cheapest and safest way to go."[31]

The political economy of the Folk in Nova Scotia involved even fewer relations of reciprocity than was the case in the Appalachians, and the charge of superficiality and acquiescence in relations of oppression is for that reason all the more plausible. So often in Nova

Scotia there was no interplay between middle-class interpreters and their working-class informants, but rather an outright appropriation of culture and a one-sided process of commodification. Folk forms were all too easily and complacently absorbed. As one left-wing critic of this process of cultural appropriation on a world scale has observed,

By an act of magical naming, all the peasantries and technologically primitive peoples of the world can be turned into "folk." They are certainly more palatable that way. The peasants exploited by nearby urban centers or the tribes trapped in the coils of more distant imperial powers might make us feel guilty or ashamed if we could transform them into charming sources of inspiration. A world of misery and stolen pleasures can become a staged world of song and dance and ever so colorful costumes ...

By now quite a few middle-class people in the industrialized nations become folk one way or another on their weekends, and their children can explore the various options of becoming fully professional "folk" via the media, of remaining amateur "folk" in the counterculture, or of becoming professional and amateur folklorists – collectors and appreciators of things folksy ...

Can we keep "the folk" concept and redeem it? No! and no! again. You can't, because too many Volkswagens have been built, too many folk ballets applauded, too many folksongs sold, too much aid and comfort given to the enemy. Unlike "primitive," "folk" has only a positive, friendly meaning. The folk are not the oppressed whose revolution is long overdue, but the Quaint-not-like-us, the Pleasant peasants, the Almost-like-me-and-you, to be consumed at leisure. The folk are not neutrals to be fought over by left and right. They belong to the bourgeoisie, just like "High Culchaa."[32]

Although only loosely "Marxist" in provenance, this *cri de coeur* is Marxian in sentiment. Its tactic of debunking Folk romanticism by contrasting it with the harsh realities of exploitation has become a significant feature of critical thought in the region, and is likely to remain so. Why go beyond the Folk? Because inherent in the concept itself is a reactionary sociology which, when applied to oneself or to society as a whole, removes any detailed consideration of the structure of power. It leads one to a complacently organic view of society, in which there are no fundamental social contradictions and no underlying differences in perspective.

Nonetheless, there are some serious limitations to this strategy of the "critique of ideology" (probably the single most common strategy of persuasion on the left). It is not clear that exposés of starvation, desolation, and disease in the quaint fishing-coves of the "Coast of

Songs" – realistic and needed as these exposés are – would in them-selves create unresolveable problems for Innocence. As a mytho-moteur generating a huge number of semi-autonomous myths and symbols, it is much more supple than this. It is possible, for example, to incorporate a good deal about how hard life was for the fisherfolk into romantic and essentialist treatments. (Day's *Rockbound* is a good example.) It would be more difficult, but still possible, for Innocence to incorporate a sense of fishing communities' suffering not just from the storms and stresses of life at sea, but from systematically oppres-sive class relations, provided that these relations of exploitation were falsely depicted as the work of outsiders rather than insiders. Tales of death at sea could still be comfortably blended in, provided that one edited out any bitter and unresolved sense of grievance or even the possibility of an alternative ending. Stories of economic hardship could be accommodated, provided that there was no blame attached to any individual, or to a social class, or to the state, and no consid-eration of the generation of profits out of poverty. There is no one unequivocal way of reading a particular fact. Deaths at sea might be (should be, a Marxist says), interpreted socio-historically, as aspects of a social structure in which workers' lives were held to be less important than commercial considerations. But there are alternative readings of the same facts – acts of God, the workers' careless indif-ference to Fate, a hard but traditional way of life – in which their politico-ethical meaning is very different. Innocence is in some ways invulnerable to empirical refutation, because it deals with essence.

There are additional problems. Although some people may come to question the ideologically conceived "Spirit of Nova Scotia" on the basis of empirical data, what chance is there of conveying this infor-mation to a wider public? Will the vast machinery that now manu-factures the Folk, in the interests of selling bread and political parties and Folk art, ever be adapted to an alternative reading? The problem we confront is less one of incomplete or repressed information, and more one of the conceptual frameworks within which facts acquire their significance and further the hegemony that such frameworks have achieved in society. Many people have acquired a strong interest in maintaining Innocence. If it is to work, such a mythomoteur has to generate ideological formations that seem to speak universally, to represent themselves as being in the general interest. Finally, and touching on the most ethically troubling issue, there is the tone of the simplest Marxist critiques of ideology. Those who identify with the Folk are charged with dishonesty and inauthenticity. This does not allow for an adequate view of the complex of motivations and ideals the historian is likely to find in the records of the past, and it may prompt ineffectively simplistic strategies in the present. Many of those who incorporated a Folk ideal into their deepest imaginings may have been striving for an honest and authentic response to the emptiness of life in a capitalist order. To dismiss their pain as so much illusion is to miss the point.

Traditional Marxist accounts of ideology are indispensable as starting-points, but they generally err in arguing for too instrumentalist a view of culture and the state – in seeing both as instruments wielded by a phenomenally farsighted business class and "its" pliant state. But the class interests of workers or capital cannot be simply "read" directly out of an "objective" situation. A key insight of modern linguistic theory is that all language is multireferential; there is not a one-to-one relationship between the linguistic form and the object to which it intends to refer. If this is so, Stuart Hall observes, it becomes difficult to argue that material conditions will invariably generate a single set of meanings, as if the concept of "class" meant just one thing.

So the field of language is not strictly segmented by class but is obviously more open. Yet the semiotic systems of meaning are not, therefore, entirely disconnected from the social or class positions in which the speakers are placed. The play of power between different social groups is worked out *within* language, partly by the different ways in which shared terms are accentuated, or the ways in which shared terms are inserted into different discourses, as well as by different subcultural dialectics.[33]

Class consciousness is contradictory, and there is no law that determines that workers, for example, will inevitably or "naturally" arrive at one consciousness that expresses the truth of their situation.

To arrive at a richer, less reductionist, account of modern culture and a more sophisticated political practice, certain elements of Michel Foucault's work may be useful. For Foucault, "discourses, programmes, or rational schemas are themselves fragments of reality in complex relations with other social and institutional practices ... the effects or ends which emerge generally fail to correspond with those programmed."[34] The central concern of Foucault's genealogical research is the mutual relations between systems of truth and modalities of power. This concern with "power/knowledge" neither equates the two nor commits one a priori to a self-refuting relativism.[35] Foucault usefully alerts us to the strangeness of seemingly self-evident categories. We can use his framework to begin research on how "discursive entities" such as the Folk – for a materialist and a realist position is that the Folk do not exist in the same way that a chair or a proton exists – are constructed as new objects of thought through mutual relations of knowledge and power. This approach moves one away from those instrumentalist accounts of the state and culture (which generally imply a teleology of inevitable class development) towards a sense of a socio-cultural relational field, a vast network of things and words, within which subject-positions are created. The state ceases to be a monolithic instrument and instead becomes a node within a "matrix of individualization," which "forms, shapes, and governs individuality" through the exercise of a new form of power over the social.[36]

To see things this way is to move towards a critique of accounts of ideology that reduce it to class location or interest. Metaphors such as "base" and "superstructure" are rendered unusable, for there is no absolute "top" or "bottom" in language. The new metaphors are those of grids and networks, more like "vocabularies" operating within "grammars" than "superstructures" erected on "bases." They speak to a contemporary sense of a social world in which language plays a far more critical role than had earlier been acknowledged.

It would be an understatement to say that historians and other writers disagree about how to interpret the consequences of the linguistic turn. Without reviewing a vast polemical literature, I shall merely indicate the attractions of the balanced and careful Gramscian position of Stuart Hall. Unlike many other critics, who proceed as though they had developed unproblematical and certain positions on language which they cannot be bothered to disclose to us, Hall is not willing to dismiss the Foucauldian enterprise as so much idealism. Even if we could, even if it were desirable, it does not seem possible to "unlearn" our insight into the multireferentiality of language. Moreover, from the perspective of the new social movements – which are radically contesting the drugged liberal consensus of contemporary society – these new conceptual developments have opened up spaces, and allowed analyses, once firmly relegated to the margins.[37]

The question "Why go beyond the Folk?" can be cogently answered in Marxist terms by referring to the obvious class bias and distortion of applied Folk thought. It can be no less cogently answered in terms of a critique of essentialism. A Foucauldian could answer the question, "Why go beyond the Folk?" with a critique of essentialism: "We need to go beyond the Folk in the same way, and for the same reason, that we need to go beyond 'Man' and 'Woman' and 'Homosexual' and 'Indian' as stable, bounded, trans-historical identities, whose meanings are straightforward and universal." If we work within a Foucauldian framework, we see the Folk not as something that existed prior to the category, but rather a socially constructed subject-position within antimodernity. *There never were any Folk. There were only the categories and vigorously redescribed if not invented traditions that enabled us to think there were.* This move to look at the "social construction" of the Folk simply follows what is going on in many other fields of historical inquiry influenced by the linguistic turn. The strategy of "genealogy" – reading history backwards to locate a discontinuity in the past, and stressing the past's strangeness and contingency, the better to "bestrange" the present – that this study has followed in no way entails an abandonment of historical materialism. The anti-essentialism which the method of genealogy grounds in historical research is, if anything, more rigorously anti-idealist in outlook than many Marxist works, which attribute a forward-moving "spirit" to history itself and find cultural "identities" that achieve a fixed and final form only outside any history of which we can have empirical knowledge.

Moreover, contrary to arguments that set the two traditions in absolute and unremitting opposition, on Hall's reading these approaches can complement each other in historical analysis. A myth-symbol complex such as Innocence, or a specific formation within it, such as the Folk, does not achieve widespread acceptance as an obvious "commonsense" without, Hall argues, "a process of vigorous polemic and contestation in order to become the normative-normalized structure of conceptions through which a class 'spontaneously' and authentically thinks or lives its relations to the world." In this neo-Gramscian view of ideology, dominant ideas are not "ascribed by and inscribed in the position a class holds in the structure of social relations and ... the position of dominance is guaranteed elsewhere – by class location." Rather, dominant ideas have to win ascendancy "through a specific and contingent (in the sense of open-ended, not totally determined) process of ideological struggle." The ideology of the bourgeoisie is not an unequivocal marker, attached to a homogeneous class as a licence-plate is attached to a car.

We are looking here at a significant *shift* in thinking. Far from one whole unified class outlook being locked in permanent struggle with the class outlook of an opposing class, we are obliged to explain an ideology that has effectively penetrated, fractured, and fragmented the territory of the dominated classes, precipitating a rupture in their traditional discourses (laborism, reformism, welfarism, Keynesianism) and actively working on the discursive space, the occupancy or mastery of which alone enables it to become a leading popular ideological force.[38]

This is a helpful guideline for interpreting what happened in Nova Scotia. And against any "critical theory" move, which would dissolve everything into the free play of "discourses," Hall argues:

The social distribution of knowledge *is* skewed. And since the social institutions most directly implicated in its formation and transmission – the family/school/media triplet – are grounded in and structured by the class relations that surround them, the distribution of the available codes with which to decode or unscramble the meaning of events in the world, and the languages we use to construct interests, are bound to reflect the unequal relations of power that obtain in the area of symbolic production as in other spheres. Ruling or dominant conceptions of the world do not directly prescribe the mental content of the illusions that supposedly fill the heads of the dominant classes. But the circle of dominant ideas *does* accumulate the symbolic power to map or classify the world for others; its classifications do acquire not only the constraining power of dominance over other modes of thought but also the inertial authority of habit and instinct. It becomes the horizon of the taken for granted; what the world is and how it works, for all practical purposes. Ruling ideas may dominate other conceptions of the social world by setting the limit to what will appear as rational, reasonable, credible, indeed sayable or thinkable, within the given vocabularies of motive and action available to us. Their dominance lies precisely in the power they have to contain within their limits, to frame within the circumference of thought, the reasoning and calculation of other social groups. The "monopoly of the means of mental production" – or of the "cultural apparatuses," to use a more modern phrase – is not, of course, irrelevant to this acquisition over time of symbolic dominance vis-a-vis other, less coherent and comprehensive accounts of the world. Nor do they have literally to displace other ideas with illusions in order to acquire a hegemonic position over them. Ideologies may not be affixed, as organic entities, to their appropriate classes, but this does not mean that the production and transformation of ideology in society could proceed for or outside the structuring lines of force of power and class.[39]

This theoretical position secures the materialism of ideology without taking us back to either culturalism or economism; and it acknowledges the importance of language without requiring everything to be turned into "discourse."

Innocence constructed the "Folk" as an imaginary position from which Nova Scotians could respond to antimodernism. This new subject-position interrupted and partially replaced older, progressive ones. (Hugh MacLennan's curious sense of himself as a member of a pre-modern society was a product of the turn to Innocence, just as

T.C. Haliburton's conviction that he was affiliated with a metropolitan culture was an aspect of a British imperial subject-position disrupted by the crisis of the early twentieth century.) Innocence as an ideology had to articulate itself on and through subjectivities, fractured and rendered contradictory through a wrenching socio-economic crisis. In a reconstitution of subject-positions, the category "Folk" came to assume special significance as a central term in a reconstituted Nova Scotian subjectivity.

This antiessentialism represents a distinct gain over the accounts of ideology offered by classical political economy and vulgar petit-bourgeois culturalism. Nonetheless, Foucauldian analysis on its own leads to unresolvable problems. Political antiessentialism can lead analysis too far away from the state as the place where symbolic violence is ultimately ratified. As a historical generalization, an infinitely diffuse sense of power/knowledge in society seems vulnerable to the abundant empirical evidence of the continuing centrality of the state as a site where some words and things are made "truer" than others – the arena in which the ultimate (although not the only or necessarily the most important) battles over politico-ethical commonsense are waged. In this local study, one thinks of the positive pre-eminence of the state in securing a place for handicrafts and the Folk. We should also remember the potency of cultural non-decision, the state's undeclared but crucial strategy (through the chronic underfunding of cultural producers and a bourgeois insistence that cultural activities pay a return on investment) of abandoning many spheres of culture to the workings of the market. More attention to how the state actually functions could mitigate the ironic tendency of Foucauldian theory to treat as "essential" certain strategies of control – the panopticon, most notoriously – whose application within the state may have been much more limited, and less successful, than is implied. If the complex gaze of the state has intensified immeasurably over the past century, this does not mean that we are all now metaphorically living in the shadow of the prison tower. As Frederic Jameson observes, the more persuasively and massively Foucauldian theorists developed their crushing images of panopticism, governmentalization, and the "matrix of individualization," the more this tendency undermined its own emancipatory potential. By "winning" readers over to a vision of the carceral universe of modern society, it "loses" them as people who might effectively resist it, and who might draw inspiration from the (often relatively successful) countermovements that have contested the terms of their subaltern position.[40] Visions of postmodern cultural catastrophe, so pervasive as we near the end of the millennium, immobilize those who might challenge a dying social order – especially when the catastrophe in question relates to so vast and ill-defined a cultural complex as post-modernity. R. Radhakrishnan has tellingly probed the deeper logic of the "winner loses" syndrome common in so much contemporary cultural theory. Foucault's attractive debunking of the claims of the universal intellectual, and his claim that "truth" is a thing of this world, is accompanied by a perplexed inability to work out any alternative subject-position (the imaginary position of knowledge from which alone a text can be unproblematicaly read or spoken). "This self-critical and deconstructive rhetoric certainly sounds correct and politically wholesome except for one little problem," Radhak-rishnan remarks apropos of Foucault's critique of the universal intel-lectual. "It is not clear 'who' is speaking here, and 'why,' and 'about whom,' and from what point of view."[41] The fastidious refusal to work out a political ethic for fear of complicity in the impurities of actual day-to-day political life leaves the Foucauldian with a romantic, essentialist notion of constituencies of the dominated. In an odd way, such Foucauldian thought returns us to the Folk, whose essential "innocence" is once again underwritten by their isolation and their distance from theory, that new symptom of overcivilization. It evades a recognition of the difficult and necessarily abstract and concrete work of constructing a counter-hegemonic practice. Theory rages against Identity, the Voice, and the Self, while the constituencies in which it vests what remains of its hopes for resistance voice them-selves "with conviction into Self and Identity."[42] The struggles of gays and lesbians are eloquent in this regard.

As Hall suggests, Foucauldian insights into the workings of power/ knowledge can be incorporated into a neo-Marxist approach without necessarily committing the researcher to accepting a self-refuting relativism or abstention from active politics. It is necessary to go beyond the enraged critique of the Folk as bourgeois ideology to a more sophisticated analysis of how this network of things and words actually worked as a body of applied social thought. In particular, such valuable work on the constitution of subject-positions could be brought into relationship with the Gramscian concept of hegemony, because Gramsci, an orthodox Marxist in many respects, nonetheless made a decisive and irrevocable break with both culturalism and economism. Transforming such hypotheses as that of direct transla-tion into politics of the economic needs of the capitalist class, or that of the predominant place of coercion and force in cementing capitalist control over a pliant state, Gramsci opened the way to a far different sense of how power works in a modern capitalist state. By focusing attention on those components of the dominant culture that require the consent of subordinates, Gramsci suggested a culture in constant process, where the state of play between the classes can be changed very rapidly. Against the closed and complete world of essentialist antimodernism, Gramsci's concept of hegemony stressed incompleteness and unevenness, the overlapping and confusion of identities, and (by inference) the non-reducibility of the cultural to the economic. Thus, to go back to our question, "Why go beyond the folk?" the neo-Gramscian might answer – and in my opinion this answer is better than that of either the classical Marxist or the poststructuralist theorist – "Constructed as a subject-position within a new hegemonic framework in the 1920s, the concept of the Folk was and remains a powerful obstacle to the formation of a counter-hegemonic cultural politics, without which a new, profoundly emancipatory politics of class, gender, and racial equality is inconceivable."

A neo-Gramscian approach which has learned from but not capitulated to critical theory can, in resisting the temptations of economistic and culturalist reductionisms, help us understand both the power and fragility of ideologies in a fragmented and fragmenting postmodern world. "Ideological formations operating through discursive regularities 'formulate' their own objects of knowledge and their own subjects; they have their own repertoire of concepts, are driven by their own logics, operate their own enunciative modality, constitute their own way of acknowledging what is true and excluding what is false within their own regime of truth," Stuart Hall argues. "They establish through their regularities a 'space of formation' in which certain statements can be enunciated; one constellation constantly interrupts, displaces, and rearranges another."[43] The naturalization of the Folk required just this interruption and displacement of such alternative categories of the "worker" and the "producer," with their very different logics and truths. Yet the "Folk" was hardly conceivable as an idea without the project of capitalist modernity, without the liberal state, and without the efforts of actual capitalist modernizers – the succession of cultural entrepreneurs with whom we have dealt in this study – to make it an authoritative, influential reading. And this, I believe, my study of the Folk has clearly shown.

IN SEARCH OF THE COMPLEX LIFE

Ultimately the Folk offered Nova Scotians a flawed answer to a question that was suddenly urgent at a time of great crisis: who are "we"? The myths and symbols generated by the mythomoteur of Innocence answered by tracing an imagined path of descent from a vanished Golden Age of Folk authenticity, whose last traces were always already vanishing before the eyes of the present. It flattered certain things about Maritime society – such as the continuity of communities and the persistence of tradition – and offered an explanation of that which could not be flattered in essentialist and culturalist terms. (Underdevelopment could thus be explained by a deficiency in entrepreneurial spirit, or the outcome of regional conservatism.) The category thus provided both a means of sustaining subjective self-esteem and of shielding, from subaltern critique and activism, those political and social leaders who had led their society into such a crisis.

Folk forms in a postmodern society are planets circling a dead sun, for there can be little doubt that, among those who have given it the most sustained attention over the years, the very concept of the Folk has entered a profound crisis. The crisis of ethnographic authority and the concept of "culture" (at least as an explanation of anything) experienced with full force in modern anthropology has had its echoes in uncertainties about the epistemological status of the Folk. After all, why did only *European* peasants count as Folk? Why not people in the Third World? Was someone a Folk performer who had learned one traditional ballad from a book and another from his grandfather? What was it, exactly, about the printed word that was held to be so contaminated that a broadside would never rank with a ballad? One hardly needed to be a theorist of language to notice the difficulty in creating any agreement over what the term "Folk" meant. The international Quest of the Folk came down to this: the Folk did not exist. There was even a general crisis of faith in the existence of a unitary concept of folk music, dramatized in 1981 by the dropping of the word itself from the title of the International Folk Music Council.[44] In academic folklore studies, the explosive polemics concerning the concept of "folklorismus" – which might be roughly translated as "fakelore" – have inevitably brought into question the conventional culturalist calculus of authenticity that had once given folklorists a sure grasp of the true folklore. The perhaps rather desperate attempt to salvage "folklore" by expanding the boundaries of the Folk to refer to *"any group of people whatsoever* who share at least one common factor, be it occupation, language, etc.," begged the question of what additional information or insight was gained into the group in question by calling them "folk" (or, for that matter, by calling their shared understandings "lore.")[45]

Under conditions of postmodernity, then, Folk forms are widely dispersed and popular, but belief in the Folk themselves is waning. The Quest of the Folk may well continue – *Good Morning America* recently discovered Peggy's Cove, although to audible guffaws in the region, and certain central Canadians will probably always have a soft spot for the notion of the happily underdeveloped east coast Folk – but probably not as a source of powerfully unifying myths and songs in Nova Scotia itself. Illusions of Folk isolation are hard to sustain in a fully wired society, much of it tuned in, via cable television, directly to Detroit. The romance of the rural Folk has run aground on the shoals of its own implausibility. In the context of a countryside that bristles with satellite dishes and shopping-malls, populated with people who often work at urban jobs to support rural homes, and that is in a hundred other ways so evidently *not* a haven set apart from late twentieth-century capitalism, the notion of the "simple life" of the Folk can only be ironic. In the dissolution of one powerful form of hegemonic ideology, there is perhaps a moment of opportunity for creative cultural opposition.

A reading of identity alternative to that of the Folk will have to address very carefully the important political and symbolic functions once filled by the concept it seeks to displace. The task that faces any possible left is to imagine another Nova Scotian community, one that opens the doors that Innocence so firmly closed to people of colour, to women, to gays and lesbians, to workers, and to rural producers, to the history of popular struggle and resistance, and to an optimistic, open-ended sense of a common future. New heroes, a new canon of significant events, and a new language of belonging could emerge as the old canon and the old pantheon of heroes are transformed to accommodate a new politics of culture. There will probably always be, in any readily imaginable Nova Scotia, a "politics of cultural selection," but this politics could conceivably be divorced from the narrow class and commercial criteria and the vulgar culturalism that since the 1920s have decisively shaped it.

This description of a moment of cultural possibility would be starry-eyed utopianism were it not for indications that it is already underway, in a remarkable if unheralded movement of cultural renaissance in Nova Scotia and the Atlantic region as a whole. Alden Nowlan incompletely yet brilliantly caught the sense of this feeling. In one of the most memorable scenes in *Various Persons Named Kevin O'Brien*, Kevin O'Brien cruelly terrorizes his sister by bounding after her in an outsized black cloak: she falls in a "vertigo of humiliation," and Nowlan savagely imagines a passing driver thinking, as he watches the children run across the field, "'The country ... it's still the best place to bring kids up.'"[46] It is a defining moment in the culture of Nova Scotia, in which the fond patronage of the outside observer is thrown back, is *refused*: the lure of Innocence is resisted.

In ways Nowlan never developed, much new cultural work in the Maritimes extends the political implications of this seminal moment in which the gaze is refused. A powerful and dynamic environmental movement (the neo-pioneers' best gift to the region) has overturned the easy division of society along urban–rural lines that for so long seemed like a natural and obvious way of seeing. In the emergent environmentalist framework, there are no Folk living tranquil lives in a pastoral countryside, to be envied by the harried citizens of the city. Instead, there are people in rural areas fighting many of the same political and social dilemmas as their urban friends. In the feminist movement, the illusion of a happy seaside patriarchy has been challenged by very different stories. Perhaps the best single feminist critique of the Folk can be found in M.T. Dohaney's *The Corrigan Women*, a wrenching account of growing up in a Newfoundland fishing cove, which implicitly sketches a path beyond the repression it details. Within the Cape Breton cultural community, wrestling with the legacy of seven decades of an intrusive tourism state, there are important indications of resistance and refusal, as Ellison Robertson's deeply compassionate if pessimistic fiction has suggested. Erik Kristiansen's emergent critical study of Maritime literature is reshaping our understanding of how the region's writers have responded to capitalism, and George Elliott Clarke's brilliant poems on the rural black experience combine gospel songs, social critique, and a vision of justice.[47] New energies are everywhere. Thanks to a limited but valuable democratization of culture since the 1960s, state money has been made more readily available to a wider range of cultural producers. Writers no longer have to tailor their books for the tourist market; artists can paint things other than lobsters and picturesque fishing-coves (or, like Gerald Ferguson, can do so with an arch postmodern irony); and a civil society outside the business of tourism can take shape. Paradoxically, the state, which is fuelling postmodern tourism so massively, is in another way attempting to legitimate itself by sustaining a critical mass of writers and artists in a new Maritimes that is now imagining a very different community. This cultural transition has been partial and is vulnerable, but for the first time since the 1920s Innocence, this strange local variant of antimodernism, is encountering an opposition intelligent enough to realize that the ideals of community and belonging are too important to be abandoned to a commercialized antimodernism.

The paradox of postmodernity is that the more the notion of the Folk essence became a conventional truth, the more it was opposed as a realistic way of seeing Nova Scotia. On the one hand, the images of the Folk and their handicrafts are everywhere. On the other hand, the consumers of these images and crafts surely know very well that what they are buying is a kind of counterfeit. The state spends lavishly to support those who produce conventionalized commercial images of the Folk. Nonetheless, even limited state funding has enabled an entirely new group of cultural producers to emerge, people whose work has undercut such images at every turn. Paradoxically, then, as the Folk image was spread far and wide as one of the many styles cannibalized by postmodernism, it became more contested as a commonsense. It has come to be a thinly spread rhetoric, vulnerable to articulate and subtle moral critiques, including those of people who were brought up in the rural areas it romanticizes. The old way of seeing is now starting to fade: who will be able to articulate a new imagined community to take its place?

Alistair MacLeod's is perhaps the best single example of the new voices that are unsettling the old truths of the Folk. In his brilliant story "The Boat," he develops a sustained fictional critique of emergence of the Folk through a politics of cultural selection. The fisherman father in the story is not an imagined Ben Henneberry gratefully yielding up his cultural treasures to Helen Creighton and the urban gaze, nor is he a man at peace with himself and his humble existence, spontaneously finding contentment in his unreflectingly simple life. MacLeod's imagined father is a tormented figure, longing for things his environment denies him – a university education and a deeper knowledge of literature. (One could say that he wants participation and honour in a common culture.) This is a profoundly subversive story, unthinkable within the framework of Innocence: how could one even imagine a man of the Folk bitterly divided against himself and his family? MacLeod subtly undermines the fundamental fond illusion of the idea of the Folk: that of a deep understanding, a loving, reciprocal, uncomplicated relationship between the rich and the poor, the powerful and the dominated.

One day the tourists arrive in a small fishing community. The narrator's troubled father takes them out to sea on his boat and drinks with them. The tourists are delighted to find a real live ballad-singing primitive: he perfectly fulfils their romantic conception of the Folk. They think – did not all "interpreters" of the Folk share this illusion? – that they understand him. Actually, they understand nothing. They have him framed in the category "Folk," and for them this has the quality of a life sentence: he can never escape it. His son remembers how his father responded to them:

I was just approaching the wharf ... when he began, and the familiar yet unfamiliar voice that rolled down from the cabins made me feel as I had never felt before in my young life or perhaps as I had always felt without really knowing it, and I was ashamed yet proud, young yet old and saved yet forever lost, and there was nothing I could do to control my legs which trembled nor my eyes which wept for what they could not tell.

The tourists were equipped with tape recorders and my father sang for more than three hours.[48]

There was tragedy as well as farce in this long Quest, this anxious search through the empty confusion of modernity, as middle-class Innocents destroyed the very haven they had sought, the very solace they had so inchoately longed for, when they finally found their Folk.

Notes

ABBREVIATIONS

CMC	Canadian Museum of Civilization
DUA	Dalhousie University Archives
MUNFLA	Memorial University of Newfoundland, Folklore and Language Archives
PANS	Public Archives of Nova Scotia
QUA	Queen's University Archives
RAC	Rockefeller Foundation Archival Centre

FOREWORD TO THE CLS EDITION

1 See D.C.Harvey, ed., *The Diary of Simeon Perkins 1780-1789* (Toronto: The Champlain Society, 1958).

2 For an engaging discussion from various perspectives of the book's first decade, see "Forum: The Quest of the Folk," *Acadiensis* 35, 1 (Autumn 2005), with contributions from David Creelman, Stephen Dutcher, Greg Marquis, and Miriam Wright. This introduction builds on my own contribution to this forum.

3 See Geoff Eley and Keith Nield, *The Future of Class in History: What's Left of the Social?* (Ann Arbor: University of Michigan Press, 2007), 157.

PROLOGUE

1 Photograph Collection, PANS N-2382.

2 Withrow, *St. Margaret's Bay*, 105.

3 Barthes, *Camera Lucida*, passim.

4 Sekula, "Photography between Capital and Labour," 195.

5 Tagg, *The Burden of Representation*, 3.

6 Berger, *Ways of Seeing*, 8–9.

7 See McKay, "Among the Fisherfolk," 23–45.

8 On the concept of the "structure of feeling," which is admittedly very general, see Williams, *Politics and Letters*, 158–9.

9 Sekula, "Photography between Capital and Labour," 250.

10 Tagg, *The Burden of Representation*, 211.

11 Benjamin, *Illuminations*, 255.

CHAPTER ONE

1 Creighton, *A Life in Folklore*, 50; Sclanders, "She's Collecting Long Lost Songs," 14–15, 54–7.
2 Dartmouth itself was a small town with a population of less than ten thousand, but it was and is socially and economically integrated with Halifax, the capital, whose 1931 population of 59,273 made it the largest urban centre in the province and the region. Throughout this book, "Greater Halifax" designates the City of Halifax and its satellites: Bedford, Dartmouth, etc.
3 Creighton, *A Life in Folklore*, 56, gives June 1928 as the date of this first journey to Devil's Island. But this seems unlikely, given the evidence that her first interest in folklore was aroused in "late spring" 1928 (48), and given that she had had time in her narrative to work up and down the coast collecting folklore before going to Devil's Island for the first time. The case for "June 1929" as the likelier date is in my view proved by this passage in a letter of 1929: " ... if Mr Ben Henneberry has as large a [repertoire] as people say he has ... " in the context of a passage hinting at the additional songs she might be able to send to her correspondent. Helen Creighton to J. Murray Gibbon, 30 August 1929 (copy), Creighton Papers, MG 1, vol. 2811, f. 162, PANS. This reference also suggests that the period from her first arrival on the Island to the exploration of Henneberry's repertoire may have been telescoped, for dramatic effect, in later retelling.
4 Creighton Papers, MG 1, vol. 2793, no. 5. draft manuscript, "First Collecting Days," 1, PANS.
5 Ibid., 33.
6 Mary Louise Pratt, "Fieldwork in Common Places," in Clifford and Marcus, eds., *Writing Culture*, 27–50.
7 "First Collecting Days," 41, 72.
8 Creighton, *Songs and Ballads from Nova Scotia*, xiii.
9 Creighton to Howard Angus, CAA national secretary, n.d. [1931?] (copy), Creighton Papers, MG 1, vol. 2811, f. 162, PANS.
10 Williams, *The Country and the City*, 313.
11 Cocchiara, *The History of Folklore*, 28.
12 Ibid., 168.
13 Herder, cited in Bohlman, *The Study of Folk Music in the Modern World*, 52.
14 Barnard, *Herder's Social and Political Thought*, 144.
15 Bohlman, *The Study of Folk Music*, 54.
16 Collingwood, in *The Idea of History*, may have been overdoing it a bit when he argued that "Once Herder's theory of race is accepted, there is no escaping the Nazi marriage laws" (92).

17 Williams, *Keywords*, 189–92.
18 Rosenberg, "Folklore in Atlantic Canada: The Enigmatic Symbol," 79–86. See also Smith, *The Ethnic Origins of Nations*, 33.
19 For an outline of theoretical debates in American folklore, see McNeil, "A History of American Folklore Scholarship before 1908," vol. 2.
20 See the useful discussion in Adamson, *Marx and the Disillusionment of Marxism*, 17–20.
21 Anderson, *Imagined Communities*, 15.
22 Smith, *The Ethnic Origins of Nations*, 15; 22–31.
23 See especially Hobsbawm, *Nations and Nationalism since 1780* and Gellner, *Nations and Nationalism*.
24 See Forgacs, ed., *An Antonio Gramsci Reader*, 422–4.
25 Bohlman, *The Study of Folk Music*, 54.
26 Ibid., 109.
27 Ibid., xviii-xix. See also Harker's more polemical study *Fakesong*.
28 See, however, one scholar's strong defence of the intelligence that crafted Child's "ballad aristocracy" in Buchan, *The Ballad and the Folk*.
29 See McNeil, "A History of American Folklore Scholarship," vol. 2, 551, on Kittredge's "truly staggering" influence.
30 Ibid., 787: McNeil refers to this as a form of "*gesunkenes Kulturgut.*"
31 Wilgus, *Anglo-American Folksong Scholarship*, xiv-xv.
32 Ibid., 132.
33 Howkins, "Greensleeves and the Idea of National Music," in Samuel, ed., *Patriotism*, vol. 3, 89–98.
34 See Wilgus, *Anglo-American Folksong Scholarship*, 59–63; Harker, *Fakesong*, 172–231.
35 Ives, "Maine Woods Ballads and Creative Tradition," 22.
36 Whisnant, *All That Is Native and Fine*, 79–81.
37 Wilgus, *Anglo-American Folksong Scholarship*, 7.
38 Whisnant, *All That Is Native and Fine*, 56.
39 Ibid., 115.
40 Buchan, *The Ballad and the Folk*, 1; for a markedly different treatment of "the Folk" in Scotland, less oriented to questions of the survival of oral literature, see Henderson, *Alias MacAlias*.
41 Whisnant, *All That Is Native and Fine*, 57. Note also the emphasis on the "Elizabethan" words still current in the South Shore in Poteet's *The Second South Shore Phrase Book*.
42 Frank, "The Industrial Folk Song in Cape Breton," 22.
43 Wilgus, *Anglo-American Folksong Scholarship*, 225.
44 See Denisoff, *Great Day Coming*.
45 Zumwalt, *American Folklore Scholarship*, 6.
46 Ibid., 7.
47 Ibid., 122.

48 For an interesting discussion, see Handler, "In Search of the Folk Society," 103–14. For the impact of the "Chicago School" on analyses of Quebec, see Guindon, "The Social Evolution of Quebec Reconsidered," in *Quebec Society*, 3–26. Rev. S.H. Prince, the pioneering sociologist at King's College, Halifax, might be associated loosely with this tradition of thought, but his various plans for rural reform actually assumed that rural society was in need of urban amenities and cultural facilities in order to stem the exodus from the farms. See Prince, *The Architecture of Rural Society*. Note, however, for New Brunswick, Baker, "Negotiated Objectivity: Weekly Newspaper Reporting and Social Relations in the New Brunswick Communities," in McCann, ed., *People and Place*, 211–25, which does warily use Tonnies's notion of *gemeinschaft*.

49 On this theme, see Ian McKay, "The 1910s: The Stillborn Triumph of Progressive Reform," in Del Muise and E.R. Forbes, eds., *The Atlantic Provinces in Confederation*, 192–229.

50 See Forbes, *Maritime Rights: The Maritime Rights Movement*.

51 See Barrett, "Capital and the State in Atlantic Canada: The Structural Context of Fishery Policy between 1939 and 1977," in Lamson and Hanson, eds., *Atlantic Fisheries and Coastal Communities*, 77–104.

52 No doubt one could call Innocence a "discourse," which would usefully suggest the ways in which it often called into being the very traditionalism about which it spoke (much as nationalists called forth "the nation" and folklorists "the Folk"). The extent to which my account of Innocence draws on critical theory will be evident, but I prefer not to emphasize the word "discourse," which I find conceptually ambiguous. A "network of words and things" seems preferable as a way of capturing the way in which Innocence operated both "materially" and "ideally" – in hotels and highway paving as much as in conceptions of beautiful landscapes and pastoral people. Whenever "discourse" is used, the reader should take it in this materialist sense.

53 See Lears, *No Place of Grace*, xv; Dancy and Sosa, eds., *A Companion to Epistemology*, 300–1.

54 Williams, *The Country and the City*.

55 Tippett, *Making Culture*.

56 Urry, *The Tourist Gaze*, 1.

57 See Morton and McKay, "The Maritimes," in Craig Heron, ed., *The Canadian Labour Revolt* (forthcoming).

58 See Overton, "Toward a Critical Analysis of Neo-Nationalism in Newfoundland," in Brym and Sacouman, eds., *Underdevelopment and Social Movements in Atlantic Canada*, 219–49, for a related usage of the term "neo-nationalism" in the context of a Canadian province.

59 Williams, "Literature and Sociology: In Memory of Lucien Goldmann," 7.

60 Whisnant, *All That Is Native and Fine*, 263–4.
61 Harker, *Fakesong*, xiii.
62 See Smart, "The Politics of Truth and the Problems of Hegemony," in Hoy, ed., *Foucault*, 157–73, for an interesting discussion of some of these points.

CHAPTER TWO

1 The inauguration of an annual Helen Creighton festival and the establishment of a Helen Creighton Foundation provide evidence on this point. With the exception of Thomas Raddall, whose name is attached to a regular conference on cultural studies at Acadia University, no other twentieth-century writer in the province has been recognized so fully.
2 For a useful outline and many references, see Carole Henderson Carpenter, *Many Voices*.
3 Frank, "The Industrial Folk Song in Cape Breton," 21–42.
4 Thus Fanny D. Bergen, whose first book was *A Primer on Darwinism and Organic Evolution*, felt the most fruitful areas for collecting folklore included sparsely populated parts of the American South, isolated New England villages, and "secluded parts of Canada." McNeil, "A History of American Folklore," vol. 2, 802.
5 Doerflinger, "Cruising for Ballads in Nova Scotia," in Fowke, ed., *Explorations in Canadian Folklore*, 130.
6 Maud Karpeles to Helen Creighton, 29 September 1930, Creighton Papers, MG 1, vol. 5814, f. 50, PANS.
7 Useful analyses of the folklore tradition in the region include Tallman, "Folklore Research in Atlantic Canada"; Rosenberg, "Folk Music, Anglo-Canadian: Newfoundland," in Kallman et al., eds., *Encyclopedia of Music in Canada*; Rosenberg, "Folklore in Atlantic Canada"; Carpenter, "Forty Years Later"; Fowke, *Canadian Folklore*; Ives, "Oral and Written Tradition."
8 John B. Calkin, *Old Time Customs*.
9 See Samson, "Family Formation," for a discussion.
10 Mackenzie, *Quest*, 63.
11 Mackenzie, "Ballad-Singing in Nova Scotia," 327–31.
12 Mackenzie, *Quest*, 49.
13 Ibid., 29.
14 For a discussion of this theme, see Trumpener, "The Voice of the Past," 337.
15 Ibid., 32.
16 Mackenzie, *Quest*, 33.
17 Tallman, "Folklore Research in Atlantic Canada," 118–30.

18 Mackenzie, *Quest*, 49.
19 Ibid., 62.
20 Mackenzie, *Ballads and Sea Songs of Nova Scotia*, xxiii.
21 Sturtevant, review of Mackenzie, *Ballads and Sea-Songs from Nova Scotia*.
22 Mackenzie, *Quest*, 41.
23 Carl Sandburg, typescript review, W.R. Mackenzie papers, DAL MS. 2.296.C.2., Dalhousie University Archives.
24 Clara Dennis to the Princeton University Press, Princeton, New Jersey, 23 November 1939, Dennis Papers, MG 1, vol. 2865, no. 9, PANS.
25 Mackenzie, *Quest*, 43–5.
26 Ibid., 1.
27 On "salvage ethnography," see Clifford, *The Predicament of Culture*, 220–48.
28 Mackenzie, *Quest*, 34.
29 Ibid., 33.
30 "The Butcher Boy," in Mackenzie, *Ballads and Sea Songs from Nova Scotia*, 157–60.
31 Mackenzie, *Quest*, 12.
32 Ibid., 20.
33 Ibid., 22–3.
34 Ibid., 20.
35 Creighton, "W. Roy Mackenzie, Pioneer."
36 Creighton, *A Life in Folklore*, 48–9.
37 Creighton to A.J. Campbell, 8 September 1936, Creighton Papers, MG 1, vol. 2811, f. 162, PANS.
38 Helen Creighton to Hayward Cirker, 4 August 1965, Creighton Papers, vol. 2811, f. 162, PANS.
39 J.M. Gibbon to Helen Creighton, Creighton Papers, MG 1, vol. 2813, f. 21, PANS.
40 Helen Creighton to Carmen Roy, 8 March 1969, Creighton Collection, CR-K-1.20, CMC.
41 Creighton, *Songs and Ballads from Nova Scotia*, xii.
42 Carole Carpenter, interview with Helen Creighton, 1970, tape, MUNFLA.
43 Creighton, *A Life in Folklore*, 62.
44 Carole Carpenter, interview with Helen Creighton, 1970, tape, MUNFLA.
45 Cf. J.D. Robins to Helen Creighton, 12 May 1938, 30 March 1938; 21 February 1938, Creighton Papers, MG 1, vol. 2817, f. 60.; 30 March 1938; 21 February 1938, PANS.
46 Creighton, *A Life in Folklore*, 61.
47 Marius Barbeau to Dr Duncan Emrich, 14 February 1947, Creighton Collection, CR-K-2.2, CMC.

48 D.C. Harvey to Helen Creighton, Creighton Papers, MG 1, vol. 2813, f. 21, PANS; D.C. Harvey to John Marshall, 19 April 1943, RG 1.1, series 427 (Canada), box 28, file 279, RAC. In this letter to the foundation, Harvey reported that PANS endorsed the work of Creighton, even though he would not hire her. I owe this and all further references to the Rockefeller papers to Mr Jeff Brison, who kindly let me look at his research on the role of the foundation in Canada.

49 In *Canadian Mosaic*, ix, Gibbon attributes authorship of the metaphor of the Canadian "mosaic" to Victoria Hayward, an American writer.

50 Janet McNaughton, "John Murray Gibbon," 66–73.

51 Gibbon, *The Canadian Mosaic*, 413.

52 See Bohlman, *The Study of Folk Music in the Modern World*; Bohlman perceptively adds: "The size of food booths, for example, is often uniform. Musical performances may likewise be uniform, with each ethnic group performing a medley that lasts for a prescribed period and choosing from limited dance forms and musical genres – perhaps circle dances and harvest songs – that all groups presumably share. The differences between groups that could perform for hours and those that do well to prepare fifteen minutes are minimized by the festival" (66).

53 J.M. Gibbon to Helen Creighton, 22 July 1929, Creighton Papers, MG 1, vol. 2813, f. 21, PANS.

54 Helen Creighton to J. Murray Gibbon, 30 August 1929 (copy), Creighton Papers, MG 1, vol. 2811, f. 162, PANS.

55 J.M. Gibbon to Helen Creighton, 22 July 1929, Creighton Papers, MG 1, vol. 2813, f. 21, PANS.

56 J.M. Gibbon to Helen Creighton, 1 October 1929, Creighton Papers, MG 1, vol. 2813, f. 21, PANS.

57 J.M. Gibbon to Helen Creighton, Creighton Papers, 17 March 1931, MG 1, vol. 2813, f. 21, PANS.

58 Helen Creighton to Lorne Pierce, 21 June 1949, Pierce Papers, box 18, file 1, item 95, QUA.

59 Creighton, *A Life in Folklore*, 8.

60 As Dave Harker emphasizes in *Fakesong*, 147.

61 Tippett, *Making Culture*, 38.

62 See, for instance, Helen Creighton to Frank Flemington, 10 June 1950, Pierce Papers, box 19, f. 2, item 23, QUA.

63 Helen Creighton to Lorne Pierce, 24 July 1945, Pierce Papers, box 11, f. 8, item 55, QUA.

64 Creighton, *Bluenose Ghosts*, 198.

65 As is suggested by Tye, "Women and Folklore Fieldwork," passim.

66 Helen Creighton to Marius Barbeau, 11 October 1941, Creighton Papers, MG 1, vol. 2811, f. 162, PANS.

67 Helen Creighton, *A Life in Folklore*, 54.
68 Carole Carpenter, interview with Helen Creighton, 1970, MUNFLA.
69 Helen Creighton, "Halifax Little Theatre," *Mayfair*, April 1932, 38. My thanks to Marianne Rude for drawing this and other items from *Mayfair* to my attention.
70 Creighton, "Mayfair's Maritime Letter," *Mayfair*, October 1931, 64, 68.
71 Creighton, "Mayfair's Halifax Letter," *Mayfair*, December 1931, 56, 64.
72 Creighton, "Mayfair's Maritime Letter," *Mayfair*, March 1931, 48.
73 Creighton, "Mayfair's Maritime Letter," *Mayfair*, October 1931, 64, 68.
74 See Helen Creighton to Carmen Roy, 21 November 1950, Creighton Collection, CR-K-1.21, CMC.
75 Creighton, *A Life in Folklore*, 47.
76 Ibid., 62–3.
77 Ibid., 88.
78 Ibid., 10.
79 Creighton, "Rudyard Kipling and the Halifax Doctor," 53.
80 Creighton Papers, MG 1, vol. 2793, no. 8, file "Helen Creighton Papers: Poetry, Helen Creighton," PANS.
81 See, for example, Tippett, *Making Culture*, 63–70, for the seminal role of British viceroys in Canada.
82 Creighton, *A Life in Folklore*, 45.
83 Tallman, "Folklore Research in Atlantic Canada," 120.
84 Creighton Papers, MG 1, vol. 2793, nos. 1–24, rough list of articles, poems and stories, c. 1913–1972, PANS.
85 Creighton Papers, MG 1, vol. 2793, rough list of articles, c. 1927, with rates, PANS.
86 Creighton to Henry Button, 9 November 1932 (copy with enclosure), Creighton Papers, MG 1, vol. 2811, f. 162., PANS.
87 Carpenter, interview with Helen Creighton, MUNFLA.
88 Creighton to Howard Angus, CAA national secretary, n.d. [1931?] (copy), MG 1, vol. 2811, f. 162.
89 Creighton, *Songs and Ballads from Nova Scotia*, vii.
90 Ibid.
91 Ibid., 313.
92 Henry Button (of J.M. Dent & Sons (Canada) Limited) to Helen Creighton, 17 April 1939, Creighton Papers, MG 1, vol. 2811, f. 34, PANS.
93 Lorne Pierce to Helen Creighton, 21 June 1946, Helen Creighton Papers, MG 1, vol. 2816, f. 154, PANS.
94 Creighton, "Sable Island," 14.
95 Helen Creighton to W.A. Irwin, 9 December 1931 (copy), Creighton Papers, MG 1, vol. 2811, f. 162.
96 Helen Creighton, "Song Singers," 32.

97 Creighton to Hugh R. Dent, Aldine House, London, 21 May 1935, 9 November 1936, MG 1, vol. 2811, f. 162, PANS.
98 Creighton to Mrs Charlotte Barbour, 12 January 1937, Creighton Papers, MG 1, vol. 2811, f. 162, PANS.
99 Creighton to A.J. Campbell, 8 September 1936, Creighton Papers, MG 1, vol. 2811, f. 162, PANS.
100 See Brison, "Consent and Coercion," passim.
101 Helen Creighton to F.C. Badgley, Motion Picture Bureau, Ottawa, 15 January 1937, Creighton Papers, MG 1, vol. 2811, f. 162, PANS.
102 Helen Creighton to H. Button, 29 December 1936, Creighton Papers, MG 1, vol. 2811, f. 162, PANS.
103 Helen Creighton to Marius Barbeau, 22 January 1937, Creighton Papers, MG 1, vol. 2811, f. 162, PANS.
104 Creighton to Mr Gordon Sparling of Associated Screen News, 15 February 1937, Creighton Papers, MG 1, vol. 2811, f. 162, PANS.
105 Creighton to Button, 14 February 1938, Creighton Papers, MG 1, vol. 2811, f. 162, PANS.
106 Fellowship cards, "Creighton, Miss Mary Helen," RAC. Overall, the foundation's support for Creighton in the 1940s appears to have been in the range of $2,450.
107 Ibid.
108 Harold Spivak to John Marshall, 3 September 1942, RG 1.1, box 28, series 427, Canada, folder 279, RAC.
109 Ibid. On the reluctance of the foundation to make folklore a priority, see John Marshall to Creighton, 9 October 1942, RG 1.1, box 28, series 427, Canada, folder 279, RAC.
110 Helen Creighton to Alan Lomax, 17 September 1942, RG 1.1, box 28, series 427, Canada, folder 279, RAC.
111 Fellowship cards, RAC. In addition to its initial expenditure of $500 to cover Creighton's attendance at the University of Indiana summer school, the foundation gave her a grant-in-aid of $600 for the six-month period beginning 1 July 1943, to be administered through PANS; a further grant-in-aid of $600 to assist her in recording for the six-month period beginning 1 January 1944; and, on 21 December 1945, a $750 grant-in-aid for completion of her manuscript on Lunenburg to cover her expenses in a second trip to Indiana to work with Stith Thompson for three months in 1946.
112 B.A. Botkin to John Marshall, 20 December 1943, RG 1.1, box 28, series 427, Canada, folder 279, RAC.
113 In 1950 and 1953 Creighton applied to the Rockefeller Foundation for financial assistance to return to Indiana for a conference and to attend a folk festival in Pennsylvania; both requests were turned down on the grounds that folklore was no longer a Rockefeller Foundation priority.

114 Kirkconnell, *Canadians All*, 7.

115 Ibid., 20; 9.

116 Helen Creighton to Marius Barbeau, 4 December 1940, Barbeau Collection, B-MC-5729, CMC.

117 Helen Creighton to Ryerson Press, 10 January 1944 [1945], Pierce Papers, box 11, f. 8, item 55, QUA.

118 Helen Creighton to Lorne Pierce, 23 January 1945, Pierce Papers, box 11, f. 8, item 49, QUA.

119 Helen Creighton to Lorne Pierce, 17 April 1945, Pierce Papers, box 11, f. 8, item 50, QUA.

120 Creighton to Lorne Pierce, 21 May 1945, Pierce Papers, box 11, f. 8, item 53, QUA.

121 Lorne Pierce to Helen Creighton, 6 June 1945, Pierce Papers, box 11, f. 8, item 54, QUA.

122 Helen Creighton to Marius Barbeau, 28 April 1945, Barbeau Papers, B-MC-5733, CMC.

123 Lorne Pierce to Helen Creighton, 23 July 1948, Creighton Papers, MG 1, vol. 2816, f. 154, PANS.

124 J. Frank Willis to Helen Creighton, 7 January 1949, Creighton Papers, MG 1, vol. 2819, PANS..

125 Helen Creighton to Frank Flemington, 6 October 1950, Pierce Papers, box 19, f. 2, item 25, QUA.

126 Helen Creighton to Lorne Pierce, 20 November 1950, Pierce Papers, box 19, f. 2, item 29, QUA.

127 Helen Creighton to Frank Flemington, 15 November 1949, Pierce Papers, box 18, f. 1, item 97, QUA.

128 Fowke, *Canadian Folklore*, 15.

129 "Sketch for the instructions to Miss Helen Creighton," n.d. [1947], Creighton Collection, CR-K-1.1, CMC.

130 "Report of Field Work from Helen Creighton," summer 1947, Creighton Collection, CR-K-1.1, CMC.

131 Tye, "Women and Folklore Fieldwork."

132 Ibid., 7. For a solid general account of regional folklore, see the relevant chapters of Carpenter, *Many Voices*.

133 Helen Creighton to Carmen Roy, 8 September 1958, 5 November 1958, Creighton Collection, CR-K-1.9, CMC.

134 Helen Creighton, "Canada's Maritime Provinces – An Ethnomusicological Survey," 406–7.

135 Helen Creighton to Carmen Roy, 9 February 1960, Creighton Collection, CR-K-1.11, CMC.

136 Helen Creighton to Carmen Roy, 13 February 1958, Creighton Collection, CR-K-1.9, CMC.

137 Helen Creighton to Carmen Roy, 7 July 1958, Creighton Collection, CR-K-1.9, CMC.

138 Helen Creighton to Marius Barbeau, 7 November 1963, Barbeau Papers, B-MC-5773, CMC.

139 Helen Creighton to Carmen Roy, 4 November 1963, Creighton Collection, CR-K-1.14, CMC.

140 Helen Creighton to Jeanne Monette, 10 July 1964, Creighton Collection, CR-K-1.15, CMC.

141 Carmen Roy to Helen Creighton, 28 September 1964, Creighton Collection, CR-K-1.15, CMC.

142 Helen Creighton to Carmen Roy, 21 November 1970, Creighton Collection, CR-K-1.21, CMC.

143 Helen Creighton to Carmen Roy, 3 February 1965, Creighton Collection, CR-K-1.16, CMC.

144 Helen Creighton to Carmen Roy, 21 March 1960, Creighton Collection, CR-K-1.11, CMC.

145 Carmen Roy to Helen Creighton, 30 March 1960, Creighton Collection, CR-K-1.11, CMC.

146 Carmen Roy to L.S. Russell, memorandum, n.d. [March 1960], Creighton Collection, CR-K-1.11, CMC.

147 Helen Creighton to Carmen Roy, 9 February 1960, Creighton Collection, CR-K-1.11, CMC.

148 Helen Creighton to Carmen Roy, 10 March 1960, Creighton Collection, CR-K-1.11, CMC.

149 Carmen Roy to Helen Creighton, 21 April 1960, Creighton Collection, CR-K-1.11, CMC.

150 Carmen Roy to Helen Creighton, 19 May 1960, Creighton Collection, CR-K-1.11, CMC.

151 Carmen Roy to Helen Creighton, 22 February 1960, Creighton Collection, CR-K-1.11, CMC.

152 Note, for example, Barbeau, "Kinship Recognition and Urbanization," 1–11, in which the kinship recognition pattern of Chéticamp in Cape Breton is compared with that prevailing in Montreal, in support of Redfield's thesis that as one goes from folk to urban groups, the importance of kinship decreases. The Chicago style of social analysis, a combination of romanticism and functionalism, would have an imponderable impact, via Horace Miner and Everett Hughes, on the study of twentieth-century Quebec.

153 Helen Creighton to Carmen Roy, 25 February 1960, Creighton Collection, CR-K-1.11, CMC.

154 Carmen Roy to Helen Creighton, 15 February 1966, Creighton Collection, CR-K-1.17, CMC.

155 Helen Creighton to Carmen Roy, 16 February 1966, Creighton Collection, CR-K-1.17, CMC.
156 Helen Creighton to Miss Dorothy Burke, 2 September 1966, Creighton Collection, CR-K-1.17, CMC.
157 Helen Creighton to Carmen Roy, 13 November 1958, Creighton Collection, CR-K-1.9, CMC.
158 Creighton, *A Life in Folklore*, 174.
159 Ibid., 186.
160 Ibid., 244.
161 Helen Creighton to Marius Barbeau, 28 January 1957, Barbeau Papers, B-MC-5756, CMC.
162 Helen Creighton to Carmen Roy, 31 January 1967, Creighton Collection, CR-K-1.18, CMC.
163 Helen Creighton to Carmen Roy, 23 March 1959, Creighton Collection, CR-K-1.10, CMC.
164 Helen Creighton to Jeanne Monette, 6 July 1964 (copy), Creighton Collection, CR-K-1.15, CMC.
165 Helen Creighton to Carmen Roy, 21 March 1960, Creighton Collection, CR-K-1.11, CMC.
166 Carmen Roy to Helen Creighton, 30 March 1960, Creighton Collection, CR-K-1.11, CMC.
167 Helen Creighton to F.J. Alcock, 26 January 1956, Creighton Collection, CR-K-1.7, CMC.
168 Helen Creighton to Carmen Roy, 16 April 1962, Creighton Collection, CR-K-1.13, CMC.
169 Helen Creighton to Carmen Roy, 3 April 1964, 30 September 1964, Creighton Collection, CR-K-1.15, CMC.
170 Helen Creighton to Carmen Roy, 3 February 1965, Creighton Collection, CR-K-1.16, CMC.
171 Helen Creighton to Carmen Roy, 16 April 1962, Creighton Collection, CR-K-1.13, CMC.
172 Carmen Roy to Helen Creighton, 1 May 1962, Creighton Collection, CR-K-1.13, CMC.
173 Carmen Roy to Helen Creighton, 8 February 1965, Creighton Collection, CR-K-1.16, CMC.
174 Creighton, *A Life in Folklore*, 229.
175 Carmen Roy to Helen Creighton, 10 April 1964, Creighton Collection, CR-K-1.15, CMC.
176 Carmen Roy to Helen Creighton, 5 November 1965, Creighton Collection, CR-K-1.16, CMC.
177 Helen Creighton to Carmen Roy, 13 November 1958, Creighton Collection, CR-K-1.9, CMC.

178 Helen Creighton to Carmen Roy, 13 September 1963, Creighton Collection, CR-K-1.14, CMC.

179 Carmen Roy to Helen Creighton, 21 November 1963, Creighton Collection, CR-K-1.14, CMC.

180 Helen Creighton to Carmen Roy, 1 October 1963, Creighton Collection, CR-K-1.14, CMC.

181 Helen Creighton to Jeanne Monette, n.d. [July 1964] (copy), Creighton Collection, CR-K-1.15, CMC.

182 Helen Creighton to Carmen Roy, 7 May 1965, Creighton Collection, CR-K-1.16, CMC.

183 Helen Creighton to Carmen Roy, 13 May 1965, Creighton Collection, CR-K-1.16, CMC.

184 Helen Creighton to Carmen Roy, 26 May 1966, Creighton Collection, CR-K-1.17, CMC.

185 Carole Carpenter, interview with Helen Creighton, MUNFLA.

186 Helen Creighton to Carmen Roy, 4 May 1968, Creighton Collection, CR-K-1.19, CMC.

187 Whisnant, *All That Is Native and Fine*, 126.

188 Creighton, *Bluenose Magic*, 67.

189 Ibid., 73.

190 Creighton, *Bluenose Ghosts*, 263.

191 Harker, *Fakesong*, 129.

192 Creighton, *Bluenose Magic*, 32.

193 Dan Livingston to Helen Creighton, 19 March 1951, Creighton Papers, MG 1, vol. 2814, f. 163, PANS.

194 Helen Creighton to Mr Forrest Bahruth, Epcot Centre, Walt Disney World, 6 April 1981, Creighton Papers, MG 1, vol. 2811, f. 162, PANS.

195 Creighton, *Folklore of Lunenburg County*, 134, note 1.

196 Winsor, "Solving a Problem," 68–84.

197 Nesbit, "'Free Enterprise at Its Best'"; Wright, "'The Smile of Modernity.'"

198 "Report of Fishermen's Union over C.H.N.S., March 23, 1947," Angus J. Walters Papers, MS 2, 226, E2, DUA.

199 Barss, *Images of Lunenburg County*, 42–3.

200 Williams, *The Country and the City*, 51.

201 Helen Creighton to Mr H. Bramwel Chandler, 15 March 1947, Creighton Papers, MG 1, vol. 2811, f. 162, PANS.

202 Helen Creighton to Marius Barbeau, 2 October 1947, Barbeau Collection, B-MC-5742, CMC.

203 Helen Creighton to Sparlin, Associated Screen News Limited, Montreal, 25 January 1937, Creighton Papers, MG 1, vol. 2811, f. 162, PANS.

204 Helen Creighton to Mrs Gallagher, 3 March 1938, Creighton Papers, MG 1, vol. 2811, f. 162, PANS.

205 Helen Creighton to Mr Forrest Bahruth, Epcot Centre, Walt Disney World, 6 April 1981, Creighton Papers, MG 1, vol. 2811, f. 162, PANS.

206 Helen Creighton to Sandy Ives, 5 February 1983, Creighton Papers, MG 1, vol. 2811, f. 162, PANS.

207 Helen Creighton to Carmen Roy, 2 April 1960, Creighton Collection, CR-K-1.11, CMC.

208 Creighton, *Bluenose Magic*, vi-vii.

209 Helen Creighton to Pauline Greenhill, 23 July 1987, Creighton Papers, MG 1, vol. 2811, f. 162, PANS.

210 Angelo Dornan to Helen Creighton, 7 August 1955, Creighton Papers, MG 1, vol. 2812, f. 52, PANS.

211 Beck, "'Enough to Charm the Heat of a Wheelbarrow and Make a Shovel Dance,'" 8.

212 Helen Creighton to Howard Angus, n.d., MG 1, vol. 2811, f. 162, PANS.

213 Helen Creighton, "Song Singers," 32.

214 Creighton to A.J. Campbell, 9 September 1936, Creighton Papers, MG 1, vol. 2811, f. 162, PANS.

215 Williams, *The Country and the City*, 208.

216 Creighton Papers, MG 1, vol. 2793, no. 5, draft manuscript, "First Collecting Days," 72, PANS.

217 Creighton, *A Life in Folklore*, 95.

218 Creighton to A.J. Campbell, 8 September 1936, Creighton Papers, MG 1, vol. 2811, f. 162, PANS.

219 Helen Creighton to Charles L. Glett, Audio Productions Inc., New York, 25 January 1937, Creighton Papers, MG 1, vol. 2811, f. 162, PANS.

220 Creighton, "Song Singers," 33.

221 Rosenberg, "Folklore in Atlantic Canada," 83.

222 Creighton, *A Life in Folklore*, 116.

223 Helen Creighton to Miss Jocelyne Quevillon, Centennial Commission, 17 February 1966, Creighton Papers, MG 1, vol. 2811, f. 162, PANS.

224 The same delicacy made Creighton glad that she had not mentioned names when she used one scandalous ghost story in her collection, since she later bumped into a doctor who was related to the family. Helen Creighton to Carmen Roy, 3 March 1959, Creighton Collection, CR-K-1.10, CMC.

225 Helen Creighton to C.J. Eustace, 24 September 1932 (copy), Creighton Papers, MG 1, vol. 2811, f. 162, PANS.

226 Creighton, *Songs and Ballads from Nova Scotia*, 259; 233.

227 Creighton, "W. Roy Mackenzie, Pioneer," 20.

228 Creighton, *A Life in Folklore*, 68–9.

229 Mackenzie, *Quest*, 53.

230 Creighton Papers, MG 1, vol. 2793, no. 11, draft of "Folklore of St. Margaret's Bay," PANS.

231 Creighton, "Folk-Singers of Nova Scotia," 87.

232 Creighton, "W. Roy Mackenzie, Pioneer," 18.

233 Creighton, *A Life in Folklore*, 102–3.

234 Ibid., 103.

235 MacIntyre, "Bootlegging," 11–14.

236 Mackenzie, *Quest*, 22.

237 Creighton, *A Life in Folklore*, 60.

238 Ibid., 102–3.

239 Ibid., 125.

240 Helen Creighton to Pauline Greenhill, 23 July 1987, Creighton Papers, MG 1, vol. 2811, f. 162, PANS.

241 Tye, "Women and Folklore Fieldwork in English-speaking Atlantic Canada," passim.

242 Helen Creighton to Pauline Greenhill, 23 July 1987, Helen Creighton Papers, MG 1, vol. 2811, f. 162, PANS.

243 Creighton, *A Life in Folklore*, 162.

244 Wilgus, *Anglo-American Folksong Scholarship*, 237. See also Harker, *Fakesong*, 118.

245 G. Legman to M. Barbeau, 29 February 1956, Creighton Collection, CR-K-1.7, CMC. For some reflections on this issue, see Green, "Folk Is a Four-Letter Word," 525–32. For Legman's published work, see *No Laughing Matter*.

246 In general, Creighton did not collect from the lumber camps, although she did collaborate with Ives on presenting this tradition to the public: see Creighton (with Ives), "Eight Folktales from Miramichi," which were shaped by the lumbercamps. Of course, many of her fisherfolk worked as lumbermen in the winter.

247 Ives, *Joe Scott*, 391–6.

248 Creighton, *Songs and Ballads from Nova Scotia*, 226–7.

249 Creighton, *Bluenose Magic*, 23. With the possible exception of the enigmatic "Old Men's Troubles," cured by the juniper or hemlock berries and possibly a euphemism for sexual dysfunction?

250 Helen Creighton to Carmen Roy, 1 December 1964, Creighton Collection, CR-K-1.15, CMC.

251 Fowke, *Canadian Folklore*, 57.

252 Creighton, *Bluenose Magic*, 81.

253 See Ernest Forbes, "The 1930s: Depression and Retrenchment," in Forbes and Muise, eds., *Atlantic Provinces in Confederation*, 283.

254 Helen Creighton to Mr John Marshall of the Rockefeller Foundation, 3 October 1942, Creighton Papers, MG 1, vol. 2811, f. 162, PANS.

255 Helen Creighton to Dr Kenneth Goldstein, 12 April 1978, Creighton Papers, MG 1, vol. 2811, f. 162, PANS. See also RG 1.1, series 427, Canada, box 28, f. 279, RAC.

256 Helen Creighton to Carmen Roy, 25 January 1972, Creighton Collection, CR-K-1.23, CMC.

257 Sclanders, "She's Collecting Long Lost Songs," 56–7.

258 Helen Creighton to Carmen Roy, 8 March 1963, Creighton Collection, CR-K-1.14, CMC.

259 Creighton, "Collecting Songs of Nova Scotia Blacks," 142–3.

260 Creighton, *A Life in Folklore*, 137.

261 Helen Creighton to Alan [Lomax], 8 October 1942, Creighton Papers, MG 1, vol. 2811, f. 162, PANS.

262 Whisnant, *All That Is Native and Fine*, 56.

263 Creighton, *A Life in Folklore*, 181.

264 Creighton, *Bluenose Ghosts*, x-xi.

265 Creighton, *Bluenose Magic*, 19.

266 Helen Creighton to Carmen Roy, 21 March 1960, Creighton Collection, CR-K-1.11, CMC.

267 Helen Creighton to Carmen Roy, 2 December 1966, Creighton Collection, CR-K-1.17, CMC.

268 Helen Creighton to Carmen Roy, 28 February 1962, Creighton Collection, CR-K-1.13, CMC.

269 Creighton, *Bluenose Ghosts*, xi.

270 Helen Creighton to Carmen Roy, 2 April 1960, Creighton Collection, CR-K-1.11, CMC.

271 Creighton, *Bluenose Magic*, 115.

272 Creighton, *Bluenose Ghosts*, 80.

273 Ibid., 279–80.

274 Raddall, *In My Time*, 164.

275 Lears, *No Place of Grace*, 168, 173.

276 Howkins, "Greensleeves," 89–98.

277 See Bird, "Ghosts and Haunted Places." Strangely, nineteenth-century tales of a sea-serpent in Bras d'Or, which would fit in nicely with contemporary Scottish tourist "theming", have yet to be exploited. See *Trades Journal* (Stellarton), 19 September 1883.

278 Tallman, "Folklore Research," 120.

279 Helen Creighton to Carmen Roy, 16 February 1966, Creighton Collection, CR-K-1.17, CMC.

280 Creighton, *A Life in Folklore*, 44.

281 Creighton to Hugh R. Dent, Aldine House, London, 21 May 1935, Creighton Papers, MG 1, vol. 2811, f. 162, PANS.

282 Creighton Papers, MG 1, vol. 2793, no. 8, file "Poetry, Helen Creighton," PANS.

283 *Busy East*, April 1913, 15.

284 Helen Creighton to Carmen Roy, 10 July 1971, Creighton Collection, CR-K-1.22, CMC.

285 Helen Creighton to Charles L. Glett, Audio Productions Inc., New York, 25 January 1937, Creighton Papers, MG 1, vol. 2811, f. 162, PANS.
286 Fowke, "Labour and Industrial Protest Songs in Canada," 40.
287 Helen Creighton to Marius Barbeau, 28 September 1932 (copy), Creighton Papers, MG 1, vol. 2811, f. 162, PANS.
288 For this Cape Breton tradition, see, in addition to the work of David Frank, O'Donnell, "Labour's Cultural Impact on the Community," 49–59, 64.
289 Creighton, *Bluenose Magic*, passim.
290 Helen Creighton to Lorne Pierce, 4 October 1957, Pierce Papers, box 26, f. 1, item 49, QUA.
291 Lovelace, "W. Roy Mackenzie," 10.
292 Helen Creighton to Pauline Greenhill, 23 July 1987, Creighton Papers, MG 1, vol. 2811, f. 162, PANS.
293 Creighton, *A Life in Folklore*, 95.
294 Helen Creighton to Lorne Pierce, 23 January 1945, Pierce Papers, box 11, f. 8, item 49, QUA.
295 Helen Creighton to Mr H. Bramwell Chandler, 15 March 1947, Creighton Papers, MG 1, vol. 2811, f. 162, PANS.
296 Helen Creighton to H. Button, 25 February 1933 (copy), Creighton Papers, MG 1, vol. 2811, f. 162, PANS.
297 Creighton, *A Life in Folklore*, 28.
298 Helen Creighton to Doreen Senior, 30 March 1943, Creighton Papers, MG 1, vol. 2811, f. 162, PANS.
299 Helen Creighton to A.J. Campbell, 8 September 1936, Creighton Papers, MG 1, vol. 2811, f. 162, PANS.
300 Helen Creighton to Mr McDonald, 22 November 1936, Creighton Papers, MG 1, vol. 2811, f. 162, PANS.
301 Dan Livingston to Helen Creighton, 19 March 1951, Creighton Papers, MG 1, vol. 2814, f. 163, PANS.
302 Helen Creighton, "Song Singers," 18.
303 Doucette and Quigley, "The Child Ballad in Canada," 3–19. On the rarity of Child ballads in the lumbercamp tradition, see Ives, *Joe Scott*, 392.
304 Mackenzie, *Quest*, 8.
305 Alan Lomax to Helen Creighton, 28 January 1957, Creighton Papers, MG 1, vol. 2814, f. 163, PANS.
306 As noted by Ives, "Maine Woods Ballads," 22.
307 J.M. Gibbon to Helen Creighton, 17 March 1931, 9 January 1937, Creighton Papers, MG 1, vol. 2813, f. 21, PANS; F.W. Wallace to Helen Creighton, 23 April 1931, Creighton Papers, MG 1, vol. 2818, f. 202, PANS. (This song, although written by F.W. Wallace, somehow later became the property of Creighton. See Alan Lomax to Helen

Creighton, 28 January 1957, Creighton Papers, MG 1, vol. 2814, f. 163, PANS.

308 Stallabrass, "The Idea of the Primitive," 101.

309 Bohlman, *The Study of Folk Music*, xiv.

310 Ibid., 30.

311 Ibid., 58.

312 MacNeil, *Tales until Dawn*.

313 For the rise of academic folklore in Canada and the United States, see Baker, "Folklore and Folklife Studies," 50–74.

314 Her collection at the National Museum has been itemized as follows: English folksongs 2,227; French folksongs 108; Gaelic folksongs 150; fiddle tunes 108; folktales (English) 94; Indian (Micmac) chants 30; Austrian songs 7; Danish songs 8; Finnish songs 22; German songs 5; Latvian songs 6; Italian songs 1. In manuscript, there are 26 English folksongs. Note, "Collection Dr Helen Creighton," 1974, Creighton Collection, CR-K-1.25, CMC.

315 *The Dr Helen Creighton Foundation* (pamphlet).

316 *Daily News* (Halifax), 23 September 1990.

317 Helen Creighton to A.J. Campbell, 8 September 1936, Creighton Papers, MG 1, vol. 2811, f. 162, PANS.

318 Helen Creighton to C.J. Eustace, 19 November 1932 (copy), Creighton Papers, MG 1, vol. 2811, f. 162, PANS.

319 Helen Creighton to Thompson, 17 September 1945, Creighton Papers, MG 1, vol. 2811, f. 162, PANS.

320 Creighton, "Fiddles, Folk Songs and Fisherman's Yarns," 19.

321 Creighton, *A Life in Folklore*, 167.

322 Ibid., 244.

323 Tallman, "Folklore Research in Atlantic Canada," 122–3.

324 This was not invariably the case. From the perspective of one listener (admittedly a Henneberry), the star of Creighton's 1938 radio show was Edmund Henneberry, whose "voice was wonderful over the air … I think he can be called a Radio Star." Mrs Alice Henneberry to Helen Creighton, n.d. [c.1938] (copy), Creighton Papers, MG 1, vol. 2813, f. 172, PANS.

325 Angelo Dornan to Helen Creighton, 15 May 1958, Creighton Papers, MG 1, vol. 2812, f. 52, PANS.

326 Denisoff, *Great Day Coming*, 170.

327 Helen Creighton to Howard Angus, n.d., Creighton Papers, MG 1, vol. 2811, f. 162, PANS.

328 Creighton, *A Life in Folklore*, 196.

329 Cf. Creighton, *A Life in Folklore*, 59.

330 Helen Creighton to Charles L. Glett, Audio Productions Inc., New York, 25 January 1937, Creighton Papers, MG 1, vol. 2811, f. 162, PANS.

331 Helen Creighton to A.J. Campbell, 8 September 1936, Creighton Papers, MG 1, vol. 2811, f. 162, PANS.

332 Helen Creighton to Philip Tilney, n.d. [1979], Creighton Papers, MG 1, vol. 2811, f. 162, PANS.

333 Alan Mills to Helen Creighton, 13 October 1950, Creighton Papers, MG 1, vol. 2816, f. 1, PANS. In 1981 Fowke brought out *Sea Songs and Ballads from Nineteenth-Century Nova Scotia.*

334 Helen Creighton to J. Murray Gibbon, 13 July 1929 (copy), Creighton Papers, MG 1, vol. 2811, f. 162, PANS.

335 Lorne Pierce to Helen Creighton, 27 October 1948, Creighton Papers, MG 1, vol. 2816, f. 154, PANS.

336 Helen Creighton to F.C. Badgley, Motion Picture Bureau, Ottawa, 15 January 1937, Creighton Papers, MG 1, vol. 2811, f. 162, PANS.

337 Helen Creighton to William M. Doerflinger, 1 March 1939, Creighton Papers, MG 1, vol. 2811, f. 162, PANS.

338 Statement by Allan Mills re the "Farmer's Curst Wife" (copy), Creighton Papers, MG 1, vol. 2811, f. 34, PANS.

339 Helen Creighton to Dr Douglas Leechman, 3 February 1949, Creighton Collection, CR-K-1.3, CMC.

340 F.J. Alcock to Helen Creighton, 24 January 1949, Creighton Collection, CR-K-1.3, CMC.

341 Helen Creighton to Frank Flemington, 17 October 1950, Pierce Papers, box 19, f. 2, item 26, QUA.

342 Creighton to A.J. Campbell, 8 September 1936, Creighton Papers, MG 1, vol. 2811, f. 162, PANS.

343 M.E. DeLory to Helen Creighton, 30 May 1977, Creighton Papers, MG 1, vol. 2812, f. 32, PANS.

344 Lorne Pierce to Helen Creighton, 1 March 1949, Creighton Papers, MG 1, vol. 2816, f. 154, PANS.

345 See Helen Creighton to Angus L. Macdonald, 22 November 1936, in Macdonald Papers, MG 2, vol. 1535, f. 1384/36, PANS, for reports on her trip to Cape Breton and thanks for the local government's preparation of programs for her American tour; and see D.C. Harvey to Helen Creighton, Creighton Papers, MG 1, vol. 2813, f. 21, PANS, on arranging the subsidy.

346 Fowke, "A Personal Odyssey," 7.

347 Fowke, "Labour and Industrial Protest Songs in Canada," 34–50.

348 Helen Creighton to Carmen Roy, 3 January 1959, Creighton Collection, CR-K-1.10, CMC.

349 As it turned out, Fowke was not herself responsible for the use of Creighton's songs. Carmen Roy to Helen Creighton, 5 January 1959, and Helen Creighton to Carmen Roy, 8 January 1959, Creighton Collection, CR-K-1.10, CMC.

350 Helen Creighton to Carmen Roy, 29 April 1959, Creighton Collection, CR-K-1.10, CMC.

351 "I was delighted you were able to come over after the meeting. Hope you didn't mind Edith's 'shockers' too much. At the early summer meeting Sam and I were kidding Edith about her 'dirty' songs, so I suppose she felt bound to prove at least some of them were musically interesting as well." Kenneth Peacock to Helen Creighton, 18 November 1959, Creighton Papers, MG 1, vol. 2816, no. 133, PANS.

352 Roger de C. Nantel to Helen Creighton, 10 May 1977, Creighton Papers, MG 1, vol. 2816, no. 69, PANS.

353 Creighton had other differences of opinion with Seeger, who she believed had "belittled" the Nova Scotia song tradition in comments at a student concert in Halifax. According to Creighton, the two patched up their differences and proceeded to have an enjoyable visit. Creighton, *A Life in Folklore*, 174. Ewan McColl and Peggy Seeger had also visited Halifax in 1959 and were impressed by the ease with which Creighton could visit the Folk from her urban base. Helen Creighton to Carmen Roy, 24 November 1959, Creighton Collection, CR-K-1.10, CMC.

354 Denisoff, *Great Day Coming*, 142–57. For the parallel British tradition, whose most prominent exponent was A.L. Lloyd, see Harker, *Fakesong*, 241–50.

355 Helen Creighton to Carmen Roy, 27 March 1960, Creighton Collection, CR-K-1.11, CMC.

356 Helen Creighton to Edith [Fowke], 29 March 1960, Creighton Papers, MG 1, vol. 2811, f. 162, PANS. For a further description of the incident involving the injured workman, see Helen Creighton to Carmen Roy, n.d. [1959], Creighton Collection, CR-K-1.10, CMC: "We had a bit of unwelcome excitement here last week when a carpenter fell off my roof and went hurtling down as I was sitting at the table having lunch. He has multiple injuries, so it was very upsetting. And he apologized for falling, bless him. He said, 'And to think I had been working on your house for such a short time and then had to cause you all that trouble.' His hat had blown off in the strong wind and he jumped from the scaffold to catch it. A strong gust of wind threw him off balance, and away he went."

357 Carmen Roy to Helen Creighton, 31 March 1960, Creighton Collection, CR-K-1.11, CMC.

358 Helen Creighton to Carmen Roy, 2 April 1960, Creighton Collection, CR-K-1.11, CMC.

359 Creighton, *A Life in Folklore*, 204.

360 The Public Archives of Nova Scotia has requested that letters in the closed files of the Creighton Papers, which include Fowke's reply to Creighton, not be cited.

361 Helen Creighton to Carmen Roy, 4 April 1960, Creighton Collection, CR-K-1.11, CMC.

362 Carmen Roy to Helen Creighton, 12 April 1960, Creighton Collection, CR-K-1.11, CMC.

CHAPTER THREE

1 See, in addition to Lears and Whisnant, Shi, *The Simple Life*, and Boris, *Art and Labor*.

2 Hutchinson, "The Trend in Handicrafts."

3 Gibbon, "Canadian Handicraft Old and New," 130–43.

4 *Older Ways: Traditional Nova Scotian Craftsmen*, pamphlet advertising exhibit organized by the Art Gallery, Mount Saint Vincent University, circulated by the Nova Scotia Museum as part of the National Museums Programme, 25 November 1977–1 January 1978. PANS, vertical file 150, no. 14.

5 In a growing literature concerning souvenirs, see especially Nason, "Tourism, Handicrafts, and Ethnic Identity in Micronesia."

6 *Maritime Co-Operator*, 1 April 1943.

7 Lotz, *Head, Heart and Hands*, 41.

8 See McKay, *The Craft Transformed*; "Class Struggle and Mercantile Capitalism."

9 As argued, for example, in *Keep Me Warm One Night*, 6.

10 Angie A. MacKenzie to Angus L. Macdonald, 1 March 1947, Macdonald Papers, MG 2, vol. 921, f. 31–9h/62, PANS.

11 See Mary Black, Diary Notes, 23 June 1943, Black Papers, MG 1, vol. 2878, PANS (hereinafter "Black diary notes").

12 Gibbon, "Canada's Million and More Needlecraft Workers," 144–55.

13 McNaughton, "CPR-Sponsored Quebec Folk Song and Handicraft Festivals," passim.

14 Bériau, "Home Weaving in Canada," 22. See also Green, ed., *A Heritage of Canadian Handicrafts* 113–14.

15 *Agricultural and Industrial Progress in Canada*, April 1943, clipping in Black Papers, MG 1, vol. 2878, f. 30, PANS.

16 Black diary notes, 16 February 1945.

17 Barbeau, "Are the Real Folk Arts and Crafts Dying Out?" 132–3.

18 Bériau, "Home Weaving in Canada," 29.

19 Black, "We," 1–3; *Herald* (Halifax), 11 April 1942.

20 *Journals of the House of Assembly, Nova Scotia* (hereinafter JHA) (Highways and Public Works) 1939, 5.

21 Prins, "Indian Artifacts and Lost Identity," 10–16. Native basketry remained a minor part of the provincial tourism repertoire; both Indian baskets and Indian games were, for example, part of the Nova

Scotia exhibit at the Sportsmen's Shows in Boston, Hartford, and New York City from January to March 1936. *JHA* (Highways) 1937.

22 See McKay, "Tartanism Triumphant."

23 *The Saga of Terence Bay*, n.p.

24 Black diary notes, 19 February 1943.

25 *JHA* (Agriculture) 1881, prize list, Provincial Exhibition of 1881.

26 Lotz, *Head, Heart and Hands*, 16.

27 *JHA* (Industry and Publicity) 1946, 44.

28 Henrietta B. Andrews to Clara Dennis, 21 January 1941, Dennis Papers, MG 1, vol. 2865, no. 12, PANS.

29 Traquair, "Hooked Rugs in Canada," 240–54; Law, "The Hooked Rugs of Nova Scotia," 58.

30 Scott Robson, "Textiles in Nova Scotia," 33.

31 "The Story of the Cheticamp Carpets," 43.

32 Creighton, "Hooked Rugs for Color," 19.

33 *JHA* (Highways and Public Works) 1941, 9; *JHA* (Industry and Publicity) 1942, 44.

34 *Nova Scotia, Canada's Ocean Playground*.

35 See, for example, Laidlaw, ed., *The Man from Margaree*, 124.

36 *Herald* (Halifax), 10 April 1942.

37 Ibid., 16 April 1942.

38 "Nova Scotia Urges Wider Interest in Handicrafts," undated clipping, Black Papers, MG 1, vol. 2878, f. 30, PANS.

39 On 10 November 1948 the Halifax *Herald* remarked, "It would be difficult to exaggerate the significance of the spread of this good and wholesome work. Leadership is provided by the Handcrafts and Home Industries branch of the Provincial Department of Trade and Industry. It is a work deserving of every encouragement, all possible co-operation, not from the cultural viewpoint alone, but as a valuable contribution to the economic strength of the Province."

40 Harold Connolly to Mary Black, 18 August 1942, Black Papers, MG 1, vol. 2878, f. 30, PANS.

41 *Chronicle-Herald*, 31 December 1955.

42 See the profile of Mary Black in Lotz, *Head, Heart and Hands*, 19–24.

43 From 1945 a stream of books consolidated her position in the field: *Weaving for Beginners* (1953), *Handweavers' Reference* (1954), *The Sett and Weaving of Tartans* (1954), and, with Joyce Chown, *The Ready Reference Tables* (1956), the *Colour Guide for Handweavers* (1958), and the *Thread Guide for Handweavers* (1959). *The Key to Weaving* was reprinted nineteen times and sold over 100,000 copies in Black's lifetime. The *Shuttlecraft Bulletins*, edited from 1957 to 1960 by Joyce Chown and Mary Black, were mailed to weavers in Australia, New Zealand, South

Africa, and Korea from Bedford, Nova Scotia. See Black Papers, MG 1, vol. 2144, f. 4, PANS.

44 Mary Black to secretary, Halifax Board of Trade, 7 April 1940, and Mary Black to John A. Mcdonald, 7 May 1940, in Black Papers, MG 1, vol. 2878, f. 30, PANS.

45 Norma Nelsen for Civil Service Commissioner to Mary Black, Black Papers, MG 1, vol. 2878, f. 28, PANS.

46 Mary Black to Charles Bruce, 1 December 1956, in Black Papers, MG 1, vol. 2878, f. 29, PANS.

47 Mary Black to Harold B. Burnham, 24 May 1966, Black Papers, MG 1, vol. 2144, f. 3, PANS.

48 Black, "Weaving in Nova Scotia – Yesterday and Today" 5–6.

49 Whisnant, *All That Is Native and Fine*, 175.

50 Black diary notes, 2 February 1943.

51 Ibid., 23 July 1943.

52 Ibid., 2 April 1943.

53 Ibid., 17 April 1943.

54 Ibid., 26 September 1944.

55 Speaker's Notes, Black Papers, MG 1, vol. 2144, f. 3, PANS.

56 *JHA* (Trade and Industry) 1949, 2.

57 *JHA* (Industry and Publicity) 1948, 153.

58 Ibid., 119.

59 *JHA* (Trade and Industry) 1950, 150.

60 Black diary notes, 3 March 1943.

61 Ibid., 4 January 1951.

62 Ibid., date illegible, c.November–December 1951.

63 Ibid., 21 to 28 July 1955.

64 Ibid., December 1955.

65 Ibid., 27 April 1943.

66 Ibid., December 1954; comment added March 1972.

67 *JHA* 1950, 147–8. Besides Mary Black, the "Director of Handcrafts and Home Industries," there was an assistant director; an instructor in silver jewellery, woodcarving, and leather-tooling; a general instructor; two weaving instructors and a tapestry-weaving instructor; a pottery instructor; a librarian; and a secretary.

68 Black diary notes, 28 January 1943.

69 Ibid., 20 March 1943.

70 Ibid., 9–19 July 1954.

71 Ibid., 4 May 1949.

72 Ibid., 21 May 1946.

73 Ibid., 4 February 1943.

74 Ibid., 12 March 1943.

75 Ibid., 12 March 1945.

76 Ibid., 16 May 1945.

77 Ibid., 8 June 1946.

78 Mary Black, "Handcrafts in Nova Scotia," 1944, Black Papers, MG 1, vol. 2878, f. 28, PANS.

79 JHA (Industry and Publicity) 1946, 43.

80 Ibid. 1945, 44.

81 Ibid. 1946, 34.

82 Ibid. 1945, 51.

83 Ibid., 39.

84 Black diary notes, 22–27 October 1945.

85 Black Papers, MG 1, vol. 2144, f. 1, "Craftsmen at Work"; Black, "We," 1–3, in Black Papers, MG 1, vol. 2878, f. 30, PANS.

86 "Handcrafts Report, April through March, 1952," Black Papers, MG 1, vol. 2878, PANS.

87 JHA (Industry and Publicity) 1944, 57.

88 Ibid. 1948, 157–8.

89 Ibid., 159.

90 Ibid. 1945, 49.

91 Star (Halifax), 14 October 1944.

92 Black diary notes, 11 February 1944.

93 JHA (Industry and Publicity) 1945, 49.

94 Ibid. 1949, 159.

95 Ibid. 1948, 158.

96 Ibid. 1945, 43, 51.

97 Ibid. 1946, 41.

98 Herald (Halifax), 25 January 1946; clipping from Coast Guard in Macdonald Papers, MG 2, vol. 997, f. "Industry and Publicity," PANS.

99 JHA (Industry and Publicity) 1946, 42.

100 Ibid. 1948, 162.

101 Memorandum of D. MacDonald, 21 March 1951, in Black Papers, MG 1, vol. 2878, f. 29, PANS.

102 JHA (Industry and Publicity) 1946, 42; Black diary notes, 20 May 1949.

103 Black diary notes, 29 September 1945.

104 Lotz, Head, Heart and Hands, 22.

105 Black diary notes, 20 May 1949.

106 JHA (Industry and Publicity) 1945, 46.

107 Canadian Museum of Civilization, "The Turning Point: The Deichmann Studio," exhibition, 1991.

108 Canadian Art (Summer 1952), 160–1.

109 Advertiser (Kentville), 1 October 1980.

110 Unidentified clipping, Black Papers, MG 1, vol. 2878, f. 28, PANS; Black, "We," 3.

111 Black, "The Therapeutics of Weaving," 397–405.

112 Black, "Challenge to a Therapist," 45–6.

113 Mary Black to the president, St. Francis Xavier College, 16 February 1942, Black Papers, MG 1, vol. 2878, f. 30, PANS.

114 Black diary notes, 21 May 1945.

115 Ibid., February 1949.

116 JHA (Industry and Publicity) 1948, 160.

117 Mary Black, Memorandum to Montgomery re Handcrafts, n.d. [1945], Black Papers, MG 1, vol. 2878, f. 28, PANS.

118 Harold Connolly to Angus L.Macdonald, 13 September 1945, in Macdonald Papers, MG 2, vol. 907, f. 37B/3, PANS.

119 JHA (Industry and Publicity) 1947, 106.

120 JHA (Trade and Industry) 1949, 158.

121 Ibid. 1950, 145–6.

122 Mary Black, undated memorandum to S.J. Montgomery, Black Papers, MG 1, vol. 2878, f. 28, PANS.

123 Barthes, *Mythologies*, 151.

124 Memorandum of D. MacDonald, 21 March 1951, in Black Papers, MG 1, vol. 2878, f. 29, PANS.

125 Mary Black, Memorandum on Handicrafts, c. 1943, Black Papers, MG 1, vol. 2878, f. 28, PANS. She mentioned similar arrangements in Israel, China, and Japan.

126 Mary Black, "Proposed Outline for a Handcrafts Program," January 1956, Black Papers, MG 1, vol. 2878, f. 28, PANS.

127 JHA (Industry and Publicity) 1948, 160.

128 Mary Black, "Handcrafts in Nova Scotia," undated note [c.1945 or early 1946], Black Papers, MG 1, vol. 2878, f. 28, PANS.

129 *Canadian Art* (Summer 1952), 158–9.

130 JHA (Trade and Industry) 1949, 16.

131 Ibid. 1950, 152.

132 Black was a student at the Saterglantan Vavskola in Sweden from 28 April to 15 May 1937.

133 Mary Black, "You, Your Home & Handcrafts," unpublished article, Black Papers, MG 1, vol. 2878, f. 30, "Drafts, typescripts, copies of articles by M.E.B. for newspapers," PANS.

134 Black diary notes, 15 September 1953.

135 Ibid., 8 January 1945.

136 Auville Eager to Angus L. Macdonald, 31 January 1951, Macdonald Papers, MG 2, vol. 962, f. 21/2, PANS.

137 Chiasson, *L'histoire des tapis*, 49–50.

138 JHA (Industry and Publicity) 1944, 64; JHA (Trade and Industry) 1950, 146.

139 *Herald* (Halifax), 6 April 1949; JHA (Industry and Publicity) 1948, 160–1.

140 When she visited a subordinate in Comeauville, she remarked in her diary notes: "Colours etc. in home, which seemed very comfortable, rather wild." 16 August 1943.

141 *JHA* (Industry and Publicity) 1945, 44.

142 Mary Black, "Handcrafts in Nova Scotia," undated note [c. 1945 or early 1946], Black Papers, MG 1, vol. 2878, f. 28, PANS.

143 *Canadian Art* (Summer 1952), 159.

144 Mary Black, "Growth of Design in a Handcrafts Program," unpublished essay, Black Papers, MG 1, vol. 2878, f. 29, PANS.

145 See Whisnant, *All That Is Native and Fine*, 163–72.

146 Black diary notes, 13 August 1943.

147 Mary Black, "Handcrafts in Nova Scotia," undated note [c. 1945 or early 1946], Black Papers, MG 1, vol. 2878, f. 28, PANS.

148 Mary Black, "Growth of Design in a Handcrafts Program," unpublished essay, Black Papers, MG 1, vol. 2878, f. 29, PANS.

149 *Canadian Art* (Summer 1952) 162; 159–60.

150 *JHA* (Industry and Publicity) 1944, 62.

151 *Canadian Art* (Summer 1952), 161–2.

152 Ibid., 162, 159–60.

153 Mary Black, "Growth of Design in a Handcrafts Program," unpublished essay, Black Papers, MG 1, vol. 2878, f. 29, PANS.

154 Mary Black, "We Don't Understand," *Handcrafts* , 1956 (n.p.), Black papers, MG 1, vol. 2878, f. 29, PANS.

155 Mary Black, "Handcrafts in Nova Scotia," *Family Herald and Weekly Star,* 25 January 1950.

156 One might draw an interesting parallel with the rhetoric of the Union Nationale in Quebec: see Bourque and Duchastel, *Restons traditionnels et progressifs.*

157 Province of Nova Scotia, Department of Trade and Industry, Handcrafts Division, *Weaving Course* (June, 1950), in Black Papers, MG 1, vol. 2144, f. 6, PANS.

158 *JHA* (Industry and Publicity) 1946, 36.

159 Ibid. 1948, 152.

160 See Black diary notes, 5 July 1943, for remarks on the inadequacies of convent training: she considered training at St. Ann's and Antigonish "all in all ... very poor training for a competent craftsman-instructor, however as no other prospects are in view we will have to make out."

161 *JHA* (Industry and Publicity) 1948, 152.

162 *JHA* (Trade and Industry) 1949, 154.

163 *JHA* (Industry and Publicity) 1948, 153; 1953, 35.

164 Mary Black, "Growth of Design in a Handcrafts Program," unpublished essay, Black Papers, MG 1, vol. 2878, f. 29, PANS.

165 *The Cross-Country Craftsman* (August 1951), 1.

166 *JHA* (Trade and Industry) 1958, 60.

167 Ibid. 1959, 55.

168 At the Star of the Sea in Terence Bay, for example, the leading activist had studied in Montreal with Karen Bulow, a noted Danish expert. See Green, ed., *A Heritage of Canadian Handicrafts*, 49.

169 Mary Black, "Growth of Design in a Handcrafts Program," unpublished essay, Black Papers, MG 1, vol. 2878, f. 29, PANS.

170 Black diary notes, 31 March 1948; see also *JHA* 1950, 150.

171 Krystyna and Konrad Sadowski to Angus L.Macdonald, 22 January 1953, in Macdonald Papers, MG 2, vol. 976, f. 21/1, PANS; see also Sadowski to Nauman, 22 January 1953, ibid., f. 21/2.

172 Black diary notes, 29 March 1949.

173 Gobelin tapestries epitomized the European craft ideal for Nova Scotian handicrafts advocates: instructors were imported from the United States to talk about them, and drawn perhaps by the fame of the European tapestry works as a centre of tourism, local planners dreamed of creating something like the tapestry works in Nova Scotia. See MacCannell, *The Tourist*, 68–9, for the Gobelin tapestry works as a tourist attraction.

174 Black diary notes, 9 April 1951.

175 Ibid., 14 February 1941; 3 March 1941.

176 *JHA* (Industry and Publicity) 1946, 32.

177 Major, "History of the Nova Scotia Tartan," 210–11.

178 Black diary notes, 16 March 1943.

179 Mary Black to D.W. Buchanan, Ottawa, 14 February 1952, Black Papers, MG 1, vol. 2878, f. 29, PANS. In New Brunswick, although one National Film Board documentary was called *Crafts of My Province*, it focused exclusively on the Deichmanns' studio.

180 Black diary notes, 29 March 1943.

181 *JHA* (Trade and Industry) 1952, 61–2.

182 *Chronicle-Herald* (Halifax), clipping, n.d. [but October 1950], in Black Papers, MG 1, vol. 2878, f. 29, PANS.

183 Mary Black to Mrs Angus L. Mac Donald [sic], "Winwick," Marlboro Woods, Halifax, 13 May 1961, Black Papers, MG 1, vol. 2144, f. 2, PANS.

184 Black diary notes, 26 April 1956.

185 *JHA* (Trade and Industry), 1952, 60 (loans); Memorandum of D. MacDonald, 21 March 1951, in Black Papers, MG 1, vol. 2878, f. 29, PANS.

186 *JHA* (Trade and Industry) 1956, 55 (Handcrafts); Mary Black, Memorandum to Montgomery re Handcrafts, n.d. [1945], suggested agreement between Department of Trade and Industry and Handcraft Shop Managers Covering Rental of Shops Owned By the Province. Black Papers, MG 1, vol. 2878, f. 28, PANS.

187 Black, "Nova Scotia Handcrafts."
188 Black diary notes, 21 May 1946.
189 *JHA* (Trade and Industry) 1949, 16.
190 Ibid. 1956, 55.
191 Judith Crawley to Miss Mary Black, 7 February 1957, in Black Papers, MG 1, vol. 2878, f. 29, PANS.
192 *Star* (Halifax), 14 October 1944.
193 *JHA* (Industry and Publicity) 1947, 109.
194 Cf. Green, ed., *A Heritage of Canadian Handicrafts.*
195 *JHA* (Industry and Publicity) 1946, 43; 1947, 118.
196 *JHA* (Trade and Industry), 1949, 161.
197 *JHA* (Industry and Publicity) 1945, 47; J.F.B. Livesay, *Peggy's Cove*, 98.
198 Mary Black to D.W. Buchanan, Ottawa, 14 February 1952, Black Papers, MG 1, vol. 2878, f. 29, PANS.
199 Black diary notes, addition of March 1972 to notes on 1954.
200 *JHA* (Trade and Industry) 1958, 62.
201 Ibid. 1960, 53.
202 Ibid. 1961, 63.
203 Lotz, *Head, Heart and Hands*, 35.
204 New York *Times*, 25 May 1958.
205 *The Cross-Country Craftsman* (August 1951), 1.
206 *JHA* (Trade and Industry) 1957, 65.
207 Burnham and Burnham, *'Keep Me Warm One Night.'*
208 *Museum of Cape Breton Heritage, North East Margaree, Cape Breton Island*; Mackley, *Handweaving in Cape Breton*, 62.
209 Black, "Nova Scotia's Gifts to Princess Elizabeth and the People Who Made Them," unpublished article, 1951, Black Papers, MG 1, vol. 2787, PANS.
210 Black diary notes, 18 September 1951.
211 Creighton, "Hooked Rugs," 19, remarks that "Nova Scotia rugs are not perfect by any means. In fact many of the colors are so gaudy as to leave one blinking."
212 Chiasson, *L'histoire des tapis*, 41.
213 Ibid., 58; see also Fairchild, "Cape Breton's Debt to Lilian Burke."
214 "A Note About Miss Lillian Burke" (interview with G.B. Fairchild), 47.
215 Chiasson, *L'histoire des tapis*, 51.
216 Brown, "Salty Nova Scotia," 614.
217 Chiasson, *L'histoire des tapis*, 59.
218 Lotz, *Head, Heart and Hands*, 15.
219 Chiasson, *L'histoire des tapis*, chapter 9.
220 See McKay, "Tartanism," passim.
221 Mackley, *Handweaving in Cape Breton*, 43.
222 Black diary notes, 2 August 1943.

223 Mrs A.W.R. (Angie) MacKenzie to A.L. Macdonald, Macdonald Papers, MG 2, vol. 921, f. 31–9h/62, PANS.

224 Mary Black to Angus L. Macdonald, 20 November 1946, Macdonald Papers, MG 2, vol. 921, f. 31–9L/56, PANS.

225 *JHA* (Industry and Publicity) 1947, 112.

226 Major, "History of the Nova Scotia Tartan," 197. It should be noted that Black fiercely contested some of the details of Major's account of the emergence of the tartan, and even had a pamphlet entitled "How Nova Scotia Got Its Tartan," published by Petheric Press, withdrawn from circulation on the grounds that it slighted Murray's contribution in favour of that of Mrs Isobel MacAulay. As late as 1 July 1984, Black was willing to defend Murray's claim to have invented the tartan (See Mary Black to Editor, *Atlantic Advocate*, 22 January 1962; Black to Chris [Tyler], craft advisor, Cultural Affairs, Nova Scotia Department of Culture, Recreation and Fitness, 1 July 1984, Black Papers, MG 1, vol. 2880, PANS). However, she was in agreement with Major on the inspirational role of the local landscape.

227 Mary Black, "To Whom It May Concern," n.d., "Re Origin of the Nova Scotia Tartan," Black Papers, MG 1, vol. 2880, f. 62, PANS. Black's concern was to defend the sole authorship of Bessie Murray.

228 Mary Black to Eleanor C. Hayes, Lily Mills Co., 22 January 1957, Black Papers, MG 1, vol. 2142, f. 3, PANS.

229 Bessie Murray to Mary Black, 14 September 1961, Black Papers, MG 1, vol. 2880, f. 63, PANS.

230 Major, "History of the Nova Scotia Tartan," 198–9.

231 Mary Black, "The Nova Scotia Tartan and a Cloth of Gold Dress," Black Papers, MG 1, vol. 2878, f. 30, PANS.

232 Major, "History of the Nova Scotia Tartan," 206–7; Black diary notes, 19 August 1953, 1 May 1954, 4, 23, 26 August 1954, 3 September 1954; *JHA* (Trade and Industry) 1956, 56–7.

233 *Mail-Star* (Halifax), 7 July 1967: "Nova Scotian Products Featured at Eaton's Right Now!"

234 Minutes of the annual meeting of Nova Scotia Tartan Limited, 18 August 1964, Black Papers, vol. 2880, PANS. For the purposes of identification and advertising, it was not possible to state explicitly that the dress tartan was the "dress version" of the official Nova Scotia tartan, because the rights in connection with the official tartan had been vested by statute in the government of Nova Scotia. This was neatly and misleadingly circumvented by a card attached to the garments in the dress tartan, which read, "Dress Tartan, Nova Scotia Tartan Limited." See Black Papers, vol. 2880, no. 63, file "Nova Scotia Tartan Ltd. (Halifax): 1955–1973," PANS.

235 Bessie Murray to Mr J. DeGooyer, Bonda Textiles, 29 September 1973 (copy), Black Papers, MG 1, vol. 2880, f. 63, PANS.

236 *Casket* (Antigonish), 2 December 1954.

237 Whisnant, *All That Is Native and Fine*, 100.

238 *Chronicle-Herald* (Halifax), 3 January 1956.

CHAPTER FOUR

1 Hall, "The Toad in the Garden," 35–73.

2 See Margaret Conrad, "The 1950s: The Decade of Development," in Forbes and Muise, eds., *The Atlantic Provinces in Confederation*, 382–420.

3 See Morton, "Men and Women in a Halifax Working-Class Neighbourhood."

4 Shi, *The Simple Life*, 3.

5 Turner and Ash, *The Golden Hordes*, 77.

6 See Cameron, *MacLennan*, chapter 2.

7 Duncan, *Bluenose*, 67–8.

8 Ibid., 70.

9 MacLennan, "The Miracle That's Changing Nova Scotia," 31.

10 Cameron, *MacLennan*, 6.

11 Sharp, "Do You Know Who We Are?," 9–13, 16.

12 Shi, *The Simple Life*, 277. See also Bové, *Mastering Discourse*, chapter 6.

13 See Bourque and Duchastel, *Restons traditionnels et progressifs*.

14 See Moody, "The Novelist as Historian," 150–1.

15 Raddall, "Blind McNair," in *Tambour*, 371–2.

16 V.D. Kyte to Thomas Raddall, 12 December 1946, in Raddall Papers, MS 2, 202, S621, correspondence V.D. Kyte, DUA.

17 For discussions, see Clary Croft, "The Use of Folklore in Selected Works of Thomas H. Raddall," in Young, ed., *Time and Place* 109–19; Fowke, "'Blind McNair,'" 173–86.

18 Fowke, ed., *Sea Songs*, 1–8.

19 Thomas Raddall, introduction to Wallace R. MacAskill, *Lure of the Sea*, n.p.

20 Raddall, *The Wings of Night*, 135, 138.

21 Ibid., 138.

22 See MacNeil, "Society and Economy in Rural Nova Scotia," for evidence that flatly contradicts impressions of rural stagnation.

23 McDonald, "Tourism," 127.

24 Ibid., 121–2.

25 "There are about a dozen fishermen's huts on the beach outside the walls of the old town of Louisburgh [Louisbourg]. When you enter one it reminds you of the descriptive play-bill of the melo-drama – 'Scene II.: Interior of a Fisherman's Cottage on the Sea-shore: Ocean in

the Distance.' The walls are built of heavy timbers laid one upon another, and caulked with moss or oakum. Overhead are square beams, with pegs for nets, poles, guns, boots, the [heterogeneous] and picturesque tackle with which such ceilings are usually ornamented. But oh! how clean everything is! The knots are fairly scrubbed out of the floor-planks, the hearth-bricks red as cherries, the dresser-shelves worn thin with soap and sand, and white as the sand with which they have been scoured. I never saw drawing-room that could compare with the purity of that interior." Frederic S. Cozzens, *Acadia*, 114–15.

26 Forbes, "In Search of a Post-Confederation Maritime Historiography, 1900–1967," in Forbes, ed., *Challenging the Regional Stereotype*, 48–66.

27 Davies, "The Song Fishermen," 138.

28 "Song Fishermen's Song Sheet" (mimeo), in Merkel Papers, MS 2, 326, K.1, DUA.

29 Raddall, *In My Time*, 223. Raddall visited Peggy's Cove in the company of Merkel, who later became known as the author of an important book on the *Bluenose*.

30 Davies, "The Song Fishermen," 141.

31 "Announcement," The Song Fishermen's Song Sheet, 29 July 1929, no. 15, "Issued Every So Often." Merkel Papers, MS 2, 326, K.1, DUA. See, for discussion, Davies, "The Song Fishermen," 144–5.

32 Davies, "The Song Fishermen," 148.

33 G.F. Parker had some good fun at the expense of a friend who had just arrived from Worcester full, as he says, "of Longfellow sentiment." Parker asked his friend if he would like to see the cream pot and churn? "Sure," he answered, "Perhaps we might see Evangeline's heifer." The "churn" in question was so named because of the action of waves along the coast, and had nothing to do with Evangeline or her cow. Parker, *A Tripod Trip*, 6.

34 Breck, *Sporting Guide*, 9.

35 Squier, *On Autumn Trails*, 9.

36 Brown, "Salty Nova Scotia," 111.

37 *Nova Scotia by the Sea* [1928].

38 MacLennan, "Nova Scotia," 98.

39 Call, *The Spell of Acadia*, 402–3.

40 Fisher, "The Charm of Nova Scotia," 14–16.

41 *Nova Scotia, Canada's Ocean Playground* [1950], 58.

42 Adams, *Glimpses of Nova Scotia*, 1.

43 Ibid., 32.

44 Bird, *This Is Nova Scotia*, 1.

45 Ibid., 19.

46 Ibid., 69.

47 Ibid., 28–9.
48 Ibid., 204; 44–5; 64; 169; 258.
49 Ibid., 67.
50 Adams, *Glimpses of Nova Scotia*, 32.
51 Bird, *This Is Nova Scotia*, 127.
52 Ibid., 128.
53 Ibid., 127.
54 Will R. Bird on summertime for the fisherfolk in the Eastern Shore: "Then the hay patches are ripe for the scythe, nets and boats are abandoned for a day, and the cheerful raspings of stone on steel ring along from field to field" (*This Is Nova Scotia*, 223). Livesay: "But when at last the sun comes out and the little rockgirt hay patches are ripe for the scythe, nets are abandoned and the Cove is merry to the sound of stone on steel" (*Peggy's Cove*, 32). Bird also copies Livesay in remarking on fish-heads and finding their stares melancholy.
55 Bird, *This Is Nova Scotia*, 221.
56 Ibid., 295.
57 Deacon, *The Four Jameses*.
58 John G. MacPherson, "James D. Gillis Teacher and Author, An Appreciation of his literary and poetic genius," undated clipping enclosed with P.S. Campton to Angus L. Macdonald, 9 April 1936, Macdonald Papers, MG 1, PANS.
59 Rankin, *Our Ain Folk*, 45–6.
60 Adams, *Glimpses of Nova Scotia*, 22.
61 Gillis, *The Cape Breton Giant*, dedication page and 56.
62 Raddall, *In My Time*, 227–8.
63 Ibid., 229.
64 Gillis, *The Cape Breton Giant*, memoir of James D. Gillis by Thomas H. Raddall, 66. In this version, Gillis says: "My, that is a very big house. It has more rooms than a university."
65 Ibid., 60.
66 D.J. Rankin, *Our Ain Folk*, v.
67 Ibid., 162.
68 Ibid., 59.
69 Ibid., vi.
70 Ibid., 207–8.
71 Ibid., 9.
72 Ibid., 111.
73 Ibid., 73.
74 Ibid., 39–40.
75 Ibid., 155.
76 Ibid., 49–53.
77 Ibid., 90.

78 Ibid., 167–8.

79 D.J. Rankin, *On This Rock*, 107–9.

80 MacLennan, *Barometer Rising*, 124. The best work on MacLennan in his regional context is as yet unpublished: see Kristiansen, "Time, Memory and Transformation: Capitalism and the Countryside in the Maritime Novel."

81 Gwen Davies, "Afterword," to Day, *Rockbound*, 302–5.

82 Day, *Rockbound*, 202.

83 Watson, "Rockbound, by Frank Parker Day: Novel and Ethnography," 75.

84 Keefer, *Under Eastern Eyes*, 72.

85 Bevan, "Introduction" to Day, *Rockbound*, xviii.

86 "To instill into the Established Order the complacent portrayal of its drawbacks has nowadays become a paradoxical but incontrovertible means of exalting it" (Barthes, *Mythologies*, 41).

87 Lowenthal, *Literature, Popular Culture and Society*, 152.

88 Day, *Rockbound*, 106.

89 Wallace, "Some Fishing!" 109.

90 Davies, "Afterword," 306.

91 Ibid., 295–6.

92 Thomas Raddall was savagely critical of Day: "In the mid-1920s a literary professor named Frank Parker Day had spent two or three summers on Tancook's small neighbour, Ironbound Island, whose people are all close blood relations of the Tancookers. In 1928 he published a pseudo-novel called *Rockbound*, portraying the Ironbounders as a backward folk, the result of generations of intermarriage, speaking English with a thick Old German accent, and lusty in the quarrels and amours." Raddall, *In My Time*, 256. Yet it seems that Raddall is scarcely in a position to dismiss Day's novels on aesthetic or ethical grounds; his own work was no less reductionist in its treatment of the Folk. He also found himself in almost exactly the same position as Day when he sold an article to *Maclean's* depicting the folk ways of the residents of Tancook Island; the islanders bitterly complained that he had made fun of their dialect. Raddall, *In My Time*, 257.

93 Ferguson, ed., *Marsden Hartley and Nova Scotia*, 40.

94 See Ludington, *Marsden Hartley*.

95 Ferguson, ed., *Marsden Hartley and Nova Scotia*, 45.

96 John Coldwell Adams, "Introduction," to Duncan, *The Way of the Sea*, vii-xiii.

97 Raddall, *In My Time*, 259–61.

98 Duncan, *Bluenose*, 139.

99 Ibid., 138.

100 Ibid., 140.

101 Ibid., 224.
102 See, for example, DesBrisay, *History of the County of Lunenburg*, 396–406.
103 Duncan, *Bluenose*, 150.
104 D'Emilio and Freedman, *Intimate Matters*, xv–xvi.
105 *Herald* (Halifax) 2, 5, 6 April 1920.
106 Ironically, local cultural producers at times even went beyond what their British or American publishers wanted to publish. In 1939 one British editor turned down a Raddall novel with polite remarks, but significantly added a handwritten note: "I also feel that there is too much 'sex.'" G.W. Blackwood to Thomas Raddall, 15 March 1939, Raddall Papers, Dal MS 2, 202, correspondence "Blackwoods," s. 41–89, DUA.
107 On this "crisis of masculinity," see especially Weeks, *Sex, Politics and Society*; Kimmel, "The Contemporary 'Crisis' of Masculinity"; Rotundo, "Manhood in America"; Morton, "Men and Women in a Halifax Working-Class Neighbourhood," chapter 6; Maynard, "Rough Work and Rugged Men," 159–69.
108 Pope, *DeGarthe*, 58.
109 Raddall, *In My Time*, 96.
110 Duncan, *Bluenose*, 141.
111 Stuart McCawley, letter, "News from the Tall Man's Brother," The Song Fishermen's Song Sheet, sheet Two, no. 12, Merkel Papers, DUA; D.J. Rankin defended those who admired McAskill, "for he was possessed of physical proportions, and strength, seldom equalled in modern times." Rankin, *Our Ain Folk*, 38.
112 For an interesting discussion, see Stallabrass, "The Idea of the Primitive," 108.
113 Day, *Rockbound* [1973 ed.], 50–1.
114 Davies, "Afterword," 315.
115 Cited, Allan Bevan, Introduction to Day, *Rockbound*, xvii–xviii.
116 For the debate over Beckles Willson's *Nova Scotia, The Province That Has Been Passed By*, see *Herald* (Halifax) 21 March 1913. J.F.B. Livesay's mention of premarital conception in Peggy's Cove was also quite controversial, and was withdrawn from his book's second edition: Livesay, *Peggy's Cove*, 96.
117 There are, admittedly, other MacAskills that do include women (one finds a few, including the inevitable "bathing beauties", in the tourism pamphlets he illustrated, and a fisherman and his wife are to be seen in his photographs for a spread in *National Geographic*); but none of the major photographs in the MacAskill canon, the most pervasively circulated visual images of the province, and those brought together in the book on him, contains a single woman. See MacAskill, *MacAskill: Seascapes and Sailing Ships*, passim.

118 Buckler, "The First Born Son," 38.

119 Raddall, *The Nymph and the Lamp*, 365; 321–2.

120 Hartley, "Cleophas and His Own," 93.

121 Marsden Hartley to Adelaide Kuntz, 6 October 1935, in Ferguson, ed., *Marsden Hartley*, 36–7.

122 Hartley, "Cleophas and His Own," 97, 101.

123 Ibid., 91.

124 Ibid., 92.

125 Hartley to Adelaide Kuntz, 4 November 1935, in Ferguson, ed., *Marsden Hartley*, 39.

126 Hartley to Adelaide Kuntz, 6 November 1935, ibid., 43.

127 Hartley, "Cleophas and His Own," 99.

128 Hartley to Adelaide Kuntz, 23 September 1936, in Ferguson, ed., *Marsden Hartley*, 49.

129 Hartley, "Cleophas and His Own," 98.

130 Ronald Paulson, "Marsden Hartley's Search for the Father(land)," 23.

131 *JHA* (Trade and Industry) 1947, 85.

132 Forbes, "Battles in Another War: Edith Archibald and the Halifax Feminist Movement," in E.R.Forbes, *Challenging the Regional Stereotype*, 67–89.

133 Chapin, *Atlantic Canada*, 79.

134 Cozzens, *Acadia*, 39.

135 *Nova Scotia: The Doers and Dreamers Complete Guide to the Festival Province of Canada*, cover and 2.

136 Kenneth Leslie, "Windward Rock," in Leslie, *The Poems of Kenneth Leslie*, 28.

137 *Nova Scotia Pictures. Catalogue of the Third Travelling Exhibition*, comments on "Cape Breton."

138 *Nova Scotia Pictures. Catalogue of the Seventh Travelling Exhibition*, 1.

139 Adams, *Glimpses of Nova Scotia*, 10.

140 Fraser, "The Spirit of the Maritimes."

141 On divorce, see Snell, "Marital Cruelty," 3–32. He notes that between 1900 and 1939 the Nova Scotia Divorce Court applied a stricter and more inclusive definition of cruelty, and to some extent, at least, undermined the doctrine that a wife was the property or the servant of the husband in sexual life.

142 Fingard, *The Dark Side of Life*; Fingard, "The Prevention of Cruelty," 84–101; Dubinsky, "Improper Advances."

143 See David Frank, "The 1920s: Class and Region, Resistance and Accommodation," in Forbes and Muise, eds., *The Atlantic Provinces in Confederation*, 233–71.

144 Sharp, "Do You Know Who We Are?" 9–13, 16.

145 Fraser, "The Spirit of the Maritimes."

146 Rankin, *On This Rock*, 147.

147 Ibid., 133.

CHAPTER FIVE

1 Dobbs, *The Living Heritage*, n.p.
2 Jameson, "Postmodernism," 56. For an interesting critique of Jameson which detects a tendency to reduce the diversity of social life to exemplars of a single essence, see Callinicos, *Against Postmodernism*, 128–32.
3 Jameson, "Postmodernism," 66.
4 See Harvey's insightful discussion in *The Condition of Postmodernity*, part I.
5 In 1989, according to its former director, the park lost $2 million in its operations, which prompted wage reductions of craftspeople from $12 to a "more manageable $9.25 an hour." *Daily News* (Halifax), 18 July 1990.
6 Benjamin, *Illuminations*, 221.
7 Cited, O'Donnell [MacLean], *Leading the Way*, 36–7.
8 See Bruce, *Frank Sobey*, and *R.A.: The Story of R.A. Jodrey*.
9 Note Giddens, *The Consequences of Modernity*, 63–78.
10 Culler, "Semiotics of Tourism," 127–8.
11 *Buskers 88. The International Street Performers Festival, August 11–27, 1988*, 4.
12 Ross, "The Rise and Fall of Pictou Island," 186.
13 Ibid., 185.
14 Cameron, *The Education of Everett Richardson*, 170.
15 Choyce, *An Avalanche of Ocean*; Keefer, *Constellations*; Carver, *Compassionate Landscape*, 233.
16 The "Sterling County" studies, conducted by scholars from Cornell University, further developed the notion that there was something intrinsically wrong with the "people of cove and woodlot," by purporting to find a higher incidence of mental illness in depressed areas. See Margaret Conrad, "The 1950s: The Decade of Development," in Muise and Forbes, eds., *The Atlantic Provinces in Confederation*, 394.
17 Lotz, *Head, Heart and Hands*, 41.
18 The empirical detail in this paragraph is drawn entirely from Lotz, *Head, Heart and Hands*, 31–40.
19 Lotz, "Crafty Entrepreneurs," 34–5.
20 Aikenhead, "The Business of Crafts," 13. See also Macpherson, "Crafts."
21 Nova Scotia Designer Crafts Council, *Nova Scotia Crafts Catalogue*.
22 Harper, *A People's Art*, 3.
23 Stallabrass, "The Idea of the Primitive," 96–103. For an interesting case study of tourism and "folk art," see Tye, "Folk and Tourist Art in the Life of Patrick Murphy," 54–67.

24 *Daily News* (Halifax), 5 August 1989.

25 Huntington, "Charlie Tanner," n.p.

26 Ibid.

27 Field, *Spirit of Nova Scotia*, 3.

28 Cited, Wright, "'The Smile of Modernity,'" 129–30.

29 For references, see "The Tragedy of the Commons or the Common Tragedy of Capital?", chapter 1 of Burrill and McKay, eds., *People, Resources and Power.* Jeanette Neeson's forthcoming work on the actual "Commons" and Enclosures will be of great significance in reducing the allure of the "Tragedy of the Commons" metaphor.

30 Hall, "The Toad in the Garden," 36.

31 Whisnant, *All That Is Native and Fine*, 261.

32 Keil, "Who Needs 'the Folk'?" 263–5.

33 Hall, "The Toad in the Garden," 60.

34 Smart, "The Politics of Truth," 168.

35 Davidson, "Archaeology, Genealogy, Ethics."

36 Smart, "The Politics of Truth," 162.

37 As conceded by Harvey, for example, in *The Condition of Postmodernity*, 353.

38 Hall, "The Toad in the Garden," 42.

39 Ibid., 44–5.

40 Jameson, "Postmodernism," 57.

41 Radhakrishnan, "Toward an Effective Intellectual," 68.

42 Ibid., 57.

43 Hall, "The Toad in the Garden," 51.

44 Bohlman, *The Study of Folk Music*, 1.

45 Dundes, "Defining Identity through Folklore," 150.

46 Nowlan, *Various Persons Named Kevin O'Brien*, 69.

47 Dohaney, *The Corrigan Women*; Ellison Robertson, "A Parting Shot"; Erik Kristiansen, "Realism and the Crisis of Rural Community."

48 MacLeod, "The Boat," in *The Lost Salt Gift of Blood*, 139–40.

Bibliography

ARCHIVAL SOURCES

Manuscript Collections

CANADIAN MUSEUM OF CIVILIZATION (HULL)
Marius Barbeau Collection
Helen Creighton Collection

DALHOUSIE UNIVERSITY ARCHIVES (HALIFAX)
W.R. Mackenzie Papers
Andrew Merkel Papers
Thomas Raddall Papers
Angus Walters Papers

MEMORIAL UNIVERSITY OF NEWFOUNDLAND, FOLKLORE
AND LANGUAGE ARCHIVE (ST. JOHN'S)
M. Carole Henderson, interviews with Helen Creighton, MUNFLA 78–57/
    C-3927–29

ROCKEFELLER ARCHIVAL CENTRE (POCANTICO HILLS,
NEW YORK)
Fellowship Cards
RG 1.1, series 427, Canada, box 28

PUBLIC ARCHIVES OF NOVA SCOTIA (HALIFAX)
Mary Black Papers
Helen Creighton Papers

Clara Dennis Papers
Angus L. Macdonald Papers
Society for the Propagation of the Gospel in Foreign Parts, originals,
microfilm

QUEEN'S UNIVERSITY ARCHIVES (KINGSTON)
Lorne Pierce Papers

Newspapers and Periodicals

Advertiser [Kentville], 1 October 1980
American Journal of Occupational Therapy, 1949
Canadian Art (Summer 1952)
Casket (Antigonish), 2 December 1954
Chronicle-Herald (Halifax), 31 December 1955
The Cross-Country Craftsman (Washington, DC), August 1951
Daily News (Halifax), 1988–
Handcrafts (Halifax), 1946–56
Herald (Halifax), 1910–22; 1942
Maritime Co-Operator, 1 April 1943
Mail-Star (Halifax), July 1967
Mayfair, 1928–39
Star (Halifax), 14 October 1944
Trades Journal (Stellarton), 1883

OTHER SOURCES

Adams, George Matthew. *Glimpses of Nova Scotia*. Halifax: Bureau of Infor-
mation, Government of Nova Scotia, n.d. (c. 1932).
Adamson, Walter L. *Marx and the Disillusionment of Marxism*. Berkeley and
Los Angeles: University of California Press 1985.
Aikenhead, Sheri. "The Business of Crafts: Making a Buck on Beauty." *Com-
mercial News* (December 1983).
Anderson, Benedict. *Imagined Communities: Reflections on the Origin and Spread
of Nationalism*. London: Verso 1983.
"A Note about Miss Lillian Burke." *Cape Breton's Magazine*, 19, n.d. (interview
with G.B. Fairchild): 47.
Baker, Patrick L. "Negotiated Objectivity: Weekly Newspaper Reporting and
Social Relations in the New Brunswick Communities." In *People and Place:
Studies of Small Town Life in the Maritimes*, edited by Larry McCann.
Fredericton: Acadiensis Press and Sackville: Mount Allison University,
1987.
Baker, Ronald. "Folklore and Folklife Studies in American and Canadian Colleges
and Universities," (1986) 99 *Journal of American Folklore*, no. 391: 50–74.

Barbeau, Marius. "Kinship Recognition and Urbanization in French Canada." In *Contributions to Anthropology, 1959*. Ottawa: National Museum of Canada, Bulletin no. 173, Anthropological Series no. 50, 1961.

– "Are the Real Folk Arts and Crafts Dying Out?" (1948) 5 *Canadian Art*: 128–133.

Barnard, F.M. *Herder's Social and Political Thought: From Enlightenment to Nationalism*. Oxford: Clarendon Press, 1965.

Barrett, L. Gene. "Capital and the State in Atlantic Canada: The Structural Context of Fishery Policy between 1939 and 1977." In *Atlantic Fisheries and Coastal Communities: Fisheries Decision-Making Case Studies*, edited by Cynthia Lamson and Arthur J. Hanson. Halifax: Dalhousie University, 1984.

Barss, Peter. *Images of Lunenburg County*. Toronto: McClelland and Stewart, 1978.

Barthes, Roland. *Mythologies* (1972). Reprinted with translation by Annette Lavers. Frogmore, St Albans: Paladin, 1973.

Bausinger, Hermann. "Towards a Critique of Folklorism Criticism." In *German Volksunde*, edited by James R. Dow and Hannjost Lixfeld. Bloomington: Indiana University Press, 1986.

Beck, Jane C. "'Enough to Charm the Heart of a Wheelbarrow and Make a Shovel Dance': Helen Creighton, Pioneer Collector." (1985) *Canadian Folklore Canadien*: 5–20.

Benjamin, Walter. *Illuminations*. Translated by Harry Zohn. New York: Schocken Books, 1969.

Berger, John. *Ways of Seeing*. Harmondsworth: Penguin Books, 1972.

Bériau, Oscar A. "Home Weaving in Canada." (1943) 27 *Canadian Geographical Journal*, no. 1: 18–29.

Bird, Will R. "Ghosts and Haunted Places." *Busy East* (September–October 1926).

– *This Is Nova Scotia*. Toronto: Ryerson, 1950.

Black, Mary. "Challenge to a Therapist." (1949) 3 *American Journal of Occupational Therapy*, no. 1: 45–6.

– "Handcrafts in Nova Scotia." *Family Herald and Weekly Star*, 25 January 1950.

– *Handweavers' Reference*. Bedford: the author, n.d. [1954].

– "Improving Design in Handcrafts." (1952) 9 *Canadian Art*, no. 4: 158–62.

– *The Key to Weaving: A Textbook of Hand Weaving for the Beginning Weaver* (1945). Reprinted New York: Macmillan, 1980.

– "Maritime Handcrafts." (April 1955) *Journal of the Royal Architectural Institute of Canada*: 131–3.

– "Nova Scotia Handcrafts." (August 1953) *Smoke Signals: A Circular for Craftsmen*, no. 8.

– *The Sett and Weaving of Tartans*. Shelby, NC: Lily Mills Company, 1954.

– "The Therapeutics of Weaving." (1938) 17 *Occupational Therapy and Rehabilitation*, no. 6: 397–405.

– "We." (January 1956) 13 *Handcrafts*

– *Weaving for Beginners*. Ottawa: Department of National Health and Welfare, 1953.

– "Weaving in Nova Scotia – Yesterday and Today." *Handweaver and Craftsman* (Fall 1951): 5–6.

Black, Mary, and Joyce M. Chown. *Ready Reference Tables for Handweavers*. Bedford, Nova Scotia: the authors, 1959.

Bohlman, Philip V. *The Study of Folk Music in the Modern World*. Bloomington and Indianapolis: Indiana University Press, 1988.

Boris, Eileen. *Art and Labor: Ruskin, Morris, and the Craftsman Ideal in America*. Philadelphia: Temple University Press, 1986.

Bourque, Gilles, and Jules Duchastel. *Restons traditionnels et progressifs. Pour une nouvelle analyse du discours politique: Le cas du régime Duplessis au Québec*. Montréal: Boréal, 1988.

Bové, Paul A. *Mastering Discourse: The Politics of Intellectual Culture*. Durham and London: Duke University Press, 1992.

Breck, Edward. *Sporting Guide to Nova Scotia*. Halifax: Imperial Publishing Company, 1909.

Brison, Jeffrey. "Consent and Coercion: A Comparative Study of Work Relief in the United States and Canada during the Depression." MA thesis, Queen's University, 1990.

Brown, Andrew H. "Salty Nova Scotia: In Friendly New Scotland Gaelic Songs Still Answer the Skirling Bagpipes." *National Geographic Magazine* (1940): 575–624.

Bruce, Harry. *Frank Sobey: The Man and the Empire*. Toronto: Macmillan, 1985.

– "Marine Photographer par Excellence." *Canadian Geographic* (February–March 1986): 44–51.

– *R.A.: The Story of R.A. Jodrey*. Toronto: McClelland and Stewart, 1979.

Buchan, David. *The Ballad and the Folk*. London and Boston: Routledge and Kegan Paul, 1972.

Buckler, Ernest. "The First Born Son." In *The Maritime Experience*, edited by Michael O. Nowlan. Toronto: Macmillan, 1975.

Burnham, Harold B., and Dorothy K. Burnham. *'Keep Me Warm One Night': Early Handweaving in Eastern Canada*. Toronto: University of Toronto Press, 1972.

Burrill, Gary, and Ian McKay, eds. *People, Resources, and Power: Critical Perspectives on Underdevelopment and Primary Industries in the Atlantic Region*. Fredericton: Acadiensis Press for the Gorsebrook Research Institute, 1987.

Buskers 88: The International Street Performers Festival, August 11–27, 1988. N.p., n.d. [1988].

Calkin, J.B. *Old Time Customs: Memories and Traditions*. Halifax: A. & W. MacKinlay, 1918.

Call, Frank Oliver. *The Spell of Acadia*. Boston: L.C. Page, 1930.

Callinicos, Alex. *Against Postmodernism: A Marxist Critique*. New York: St Martin's Press, 1990.

Cameron, Elspeth. *Hugh MacLennan: A Writer's Life* (1981). Reprinted Halifax: Formac Publishing, 1983.

Cameron, Silver Donald. *The Education of Everett Richardson: The Nova Scotia Fishermen's Strike 1970–71*. Toronto: McClelland and Stewart, 1977.

Carpenter, Carole Henderson. *Many Voices: A Study of Folklore Activities in Canada and Their Role in Canadian Culture*. Ottawa: National Museums of Canada, Canadian Centre for Folk Culture Studies, paper no. 16, 1979.

– "Forty Years Later: Maud Karpeles in Newfoundland." In *Folklore Studies in Honour of Herbert Halpert*, edited by Kenneth S. Goldstein and Neil V. Rosenberg. St John's: Memorial University, 1980.

Carver, Humphrey. *Compassionate Landscape: People and Places in a Man's Life*. Toronto: University of Toronto Press, 1975.

Chapin, Miriam. *Atlantic Canada*. Toronto: Ryerson Press, 1956.

Chiasson, Anselme, and Anne-Rosie Deveau. *L'histoire des tapis «hookés» de Chéticamp et de leurs artisans*. N.p.: Les Editions Lescarbot, 1986.

Choyce, Lesley. *An Avalanche of Ocean: The Life and Times of a Nova Scotia Immigrant*. Fredericton: Goose Lane Editions, 1988.

Clark, George Frederick. *Thetis Saxon*. Toronto: Longmans, 1927.

Clifford, James. *The Predicament of Culture: Twentieth-Century Ethnography, Literature and Art*. Cambridge: Harvard University Press, 1989.

Clifford, James, and George E. Marcus. *Writing Culture: The Poetics and Politics of Ethnography*. Berkeley: University of California Press, 1986.

Cocchiara, Giuseppe. *The History of Folklore in Europe*. Philadelphia: Institute for the Study of Human Issues, 1981.

Collingwood, R.G. *The Idea of History* (1946). Reprinted New York: Galaxy, 1956.

Cozzens, Frederic S. *Acadia, or, A Month with the Blue Noses*. New York: Derby and Jackson, 1859.

Creighton, Helen. "Ballads from Devil's Island." (1935) 32 *Dalhousie Review*: 503–10.

– *Bluenose Ghosts*. Toronto: Ryerson Press, 1957.

– *Bluenose Magic: Popular Beliefs and Superstitions in Nova Scotia*. Toronto: Ryerson Press, 1968.

– "Canada's Maritime Provinces – An Ethnomusicological Survey (Personal Observations and Recollections." (1972) 16 *Ethnomusicology*: 404–14.

– "Collecting Songs of Nova Scotia Blacks." In *Folklore Studies in Honour of Herbert Halpert*, edited by Kenneth S. Goldstein and Neil V. Rosenberg. St John's: Memorial University, 1980.

– "Easter on Cape Sable Island." (1964) 54 *Atlantic Advocate*.

– "Fiddles, Folk-Songs and Fishermen's Yarns." (1955) 51 *Canadian Geographical Journal*, no. 6: 212–21.

- "Fishing for Albacore." (1931) 3 *Canadian Geographical Journal*: 65–76.
- *Folklore of Lunenburg County, Nova Scotia*. Ottawa: National Museum of Canada, bulletin no. 117, Anthropological Series no. 29 (1950). Reprinted Toronto: McGraw-Hill Ryerson, 1976.
- "Folklore of Victoria Beach." (1950) 63 *Journal of American Folklore*: 131–46.
- "Folk-Singers of Nova Scotia." *Canadian Forum* (July 1952).
- *Folksongs from Southern New Brunswick*. Ottawa: National Museums of Canada, 1971.
- "Hooked Rugs for Color: Nova Scotia's Great Home Industry." *The Chatelaine* (May 1929).
- *A Life in Folklore*. Toronto: McGraw-Hill Ryerson, 1975.
- *Maritime Folk Songs*. Toronto: Ryerson Press, 1962. Reprinted St John's: Breakwater, 1979.
- "Nova Scotia Folksongs." (1937) 4 *Nova Scotia Journal of Education*, no. 8.
- "Rudyard Kipling and the Halifax Doctor." (June 1965) 55 *Atlantic Advocate*: 50–5.
- "Sable Island." *Maclean's* (1 December 1931).
- *Songs and Ballads from Nova Scotia*. Toronto and Vancouver: J.M. Dent and Sons, 1932. Reprinted New York: Dover, 1966.
- "Song Singers." *Maclean's* (15 December 1937).
- "Songs of Nathan Hatt." (1953) 32 *Dalhousie Review*: 259–66.
- "Teachers as Folklorists." (1943) 14 *Nova Scotia Journal of Education*, no. 7.
- "W. Roy Mackenzie, Pioneer." (July 1967) 2 *Newsletter of the Canadian Folk Music Society*: 15–22.
Creighton, Helen, with Sandy Ives. "Eight Folktales from Miramichi as Told by Wilmot MacDonald." (1962) 4 *Northeast Folklore*: 3–70.
Creighton, Helen, and Calum MacLeod. *Gaelic Songs in Nova Scotia*. Ottawa: National Museum, bulletin no. 198 (1964).
Creighton, Helen, and Doreen Senior. *Twelve Folksongs from Nova Scotia*. London: Novello, 1940.
Creighton, Helen, and Doreen Senior. *Traditional Songs from Nova Scotia*. Toronto: Ryerson Press, 1950.
Culler, Jonathan. *Barthes*. N.p.: Fontana Paperbacks, 1983.
- "Semiotics of Tourism." (1981) 1 *American Journal of Semiotics*: 127–40.
Dancy, Jonathan, and Ernest Sosa. *A Companion to Epistemology*. Oxford: Basil Blackwell, 1992.
Davidson, Arnold I. "Archaeology, Genealogy, Ethics." In *Foucault: A Critical Reader*, edited by David Couzens Hoy. Oxford: Basil Blackwell, 1986.
Davies, Gwendolyn. "The Song Fishermen: A Regional Poetry Celebration." In *People and Place: Studies of Small Town Life in the Maritimes*, edited by Larry McCann. Fredericton: Acadiensis Press, and Sackville: Mount Allison University, 1987.

Day, Frank Parker. *Rockbound* (1940). Reprinted with forward by Allan Bevan, Toronto: University of Toronto Press, 1973; reprinted with forward by Glendolyn Davies, Toronto: University of Toronto Press, 1989.

Deacon, William Arthur. *The Four Jameses*. Toronto: Ryerson Press, 1953.

D'Emilio, John, and Estelle B. Freedman. *Intimate Matters: A History of Sexuality in America*. New York: Harper and Row, 1988.

Denisoff, R. Serge. *Great Day Coming: Folk Music and the American Left*. Urbana: University of Illinois Press, 1971.

Devanney, Burris. "Shouting His Wares: The Politics and Poetry of Kenneth Leslie." *New Maritimes* (June 1986).

Dobbs, Kildare. *The Living Heritage: Nova Scotia*. Halifax: Nova Scotia Department of Culture, Recreation and Fitness, n.d. [1986] (pamphlet).

Dr Helen Creighton Foundation. *The Dr Helen Creighton Foundation*. N.p. [Halifax], n.d. [1989] (pamphlet).

Doerflinger, W.M. "Cruising for Ballads in Nova Scotia." In *Explorations in Canadian Folklore*, edited by Edith Fowke. Toronto: McClelland and Stewart, 1985.

Dohaney, M.T. *The Corrigan Women*. Charlottetown: Ragweed Press, 1988.

Dorson, Richard. *The British Folklorists: A History*. Chicago: University of Chicago Press, 1968.

– *Folklore and Fakelore: Essays towards a Discipline of Folk Studies*. Cambridge: Harvard University Press, 1976.

Doucette, Laurel, and Colin Quigley. "The Child Ballad in Canada: A Survey." (1981) 9 *Canadian Folk Music Journal*: 3–19.

Dubinsky, Karen. "Improper Advances: Sexual Danger and Pleasure in Rural and Northern Ontario 1880–1929." PHD thesis, Queen's University, 1990.

Duncan, Dorothy. *Bluenose: A Portrait of Nova Scotia*. New York: Harper and Brothers, 1942.

Duncan, Norman. *The Way of the Sea* (1903). Reprinted with introduction by John Coldwell Adams, Ottawa: Tecumseh Press, 1982.

Dundes, Alan. "Defining Identity through Folklore." (1984) 21 *Journal of Folklore Research*: 149–52.

Fauset, Arthur H. *Folklore from Nova Scotia*. New York: American Folklore Society, Memoir Series 24, 1931.

Field, Richard Henning. *Spirit of Nova Scotia: Traditional Decorative Folk Art, 1780–1930*. Halifax: Art Gallery of Nova Scotia; Hamilton and Toronto: Dundurn Press, 1985.

Fingard, Judith. *The Dark Side of Life in Victorian Halifax*. Porter's Lake: Pottersfield Press, 1990.

– "The Prevention of Cruelty: Marriage Breakdown and the Rights of Wives in Nova Scotia, 1880–1900." (Spring 1993) 22 *Acadiensis*: 84–101.

Fisher, Claude Laing. "The Charm of Nova Scotia." *National Home Monthly* (March 1946): 14–16.

Forbes, E.R. *Challenging the Regional Stereotype: Essays on the 20th Century Maritimes.* Fredericton: Acadiensis Press, 1989.

– *Maritime Rights: The Maritime Rights Movement, 1919–1927: A Study in Canadian Regionalism.* Montreal: McGill-Queen's University Press, 1979.

Forbes, E.R., and D.A. Muise, eds. *The Atlantic Provinces in Confederation.* Toronto: University of Toronto Press; Fredericton: Acadiensis Press, 1993.

Forgacs, David. ed. *An Antonio Gramsci Reader: Selected Writings 1916–1935.* New York: Schocken, 1988.

Fowke, Edith. "'Blind McNair': A Canadian Short Story and Its Sources." In *Folklore Studies in Honour of Herbert Halpert,* edited by Kenneth S. Goldstein and Neil V. Rosenberg. St John's: Memorial University, 1980.

– *Canadian Folklore.* Toronto: Oxford University Press, 1988.

– "Labour and Industrial Protest Songs in Canada." (1969) 82 *Journal of American Folklore:* 34–50.

– "A Personal Odyssey and Personal Prejudices." (1978) 2 *Folklore: Bulletin of the Folklore Studies Association of Canada:* 7–13.

– *Sea Songs and Ballads from Nineteenth-Century Nova Scotia: The William H. Smith and Fenwick Hatt Manuscripts.* New York and Philadelphia: Folklorica, 1981.

Fowke, Edith, and Alan Mills. *Canada's Story in Song.* Toronto: Gage, 1960.

Frank, David. "The Industrial Folk Song in Cape Breton." (1986) 8 *Canadian Folklore Canadien:* 21–42.

Fraser, Mary L. *Folklore of Nova Scotia.* N.p., n.d. [1931].

Fraser, Thomas M. "The Spirit of the Maritimes." *Busy East* (July 1919).

Gellner, Ernest. *Nations and Nationalism.* Ithaca: Cornell University Press, 1983.

Gibbon, J. Murray. *Canadian Mosaic: The Making of a Northern Nation.* Toronto: McClelland and Stewart, 1938.

– "Canadian Handicraft Old and New." (1943) 24 *Canadian Geographical Journal:* 130–43.

– "Canada's Million and More Needlecraft Workers." (1945) 26 *Canadian Geographical Journal:* 144–55.

Gillis, James D. *The Cape Breton Giant* (1898). Reprinted with afterword by Thomas Raddall, Wreck Cove: Breton Books, 1988.

Gordon, Joleen. "Ancient Handicrafts Survive in Nova Scotia." (1979) 98 *Canadian Geographical Journal:* 50–5.

– "A Sense of the Past: Traditional Crafts in Nova Scotia Today." *Canadian Collector* (January–February 1972).

Graburn, Nelson, ed. *Ethnic and Tourist Arts: Cultural Expressions from the Fourth World.* Berkeley: University of California Press, 1976.

Gramsci, Antonio. *Selections from the Prison Notebooks of Antonio Gramsci.* Edited and translated by Quintin Hoare and Geoffrey Nowell Smith. London: Lawrence and Wishart, 1973.

Gray, Richard. *Writing the South: Ideas of an American Region*. Cambridge: Cambridge University Press, 1986.

Green, H. Gordon, ed. *A Heritage of Canadian Handicrafts*. Toronto and Montreal: McClelland and Stewart, 1967.

Green, Rayna. "Folk Is a Four-Letter Word: Dealing with Traditional * * * * in Fieldwork, Analysis, and Presentation." In *Handbook of American Folklore*, edited by Richard M. Dorson. Bloomington: Indiana University Press, 1983.

Guildford, Janet. "Coping with De-industrialization: The Nova Scotia Department of Technical Education, 1907–1930." (1987) 16 *Acadiensis*, no. 2: 69–84.

Guindon, Hubert. *Quebec Society: Tradition, Modernity, and Nationhood*. Toronto and Buffalo: University of Toronto Press, 1988.

Hall, Stuart. "The Toad in the Garden: Thatcherism among the Theorists." In *Marxism and the Interpretation of Culture*, edited by Cary Nelson and Lawrence Grossberg. Urbana and Chicago: University of Illinois Press, 1988.

Handler, Richard. "In Search of the Folk Society: Nationalism and Folklore Studies in Quebec." (1983) 3 *Culture*: 103–14.

– *Nationalism and the Politics of Culture in Quebec*. Madison: University of Wisconsin Press, 1988.

Harker, Dave. *Fakesong: The Manufacture of British "Folksong" 1700 to the Present Day*. Philadelphia and Milton Keynes: Open University Press, 1985.

Harper, J. Russell. *A People's Art: Primitive, Naive, Provincial and Folk Painting in Canada*. Toronto: University of Toronto Press, 1974.

Hartley, Marsden. *Cleophas and His Own: A North Atlantic Tragedy*. Halifax: A Press, 1982.

– "Cleophas and His Own: A North Atlantic Tragedy." In *Marsden Hartley and Nova Scotia*, edited by Gerald Ferguson. Halifax: Mount Saint Vincent University Art Gallery, 1987.

Harvey, David. *The Condition of Postmodernity: An Enquiry into the Origins of Cultural Change*. Oxford: Basil Blackwell, 1989.

Henderson, Hamish. *Alias MacAlias: Writings in Songs, Folk and Literature*. Edinburgh: Polygon, 1993.

Hobsbawm, E.J. *Nations and Nationalism since 1780: Programme, Myth, Reality*. Cambridge: Cambridge University Press, 1990.

Howkins, Alun. "Greensleeves and the Idea of National Music." In *Patriotism: The Making and Unmaking of British National Identity*, vol. 3, *National Fictions*, edited by Raphael Samuel. London and New York: Routledge, 1989.

Hunt, Lynn, ed. *The New Cultural History*. Berkeley: University of California Press, 1989.

Huntington, Christopher. "Charlie Tanner 1904–1982." In *Charlie Tanner: Retrospective*. Halifax: Art Gallery of Nova Scotia, n.d. [1984] (exhibition catalogue).

Hutchinson, Helen. "The Trend in Handicrafts." *Family Herald and Weekly Star* (Montreal), 2 July 1953.

Ives, Edward D. *Joe Scott: The Woodsman-Songmaker*. Urbana, Chicago, and London: University of Illinois Press, 1978.

– "Maine Woods Ballads and Creative Tradition." *Salt Magazine* (July 1990).

– "Oral and Written Tradition: A Micro-view of the Miramichi." (Autumn 1988) 18 *Acadiensis*: 148–56.

Jameson, Frederic. "Postmodernism, or the Cultural Logic of Late Capitalism." (July–August 1984) 146 *New Left Review*: 53–92.

Keefer, Janice Kulyk. *Constellations*. Toronto: Random House, 1988.

– *Under Eastern Eyes: A Critical Reading of Maritime Fiction*. Toronto: University of Toronto Press, 1987.

Keil, Charles. "Who Needs 'the Folk'?" (September–December 1985) 15 *Journal of the Folklore Institute*: 263–5.

Kimmel, Michael. "The Contemporary 'Crisis' of Masculinity in Historical Perspective." In *The Making of Masculinities: The New Men's Studies*, edited by Harry Brod. Boston: Allen and Unwin, 1987.

Kirkconnell, Watson. *Canadians All: A Primer of Canadian National Unity*. Ottawa: Director of Public Information, 1941.

Knott, Sarah Gertrude. "The Folk Festival Movement in America." (1953) 17 *Southern Folklore Quarterly*: 143–55.

Kristiansen, Erik. "Time, Memory and Transformation: Capitalism and the Countryside in the Maritime Novel." Unpublished paper delivered to the Rural Workers in Atlantic Canada Conference, St Mary's University, October 1990.

Laidlaw, Alexander F., ed. *The Man from Margaree: Writings and Speeches of M.M. Coady*. Toronto: McClelland and Stewart, 1971.

Law, Margaret Lathrop. "The Hooked Rugs of Nova Scotia." *House Beautiful* (July 1928).

Lears, T.J. Jackson. "The Concept of Cultural Hegemony: Problems and Possibilities." (1985) 90 *American Historical Review*: 567–93.

– *No Place of Grace: Antimodernism and the Transformation of American Culture*. New York: Pantheon Books, 1981.

Legman, Gershon. *No Laughing Matter: An Analysis of Sexual Humor*, 2 vols. Bloomington: Indiana University Press, 1982.

Leslie, Kenneth. "In Halfway Cove." (1937) 5 *The Commonweal*: 490.

– *The Poems of Kenneth Leslie*. Ladysmith, Quebec: Ladysmith Press, 1971.

Livesay, J.F.B. *Peggy's Cove*. Toronto: Ryerson Press, 1944.

Lotz, Jim. "Crafty Entrepreneurs." (June 1990) *Policy Options Politiques*: 34–5.

– *Head, Heart and Hands: Craftspeople in Nova Scotia*. Halifax: Braemar Publishing, n.d.

Lovelace, Martin. "W. Roy Mackenzie as a Collector of Folksong." (1977) 5 *Canadian Folk Music Journal*: 5–11.

Lowenthal, Leo. *Literature, Popular Culture and Society*. Englewood Cliffs, NJ: Prentice-Hall, 1961.

Ludington, Townsend. *Marsden Hartley: The Biography of an American Artist*. New York: Little, Brown, 1993.

MacAskill, Wallace. *MacAskill: Seascapes and Sailing Ships*. Halifax: Nimbus, 1987.

MacCannell, Dean. *The Tourist: A New Theory of the Leisure Class*. New York: Schocken, 1976.

McDonald, Maryon. "Tourism: Chasing Culture and Tradition in Brittany." In *Who from Their Labours Rest? Conflict and Practice in Rural Tourism*, edited by Mary Bouquet and Michael Winter. Aldershot: Avebury, 1987.

MacIntyre, John. "Bootlegging: A Slowly Evaporating Enterprise." *New Maritimes* (March–April 1991).

McKay, Ian. "Capital and Labour in the Halifax Baking and Confectionery Industry during the Last Half of the Nineteenth Century." In *Essays in Canadian Business History*, edited by Tom Traves. Toronto: McClelland and Stewart, 1983.

– "Class Struggle and Mercantile Capitalism: Craftsmen and Labourers on the Halifax Waterfront, 1850–1902." In *Working Men Who Got Wet*, edited by Rosemary Ommer and Gerald Panting. St John's: Memorial University, 1980.

– *The Craft Transformed: An Essay on the Halifax Carpenters, 1885–1985*. Halifax Holdfast Press, 1985.

– "Among the Fisherfolk: J.F.B. Livesay and the Invention of Peggy's Cove." (Spring 1988) 23 *Journal of Canadian Studies*, nos. 1 and 2: 23–45; reprinted in J.M. Bumsted, ed., *Interpreting Canada's Past*, vol. 2: *Post-Confederation*. Don Mills, Ont.: Oxford University Press, 1993.

Mackenzie, W. Roy. "Ballad-Singing in Nova Scotia." (1909) 22 *Journal of American Folk-Lore*: 327–31.

– *Ballads and Sea Songs of Nova Scotia*. Cambridge: Harvard University Press, 1928.

– *The Quest of the Ballad*. Princeton: Princeton University Press, 1919.

Mackley, Florence. *Handweaving in Cape Breton*. Sydney: privately printed, 1967.

MacLennan, Hugh. *Barometer Rising*. 1941. Reprinted with a foreword by Hugo McPherson, Toronto: McClelland and Stewart, 1969.

– "The Miracle That's Changing Nova Scotia." *Mayfair* (July 1953).

– "Nova Scotia." *Holiday* (September 1953).

MacLeod, Alistair. *The Lost Salt Gift of Blood*. Toronto: McClelland and Stewart, 1976.

McNaughton, Janet Elizabeth. "A Study of the CPR-Sponsored Quebec Folk Song and Handicraft Festivals, 1927–1930." MA thesis, Memorial University, 1982.

- "John Murray Gibbon and the Inter-war Folk Festivals." (1982) 1 *Journal of Canadian Folklore*: 66–73.

MacNeil, Alan Roderick. "Society and Economy in Rural Nova Scotia, 1761–1861." PHD thesis, Queen's University, 1990.

MacNeil, Joe Neil. *Tales until Dawn: The World of a Cape Breton Gaelic Story-Teller*. Kingston and Montreal: McGill-Queen's University Press, 1987.

McNeil, William K. "A History of American Folklore Scholarship Before 1908." PHD thesis, Indiana University, 1980.

Macpherson, Margaret. "Crafts: The Art of Business." *Commercial News* (December 1987).

Major, Marjorie. "History of the Nova Scotia Tartan." (June 1972) 2 *Nova Scotia Historical Quarterly*: 191–214.

Moody, Barry. "The Novelist as Historian: The Nova Scotia Identity in the Novels of Thomas H. Raddall." In *Time and Place: The Life and Works of Thomas Raddall*, edited by Alan R. Young. Fredericton: Acadiensis Press, 1991.

Morton, Suzanne. "Men and Women in a Halifax Working-Class Neighbourhood in the 1920s." PHD thesis, Dalhousie University, 1990.

Morton, Suzanne, and Ian McKay. "The Maritimes." In *The Canadian Labour Revolt*, edited by Craig Heron (forthcoming).

Museum of Cape Breton Heritage, North East Margaree, Cape Breton Island. N.p., n.d. (pamphlet).

Nason, James D. "Tourism, Handicrafts, and Ethnic Identity in Micronesia." (1984) 11 *Annals of Tourism Research*: 421–50.

Nesbit, E. Jean. "'Free Enterprise at Its Best': The State, National Sea, and the Defeat of the Nova Scotia Fishermen, 1946–1947." In *Workers and the State in Twentieth-Century Nova Scotia*, edited by Michael Earle. Fredericton: Acadiensis Press, 1989.

Nova Scotia by the Sea. N.p. [Halifax], n.d. [1928].

Nova Scotia. Canada's Ocean Playground. Halifax: Bureau of Information, Government of Nova Scotia, 1932.

Nova Scotia. Canada's Ocean Playground. Halifax: Bureau of Information, Government of Nova Scotia, 1936.

Nova Scotia, Canada's Ocean Playground. N.p. [Halifax], n.d. [1950].

Nova Scotia. Department of Education. *Catalogue of the Third Travelling Exhibition*. Halifax: the department, 1949.

Nova Scotia. Department of Education. *Catalogue of the Seventh Travelling Exhibition*. Halifax: the department, 1953.

Nova Scotia. House of Assembly. *Journals* of the House of Assembly, 1920–1970.

Nova Scotia. The Doers and Dreamers Complete Guide to the Festival Province of Canada. N.p. [Halifax], n.d. [1990].

Nowlan, Alden. *Various Persons Named Kevin O'Brien*. Toronto: Clarke Irwin, 1973.

Now See Nova Scotia, Canada's Ocean Playground. N.p. [Halifax], n.d. [1940].

O'Donnell, Eleanor MacLean. *Leading the Way: An Unauthorized Guide to the Sobey Empire*. Halifax: GATT-Fly Atlantic, n.d.

O'Donnell, John C. "Labour's Cultural Impact on the Community: A Cape Breton Perspective." (1986) 14 *Canadian Folk Music Journal*: 49–59; 64.

Older Ways: Traditional Nova Scotian Craftsmen. N.p. [Halifax], Art Gallery, Mount Saint Vincent University, n.d. [1977].

Papson, Stephen. "Spuriousness and Tourism: Politics of Two Canadian Provincial Governments." (1981) 8 *Annals of Tourism Research*: 220–35.

Parker, Gilbert. *A Tripod Trip along the South Shore of Nova Scotia*. Yarmouth: The "Light" Office, 1899.

Paulson, Ronald. "Marsden Hartley's Search for the Father(land)." In *Marsden Hartley and Nova Scotia*, edited by Gerald Ferguson. Halifax: Mount Saint Vincent University Art Gallery, 1987.

Pope, Douglas. *DeGarthe: His Life, Marine Art and Sculpture*. Hantsport: Lancelot Press, 1989.

Poteet, Lewis J, comp. *The Second South Shore Phrase Book*. Hantsport: Lancelot Press, 1985.

Pratt, Mary Louise. "Fieldwork in Common Places." In *Writing Culture: The Poetics and Politics of Ethnography*, edited by James Clifford and George E. Marcus. Berkeley and Los Angeles: University of California Press, 1986.

Prince, S.H. *The Architecture of Rural Society*. Toronto: The Anglican Church of Canada, n.d.

Prins, Harold. "Indian Artifacts and Lost Identity." 10 *Salt Magazine* (June 1990).

Raddall, Thomas. *The Wings of Night* (1956). Reprinted New York: Doubleday, 1963.

– *In My Time: A Memoir*. Toronto: McClelland and Stewart, 1976.

– "Introduction" to Wallace R. MacAskill, *Lure of the Sea: Leaves from My Pictorial Log*. Halifax, 1951.

– *The Nymph and the Lamp* (1950). Reprinted Toronto: McClelland and Stewart, 1963.

– *Tambour and Other Stories*. Toronto: McClelland and Stewart, 1945.

Radhakrishnan, R. "Toward an Effective Intellectual: Foucault or Gramsci?" In *Intellectuals: Aesthetics, Politics, Academics*, edited by Bruce Robbins. Minneapolis: University of Minnesota Press, 1990.

Rankin, D.J. *On This Rock*. Ottawa: Overbrook, 1930.

– *Our Ain Folk*. Toronto: Macmillan, 1930.

Redfield, Robert. "The Folk Society." (1947) 52 *American Journal of Sociology*: 293–308.

Robertson, Ellison. "A Parting Shot." *New Maritimes* (July-August 1989).

Robson, Scott. "Textiles in Nova Scotia." In *Spirit of Nova Scotia: Traditional Decorative Folk Art, 1780–1930*, edited by Richard Henning Field. Halifax: Art Gallery of Nova Scotia, and Hamilton and Toronto: Dundurn Press, 1985.

Rosenberg, Neil. "Folklore in Atlantic Canada: The Enigmatic Symbol." In *The Marco Polo Papers*, vol. 1 (Atlantic Provinces Literature Colloquium), edited by Kenneth MacKinnon. Saint John: Atlantic Canada Institute, 1977.

Ross, Andrew. "Defenders of the Faith and the New Class." In *Intellectuals: Aesthetics, Politics, Academics*, edited by Bruce Robbins. Minneapolis: University of Minnesota Press, 1990.

Ross, Eric. "The Rise and Fall of Pictou Island." In *People and Place: Studies of Small Town Life in the Maritimes*, edited by Larry McCann. Fredericton: Acadiensis Press, and Sackville, NB: Committee for Studying Small Town Life in the Maritimes, 1987.

Rotundo, Edward Anthony. "Manhood in America: The Northern Middle Class, 1770–1920." PHD. thesis, Brandeis University, 1982.

The Saga of Terence Bay. N.p., n.d. [c.1939].

Samson, Danny. "Family Formation in Mine and Farm Households: Pictou County, Nova Scotia, 1860–1880." Unpublished paper. Queen's University, 1992.

Saunders, Marshall. *The House of Armour.* Philadelphia: Griffith and Rowland, 1897.

Sclanders, Ian. "She's Collecting Long Lost Songs." *Maclean's*, 15 September 1952.

– "She Saves The Strangest Songs." *Mayfair* (December 1953).

Sekula, Allan. "Photography between Capital and Labour." In Benjamin H.D. Buchloh and Robert Willkie, eds., *Mining Photographs and Other Pictures 1948–1968: A Selection from the Negative Archives of Shedden Studio, Glace Bay, Cape Breton.* Halifax: Press of the Nova Scotia College of Art and Design, and Sydney: University College of Cape Breton Press, 1983.

Sharp, R.V. "Do You Know Who We Are? A Question to the World At Large." *Busy East* (December 1919).

Shi, David E. *The Simple Life: Plain Living and High Thinking in American Culture.* New York: Oxford University Press, 1985.

Smart, Barry. "The Politics of Truth and the Problems of Hegemony." In *Foucault: A Critical Reader*, edited by David Cozzens Hoy. Oxford: Oxford University Press, 1986.

Smith, A.D. *The Ethnic Origin of Nations.* Oxford: Basil Blackwell, 1986.

– *The Ethnic Revival.* Cambridge: Cambridge University Press, 1981.

Snell, James. "Marital Cruelty: Women and the Nova Scotia Divorce Court, 1900–1939." (Autumn 1988) 18 *Acadiensis*: 3–32.

"The Song Fishermen's Song Sheets." Mimeo. N.p., n.d. [in the Merkel Papers, Dalhousie University Archives].

Squier, Emma-Lindsay. *On Autumn Trails and Adventures in Captivity*. London: N.p., 1925.

Stallabrass, Julian. "The Idea of the Primitive: British Art and Anthropology 1918–1930." (September–October 1990), 183 *New Left Review*: 95–115.

Stam, Robert. "Mikhail Bakhtin and Left Cultural Critique." In *Postmodernism and its Discontents: Theories, Practices*, edited by E. Ann Kaplan. London and New York: Verso, 1988.

Sturtevant, Ethel. "Review of *Ballads and Sea-Songs from Nova Scotia*, by W.Roy Mackenzie." (1928) 41 *Journal of American Folklore*: 593–4.

Tagg, John. *The Burden of Representation: Essays on Photographies and Histories*. London: Macmillan, 1988.

Tallman, Richard S. "Folklore Research in Atlantic Canada: An Overview." (Spring 1979) 8 *Acadiensis*: 118–30.

Tippett, Maria. *Making Culture: English-Canadian Institutions and the Arts before the Massey Commission*. Toronto: University of Toronto Press, 1990.

Traquair, Ramsay. "Hooked Rugs in Canada." (1943) 26 *Canadian Geographical Journal*: 240–54.

Trumpener, Katherine Maria. "The Voice of the Past: Anxieties of Cultural Transmission in Post-Enlightenment Europe. Tradition, Folklore, Textuality, History." PHD thesis, Stanford University, 1990.

Turner, L., and J. Ash. *The Golden Hordes*. London: Constable, 1975.

Tye, Diane. "Folk and Tourist Art in the Life of Patrick Murphy." (1983) 7 *Culture and Tradition*: 54–67.

– "Women and Folklore Fieldwork in English-speaking Atlantic Canada." Unpublished paper delivered to the Atlantic Canada Workshop, 1989.

Urry, John. *The Tourist Gaze: Leisure and Travel in Contemporary Societies*. London: Sage Publications, 1990.

Wallace, F.W. "Some Fishing!" In *The Shack Locker: Yarns of the Deep Sea Fishing Fleets*, 2d ed. Toronto: Hodder and Stoughton, 1922.

Watson, Nancy. "Rockbound, by Frank Parker Day: Novel and Ethnography." (1982) 6 *Culture and Tradition*: 73–83.

Weeks, Jeffrey. *Sex, Politics and Society: The Regulation of Sexuality since 1800*. London and New York: Longman, 1981.

Whisnant, David. *All That Is Native and Fine: The Politics of Culture in an American Region*. Chapel Hill and London: University of North Carolina Press, 1983.

Wilgus, D.K. *Anglo-American Folksong Scholarship since 1898*. New Brunswick, NJ: Rutgers University Press, 1959.

Williams, Raymond. *The Country and the City* (1973). Reprinted Frogmore, St Alban's: Paladin, 1973.

– *Keywords: A Vocabulary of Culture and Society*. Glasgow: Fontana, 1976.
– "Literature and Sociology: In Memory of Lucien Goldmann." (1971) 67 *New Left Review*: 3–18.
Willson, Beckles. *Nova Scotia: The Province That Has Been Passed By*. Toronto: McClelland and Goodchild, 1911.
Winsor, Fred. "'Solving a Problem": Privatizing Worker's Compensation for Nova Scotia's Offshore Fishermen, 1926–1928." In *Workers and the State in Twentieth-Century Nova Scotia*, edited by Michael Earle. Fredericton: Acadiensis Press for the Gorsebrook Research Institute, 1989.
Withrow, Alfreda. *St. Margaret's Bay: A History*, 2d ed. Tantallon: Four East Publications, 1985.
Wright, Miriam. "'The Smile of Modernity': The State and the Modernization of the Canadian Atlantic Fishery 1945–1970." MA thesis, Queen's University, 1990.
Wright, Patrick. *On Living in an Old Country: The National Past in Contemporary Britain*. London: Verso, 1985.
Zumwalt, Rosemary Lévy. *American Folklore Scholarship: A Dialogue of Dissent*. Bloomington and Indianapolis: Indiana University Press, 1988.

Index